'Adie has reinvented herself as a writer with such a delightful, light touch, such an unexpected eye for the absurd, that her memoir at times bears comparison with Evelyn Waugh. Adie shows a striking ability to convey in a few pages an era, a war or a country. She is as classy an act on the page as she is on the screen'
Independent

'*The Kindness of Strangers* is a rollicking good read – witty, well written and packed with fascinating stories'
Daily Telegraph

'Adie's autobiography is tireless and entertaining'
Observer

'Adie delivers a pacy, well-written account'
Daily Mail

'*The Kindness of Strangers*, a broadly comic and at times hilarious account of her life as, among other things, a war correspondent for the BBC'
Guardian

Kate Adie is the BBC's Chief News Correspondent and the presenter of Radio Four's *From Our Own Correspondent*. She grew up in Sunderland, read Swedish at Newcastle University and was a member of the National Youth Theatre before embarking on a career initially in radio journalism. She has been named Reporter of the Year twice by the Royal Television Society and won the premier news award – the Monte Carlo International Golden Nymph Award – in 1981 and 1990; she was awarded an OBE in 1993.

Kate has served as a judge for several literary prizes, most recently the Orange prize for fiction. She is a trustee of the Imperial War Museum and has published a book about women in uniform to coincide with an exhibition on the subject at the museum in 2003. *The Kindness of Strangers* is her first book.

The Kindness of Strangers

Kate Adie

headline

First published in 2002
by HEADLINE BOOK PUBLISHING

First published in paperback in 2003
by HEADLINE BOOK PUBLISHING

20 19 18 17 16 15

ISBN 0 7553 1073 X

Set in Janson
Designed & set by Ben Cracknell Studios
Printed and bound in Great Britain by
Clays Ltd, St Ives plc

HEADLINE BOOK PUBLISHING
A division of Hodder Headline
338 Euston Road
London NW1 3BH

www.headline.co.uk
www.hodderheadline.com

To: Babe

Acknowledgements

I would like to thank my agent Louise Greenberg for all her encouragement and good advice, Nick Marcus and Ken Lennox for help with photographs, and Anthony Massey and Brenda Griffiths for their support and friendship. I would also like to thank Heather Holden-Brown, Celia Kent and Gillian Bromley, the editorial team at Headline.

Contents

ONE

Sacked again

You're a reporter. Just stick to the facts.

All that can happen to you is attempted murder, grievous bodily harm, calls for your resignation – and years of fun, intriguing adventure and unexpected delight.

A reporter is an observer, a bystander, a witness. That's the theory. In reality, you are a privileged gnat alighting on the faces of history, part of events great and small. You discover secrets, smell the atmosphere, feel the vibrations of emotion. And every so often, someone tries to swat you.

I found these things out the obvious way – through ignorance and mistakes – for I never expected to be a reporter. As a child, a student, and then a BBC local radio producer, the world of News had never beckoned, and not for a trice had I harboured thoughts of a career in journalism. Nor had I ever desired fame. Fame in my upbringing was equated with Vanity. Also, famous people from my north-eastern home town of Sunderland appeared to be very few (the Venerable Bede – it's a short list) and very dead.

However, through an odd succession of opportunity, lucky breaks and downright curiosity, I've had over three decades of extraordinary good fortune – punctuated with frequent demands that I be sacked, or at least removed to the BBC Special Projects

1

Department, a black hole into which awkward employees are thrown, never to be seen again.

My survival owes much to the pulsating chameleon which is the Corporation. It is a peculiar institution – but not the dinosaur so often depicted. It's an eccentric creature, constantly changing, but never managing to get its camouflage quite right in order to blend in with its surroundings. Instead it highlights and reflects all manner of goings-on in society, frequently turns the wrong colour when browsing among politicians, and generates a fearsome amount of noise from its intestines, otherwise known as BBC Gossip.

Hitherto, it has kept to its path of public service broadcasting and acted as an extraordinarily benign host to those who work for it. It still has impressive impact worldwide, and generates affection and no little respect. Nevertheless, a chameleon is an embarrassing sight in a world where business management is preferred to adventure, and where character and creativity and cussedness are less welcome than convention and the bland pleasing of the customer.

On the numerous occasions when I've been hauled over the BBC carpet (green, frayed and wine-stained until the consultants arrived with tasteful grey), there was always the feeling that, whatever your sins, the BBC would vigorously fend off the critics – while pasting you to the floor. Only failing to possess a current TV licence or having sex during transmission of an Act of Worship would see you fed to the lions and dismissed. Not to mention committing a Royal to the hereafter before they'd officially dropped off the perch. Anything else – being drunk on air, crashing £45,000 worth of BBC armoured land rover, flying to the wrong country, embarrassing the government, enraging cabinet ministers, falling asleep while live on air to the *Today* programme – was treated as an internal matter, to be dealt with rigorously, while simultaneously mounting a stout public defence of the reasons for your behaviour. I should know; I've done all of these things.

As a reporter, you are only as bold as the management behind you. To deliver certain stories you need the backing of experienced editors and managers, confident in their principles and loyal to their staff. If that confidence and loyalty begin to diminish, then reporters become less able to ask hard questions and probe more deeply into sensitive subjects. And obtaining the facts becomes more difficult.

The BBC I joined was a brilliant cultural circus presided over by a tiny but wily civil service-type management. The combination was pragmatic: creative geniuses were tolerated as long as they didn't go outside and frighten the horses. I worked on a radio station where the estranged wife of an adulterous producer attempted very determinedly to brain him with a cast-iron frying-pan until four members of staff intervened. The BBC memo about this incident merely enquired whether this had happened on BBC premises. When assured that this was so, the BBC sighed with relief and promoted him.

During a party to celebrate six months of desperate struggle for survival on a local radio station, my colleagues got totally pickled, kindly remembering to send an endless supply of gin and tonic to the unfortunate creature in the studio upstairs in charge of the evening's broadcasting. Needless to say, I was legless when I had to tackle a long list of announcements on air, including the 'What's On' list of bring and buy sales, the appeals for Missing Cats, the local fatstock market prices – full of mysterious references to gilts, gimmers and fat sheep – and the weather forecast. The subsequent inquest with the station manager contained the following exchange:

'Could you explain the phrase: "stuff the gilts"?'

'Er ... possibly.'

'What about: "Who's a nice fat sheep then?"'

Having established that I was the guilty party, the station manager seemed unsure what to say. For a moment he muttered about the importance of agricultural prices to our farming listeners. Then he suddenly said:

'Did you read the weather forecast as well?'

The red light went on in my newly fledged broadcaster's brain. The BBC might tut-tut over mucking about with the price of sheep and pigs, but the weather forecast? A sacred cow, interference with which was likely to be a sackable offence.

'No, I didn't read it,' I said truthfully, and received a short lecture on alcohol and broadcasting.

Of course I didn't read it. Apparently, I sang it.

None of this happened in a Golden Age. As a junior underling in local radio, I was frequently harangued by venerable old hands who spoke in disgusted tones about 'the decline in standards', adding, 'Reith would never have stood for it, you know.' For years I was under the impression that Lord Reith, the Corporation's puritanical and high-minded founding father, had just recently left the building. It came as something of a shock to discover that he'd departed before the Second World War began. Even so, changes never occurred in the institution without a great deal of shouting, intrigue and theatrical scenes, with the staff eventually learning their fate via the newspapers.

Pop music, women reading the news, phone-in programmes – all were hot topics for radio when I joined in the late sixties, and all were thought to herald the end of broadcasting civilisation as we knew it. Added to this was the prospect of transmitting programmes after midnight (sinful), playing jingles (vulgar) and using new portable tape-recorders which didn't weigh half a ton (death of engineering standards). As I began my first local radio training course in London, the BBC was seething with resentment and anxiety.

Even so, some habits remained rock-solid. Issues which raised ethical dilemmas were picked over by meticulous-minded heads of department. Production values were subjected to academic scrutiny. Journalism was conducted according to rules which were prissy by Fleet Street standards, but which aimed for accuracy and significance. Above all, the audience was considered to be grown up and deserving of the best – and what was good for them. There was no doubting the BBC's conviction that it delivered what it thought people ought to have, rather than what they might want.

(This is not to say that as an organisation it was illiberal. True, there were rules about 'relationships', stipulating that couples were not meant to work for the same department; however, it quickly dawned that this was on the grounds of public decency, as microphones had been known to be left on while passionate staff utilised cosy, dim-lit studios. Added to this, the entire Drama Department appeared to be gay; its members, propositioning everyone in the lifts, sent us horrified radio station trainees scuttling out in provincial indignation.)

The principles of broadcasting, a distillation of over forty years' experience, were dinned into us with an assurance that verged on arrogance at times. Intellect, history and culture were pre-eminent, whether your ambition was to produce variety shows or football outside broadcasts. The audience was to be respected, but not patronised. And in news, facts came first, with opinion, speculation and personal emotion considered improper and distracting.

Of course, the BBC has changed – and it has needed to. The chameleon has to adapt, otherwise it doesn't deserve to survive. Taste and popular culture, fashion and style, public opinion and social attitudes are permanently on the move. However, in the last ten years of the twentieth century the Corporation not only saw an alteration to its outer skin, reflecting a fast-moving society, but also changed inwardly, losing many of the old certainties based on experience, and replacing them with a theory of management that owed much to business practice and an increasing sense of insecurity. The audience ceased to be respected and came to be seen as a consumer whose desires were to be catered for, and audience figures achieved a daily influence on production decisions.

As a reporter, my involvement in such matters was minimal. However, at the start of the nineties I found myself at a very glamorous free lunch at the Edinburgh television festival, sitting between two smart young men who held their discussion across me as if I were an irritating empty chair. I was curious about their conversation, which was full of yelps of enthusiasm about money. They were discussing Product, and passing figures and phone numbers to each other. I pronged my fork into one of the paws opening a filofax on my plate.

'I can't help overhearing your conversation,' I tried politely. 'So that I can spend the next forty minutes enjoying it, perhaps you'd explain what Product is?'

They looked at me as if I'd padded out of a case at the Natural History Museum.

Condescendingly, one of them said: 'Well it's what you BBC types do.'

'We do programmes,' I ventured.

'So *traditional*,' he brayed, '*so* seventies.'

I mentally padded back into my display case, musing on Product: a product of Business, of the world of economic efficiency, profits and bottom lines.

A year later, a BBC memo made its way to one of my colleagues in Bosnia, a camerawoman of considerable courage and great experience. Staff in the BBC have always been on first-name terms with each other, regardless of status; a familiarity which often shocked outsiders thirty years ago, and which was regarded as proof of degenerate behaviour by the corps of commissionaires who manned our front doors. 'Dear Sue' would have been the usual form of address from the Corporation, or perhaps 'Dear Colleague'. None of us knew what to make of her new communication, which began: 'Dear Operative'.

Gradually, we learned. The BBC was shedding its gothic past, being stripped and shredded, and cut into bite-size business-friendly chunks. Remodelling, streamlining and internal marketing were on the way, with lots and lots of Management. Management was a growth industry within the BBC, like a mad fungus which stuck its greasy stalks into every crevice and expanded to block light and logic. We 'Operatives' were no longer trusted with decision-making, and if we questioned the twaddle which was issued to justify the 'selling' of car park spaces from one department to another, it was suggested that we needed to go on A Course. On A Course, you learned that colleagues were no longer colleagues; they were Clients or Customers.

Everything was subject to cost analysis, and had its price – even pronunciation. Newsreaders were dissuaded from ringing up the venerable Pronunciation Unit because 'each call is charged to our budget', resulting in vagaries such as a Chinese politician being named in various bulletins as Ding Xiao Ping, Dung Xiao Pang and Deng Xiao Pong. Mission Statements took over from ideas and creativity: even a themed week of religious radio programming was considered incomplete without a Mission Statement. Mildly incredulous, I suggested 'I believe in one God,' and was asked to leave the room, being deemed not sufficiently sympathetic to minority views.

The place had gone unhappily loopy, mired in constant re-organisation, obsessive emphasis on administration, and volumes of gobbledygook statements on Vision and Strategy. Staff posts were disappearing; contracts ran for just a few months, and insecurity gnawed at every level. The new Management quite coolly laid into their own Operatives in public, and 'BBC stories' acquired a vicious edge, with the sight of an ancient animal chomping its own entrails too tasty to ignore.

More than anything, there was a loss of confidence. One day, a 361-page manual arrived on everyone's desk. Entitled *Producers' Guidelines*, it covered every imaginable decision that a programme-maker might have to make, from four-letter words to focus groups. In itself, it was a wordy but harmless publication, stating the obvious. That it was found imperative to exhort the staff to refer to it at all times, and treat it as the newly delivered Bible According to Birt, wherein all was to be revealed to an uncomprehending and uneducated workforce, was both depressing and enfeebling. Mr John Birt was director-general at the time, and bore most respons-ibility for the collapse of internal confidence. It was difficult to discern his personal thoughts on altering the BBC so drastically. No one could understand his Birtspeak memos and he was known to be uncomfortable talking to the staff; he seemed to think it pointless.

How all this came about has been catalogued and claimed by those who were in charge; a mixture of the great and the good, the politically well-connected and the seriously ruthless. A mixed salad of British ambition sprinkled with titles and dressed ever more sharply.

To a reporter stuck in the middle of Bosnia for much of this time, it appeared to be a long-distant farce with few laughs. However, so far the madness of managers had usually been kept separate from the function of broadcasting. Those of us at the coal-face used to hear of the goings-on among those upstairs, but assumed they'd keep their mitts off the actual programme-making – after all, there was still a mighty audience out there, and we were serving it.

Er, no.

The first indications of a major shift in the News Department were odd conversations down satellite telephones with assorted news producers and editors. With the Balkan conflict going at full blast, life was anything but simple; however, if we stuck to reporting the facts – the scenes we'd witnessed, the incidents we had verified – we managed to convey a limited but accurate picture of what was going on. Now, though, as we described how we'd spent four hours in a wet ditch being shot at in order to get vital evidence of ethnic cleansing, there'd be murmuring from London suggesting we were at cross-purposes. Again and again came the phrase, 'That's not the view from here. How *we* see it is . . .'

Initially, this was puzzling. How did a London producer see things from behind a warm desk in Shepherd's Bush, contemplating a pleasant lunch while grousing about the rigours of commuting from Islington? Not the same as we did, lying in a smelly puddle while a bunch of drunks used us for target practice and we contemplated escape via a four-hour cross-country ride in an armoured land rover towards a plate of bean soup and a widdle in the cabbage patch before retiring to a damp sleeping-bag.

The difference turned out to be not one of circumstances, but of agenda. 'London' was seeing News in a different light. According to the newly arrived thoughts from on high, news was being allowed to be far too unpredictable. All this unexpected and surprising stuff, which hadn't had time to be analysed or evaluated, never mind put in context – this was anathema to the orderly style of a well-behaved bulletin. Allowing those on the ground to gauge the significance of a story, follow events and deliver a messy slice of human life on to the screen offended instincts which denied the disorder of daily life and which had a mission to explain, instead of an obligation to report.

But there was a lot of disorder in daily life in Bosnia. It was also a test of survival for mere reporters. Over the five years we spent in the Balkans, it dawned on my colleague Martin Bell and myself that the news system we had known was being dispatched – though it dawned rather slowly, mainly because we were preoccupied with preventing ourselves being dispatched by the locals. Put simply, news was increasingly selected not for its significance, but for its interest. A growing nervousness about 'relevance' and 'accountability' was driving editors to include more items centred on consumer values and entertainment appeal, all packaged with presentation that was appealingly easy on the eye, and given pace with frequent 'live' spots. An underlying fear that viewers might be easily bored, or fail to find items 'relevant' to their own lives, narrowed horizons and widened the scope for sentiment and personal opinion. And the growth of 24-hour channels brought about a dramatic increase in speculation and comment – purely to fill the time available – from reporters who hitherto had not been expected to express opinions.

News found itself just one element in a world swirling with information of dodgy provenance, slick advertising and public relations half-truths. To stick to the facts in such circumstances was to be a dull root vegetable in a fancy box of chocolates.

However, who am I to complain? My own experience has been a journey of discovery which I never expected.

TWO

To Germany

I was a timid child. My idea of hell was being made to ask a stranger a question. Other than that, life was a sunny experience, full of meat-paste sandwiches and Sunday school, party frocks and tennis racquets, totally devoid of all the drama which makes for an interesting background of deep psychological significance. My nearest encounter with any form of violence was in the Brownies, where we Pixies occasionally tripped up the fatter Fairies, in order to win some utterly pointless game. That I have ended up interviewing strangers for a living is merely a quirk of bloody-mindedness, for I'm still rather shy. However, if that's the cost of being able to eat spare camel-rib and visit the Taj Mahal, wear old jeans and go to war, I haven't any regrets.

And I was a happy child, skipping through the fifties, a time of calm and convention for the middle classes, with parents thankful for routine and certainty after the alarms and excursions of war. A time of well-ordered conformity, with good behaviour a virtue to be prized above most others. We lived on the outskirts of Sunderland, all neat gardens and dog-walking, with so little traffic that playing in the street was natural, punctuated with only one or two cries per morning of 'There's a car coming!' We children had no concept of any threat to our existence, and were a resoundingly boring example of quite well-mannered obedience. We didn't care, for we knew no different. There was a hint of another sort of life on the huge council estates, and in the alleys of the town's east end, but, I'm ashamed to say, I was devoid of curiosity and felt there was nothing wrong with complacency. I was much loved and given all the chances that a little girl was given in those days – ballet lessons, piano tuition, a private education and a puppy. Outward Bound courses, consciousness-raising, girls' soccer and equality hadn't yet been invented. What you never have . . .

I wasn't a total vegetable, though: I bookwormed my way through anything in print, including the cereal packet on the breakfast table, and developed a habit of asking Why, as long as it didn't involve strangers. My first school report noted these habits, adding that 'Kathryn has a very loud voice', though it was a mere forty years later, after being blown up by a rocket-launched grenade while playing Scrabble in Beirut, that I was finally diagnosed as having been partially deaf in both ears since birth.

So: shy, complacent and a bit deaf – anybody like to hire me as a reporter?

To Germany. On the seafront at Sunderland there was a wooden signpost on the cliff top. It pointed out to sea, and read: To Germany.

On what was, in the north-east, classified as a hot summer's day, we took the tram and spent hours in the bracing wind, at the foot of the Cat and Dog Steps, on the preferred – for the middle classes – stretch of the three-mile beach which could rival the Riviera, according to the locals, if it weren't for the wind straight in from Siberia.

Rituals were performed. Egg and tomato sandwiches; and mass hypothermia, as we children turned blue in the North Sea next to the Cannonball Rocks. I suspect that the dedication to 'going to the beach' on every possible day when frost seemed unlikely had a touch of wartime influence. For the grown-ups, the parents, the wonderful flat, clean sand had been out of bounds for six years, with coils of barbed wire to repel Hitler. A cement pill-box lurked under the cliffs at nearby Whitburn. It ponged, and we were warned never to enter. All of us solemnly believed the pong was due to a large part of Hitler's Wehrmacht having perished therein. If it wasn't some kind of military fly-trap, we children pondered, then what was it?

Anyway, questions about such matters were brushed aside by the war-fighting generation. They all wanted to concentrate on the future. Put the war behind them. Occasionally snippets of conversation pointed to evidence that some girls' parents seemed to have had an exciting time – Spitfires and foreign places and intimations of rather too racy behaviour, especially involving mothers who'd been WAAF officers. An incomprehensible set of images. The only thing that sounded remotely like WAAF was giraffe – and although so-and-so's mother was tall, surely that was where the resemblance ended? There were also frequent references to 'the day Number 27 got it'. This referred to one of the many gaps between the houses. Curiously, rebuilding seemed out of the question. Once bombed, a place seemed to stay that way. At least, that was how we children saw it. Never mind our greenhouse.

I was baffled by the importance of our greenhouse. It had seemed to sit blamelessly at the bottom of our garden, but it was spoken of by adults as if its destruction had been one of the war's main objectives, personally identified by Herr Hitler, who would stop at nothing to win the war, via Tunstall Park and its tomato-production centre. This apparent prime target of the Luftwaffe had been the family pride and joy just beyond the rockery at the bottom of the garden. My adopting parents, Wilfrid and Maud, had acquired their brand-new house in Tunstall Park just before war broke out, obviously unaware of Nazi designs on it. The demolition of the greenhouse occurred at ten past four in the morning with the arrival of a 500-pounder, which hit the concrete in the back lane. Every nice suburban semi for 300 yards around got a bit of bomb. Our prize exhibit was lodged in the sideboard: a three-inch lump of metal, always referred to puzzlingly as 'Jerry's', when asked about by a curious child. Other bits of shrapnel regularly popped up in the garden. Small, but naggingly heavy in a tiny hand. Bomb. Not like other bits of metal.

Sunderland was the fourth most bombed town in England. As ever, it was partly Newcastle's fault. Twelve miles away the Tyne, because of its naval shipyards, had been given the benefit of a smokescreen. Sunderland, with the Wear yards producing cargo vessels, was merely given a few barrage balloons and a number of rather ancient guns. Or so I heard. The war I heard of, or rather overheard about, was seen wholly through local perspectives. The 4 a.m. raid on the greenhouse had been entirely due to unsporting strategic use of Blackpool Tower. Local legend had it that, heading for Barrow-in-Furness and its shipyards, German planes passed over the north-east coast, their loads intact. They did their damage over on the west coast, and then, scurrying for home, flew south over Morecambe Bay to get their bearings. The received wisdom in Sunderland was that a sharp left-hand turn over Blackpool Tower brought the Germans on to a line which saw Sunderland as the last British outpost before gaining the North Sea. Anything which hadn't made it on to Barrow-in-Furness was duly delivered to Sunderland – which accounted for the lateness of the raids. Whether this was complete rubbish, dreamed up in shelters all over Wearside, I haven't a clue. But to a child it seemed like a typical Nazi deed, one which had seen our plucky greenhouse sacrificed to save a newly built battleship.

A large part of the fleet must have been spared, for Sunderland was littered with bombsites. They were natural adventure playgrounds for us, with huge chunks of concrete softened by buddleia. The raids left other reminders. We never put our hands down the back of sofas in search of lost sixpences or combs: 'Mind your hands,' was the admonishment, 'there's glass in there from every window in this house.' And our dog limped, for he had defied the Hun. A wily Manchester terrier, he had trotted off from the Morrison shelter in the dining room – a construction I could never envisage, which somehow involved the dining-room table and a meat-safe – and reappeared three miles away and four days later, sporting a poorly paw, otherwise referred to, quite seriously, as his war wound.

These glimpses apart, six years of conflict, to a child born just after peace descended, was a grey period; something determinedly put to one side by the grown-ups, referred to only with occasional nostalgia, when the wartime spirit was sighed for, wistfully. Perhaps the only time the war made an honest reappearance was on those days when the air-raid siren was tested. The awful rising wowl was frightening, not just for itself, but for the jump of fear that the adults displayed. Just a little whiff of what it had really been like, amid all the tales of firewatching and searchlights. Something that scared the grown-ups.

Otherwise, it was left for us children to discover the war for ourselves – in the heroic films, the memoirs of generals, the curious fact of rationing in the early fifties: were the Germans still targeting our convoys of sweets? At school, the war was never mentioned. For a start, the twentieth century never got a look-in, the Church School's company ethos being firmly rooted in the 1880s, when most of the mistresses appeared to have been born. In history lessons, even the First World War was considered a bit too 'fresh'. At the back of the school hall, next to the house shields, were photographs of four fearsome-looking ships: *Tiger*, *Panther*, *Swift* and *Drake*. The Great War wasn't yet history. Our school houses had been named after these dreadnoughts. We weren't a patriotic Church of England girls' school for nothing.

We were also the local snobs. There was no getting away from it. In a north-east town of considerable poverty, its riverbanks still lined with festering slums, a school where everyone spoke standard northern middle-class English rather than broad Geordie, and whose hockey teams were unpopular with state schools because we were so much taller, was the target of much local abuse.

I went to school dutifully, a conformist little creature who did her homework and was expected to do well in exams. Routine dominated everything, and rebellion was never considered by any of us – until we hit our mid-teens, when the school went into overdrive to suggest that boys were 'for later' and uniform should never be 'modified'. Our future was assured: we were the housewives and mothers of the future, nicely spoken and well-behaved, unless the Almighty thought fit to send us as Anglican missionaries to minister to 'unfortunate people'.

A succession of headmistresses attempted to define our position:

'High School girls are *leaders*. Others are less *fortunate*. Do not stand idly by.'

This bemused us; social obligations were a mystery. How were housewives leaders? The word Career was never uttered at school. Politics was *never* mentioned, either at school or at home. Parents voted Tory; a symbolic gesture, as the rest of the town believed the Lord God to have put the Labour party on earth.

I loved my town – and still do, though it's now achieved city status (a memorable occasion when the Queen received a firm elbow in the ribs as the mayor solicitously decided she needed reminding about unveiling the new coat-of-arms: 'Just press the button, pet'). Ringed by acres of housing estates, parochial, and visited only by mistake by people who took the wrong turn off the A1, it had seen the slow decline of shipbuilding with disbelief. In my childhood the riverbanks still clanged and hooted, shrouded in smoke and populated with monstrous boilers and steel plates and small men in thin jackets and mufflers and flat caps. From this mysterious inferno slid chunky cargo ships with a screech of retaining chains, down the ways with a final whoosh into the water. Only once were we schoolchildren even taken to the yards, and that was a pretty tame visit. Industry lived in a separate world, rough, grown-up and not for little girls. Nor, indeed, for adult women – the world of heavy industry was male in every aspect, extending beyond the high and excluding walls of the yards to the working men's clubs, the trade unions and the town centre pubs.

And then there was a social gap. The pits, the yards, the foundries were all run by families I knew, but worked in by thousands I rarely encountered. From the garden of our semi you could sometimes see in the far distance the tip of Silksworth pit-heap, glowing demonically at night, as fire from deep within surfaced and blazed for weeks. Later, I longed to have seen more of the guts and grit of everyday work. The conformity to social niceties in a town like Sunderland in the fifties was breathtaking. Nothing dramatic; just an acceptance that accent, school and job description marked everyone indelibly, and it was rude to draw attention to such matters. Protest, criticism and reform were not the stuff of our lives; such activities would be regarded as 'making an exhibition of yourself'. Money was a subject never mentioned: we aspired to being, and indeed were, 'comfortable', with a car, and long summer holidays spent in Scotland or Cornwall. I had no inkling of the depth of wealth that suburban Surrey or Berkshire took for granted. However, the upside of narrow comfortableness was a sense of security, a conviction that the world was benign and stable.

The war lurked, but was never defined, throughout childhood. Admittedly I learned German, but as all the textbooks were prewar – one of the advantages of a private school being everyday familiarity with decaying ancient objects – and the mistresses who taught us had memories of a distinctly pre-Hitlerian period, there was little connection between the language and the recent Unpleasantness. On the other hand, I was a dab hand at reading Gothic script. Nobody had told our school that modern Germans had ditched it.

A school exchange in the late fifties to a *Gymnasium* near Frankfurt widened our horizons just a fraction. There had been mixed feelings about our trip. 'Bit too soon' was heard from the grown-ups, an attitude that baffled us, for surely it had been a lifetime since the war ended. Well, our lifetime, anyway. But we were curious. We'd seen old newsreel films of Dresden; of the Russians in Berlin, and the mounds of rubble. Our teenage years had seen Richard Todd busting the Möhne Dam, and Trevor Howard and everyone else getting out of Stalag Luft via wooden horses. And endless dogfights over the fields of Kent. And lines of refugees when we saw Pathé newsreels on trips to the 'news theatre' in Newcastle. I suppose we expected to find the Germans living in temporary accommodation. After all, Sunderland was still full of bomb sites, and the country didn't feel very affluent, when all British teenagers lusted after was an American way of life, full of huge shiny cars, drive-in movies and rock'n'roll.

Frankfurt turned out to be surprisingly substantial. It had more new buildings than we'd ever clapped eyes on – soaring modern towers, and a fabulous sports centre with a turquoise swimming pool encased in a glass palace. This did not reflect well, postwar – same war? – on Sunderland's municipal baths, which clearly doubled as a chlorine factory, and were lined with lavatory tiles. However, in Offenbach, the small town nearby where I was staying, I was disconcerted to see that every bus had two seats labelled sternly: *Für Kriegsblessierte*. The idea that so many people might have been wounded so as to need special places on buses was new to me. However, my hosts, identical twins my age, with impeccable manners, never mentioned the war – which was quite a good thing, as I'd learned that their father had been in the Luftwaffe, and was therefore immediately associated with our greenhouse. So I never raised the subject.

Some days later, though, walking in the local park, I asked the twins why this otherwise immaculate park had a building pitted with curious circular blotches. *Kugeln*, they said, a hint embarrassed. I went back to their apartment and looked up the word.

Bullets. I was fascinated. Had there been a battle? Just like in the films? The idea that soldiers had fought over a public park bewildered me. Especially as the bullet-ridden building had been identified by the twins as *Toiletten*. I was more confused by this near-encounter with actual war damage than any bomb site or pill-box had hitherto prepared me for. Toilets and greenhouses: what was war really about?

Conflict in itself, though, didn't intrigue me. I was a girl. I knew nothing of battles, and had never evinced the slightest interest in warfare, guns or soldiers. I wasn't even aware, not having grown up with brothers, that boys were infatuated with such matters. The world of toy soldiers, of pretending to be a Lancaster bomber, of shouting I'm the King of the Castle, of constructing the *Ark Royal* in matchsticks, never impinged. Decades later, I'd be amazed to meet men who had been imbibing aircraft types, categories of tank and the characteristics of Walther PPKs since they were seven – and could still recite lists of stuff. I achieved adulthood unable to distinguish between a tank and an aardvark.

Indeed, the first time I saw someone carrying a gun I was shocked.

I was eighteen and in Berlin. Having rather a good time at Newcastle University, I'd completely forgotten that a spell in Germany was necessary before I took second-year exams in the language. I was confronted by my ever-tolerant professor: 'Where are you going next week then?'

I rightly suspected that the answer was not meant to be Home. Should it perhaps be Stockholm, I thought? As I was reading Scandinavian Studies, majoring in Swedish, this seemed like a likely place.

'The capital?' I ventured.

'What on earth do you want to go to Bonn for?' he said. 'It's a boring backwater.'

I did a few calculations. Getting the odd intransitive verb wrong attracted a bit of disapproval from professors. Getting the country wrong might make a considerable dent in my degree prospects. I tried again.

'Berlin?'

'Marvellous,' said Professor Mennie. 'Politics, history, a divided city, lots to learn. All those Russians. And then there are the spies,' he added, 'but don't get too mixed up in things. I'll give you one piece of advice. We haven't got any diplomatic relations with the East Germans. I did know a nice professor at Humboldt University – but I think he's been shot. So if you get into trouble, you're on your own.'

My mind went a bit blank. Two minutes earlier I hadn't been contemplating going anywhere, never mind plunging into the world of espionage. However, Duncan Mennie was nothing if not inspirational. He spoke over thirty languages, was a brilliant teacher, and had run the BBC's counter-propaganda broadcasts to Germany's Lord Haw-Haw during the war, working with Hugh Carleton Greene, later to become director-general of the BBC. A Highland Scot from Deeside, he believed education to be the permanent acquisition of knowledge, in all its forms. Ignorance, and especially incuriosity, in his students produced snorts of frustration, followed by the instant infusion of information. Lectures on Old Icelandic literature were diverted to encompass the invasion strategy of Genghis Khan, the history of the stirrup, how to classify worms and serpents, and instructions on successful seal-spotting. Being especially ignorant about medieval warfare, I was a sitting duck for the professor's vast and entertaining fount of wisdom. After two terms, I could have personally conducted a Viking raid, twined enemy intestines round a handy tree and carved several rune stones to mark my victory.

I was reading Swedish for a degree in Scandinavian Studies entirely by chance. I'd spent the summer after leaving school with the National Youth Theatre in London and had been entranced by all things theatrical, to the extent of taking no notice of my dismal A-Level results – the product of much partying and tennis, a hefty dislike of Wordsworth and Goethe, and a fanciful desire to read Italian and French at a fashionable university such as Bristol. As September loomed, my parents and my headmistress became desperate. *Someone's* name had to be engraved on the University Entrants Board, and I was the only likely candidate that year (expensive education doesn't necessarily go hand in hand with academic prizes, but you do get bags of confidence). The head made a few phone calls, and in a year when the government was tootling a fanfare about the newly operational student admissions systems – 'fair, equable, none of this back-door stuff' – I went straight in the back door. On the first day of my student life I encountered Professor Mennie, who couldn't remember my name (it wasn't on the official list) but who had an inkling that I was the one with the dodgy results.

'You'll be expected to work hard and get a good degree,' he said, with a slight air of threat.

'Certainly,' I said, 'er, what in?'

'Swedish and German and Old Icelandic,' he replied, spelling out four years in three seconds.

I adored his breadth of learning. He was endlessly enthusiastic, and he couldn't wait to send his students away from their cosy nests to learn about life elsewhere. We were, without realising it, part of the generation which was going to venture back into Europe, but not to fight. The notion of student travel was just beginning, and we, catapulted unexpectedly into higher education as a result of the university expansion of the 1960s, were wondering about 'abroad'. To us as students the world – or at least, that attainable by a train from Calais or Ostend – the world, known to our parents as a six-year battleground, beckoned. Most of us had never been there, though I'd been lucky, as we'd ventured a couple of times on family holidays to France and Italy. The package trip was only just being invented. My school had once rashly taken the fifth and sixth forms skiing in Switzerland, only to discover, inevitably, that we were unimpressed with the Alps and rampant in the face of Alpine ski instructors. Luckily, the school had insisted that we wore uniform much of the time when we weren't actually on the slopes, and the appearance of dumpy girls in hairy grey tweed reminiscent of the Russian army acted as a sad deterrent to passion.

Now, in front of my professor, I was making swift plans.

'Berlin,' I repeated. 'But I'm not sure about the course I'm meant to go on.'

He burrowed in a file.

'Freies Universität, that's the one, I'll send them a telegram. And you can stay at the Victoria Studentinnenheim. I don't think it got bombed in the war – anyway, you'll soon find out.' He tossed me a booklet.

'Well, get going, lassie, the course starts in three days.'

'Um, via Ostend? Er, how?'

'Get a map, for God's sake. Aren't you the one with a boyfriend with a car?' (A rare catch in those days.) 'Get him to take you to London. A girl intending to get a degree should be able to find Dover. Off you go.'

And so I did. I called home, omitting references to spies and trouble. There was silence on the line. I made reassuring noises, but realised that I was thought to be heading directly for the Führer's bunker. I cajoled Jonathon into driving me south, and went out and bought Isherwood's *I Am a Camera*, the only novel I knew to mention Berlin. This being the non-gay sixties, I was puzzled by much of the book, but looked forward to meeting lots of spies in night-clubs. I omitted this in the call home, too.

To Germany . . .

I can vividly recall the thrill of standing on the station platform at Ostend, reading the destinations on the railway carriages. Berlin. Warsaw. Moscow. I could hardly believe that you could just hop on a train and head off for such exotic destinations. I felt like an explorer. The trains were mostly drab grey-green, and demanded mountaineering expertise to board. I commandeered a corner seat, and realised that I hadn't a clue what might lie ahead. I'd led what you might call a sheltered life. Streetwise I was not. But I wasn't aware of my short-comings. My main aim was to find kindred spirits on the train, preferably male, aged eighteen to twenty, good-looking and not too foreign.

By Brussels, I'd already found several likely soulmates, and was sitting on the top couchette opposite a tasty French rugby-player, singing early Simon and Garfunkel, and eating very old British sandwiches – Belgian food was a mystery, and likely to remain that way. Did such a small country, peopled by customs officers in musical comedy uniforms, actually have a cuisine? Who was Stella Artois? A giant neon sign hung in the sky as we passed through the Belgian capital – perhaps half the answer to the challenge: name two famous Belgians.

The Continent. Foreign in every way to me and my peers. Academics and wealthy independent travellers might have tasted its pleasures; but for us, it was a place which didn't feature in our culture. Growing up in the fifties, the golden glow of the future was coming from America in the shape of hula-hoops, chewing gum, Bill Haley, convertible cars, *I Love Lucy* and *Wagon Train* – and, for us students, protest, Bob Dylan and President Kennedy, the first politician we'd ever seen who didn't resemble a fossil.

The singing continued right through Belgium into West Germany. No one in the sixties travelled without a guitar, or at least the ability to join in suitable CND anthems. We were students of the world. We were the postwar children. We were all prepared to look like Peter, Paul and Mary, and demonstrate in the streets against absolutely anything. History was dead and buried. I felt hugely excited.

History was resurrected five minutes over the West German border into the territory of the East.

The train sat in a field. For ages. I produced my trusty map. We were some miles into East Germany, past the Helmstedt border crossing-point. Myself, the two other British students, the three French and the American with the guitar hadn't much notion about life in the East.

'Commies,' said the musician. 'I heard they don't have bathrooms.'

We discussed Stalinist plumbing. Meanwhile, from the field came the sound of barking Alsatians. Before we had time to survey the scene, a keen and huge dog lurched into the compartment, attached to a policeman. We stared at them.

The policeman shouted at us. Most of the words appeared to come from films about the war: *Achtung! Papiere! Heraus!* We goggled, then giggled. Then the Alsatian discovered the remains of Ye Olde British Sandwiche plus wrappings next to me, and tore them apart alarmingly. He didn't look pattable. Nor did the policeman. A confusing three minutes followed. All my German lessons up to then had concentrated on polite conversation: Good morning, could you tell me the way to the post office, please? I wasn't familiar with the German for Get your wolf off my lap and where are you going with our passports you lout?

The American lad was thoroughly upset, attempting to lecture a corridor-full of 'Commie cops', as he endearingly addressed them, on the subject of democratic rights, man. They took his guitar, shook it, then stuck a piece of bent wire through the hole and fished around in it. We gave up remonstrating about passports to stare, mesmerised. This produced further shouting, several snapped guitar strings and a shoving match to get us back into the compartment. World students that we were, we weren't having anything of this. As veterans of many a demo, we heaved purposefully against the police (I noticed the French rugby-player's muscles . . .). The cops fell over, absolutely pug-eyed. It hadn't dawned on us that opposition was an unknown concept to them. Before we all became Western martyrs for democracy, fate intervened in the form of a train whistle. Amid much shouting and universally understood gestures, the police left, tossing our passports back through the window.

God, we were naïve. We thought we'd scored a few points. We squeaked with rage in French and English. All the way to Berlin, we banged on about outrageous behaviour and Who Won The War. We were clueless. But we felt we'd made our mark. We looked forward to our next demo.

Ensconced the next morning in the Victoria Home for Female Students – seventh floor, garret, no lift, but with good view over the rooftops of Russian MiGs flying illegal low-level sorties to annoy West Berliners – I decided that the train journey had been enough excitement to last a year.

I set off for the American-backed Freies Universität, clutching a street map and a piece of paper which the student home superintendent had handed me. Room 235, ten o'clock. I clattered quickly down long cobbled streets, eager and determined. I felt very much on my own. I was sharing my garret with a Greek girl, whose German was pretty ropey. She'd come in late the night before and impersonated a dead log until after breakfast, so clearly didn't have a nice respectable language course to attend that morning. I studied the map every ten yards, and eventually galloped into the right street. I was flustered. Memories of school on the exchange visit to Frankfurt prompted fear of rigid German punctuality, and lots of strange formalities before lessons began.

There was a crowd outside the main gate, and lots of vehicles. Popular holiday course, I thought, elbowing my way politely through, head down, checking Room 235. I shoved through the throng towards the main staircase. The steps were a thick blanket of sitting students. I clambered up, excusing myself in my best German. I gained the main corridor, and luckily, with only seconds to go to ten, spotted 235 above a doorway five yards away. Just about the last thing I coherently remember. Ten o'clock must have been zero hour for the Berlin Police

Department. The sound was awesome as several hundred of Berlin's finest took on several thousand students.

This was the era of the sit-in – a student tactic used across the world, deeply irritating to authority – and, in my efforts to be punctual and possibly avoid any more foreign excitement in deference to my professor, I'd ploughed my way to the very centre of one of Berlin's bigger protests.

The next hour was a bit of a blur. Suffice it to say that not everyone went peacefully. I became aware that most Berlin cops were mountainous men, but not necessarily agile. As a dutiful English girlfriend, I'd watched a good deal of rugby. Now I found out what it was like to be in a scrum involving several hundred people. However, after a confused amount of thumping and shoving, it turned out that the most honourable action – this being the sixties – was to be carried out and hurled into a truck (they'd run out of proper police vans before they got to our floor), while chanting slogans. The latter was beyond me, as my German didn't yet include enough obscenities. Also I had no idea what the protest was about.

I got time to find out. Twenty-six hours in some anonymous barracks, squashed in a room with eighteen women and a bucket. I went through the usual catalogue: sense of outrage, anger, prissy teenage concern for personal hygiene (the bucket), and the suppression of the desire to remark to my fellow inmates Who Won The War Then, as the majority were German. It was my first taste of being utterly unable to do anything about my situation. A little lesson in what it's like to get banged up, with no kindly Dixon of Dock Green sergeant entering to say Your mother's here, or Would you like a solicitor? Instead, some old boot delivered inedible slop, and I entertained fears of being plopped down some German oubliette to moulder undiscovered for twenty years. A little shiver went down the spine. Helpless. No contacts. No influence. Nobody even knew about what had happened; and other people, who'd just given you a number of very nasty bruises, were in charge. There wasn't too much time for quiet reflection, though. The rest of the room engaged in noisy political debate all day and through the night. After several hours and a lot of very lengthy German nouns, it emerged that we'd all been demonstrating against the Berlin authorities' refusal to recognise the Communist party in the city. Not exactly what I'd ever considered going to the stake for.

Unceremoniously hoofed out of the barracks the following morning, I scuttled back to the student home, vaguely suspecting that passers-by could see the mark of the gaolbird on me. Luckily – this being the sixties – a phone call home would never have been expected, and I thought it unwise to send a postcard saying Weather fine, not seen much of it due to imprisonment.

The university closed temporarily, which was all the excuse I needed for exploring Berlin. I teamed up with two German boys from Stuttgart and the girl from Athens. Day Two, so no more Trouble, eh?

We did the sights, walking everywhere – we had little money. Berlin looked as if it had only just seen the dust settle on the war. Once-grand buildings sat around in ruins near the Tiergarten. But in the centre, a concrete monster of a shopping centre had just arisen, all modern walkways and ugliness. The city had an energy peculiar to it – or was it that I had read too much Isherwood, and was sniffing a raffishness that had not really survived? Even so, there was an odd excitement in the air. And literally in the air, as we headed past the shiny shops on the Ku'damm. Soviet MiGs overflew at frighteningly low level, part of the regular confrontation and 'show of strength' game – I later learned – that went on at that time. I'd only seen warplanes in films before; not only were these the real thing, they weren't Ours. I wondered if we should fling ourselves into a convenient ditch, only there weren't any ditches in the Ku'damm, and no one else seemed to be taking evasive action. The jets boomed through the sound barrier for good measure. I began to be fascinated. Berlin, to my delight, was not like Newcastle at all, give or take the odd bomb site.

Berlin ladies sat at pavement café tables and shook their fur-cuffed fists at the MiGs. They appeared to be dressed as if ready for church in England ten years previously: neat, buttoned-up, hat-wearing and solemn. And there seemed so many of them. I couldn't understand why the city was peopled with middle-aged females. *Die Witwe* – the widows. I hadn't realised the war had left different marks here.

We were footsore, and hungry for dinner. The German lads took us to a student-crammed bar, where I cottoned on to acknowledging modestly that I'd been part of the 'Freies-riot' the day before, and met several other European students who'd had a noisy night in the barracks. Celebration was plotted – where should we modern, pan-European students eat a stupendous dinner and drink much beer, for just a few deutschmarks? Ratskeller of course. Town Hall cellar, thought I? Sounds a bit grand.

'No, ever so cheap,' said the Greek girl, 'you and the French two head for the underground, and the rest of us'll go the other way.'

I hadn't a clue about these travel directions. Still, we scampered into the S-Bahn station. I'd given the city maps a cursory glance in the student home, and had worked out that there was something funny about them. Berlin was a divided city. So what happened, I'd wondered, when the underground line headed for the Wall? Just an idle bit of wondering, for the very notion of East Berlin was terrifying. This was the era of hideous events on the Berlin Wall; of regular attempts at escape, often with dreadful consequences. By 1964, it had matured as a barrier. It had been heightened and land on the east side laid waste, to give Ossies – Ostdeutsche, East Germans – less chance of making it through the wire and past the dogs and guards. That afternoon we'd paid the statutory visit to Checkpoint Charlie, one of the official crossing-points manned by the Americans. It was on the tourist trail, and a small room nearby was plastered with photographs of escape attempts – some full of cheering people surrounding a wild-eyed winner who'd made it to the West, others showing a dark hump of clothing flopped among the concrete and weeds in the East. It hardly seemed real as we stepped outside the room, for on an ordinary day there was traffic over the checkpoint – the four allies, Britain, France, the United States and the Soviet Union, maintaining the military agreement almost as if the Wall were invisible. Yet there it was, and half a city existed the other side, in another world.

So that evening I sat on the S-Bahn, and asked the French girl why the Germans had a cheap restaurant in the Town Hall. 'Probably nobody asked them,' she said, 'the Russians decide those things.

The penny dropped fast. Town Hall – in – in . . .

'Yes,' she said. 'City divides – West Berlin gets the Zoo, East Berlin the Town Hall.'

The S-Bahn changed its rumble as we crossed water. The Spree. I knew enough geography to realise I was trundling into another world.

I have in my memory a black-and-white scene, which I can recall every time someone talks to me about guns.

I had never seen anyone carrying a gun. I wasn't even very familiar with country shotguns, though one of our neighbours occasionally went off to Northumberland to fetch a bunch of sticky pheasanty feathers. But a revolver, or a rifle, or a semi-automatic machine gun: these were objects of film and unreality.

As we alighted at Friedrichstrasse station, I stared up at the huge semi-circle of glass arching over the tracks. There was pinkish soft evening light criss-crossed with the impressive railway ironwork. Suddenly, a figure walked along the narrow catwalk at the base of the semicircle, a silhouette – a man with a rifle. I couldn't believe my eyes. Walking, in public? Just like that, with people getting off trains below him, and him carrying a dangerous weapon?

I was so shocked. Neither then nor since have I ever accepted the idea that such weapons should form part of normal, everyday life.

An hour later, we were stuffing ourselves with *Wurst* the size of industrial tubing, paid for out of a bag of Ossie cash received in exchange for a few West German deutschmarks. Clearly, the West might feed our minds, but the East did a terrific job on the body. So began weeks of crossing the best-guarded border in Europe, in order to consume mounds of (to us) cheap food. The madness of a divided city had its roots in the war, which had given it its structure. Every day, there were ritual military patrols involving the occupying four powers, 'the allies', crossing the city as if the barbed wire and free-fire zone of unofficial no-man's-land did not exist. Presentation of a British passport in East Berlin produced a strangulated mutter about *Die Alliierte* – but it meant a privileged passage for me, one of the allied citizens; I – or my French and American friends – could travel in minutes via S-Bahn over the strip of land which citizens of the People's Republic saw as a firing range.

I began to cross during the day in order to poke around the gingerbread architecture and the war ruins. I was riveted. Naïve and rather accepting, I'd never had to teach myself about a different system. I sat in bars and met students from the Karl Marx University. They were none too keen on the off-duty Russian soldiers who drank gloomily in corners, but I wanted to meet real Reds with snow on their boots, and happily bought beers, courtesy of the ludicrous exchange rate, with my Ostmarks obtained at the obligatory currency swap at the station (a kind of entrance fee to the People's Republic). Before long, I had a very quirky acquaintance with life in Russia, oiled with hours of alcohol and song.

I walked marathons through the dowdy streets, rewarded one day with a squeaking whine from an alley of tatty lock-up garages and small workshops. Out from a garage crawled a tank. I gaped – another horrible first – and learned that the first instinct is not to cheer such things, as in all those war movies of liberation, but to leg it; even then I could not escape its persistent growling whine, like a monster in a nightmare.

There seemed to be almost no shops; only a few dusty windows full of ugly kitchen equipment and clothes which should only be bought at gunpoint. I unloaded my Ossie cash in the bookshop selling German classics. The Reklam editions were standard, and I acquired two centuries of writing printed in tiny paperbacks for a trifle. Unloading Ossie marks was a bit of a chore each day. You could only eat so much and carry so many books, and the remainder was literally shaken out of you at the railway station by stone-faced old trouts carrying inverted umbrellas into which to scatter your unused money.

Never mind; I was entranced. Each journey was an adventure. Conversations were curious, punctuated by sudden and frequent gaps. There were glaring no-go areas – in politics, in criticism, in opinion. The Karl Marx students wanted to know if we were paid a lot of money by our governments to go on demonstrations. When I explained the reality, they pondered on why we hadn't been shot by our army. I learned to avoid comparisons of societies: some students were Marxist speaking clocks of doctrinal drivel. Music, beer and food were safe bets. Still, the students – and the Russians – threw up little nuggets of information. How the authorities interfered with access to pop music. How short supplies were of certain basic foodstuffs – much of the Soviet Union's food appeared to spend its life either crossing Tajikistan in a railway wagon until it had gone off, or lurking 'under the counter'.

Here, the war seemed only an eye-blink ago. Whereas West Berlin echoed to construction work and rows about dealing with the decayed embassies in the Tiergarten, the East showed no embarrassment at the ghastly scarecrow of the Berliner Dom, the cathedral. I stood under its skeletal dome one morning, taking pictures of a shaft of sunlight in which a continuous stream of fine dust fell from the wrecked roof. The building was officially out of bounds, but I'd sneaked in via a broken side door, and ended up gossiping with the caretaker (bag of Ossie cash at the ready).

'Why isn't it being rebuilt?' I asked.

'God's not a big deal with the Visitors from Moscow,' was the caretaker's view; 'and then, of course, there's not a lot of money, of anything, because of the war.'

Problems on the Eastern side were always explained away with the words 'because of the war'. Nobody dared suggest that the looming Soviet presence might inoculate society against free thought and protest. As I walked the streets of both parts of Berlin, suffused with curiosity, the whole place seemed a *grand guignol* drama to which I had unexpectedly got a ticket. In this enclosed and loopy capital, I smelled a wider world, unthought-of horizons, so many questions.

The morning before I left, I was woken in my seventh-floor garret by the sound of my Greek room-mate trying to get under her bed. A very pale dawn light was coming through the dormer window. Greek is a linguistic closed book to me – but panic's pretty universal. I peered out over the pointy roof gables. The below-the-bed yowling yielded to a far-off rumbling. I half-crawled out of the window, craned over the tiles and stared down at Otto Suhr Allee. With headlights on, looking like giant crabs, a long column of tanks pushed slowly down the street. The noise was horrible, scraping and growling on the cobbles, welling up between the tall houses. For several seconds I succumbed to the headlines which had been blazoned across the right-wing Berlin tabloids. The Russkies were coming.

I wondered whether there was any point in investigating under-the-bed. It seemed a rather good idea. I learned in those few seconds how fear induces daftness, a need for a bolt-hole. The noise was all-enveloping. No one in the building would hear if you called out. There was no sign of anyone else, at windows or in the street. It was weird and frightening.

I decided to stare out my fate, crawled right out of the window to the ledge near the gutter and watched. I now knew the power that tanks had as they rolled into ordinary neighbourhoods – relentless, impervious beasts, against which there is nothing the citizen can sanely do. After a blank minute, logic finally took over. The column was heading *towards* the Brandenburg Gate, rather than having smashed triumphantly through it from the East. Moreover, the last in the line appeared to be flying a Union flag. Aha. One of ours. I felt very confused.

I'd never been scared of a vehicle before, or had cause to wonder about my safety. Life in Sunderland had no parallels. I felt an idiot – how come I can't recognise my own army? How could one even start to believe the propaganda about invasion and terror, so beloved of the locals and their newspapers? And I'd been physically frightened. I had one tiny crumb of bitchy comfort: I sat archly on the roof as the Greek girl crept out from hiding. 'Ours, of course,' I said, with as much disdainful cool as I could muster.

Setting off the next day, after a rather riotous night in a club which had resembled a multi-storey car park filled with competing pop groups, I contemplated a long snooze on the train. Sadly, I failed to get a seat. The world and his wife were fellow travellers, and I ended up on my suitcase in the corridor. I dozed, only to be lifted, case and all, into a compartment already stuffed to the roof. I squawked protest, but appeared to be being used to make a point by East German border guards at the Potsdam crossing from West Berlin through East Germany. *Verboten* is a word beloved of Germanic authority. Apparently sitting in corridors had been added to the *Verboten* list.

As we chugged though the East, I endeavoured to find a few square feet of room. No dice for the first hour. Then, as the border to West Germany approached, the population of several compartments began rearranging itself urgently. I nose-dived into a seat-space indicated by a nice-looking middle-aged woman, inserting myself between a mother and baby and a very ancient rigid female fossil in rather folksy clothes. Salami sandwiches appeared, followed by biscuits, cake and drink. Everyone ate very determinedly, insisting I join in. When I'd eaten more than adequately, my polite refusals were met with shrill insistence. 'Don't waste it,' they said, 'we know the Westerners will take everything – they're so short of food, you know.'

'No, they're not,' I replied.

'Well, that's what you Russians have always told us,' came the grumble. I explained myself, and produced the blue passport. Silence fell, followed by hurried consultations. They spoke a heavily accented German and turned out to be a large group of families from near the Polish border, who'd finally been allowed to travel westwards after years of bureaucratic negotiation 'because of the war'. They had all their worldly goods with them – or what they'd been allowed – in bundles stowed on the racks. They were extremely nervous.

After some prompting from granny opposite, the young mother asked shyly if I would hold her shawl-smothered baby. Certainly, I said – though I was unfamiliar with babies. Ten minutes later, the train bumped to a stop. I remembered the inbound journey, and decided to take a more determinedly British stand this time.

But this time, things started off more hectically, with every male hauled out of the carriage by the shouting-and-hungry-Alsatian method. They went meekly, adults of my parents' generation and older, fluttering their hands a bit as they passed the soldiers – part defence, part entreaty, utterly humiliating. Some bundles of belongings were tossed down and kicked apart. I sat my ground as the women started crying and the men were lined up against the train, hands in the air. I thought we'd dropped back two decades.

For several minutes a nasty shouting match took place, and I had the satisfaction of using lots of rude German, learned in bars East and West. Granny opposite also gave as good as she got, and got thumped as a result. The young mum was rigid beside me, and ponged of what I thought at the time was nervous sweat; years later I would have recognised it as the shit of fear. I hefted the baby under one arm as I dug out my passport. The border guard, a study in genetic simplicity, made a grab for it. No you don't, I said, and suggested that he was going to disappear from view with it, because he couldn't read. Granny, behind his back, made some placatory gestures, staring intently at me with her head cocked on one side. A bit thrown, I shoved the passport at him, and sat back grumpily. He read it, upside down, and threw it back at me.

More shouting and pleading came from outside. It all sounded entirely untheatrical and deeply sickening. These were travellers, ordinary people, my parents' age. Who gave anyone the right to push them around, threaten them, terrify them? I seethed with resentment.

The compartment filled to overflowing again, as the train was repacked randomly and at speed. Some bundles didn't get collected, and we set off with a lurch past bits of clothing and unidentifiable trinkets lying in the field. I couldn't think of what to say – but I found the family in the compartment relatively complacent, brushing down their clothes, checking the bundles remaining on the rack. I grew even madder. Didn't they know what an outrage it had been? Didn't they feel angry? But they just kept whispering: Are we in the West yet?

A matter of minutes later, we clanked past the Helmstedt signs. Granny stood up and uttered what I took to be prayers, until I realised she was waving her arms towards the baby, which I was still firmly clutching. She seized it and fell back on her seat, unravelling the shawl frantically. Out clinked the glinting coins, the gold jewellery, the silver family treasures.

I forced a smile, but felt a very strange feeling deep in the intestines.

I'd read the signpost To Germany, as a child, and thought it a kind of seaside joke. I had had no idea what getting to Germany would mean. In a few weeks I'd seen armed men, tanks, jets, the Wall, Russians, demonstrations and gaol. I had no inkling that such matters would become my bread and butter. What ignited deep inside of me was a sense of rage that ordinary people could be made to suffer humiliation and fear – and accepted it.

And that a very different, wide world existed all around me, and I was horrendously ignorant of it.

The window opened a little wider in my third year as a student. Because we were such a tiny band of scholars in Scandinavian Studies, we weren't farmed out to the usual foreign course for our year abroad, but placed in specific jobs. Professor Mennie had eyed me keenly, and observed: You look fit, off you go, the Arctic's fascinating. So I found myself on a train heading north of Stockholm with a seventeen-hour journey ahead, a hot-water bottle and a map on the top of my luggage.

Luleå was a dot almost at the top of the Baltic, a port dominated by a gigantic iron-ore processing plant serving the mineral mountains up in the Arctic. It was modern and efficient (I'd been expecting a frontier outpost peopled with elk-eating nomads). In every respect it emulated sixties Sweden: well-lit, clean, affluent and progressive; so progressive, indeed, that my residence permit had been issued in a glamorous civic office full of contemporary furniture by an elegant middle-aged woman who just happened to be chief executive. I was goggle-eyed. This was not what I was accustomed to; where was the fusty lino-floored Town Hall, staffed by unattractive men in cheap suits? And, I mean, a woman – how extraordinary, were Swedish women different, and not just in the much-publicised department of blond hair and free sex?

I was to spend my year in Luleå as a language-teaching assistant, later rather grandly entering on my BBC application form the phrase *the* Language Assistant for Southern Lappland – entirely accurately, seeing that no one else would be mad enough to spend a winter which reached minus 47° Fahrenheit trying to stop nine-year-olds losing fingers and earlobes to frostbite in the school playground. I also had to ski to school. How romantic, my student friends wrote back to me. They should try getting up at six and realising that two feet of snow had fallen overnight – and you'd left your skis outside. Never mind being whooshed past by seven-year-olds clearly ready for the Winter Olympics and without pity for the *engelska assitent* skidding schoolwards like a demented crab.

The teaching system was liberal towards behaviour but academically tough; the staff of the seven middle schools in Luleå were staggeringly well-paid and constantly gaining more qualifications in order to up their salaries even further. The children were relatively monstrous, coming from backwoods families attracted to the iron-ore industry; my favourite class was the sin bin, the *Specialer*, a mixture of behavioural problems and troublemakers. Heaven knows what they made of me, an untrained foreigner who cannoned into the yard with skis like busy knitting needles, but they responded to energy and interest.

I adored the Arctic north. 'Europe's last wilderness' was one of the descriptions of this vast stretch of fir-tree and moss and reindeer which began opposite my bedroom window on the edge of town and stretched to the Arctic ice. Upcountry, I saw and heard the aurora borealis – the rippling colours over a frozen forest, with a curious tinkle-crackle all around. Beneath were the reindeer: from afar, a sound of thunder as they circled in thousands during the annual round-up; up close, snuffly and adorable and very good to eat. Their herdsmen, the Lapps in their blue and red and yellow costumes, stank to high heaven. Modern life was putting a squeeze on their traditions, with pressure for them to settle – and perhaps to become acquainted with the octupus-like Swedish tax system. The Lapps were having none of it, but had nevertheless worked out a rather good wheeze for participating in the country's fiscal process. Ancient and dying reindeer were surreptitiously driven into the path of oncoming express trains from Stockholm, whereupon the government was howled at for its encroachment on traditional life – which might just be leavened by a little compensation payment. The Arctic might look primeval, but in many ways it was thoroughly modern. This included dealing with The Military Threat.

When I'd arrived in Luleå, I'd discovered that I was not only in North Bothnia, but in Defence Area 7. The Swedes, determinedly neutral, nevertheless spent a good deal on military weaponry, as befitted the inventors of dynamite and the Bofors gun. As an extra to my teaching job, I found myself giving English lessons to Swedish air force technical officers on a base to the north of the town. Only years later did I learn that I'd had to have security clearance – and that my professor, leaping at the chance of putting his wartime intelligence habits to use, had, without bothering to make any proper references to my family, cooked up an elaborate and unblemished background. He also happily told me that it had all gone on to the appropriate BBC file . . .

The Swedish technical officers must have despaired of my lack of familiarity with the French-built Draken fighter plane, as my lessons were meant to enable them to handle it properly. The technical instructions, arriving in French, had inexplicably been translated into English – and it was my job to render them intelligible. Eventually, I was taken into the control tower to get the hang of the jargon. I learned very fast, terrified that the inability to deliver words such as Fire or Eject might reflect on my tuition.

Driving occasionally to a distant airbase, I felt that the Arctic was the most peaceful and natural landscape on earth – until, one afternoon, the hills in the far distance got up and moved. A vast slab of trees and bushes slid sideways. Revealed were several holes, each with something pointing out.

I never got a straight answer to my enquiries, encountering for the first time in my life the blank wall which passes for military communication, but I did become aware of the properties of medium-range missiles, sitting in their moss-covered silos, their green camouflage munched over by the elk and reindeer. It was the local wisdom that the bad-tempered elk would do a better job than the missiles, krona for krona, seeing that no one knew how efficient the expensive weapon might be, but everyone knew how lethal the bloody elks were. Not for nothing were there road signs saying Beware Elk, many of them mangled by the antlered furies.

It was a year of novelty and feeling like a being from another planet. Sweden was a country where progress and social reform and liberal attitudes ruled the roost. Marriage, mental health, housing conditions, sexual attitudes: the Swedes stuck everything under a public magnifying glass, and then dissected mercilessly until they arrived at a solution. It was very different from my native English environment of tradition and woolly accommodation and convention. There was also a feelgood factor, with twinkling glass ornaments, beautifully bound books and chic light fittings overflowing from the first indoor shopping centres I'd ever seen. We were still postwar in Britain, despite the Swinging Sixties being upon us. The Swedes had already swung, and appeared to be thriving on the future.

The one area where they experienced major failure was with alcohol. It cost a fortune, and buying it was the exact equivalent of buying condoms in the UK: an activity loaded with furtive embarrassment and suspicion. This didn't in any way deter the Swedes, who got drunk in a spectacular collapsing manner, proud of the fact that it had cost them an arm and a leg to become legless. One of my teaching colleagues sighed sadly the morning after a major bender, and recollected a happy summer in Cambridge. 'Pubs,' he said, 'English pubs, heaven on earth – you go there every night?'

Even by Newcastle standards, this was pushing it a bit, and I said we sometimes stayed in – perhaps asked friends round for a drink.

'Where do you get it from?' he enquired, with logical Swedish habit – 'the drink, I mean.'

'Well, most people keep a bottle or two at home,' I replied.

'If you have it in the house, why do you not drink it?' he said with amazement.

No wonder one of their traditional tipples is pronounced Glug in English.

It was a year when I felt I'd discovered that the most mundane things in society could be approached differently; I too wanted elegant lamps and pine furniture and beautiful glass. The Swedes were confident, enquiring and cool in their arguments – but the glugging was a problem.

THREE

The Daily Durham

Get into trouble on BBC Radio Durham, and you were sentenced to a stint on the weekly consumer programme. Thursday evening found you sitting in the ops room for Studio 2 – the grand name for the back bedroom of the old pit manager's house – wondering what you'd done to deserve learning about nine different makes of washing machines. And what they did when on half-spin. And where you could find odd little pockets of fluff in the works. Staring through the glass panel at the earnest circle of the Durham Consumer Group, I used to wonder what motivated people to spend their lives burrowing head-first in washing machines looking for errant fluff.

The Group were a tenacious lot. Not only could they discuss vacuum-cleaner innards for up to two hours, they once continued their deliberations after the floor gave way. An unfamiliar sound had roused me from the obscure bits in *Radio Times* about Radio Three; peering into the studio, I saw that the Group seemed to have gone missing. But no, there they were: cradled in the centre of a sagging carpet, suspended above the kitchen table only by means of a few carpet tacks, and still banging on about the finer points of hoovering.

On one such evening, I was suddenly summoned by the newsroom. The newsroom: one news producer, an ex-*South Shields*

Gazette sub-editor, to be precise, working downstairs in what had probably been the pit manager's wife's tiny breakfast room. A place of four typewriters (one dead), an answering machine (which usually didn't), a very old copy of *Who's Who* (in which nobody in Durham seemed to feature) and the station cat's basket.

'Get the radio car out,' rasped the news producer. I paused. The Consumer Group didn't exactly tug at my loyalties, but the radio car was a far from glamorous alternative. Eight o'clock at night, probably no petrol, very likely still full of last night's fish-and-chip feast after the Sports Department's midweek extravaganza down the Brandon and Byshottles Working Men's Darts League.

'Why?'

The producer appeared to be absurdly animated for one dealing with news copy which usually yielded little on a Thursday evening beyond greyhound racing results from Sunderland. Perhaps plague had hit the local pigeon lofts?

'The gaol,' he said, breathing heavily. 'Someone's out.'

'Out where?'

I was only called on by the newsroom when they were absolutely desperate. I was (a) a woman and (b) not a member of the NUJ, and (c) I tended to be rather difficult about the conventions of journalism, with a tendency to ask awkward questions like What's so interesting about vicars who ride motorbikes and fancy big blond busty teenagers? Why shouldn't they?

'Out. At large.' The producer conjured up a scenario redolent of Magwitch and Jack the Ripper, in which Durham was wreathed in mist and terror, prey to a horde of stripy-clad convicts.

I raced out to the radio car. Raced back and got a tape recorder. Ditto to fetch a microphone. Spent a nasty three minutes looking for the radio car keys. Silly me. In the most obvious place. Removed station cat gently. Thank you.

Seizing the wheel of the Austin Hunter estate, emblazoned on the doors: Radio Dur m after a nasty encounter with Crook Town's goalposts the previous Saturday afternoon (well, I misjudged reversing round the pitch, and the posts didn't seem all that well embedded, I told the keeper . . .), I hurtled off down the drive.

The radio station was not in the city centre, exactly. Due to a bizarre set of circumstances, in which we were originally meant to be Radio Manchester, the premises had been acquired rather hastily. They were very pleasant: a Victorian country house, quite modest, but with large grounds and a kitchen garden, two and a half miles from the city centre, and hidden behind a modern housing estate, just off the A1. No one could ever find us. This was a mixed blessing. We rarely saw listeners – though this could have been attributable to the minimal audience figures. The inhabitants of the estate initially shut their doors to us. They'd seen our radio car with its strange mast poking out of the roof and were convinced it was the TV licence detector van. On the other hand, we never saw BBC Management from London. Most failed to get off the train at Durham, having drunk too much on realising that we were over three hours north of supposed broadcasting civilisation. The rest could never figure out the directions which involved the Bull, the Duke of Wellington, and a gate which said Private, Do Not Enter.

Still, what's two and a half miles, when you're on to a Real Story? Quite a bit, when you've missed the first turning, then realised there's a one-way system past the front of the gaol, and a dead-end; so you get clever and park the radio car next to the churchyard, where there's a little path through to the pub opposite the prison.

Clutching tape-recorder, mic dangling, stuffing spare tapes into pockets, I galloped down the narrow alleyway, nearly spreadeagling someone coming past the pub.

The scene in front of the gaol was riveting. I stood stock still, as if I'd been delivered on to a film set. Lights, action; it was all there. The little park area was a heaving throng of people, intersected by bonkers Alsatian dogs on long leads, straining everywhere. Police and prison warders were shouting, cursing. I strolled among them, fascinated. They careered in different directions like a rugby scrum on speed. Near the wall of the prison, there was a particularly wild heaving mass. I peered into it, swerving politely as the odd dog or cop scrabbled out. And, just like in the movies, the scrum parted for an instant, to reveal a rather thickset man lying quite contentedly on the ground, somewhat unbothered by the fuss. Mr Probyn had clearly done this sort of thing before.

I wondered if I should ask someone what was going on – Mr Probyn, perhaps, as he seemed to be the centre of attention. No chance. The scrum closed after an instant. No one in uniform, the people I judged to have the most official information, wanted to answer my questions. Most of them were too busy running around and shouting. I stuck my microphone ineffectually in front of any-one I encountered, and gathered an interesting array of curses and bugger-offs and the occasional snippet of information. Eventually a couple of bystanders delivered matter-of-fact descriptions of the entire event, and I began to feel slightly less bewildered.

I headed back to the pub, where I learned Mr Probyn's name. He didn't bother with a Christian name; everyone referred to him as Angel Face Probyn. He was doing a very long stretch for murder, and, as I'd niftily surmised, had made a bid for early freedom on other occasions. The pub – which the police had rather pointlessly attempted to clear – was part of the prison officers' social life, and most of the regulars had joined in the scrum. Those remaining were a fount of information, and I scribbled bits of stuff on a tape box. The idea of bringing a notebook only occurred to me later. About seven years later. Mr Probyn's short-lived bid for freedom – about six feet from the perimeter wall – was not to be compared with You Know Who, said one of the warders now back at the bar. I stood there dumbly, aware of my lack of information, lack of reporter know-how, obvious ignorance. I bought a drink – I'd seen the movies, it seemed like a good move. Not in Durham though, in the sixties. Independent bird, eh? Eventually, pink with em-barrassment and desperate for news, I pleaded for enlightenment, to be told that armed robber and top-security risk John McVicar had done a runner. And, by the look of it, unlike Mr Probyn, had made a success of it.

'All right now, pet?' said the barman. 'Good thing you're not a reporter, like that lot.' Gulping my half of lager and lime, I eyed a seedy gaggle of short men in flapping raincoats who'd just surged through the door. The press pack, down from Newcastle. I eavesdropped. I took more notes on the back of the tape box, and wondered if I should start reporting. The pack was busy trying to buy the pub's telephone – indeed, the whole of Durham's telephone service, by the sound of the offers being made. I wondered why they didn't use the phone box on the green and went to try it. A small Durham granny was ensconced, with a tall pile of coins on the shelf in front of her. I opened the heavy door, and she made a practised lunge at me with a glass bottle of lemonade. Sykes' lemonade, I noticed with irritation, as I retreated. I went to school with Marjorie Sykes. What a nerve!

Better go back to the radio car. I sprinted down the alley, remembering that leaving a boldly lettered unique radio car with the door open and the keys in was probably not the wisest of moves. However, its pit-like interior, courtesy of the Sports Department, had clearly been a deterrent. I then thanked the usually cursed Sports team, for I wrote my report on the back of an only partially grease-spotted fish-and-chip wrapper.

I managed to get the radio car into broadcasting mode – something of a near-miracle, considering BBC Engineering's evident intention to produce a cross between Apollo 13 and a mangle. I made contact with the radio station, expecting a warm glow of goodwill and gratitude. All I can say is that the ex-*South Shields Gazette*, augmented by the ex-*Newcastle Journal* who'd come in to help, was not at his most welcoming. I learned the sin of leaving the newsdesk in the dark. Not contacting it the moment you hit the ground. Taking your time. And not apologising for all these sins. Duly shredded, I offered my wares.

I can't recall what kind of report I made. I'd like to claim that it wasn't too full of novice's faults. I realised I'd found the whole scene fascinating, and just wanted to tell others about it – and did so quite successfully, I thought then. Hadn't missed out too much – except, of course, that I'd omitted to take much notice of Mr McVicar in the alleyway next to the pub, as I trotted towards the prison, and he galloped past me to freedom . . .

I was a station assistant on Radio Durham. It said so on my new passport, and meant that I spent years explaining to people that I didn't work for British Rail. It was a new title in BBC terms. Not as grand as studio manager, and minnow-like compared to the smooth salmon of BBC producers. However, it was my first real job, and paid £925 per annum. I was in seventh heaven.

Having got a highly respectable but not entirely jobworthy degree (there being only a small number of rune-stones to decipher in the UK with the help of my BA Hons Scandinavian Studies), I was eternally grateful that I was employed at all. In my final year at Newcastle University I'd seen a couple of suave men in suits describe the merits of joining the Corporation, as they visited on the annual trawl for graduates. Broadcasting sounded fun, I thought, having once taken part in a student TV quiz on the local commercial station, a not-particularly-glittering debut marred by suggestions that as the team captain was my boyfriend . . . anyway, broadcasting might be something I could do, though I wasn't sure how, or why. Sadly, the BBC mandarins perused application form No. 314 out of three hundred and fourteen applications, and made the inevitable discovery that I was female and red-brick. Wrong sex, wrong brix.

In my final term, I had a chance to redeem myself quiz-wise, this time on radio, and led my little team to glorious defeat. I personally sank our chances in a tie-breaker in the final round, on a question which haunts me still: What caused a storm in Paris in 1912? Stravinsky's *Rite of Spring*, I answered. I stayed away from campus the evening of transmission, ever to be reminded about Debussy's *L'après-midi d'un faune*. Nevertheless, it was probably my ignorance that got me my job. The radio producer and the quiz presenter, Max Robertson, were so sorry for me they took me out for a curry. After several lagers, they asked what I was going to do after university. After several lagers, I was bold enough to squeak: I want to do what you do. They seemed such a fun gang, and I'd been fascinated by the technical goings-on which put the programme on air from the university union building. Also, I was getting rather desperate, as my friends landed solid-sounding jobs in engineering, medicine and the law.

It remained a small, embarrassed, private thought at the back of my mind all through my finals and into the long summer. I applied for a job in Swedish television, hoping that my degree would impress them. Not a lot of hope there, as most Swedes speak English as well as their native tongue. I replied to an advertisement to be a 'Girl Friday' to a natural history film-maker, but he soon realised I knew nothing about furry mammals or penguins' lifestyles. I unwillingly took the civil service examinations, and to my horror, passed. I was twenty-one and totally clueless about my future.

Then, in a very odd act of serendipity, I read the local paper – the *Sunderland Echo* was no one under eighty's preferred reading, but I wasn't very busy; and there in the classifieds was an advertisement, headed BBC Radio Durham.

I can still remember the jump it gave me, as the small private thought woke up at the back of my mind and leaped around shouting silently: this is it, this is it.

I didn't dare tell anyone, not my parents, nor my friends, and I realised with some trepidation that I wanted it very much indeed. Somehow the life with the BBC might satisfy a lot of unarticulated longing for . . . I wasn't sure what; just something to do with bigger events, the wider stage, the unexpected. I associated the Beeb with style and presence at all major happenings; it had been part of history during the war, it made comedy and drama, and I was a child of radio's Home Service *Children's Hour*.

At the initial interview in BBC Newcastle (a former Lying-In Hospital), I was asked what I was prepared to do on one of these new radio stations which were starting up early the next year.

Anything, I said.

At my second interview in London, a Grand Suit leaned across the smart polished table in Portland Place waving a piece of paper. It says here you're prepared to do *anything*, he said.

Absolutely, I said.

And so it has turned out.

In February 1968 we embarked on a six-week training course fit to frighten anyone. Held in the dusty pile opposite Broadcasting House in London called the Langham – formerly an expensive hotel, now a warren of offices with corridors piled with zillions of back copies of the *Radio Times* and old scripts – the course aimed to turn us into professional broadcasters and local radio pioneers in just six weeks. We were a keen but apprehensive group, the eighth that the training team had had to handle. We were also not meant to be Radio Durham.

Local radio was the dream of Frank Gillard, a BBC man of wonderful ability, a distinguished war correspondent, and later Managing Director, Radio. The Beeb had begun with local roots, in the twenties, and he thought we ought to get back to them; he also knew that unless broadcasting changes and reflects its listeners and viewers, it no longer has either relevance or a mandate. National radio was evolving, Radio One having appeared in response to the enthusiasm for seaborne pirate stations earlier that year; now local radio was to follow.

The negotiations with government had produced a curious hybrid: local stations would be developed by the BBC, but in cooperation with local authorities. The small print was a bit woolly about the relationship, but it amounted to a local council having the final say as to whether a station could be started up. Leicester, Sheffield, Merseyside, Nottingham, Brighton, Stoke, and Leeds all agreed, and so did Manchester – at first. Then somewhere along the line, the good Mancunian burghers decided they wanted none of it, and the BBC was left with a spare station manager and a spare budget. Hawked around, they fell into the arms of Durham County Council – not hitherto known for cultural aspirations and run as a private fiefdom of the Labour party, where the main qualification for a councillor's seat seemed to be a childhood spent hauling buckets of coal underground. Heaven knows why they embraced local radio – maybe they didn't quite realise that we weren't just a transmitter mast.

There were many buzzwords in the air at the time: Community Broadcasting, Your Own Local Station, the Voice of the People, Grassroots Culture. In its wisdom, the BBC had decided that those charged with realising these ideals should be under thirty, local to the station, without any relevant experience, and possessed of boundless energy; and that's more or less what they got. Radio Durham, assembled in London, was a group of eighteen innocents, with nary a clue about the mysterious world of wireless. There was one producer – or 'programme assistant' as they were known, local radio being treated as a not-quite-respectable member of the family by the mandarins – and a studio manager who'd spent most of his career stuck on the border of Botswana and Rhodesia as part of a propaganda operation run by the Foreign Office. He wanted to get back into mainstream broadcasting, and reckoned that Radio Durham seemed nearer the action than Radio Francistown on the edge of the Kalahari Desert. Debatable.

Thrown into a training course which baffled and frightened us by turn, we nevertheless had bags of enthusiasm. We shredded our fingers learning how to edit tape using razor blades and sticky tape, chased people down Oxford Street to try out interviewing skills, and listened to lectures about transmitters which demonstrated the technological cutting edge of BBC Engineering and involved hitting things with sledgehammers when they went wrong.

There were visits to 'the real BBC' in the grand building over the way – Broadcasting House. We looked forward to meeting exciting DJs on Radio One; what was Tony Blackburn really like? Instead, they took us to *Home this Afternoon*, a kind of slippers-and-Marmite afternoon show on Radio Four, and it soon became clear that Radio One was regarded as a kind of mad animal that the BBC had had to adopt as a result of public pressure, but preferred to keep hidden in the basement.

We were lectured on every single aspect of broadcasting, including behaviour in studios – an interesting talk which centred on one's responsibility to tell people with dreadful B.O. that they had to use deodorant; studios are intimate places, they intoned, where life can become stressful. Regarding another form of intimacy, the female members of staff – the manager's secretary, and the three of us lowly station assistants – were corralled into an office and solemnly spoken to about the lengths of our skirts. We were all wearing pelmets at the time, and were unimpressed. However, we perked up when our rights regarding pregnancy (unexpected and without marital status) were mentioned, along with the assurance that the BBC was a 'pretty liberal place' and that studios could induce a 'pressured atmosphere'. Pressured? we enquired. Randy, we were told. We returned to our male colleagues refusing to divulge our private briefing, and looked at them with increased interest.

The liberal aspect of the place was made manifest when we described our moral lecture about skirts. Oh, her, said an old hand, well, she should know. She's bonking your head of technical services. Even in the swinging late sixties, this kind of thing caused us to choke on our drinks.

The hierarchy of the BBC was paraded in front of us. It wore a suit, appeared to have started broadcasting alongside Edison and Marconi, and had 'had a good war'. Its members were also charming, and possessed an eclectic fund of stories, hinting at interesting careers rubbing shoulders with important people. Several were pleasingly eccentric, and it wasn't until years later that I realised I'd seen one of the great characters in action, rubbishing his bosses.

One Friday morning, half an hour into a lecture about ethics, the front row adorned with the head of radio and sundry executive producers on a three-line whip to show support for little local radio's newcomers, a crashing sound announced the arrival of a rotund figure, swathed in a droopy cardigan with much-patched elbows. A copy of the *Daily Worker* was stuck ostentatiously under one arm.

'Christ,' said the figure, 'clearly it's a waste of bloody time if you lot are here.'

The front row looked pained.

'Morning, Reggie,' said the director of radio.

'God, you and all,' said the cardigan, heading for the back of the room, and noisily unfolding the *Worker*.

We stared saucer-eyed, but nothing else was said. Twenty minutes later, the lecture still in progress but the newspaper clearly finished, there was another furniture-bashing eruption and he was gone.

Nearly twenty years later, the BBC transmitted a highly successful drama series based on Olivia Manning's Balkan Trilogy, starring Kenneth Branagh and Emma Thompson, entitled *Fortunes of War*. A mostly autobiographical story, it centred on Manning's husband, a gifted, exasperating, larger-than-life lecturer with the British Council in Romania and Greece at the outbreak of the Second World War. This was Reggie Smith. He'd never changed, and had for years been the brilliant assistant head of radio drama, driving the BBC mandarins nuts with his passion for the Communist party and his contempt for the complacent and the conventional.

The odd, the difficult, the creative and the downright weird drifted around the corridors of the Langham and came to rest in the many bars in the building. One drinking hole was peopled with imperious men, and loud women who wore hats *à la Brief Encounter* and drank cocktails. These were the members of the Drama Repertory Company. In an alcove was the regular table for The Announcers – a chummy lot ranging from veterans of wartime to a young Terence Wogan. Their main occupation in the evening was to achieve the minimum time between leaving one's drink and getting across the road to Broadcasting House – BH – to start reading the news. An Olympic sprint was necessary, but being out of breath on air was considered bad form, with many drinks to be bought as a punishment. Serious drinking took place in the oddly named Salad Bar, where a lettuce would never have dared make an appearance. This was News territory, with a gang of slouch-shouldered blokes gripping pints and telling each other about the unfairness of the Expenses system. About half the newsroom could be found in there at any one time; the other half were in the George, a completely BBC-dominated pub the other side of BH.

I mention drink because it played a very definite role in broadcasting life. Every single major BBC establishment had The Club, an extensive organisation of sports facilities and hobbies and Lord knows what healthy pursuits. A number of employees were rumoured to take part in these; however, the mainstay of the Club was relatively cheap alcohol – on the premises. Without a doubt, more programmes, deals, stories, ideas and inspired broadcasting emanated from these cosy pits than from any departmental meeting or office discussion. On the very first day of our training course there had been a sharp exit at one o'clock by those in charge, leaving us to creep out in the hunt for a sandwich. At half-past five, the same exit occurred, but this time they took us along – Down to the Club, everyone – and we were introduced to what was as much a part of daily life as breathing.

After the first four weeks we were learning to moderate our intake – and were then rather knocked off course by the arrival of The Trolley to celebrate our diligence during the month. This laden conveyance – officially sanctioned – which clanked into the main lecture-room mid-Friday afternoon was in effect a distillery with a couple of cheese biscuits attached. We all got quite legless, and were then shown up as still in need of further training by our inability to follow the lecturers as they marched off steadily – down to the Club. I was immensely glad to have spent three years at Newcastle University, where I'd learned never to try to rival the university rugby team or the agriculture students in their efforts to drink the town dry of Newcastle Brown. I knew roughly when I needed to wimp out, and saw no point in repeating incidents involving losing bits of clothing and trying to climb

Grey's Monument, never mind falling into sundry coal sheds while looking for the loo in sundry grotty student digs.

One was now expected to be able to hold one's liquor – and to remember the solitary golden rule: Never mix booze and broadcasting.

All in all, the training course was a *tour de force* of initiation. It combined the traditional values which were the backbone of the Corporation with the new and progressive attitudes of local radio. Listeners came first. We might have wonderful ideas and want to express our own thoughts and interests – but we were told we weren't in the business for our own sakes. It was banged home that there were standards and that listeners deserved the best. It was all rather high-minded; but these earnest exhortations were delivered in an atmosphere of liberal practicality, with a healthy appreciation that out there, beyond the microphone, were not only the sensitive and the lonely, the anxious and the gullible, but also the whingers, the obsessives, the mischief-makers and the frankly mad. We couldn't wait to find out, and were dispatched to serve a month on the stations which were already operating.

My stint in Brighton was almost completely disastrous. I managed not to be asked to leave, but that was about it.

Radio Brighton was installed in a Victorian corner building next to the Royal Pavilion. It had already developed a sense of style in its first few months, breaking away from BBC stuffiness by taking a score of comments by famous people on what they'd had for breakfast – recorded as technical voice-tests before interviews – and using them to open the programme. In the late sixties, this was dangerously revolutionary. But the jingles were twee, and no one had given much thought to a music policy. As a result, every single request programme included Cliff Richard singing 'Congratulations', such is the originality of the listener.

My post of station assistant was new to the BBC, and amounted to doing everything the grander programme assistants hadn't the time to do. Much was mundane: recycling recording tape, filling in details of records played in the station log, and twiddling the knobs on the operations desk in the studio. Responding to distress calls from the receptionist was a regular duty, due to the prominence of the station; Brighton was turning out to have one of the largest collection of deranged individuals attracted to the sign 'BBC', and most days there were people who installed themselves in the small foyer and made demands of the Corporation, ranging from fixing their plumbing to invading Rhodesia. Getting rid of them politely was a challenging process.

I made my debut on air reading a short story, nervous as a kitten, but keen to deliver a bit of drama into the limp prose. Asked afterwards what I thought of my performance, I said, 'So-so,' but added that the story had been a bit wet, not knowing that original material was scarce and the wife of one of the staff had obliged with her best vapourings.

Out with the radio car to review a new film, *Dr Doolittle*, the morning programme presenter John Walmsley and myself were not familiar with the habit of 'hospitality' at 11 a.m. Neither of us made it on air at lunchtime, due to difficulties in describing Dr Doolittle's transport, a shiant pink shea shnail.

Persevering, the station's programme organiser, David Waine, decided I needed to be sent out to do some interviews. The first involved an elderly retired naval officer who'd complained about the possibility of the government bringing in metrication. He was stone deaf, and I got the recording levels a bit mixed up on the tape recorder, omitting the normal-voiced questions and instead recording my bellowing at him. The second was with a seedy junk-shop dealer in his dim cave near the main railway station. Dedication to broadcasting is all very well, but I made my exit after three minutes, having used a handy carved parrot on his left ear as his large beringed paw headed up my skirt.

In some desperation, David called me into his office one Wednesday afternoon and handed me an address in Hove: 'We set up this interview last week,' he said, 'chap's given a heap of money to a local charity, he'll give you the full story – perhaps it might run tonight?'

Glad that faith in me was not yet lost, I beetled out and caught a bus to Hove, where I found the address to be a huge pair of wrought-iron gates set in one of the town's grand avenues. As they squeaked open, I saw a small mansion with white pillars round the door at the end of a very long crunchy drive. I pressed the bell and heard nothing.

Waited, and pressed again.

The door was opened, and I launched into my well-rehearsed speech: I'm from Radio Brighton, the new local radio station, and I've an appointment to see Mr S— which was arranged last week.

The fact that I was addressing a policeman hadn't stopped me.

'You can't see him,' he said.

Panic seized me – I was failing again. 'I've got an appointment,' I insisted.

'You can't see him,' he repeated.

We stared at each other blankly.

'All right, then,' I sighed, and slunk through the gravel to the bus stop.

Back at the station, I ran straight into David.

'How'd it go?' he asked hopefully.

'It didn't,' I said, 'the policeman who answered the door said I couldn't see him.'

A mixture of expressions passed over David's face. 'Why,' he said, 'was there a policeman there?'

'Ah,' I said. And walked straight out to find the next bus.

Twenty-five minutes later, I went through another speech on the doorstep, changing a few words to '... and *why* can't I see him?'

'He's dead,' said the policeman impassively, 'he's been murdered.'

'Good God,' I said, and ran helter-skelter down the drive, flinging myself on a bus idling at the stop, hardly able to contain my first piece of real news, ever.

I crashed into David's office.

'He's dead!' I shouted. 'MURDERED!'

David put his head on one side, saying very slowly, 'Aaaand?'

I was a bit put out. David leaned towards me.

'Like: why? Like: when? Like: where? Like: how? Like: by whom?'

I was paralysed with fear, staring into the abyss of my faults. The third bus-ride passed in a mist of anxiety, and I walked slowly up the gravel. The door opened before I pressed the bell.

A still-impassive face said: 'You're new at this, aren't you?'

For reasons that I will never fathom – and earning my unending gratitude – seven years later David Waine got me my first job as a television reporter. Maybe he'd forgotten about Hove.

Back up north, I set to with determination on this, the eighth and oddest addition to local radio. My first job was to nail down the carpet in Park House, then catalogue the record library. Carpets were no problem, but I wasn't quite sure what cataloguing entailed, so I put different coloured stickers on the LPs and made a list, according to my own musical tastes. Nobody ever complained, nor did they notice that orange stickers – Mantovani and Jim Reeves for example – were listed under Yuk.

Our first hurdle was to orchestrate a Grand Opening Day. The whole staff held daily brainstorming sessions, ideas were pounced on then destroyed, and the manager, Kenneth Brown – a Mancunian stuck with a bunch of Geordies – kept demanding that we 'celebrate the local – and involve the locals'. Our automatic reaction would have been to suggest a massive session revolving round Broon Ale, but we realised more was expected. The result was an eclectic mix: garden parties aren't common in Durham, especially in a cold July, but it seemed the best solution, as every councillor for miles intended to come. To keep the guests happy in the marquee on the front lawn, we enquired about a brass band, only to discover that even pit-bands didn't come cheap for the BBC. We settled on a Gavioli fairground organ; don't ask me why, but the sports producer had a friend who knew someone who could do a deal.

On the day before opening, with the staff flat out recording and editing programmes, absolutely unaware of the impossible goal we'd set ourselves in terms of hours of broadcasting – two hours a day had been suggested by head office, but already the other stations were putting out eight to ten – we were interrupted by a cracking sound. Up the narrow drive a mammoth pantechnicon was crawling, a maroon monster emblazoned Gavioli, garlanded with a number of tree branches. After some discussion, it was directed between the rose beds to a position at a suitable distance for serenading guests crossing to the marquee. There it sat, sinking alarmingly into the lawn.

As the afternoon wore on, the caterers arrived, and various people tore their hair out as the great unknown loomed in front of us: going on air, for real, on 96.8 VHF, and possibly hearing from our listeners. To match our mood, the skies grew dark, and an ill wind blew. Towards four o'clock a massive storm broke. The caterers gave up, and the Gavioli fairground organ began to move. A puddle a yard wide had spread from the rose-bed and was creating a moat round the van. Very gently, the beast leaned over, reaching an awesome forty-five degrees.

As I was one of the most junior members of staff, it was unanimously decided that it was my problem. Three hours and two dozen phone calls later, I had exhausted all avenues involving the police, the fire brigade, garages and breakdown specialists. Ken, the manager, was beside himself: 'They'll all be here tomorrow morning, and that bloody thing will keel over and squash the leader of the County Council the minute he steps on that lawn.'

I picked up the telephone directory again and looked up Army.

A few minutes later I got through to Catterick Barracks and a charming man who sounded like a horse. I wasn't sure how to phrase things.

'Do you have anything very big for pulling something enormously big out of a lawn?'

'Bags of things,' he said, 'what would you like?'

Two hours later, a monstrous tank recovery vehicle and half a battalion arrived. They set to, and dragged and heaved, and within a very short while had the offending organ hanging like a

Dinky truck from what looked like a tank married to a crane. Swathed in mud, it was plonked on to harder standing.

Whimpering with gratitude, we raided the marquee for the caterer's supply of booze and pressed it on the soldiers.

Next day, the chains of office from Hartlepool to Gateshead arrived, and clanked and ploughed their way across matting to a quickly replenished marquee, as the fairground organ ground away, none the worse for wear. A large number of guests ignored our warning about soggy grass, and after a couple of drinks at least two mayoresses went face down into the roses. Equally face down were a posse of Radio One DJs, a motley parcel of 'stars' sent from London to lend a little sparkle to the occasion. As ever, after five hours on the train – missing Durham and having to be sent back down to us from Newcastle – we could see they'd spent the entire journey in the buffet car, so they were given another crate and banished to the back kitchen.

Most of the formal speeches and the more important guests were ignored by the staff, who were too busy with last-minute editing. Not a bad ploy, either, for a number of them became Her Majesty's guests a short while later, figuring colourfully in our news bulletins, having got themselves well and truly mired in the mud of housing development scandals.

And so we went on air. In true pioneering fashion, Radio Durham broadcast what I suspect was – and remains – a unique item. Local it certainly was. Put it this way, not many people have thought it feasible to put a pigeon race on radio. But that's how we opened, with a curious flutter.

My own minor part in this was to be stuffed into a pigeon loft on the outskirts of Ferryhill, with the birds' owner, clutching a microphone on the end of a long lead from the radio car. At the appointed time, the opening programme's presenter, Mike Hollingsworth – yes, we all start somewhere – announced that we were crossing live to the lofts – for the birds' arrival! Horrified, I scanned the skies above the little fence-railing decorations to the loft roofs. After a heart-stopping few seconds, there they were, and I breathed a sigh of relief, leading to a major dispute later over my claim that my first words on Radio Durham had been: Ah good, they're here, and not, as everyone claimed to have heard: OH GOD, they're here.

We were embarked on an experiment. No one was quite sure if local radio was, well, wanted. Within the BBC, there were mutterings about trivia and lowered standards. The regional press was having a field day with on-air boobs: 'Good morning, here is the news, and our top story is the council's complaint that the bus service oh God this is yesterday's hang on I've got today's somewhere . . .' Also: 'And now the ten o'clock summary – I know it's ten past, but we've got a bit of trouble with the photocopier which is on fire at the moment.' And there was the afternoon when I was forced to announce: 'We're sorry not to have brought you the two o'clock bulletin, as pointed out by one of our sharp-eared listeners in Hartlepool, but we'd like to assure you that there was nothing new to say anyway.'

Closeness to the listeners was a novelty – and a double-edged sword. Some took us to their hearts immediately, regarding us as family, and ringing up on a daily basis. Others regularly called to complain about *Coronation Street*, unconvinced that we had zero influence on television programmes and no connection to ITV. And then there were the phone-in programmes.

Now an integral part of all radio, the phone-in was a child of local radio, born officially out of a mission to 'put you on your own station, contribute to the community voice', but equally the result of being the cheapest kind of broadcasting ever. We coaxed and cajoled, wheedled and provoked, anxious to get the small switchboard to flash with contributors. In desperation, friends and family were rung and told to sound off about anything they could think of – and try not to give away that they were related to the presenter. Quickly we learned that the majority of our measly number of callers had every intention of appearing daily – and fitted the profile of the utterly dreadful bloke in the corner of the bar who has a strong view on the world and no knowledge of it;

or the woman who 'can't get out much, so it's nice to be able to have a good natter' (for natter read whinge). Our problem was that the audience didn't really know what the phone-in was for, coupled with a genuine and widespread reticence about getting themselves 'on air' – not only in phone-ins, but in every encounter with microphones. The very bedrock of local broadcasting, we had been taught, was the active participation of listeners, ordinary folk rather than the professional full-time broadcasters. It had been hoped that several programmes would be produced by amateur enthusiasts, and that 'access radio', in which programmes were suggested and compiled without anything more than light editorial guidance, would form a large part of the output. The newsroom was encouraged to include vox pops – those short, snippety comments gathered and strung together on one subject, masquerading as a cross-section of opinion, but more usually a chirp of light relief in a grim world.

In reality, we found ourselves up against a wall of diffidence. Time and again, I took my tape-recorder out into the streets of Durham and Darlington and Consett, and ended up imitating a collie-dog corralling unwilling sheep. So I developed a very low-key approach which didn't have people bolting at the sight of a microphone, only to have to learn to canter sideways alongside my quarry while pleading for an interview – often to no avail. There was an embedded sense of broadcasting as something 'not for the likes of us'; this was the most frequently repeated phrase, and uttered with great conviction. It was not a case of people not having the time, or not having opinions, but of an inbred constraint on 'pushing yourself forward'; women were the most timid, fearing the, 'Hark at her, making an exhibition of herself'. I actually heard the remark, 'It's not for the likes of me to talk about that, pet' on an almost daily basis, and began to wake up to the fact that my own experience and attitudes might possibly be well out of touch with a lot of our audience.

I was a product not only of the conventional fifties, but of the revolutionary, egalitarian sixties, when hairdressers and pop stars and royalty and actors and chartered accountants were meant to have 'come together'. The old class attitudes in hierarchical Britain were supposed to be a-crumbling. Liverpool accents were heard worldwide, feminism was on the march, change was in the air. With the optimism and ignorance of the young, all of us on the radio station had taken for granted that everyone would be embracing a more democratic society, where all voices would chime confidently, and where the voicing of opinion and idea in the public place would be seen as axiomatic in a lively community.

Day after day, reels of tape of gentle, polite questions followed by mutters and sorrys and not me pet would be played through by disappointed station staff. Instead of liberating and widening the airwaves, we seemed to be frightening people into silence. Few listeners responded to our invitation to come and help make programmes; indeed, some were affronted, responding that that was what we were paid to do.

Not too downhearted – we were working hundred-hour weeks and didn't have time for reflection – we pursued an intense schedule of mini-Radio Four programming, hoping that our listeners would eventually treat us with less suspicion, and open up like noisy little flowers. We put out education, religious, gardening, farming, folk music, brass bands, arts and sports programmes with virtually no resources. We lured volunteers to Park House and convinced crown green bowls fanatics and vicars that they were classic broadcasting material. In view of the vox pop problem – universal reticence compounded by Durham city being a good twenty minutes' drive away for thirty seconds' worth of comment – we developed the talents of our two cleaning ladies. An unusually forthright pair, Gladys and Doreen were soon willing and able to air their views on local government reform, pit closures and feminist bra-burning. They got ever so good, no one complained and they were only thirty seconds away – though they had to be persuaded to switch the hoover off.

We still felt we weren't fulfilling our mission; so we undertook a heavy campaign on air to make ourselves friendly, coupled with a punishing roster of visits to Townswomen's Guilds and council meetings and miners' welfare halls extolling the virtues of 'your station, your chance to make yourself heard'. It was as much a social experiment as a broadcasting one.

By now we were realising that the BBC had assumed that we needed next to no publicity to alert County Durham to a new station, on a previously unknown FM frequency, and that most people were still blissfully unaware of our existence, so we decided to engineer a little positive PR. To our joy, the BBC itself delivered us our first opportunity for national fame: it announced that it was axing its most famous radio soap opera, *Mrs Dale's Diary*. There was a national outcry – and Radio Durham went on air to announce our Save the Dales Campaign. It worked a treat. We got acres of publicity, and made lots of wild promises to any reporter who cared to ring us. Fortunately, we didn't have to fulfil any of them, for our campaign was gently brought to an end by the actual cast of *The Dales*. Despite all the anodyne and pacifying fibs from the BBC's publicity office that the series was ending because of 'changes in listeners' tastes' and other such guff, it turned out that the real reason was the cast: despite there having been several Dr and Mrs Daleses, they were now so old that some found it difficult to make their way to the studio ... certainly can't do the stairs, my dear, and I'm worried about Jim ... Our campaign gently withered, but we were on the map.

Next we went off air due to rodent activity on our cables, and advertised for a station cat. The moggie and we three station assistants (cat cute, the three of us in our shortest skirts) posed cheesily. Lots of tabloid coverage.

Then the station manager decided we needed a piano. This was not a stunt – but unfortunately he only gave me twenty-five pounds to get one, and sent me off to an auction at Crawcrook on south Tyneside. Ernie, our sharp-nosed freelance reporter, smelled a story, and rang a few people, resulting in my turning up at the auction rooms to face a lot of cameras and several TV crews. Even in the late sixties, second-hand pianos were not that cheap, and public humiliation descended on me as the bidding reached twenty-five pounds and rose to £56. 'Beeb too poor to buy an old piano' – ah well, there's no such thing as bad publicity . . .

Once the Home Office came to our aid, having for months refused to investigate reports that our VHF frequency was dangerously close to the radio wavelength used by Durham Constabulary. Listeners had occasionally alleged that they were getting the odd Calling Zed Victor One in the middle of our morning programme, but not until an odd freak of weather did the matter get serious. An entire day's broadcasting featured a gripping mix of Radio Durham programmes interlaced with a raid on a warehouse somewhere near Chester-le-Street. The switchboard lit up and the police demanded we stop broadcasting, whereupon we got a bit legalistic and said that was up to the home secretary, did they have him on the line?

Lots of lovely publicity – the only downside being that the listeners who called in tended to have preferred the police raid to our programmes.

All this left me with the impression that the national news media would swallow anything, and that journalism was a weird world in which I wanted no part. Nevertheless, we were starting to make an impact. It took more than a few months of local radio activity to make a change in the demeanour and deep-rooted diffidence of our audience; but we'd made a start, and I have no doubt that we played a small part in what became a major shift in public attitudes to participation in the media. Thirty years later, few would hurry away from a microphone because of a feeling of 'not being worthy'. The phone-in is part of public opinion, and the sense that one's voice deserves to be heard has now taken a firm grip on the media. To young people this seems natural, indeed commonplace, and it's hard to convey what public reserve was like just a few decades ago.

While generating publicity was fun, the hard slog of programme-making had to be faced. We were tackling ridiculous targets in the matter of air-time, fewer than two dozen people pretending we could be a local Radio Four, minus *Mrs Dale's Diary*. As a junior, I got up at a quarter past four, drove my little Hillman Imp seventeen miles from Sunderland to Durham (avoiding the lethal Geest banana lorries which were the only other traffic mad enough to be on the road then) and opened up the studio, taking in the milk, feeding the cat and starting up the station at five-thirty. In came the presenter of *The Daily Durham* (morning programme titles had caused us a few headaches), and I scurried around getting the essential information – calling the police for traffic reports and any crime updates, sorting record requests and taking the weather forecast from the teleprinter. More often than not, the teleprinter had chewed its own paper entrails during the night, and I was reduced to flinging open the windows of Studio 1 and staring quizzically at the sky. I thought my forecasts were pretty good – I got in all the right phrases about occasional showers and sunny periods and occasionally embellished them with suggestions that there might be dark clouds over Gateshead or unexpected turbulence in Billingham. I'll have you know I never got a single complaint.

As a leg-up the professional ladder, I'd been given the farming programme to produce. I was thrilled – and clueless. However, I've always liked farms, ever since having been found at the age of three curled up next to a new-born calf instead of snug in my holiday bed. And, in good BBC tradition, my main function was to get those on air who had experience, knowledge and varying views, merely cocking an ear to ensure that we were putting together something interesting and accurate. It also fell to me to go to the Durham County Show near Lambton Castle, trekking around with my tape-recorder, looking for likely material, and I wasn't at my most confident. But I was prepared; I wasn't going to be shown up ignorant of what was mooing or bleating in front of me; I was armed with the *I-Spy Book of Cows* and its companion volume on *Sheep*, complete with useful drawings. By God, I knew how to do research, BBC-style.

Religious programmes also fell into my remit, through the standard BBC selection process at a station meeting. Anyone particularly religious? Silence. Anyone been to church recently? No. Adie, did you go to some sort of Church School? Yes. So I spent a year fending off randy vicars and employing complex arguments against loopy fundamentalists who wanted to proselytise among the dark satanic pitheaps of County Durham.

Farming producer, brass band recordist, Thought for the Day provider, fourth-string rugby reporter (Hartlepool never actually complained about my commentaries . . .) and fifth-string cricket commentator – life was gloriously varied, and made me think. I was given access to people and homes and factories and hobby groups and institutions and workplaces to which I'd never given a thought. I began to realise how varied and complex and patchwork our society is; I was lucky, I felt I carried no terrible burden of misery or bitterness and loss or unhappiness from childhood, I was young and optimistic and fascinated, so I was honour-bound to look upon life and marvel – and learn. I found that people around one, in a Durham village, in a union meeting, in a shipyard, in a shop, were more varied and curious and unexpected than I'd ever realised. I wasn't starry-eyed or naïve, just thirsty to know how the world ticked, and spurred on by the fact that I felt I'd been slow to realise the variety and secrets of the world. I still look back on this period and bless the chance it gave me to gain a wider education, without anyone judging me or asking me why I was doing this.

I was aware that raising the matters which I saw – a murder, neglect, bad housing, the limitations imposed on those with less education and confidence, the diffidence conventionally expected of the majority – met with a sniff of indifference from my friends outside the broadcasting world, especially the older people in Sunderland among whom I'd grown up. The standard phrases – I wouldn't really want to know that, and Well, of course, you'd expect people like that to behave like animals, and What do you expect, they don't know any better? – began to make me feel rather alien. Was I a lone revolutionary, or just someone who'd been a bit dozy about noticing life around me? I began to be very wary of the convention and respectability which ruled gently comfortable lives. I realised that if you were to reflect society, put up a mirror to the community honestly, then uncomfortable, undiscussed matters were going to have to be dragged to the surface, talked about, dealt with. I began to feel that curious sense of stomach-seizing worry and outrage that I'd felt on the train from Berlin. What was the point of having fun on radio if you didn't do something worthwhile as well?

I sneaked items on social inequality and questions on unfairness into the religious slots. Nothing world-shattering, or even particularly challenging, but I wanted to have all voices heard. And I became quite puritanical about accuracy, because I saw the way misunderstanding and misinterpretation were used to further prejudice and entrench complacency.

Maybe I read too much into that period; after all, I was merely slinging together weekly programmes listened to by a minuscule audience, and slogging away at technical recordings in Birtley Working Men's Club and South Shields bus station. But I was educating myself and hungry for more.

As for news, well, it was only when completely desperate, as in the events outside Durham Gaol, that the newsroom called on my services. One day I was sent off to Hebburn, where the Boilermakers' Union were holding an emergency meeting about the possible closure of the ship repair yard. I knocked on the pub door and told the man who appeared that I'd come to interview the shop steward about the yard closure, as arranged. He looked at me kindly, and said that he was sorry, but the man in question was busy. I was slightly irritated, for I'd driven hard to arrive on time, and the interview was wanted for the lunchtime programme. Is he *very* busy, I pressed? Yes pet, came the reply, he's waiting for a reporter from the radio. But I'm a reporter from the radio, I squeaked. Ah pet, he said, eyeing me as a twenty-something trollop loaded with cheek, he's waiting for a *real* reporter.

Better stick to farming programmes.

FOUR

Bristol fashion

I learned my trade on Radio Bristol. Local radio was a sausage machine, and we fed the audience everything we could lay our hands on.

Bristol was one of the second wave of local radio stations, and even as it was mooted it had a rather fashionable air, for the BBC in Bristol was grand and well established. Its glamour was summed up by the fact that it possessed not only a canteen, but a BBC Club Bar. It also made television programmes, and the possibility of working next to those nice people from the Natural History Unit with furry things which went squeak and grunt for the cameras, seemed very exotic. In 1970, after eighteen months on home territory in Durham, I wanted pastures new; and Bristol was attractive and offered a change from the pit villages and shipbuilding of the north-east.

I was hired as the Woman's Programme producer. The application was a gamble – the odds were good on getting the job (men didn't apply), but I had little intention of spending my life delivering delicious recipes for dropscones and explaining the excitement of a new knitting pattern. Nor was I particularly committed to hours of feminist consciousness-raising confined to a women-only ghetto. So I managed a juggling act at the job interview, trying to impress the young and modern station manager, and trying not to frighten the suit from Appointments Department who was clearly looking for a sort of homely, knitted person.

The assembled staff were all sent on another training course – the veterans, scarred by the reality of other radio stations (... Our listeners were a perfectly standard local radio audience ... all of them missing one vital limb or function ... Ours had two record requests only, 'The Old Rugged Cross' and 'Congratul ...' Never? Just like ours, except that ours sometimes insisted on singing it themselves . . .), and the novices, many fresh from newspapers, including a man of keen observational talent who spotted a giant cockroach marching round his cereal bowl on the first morning in our official BBC hotel, a flop-house in Paddington.

'Bloody cheek,' said Michael Buerk, pursuing it with journalistic fervour.

'Wonder where it came from?' said his colleague Roger Bennett – showing all the signs of the unending curiosity which has never left him in a quarter of a century of presenting Bristol's morning show.

'Kill it!' bellowed Brian. Brian was clearly the news editor.

This training course was less frenetic than my initial indoctrination, but the BBC management still baulked at showing us anything of Radio One, and insisted that we go to see Radio Four's flagship news programme, *World at One*. The management can't have had the slightest idea what it was like – the bottles rolled round the floor and the editor reclined on a battered sofa in the ops room, overseeing chaos in a haze of smoke and shouting. We were hugely impressed, goggling at the mountain-ous figure of William Hardcastle in the studio, a Fleet Street veteran who was busy getting rid of the BBC tradition of playing cringing doormat to politicians. *Woman's Hour*, on the other hand, was frightening: a roomful of intellectual knitteds, who pointed to the only man at the conference table and shrilled, 'This is our token man – he's *very* well behaved for one of them.' I resolved never to go near the world of tweedy poodle-keepers.

Radio Two was a different kettle of drunken fish. After ten at night, the subterranean studios in Broadcasting House took on the aura of a night-club run on a shoestring; programmes rolled liquidly over the airwaves fuelled with cheap red wine and punctuated by bravura performances by newsreaders who were completely pissed, but succeeded in delivering two minutes of precise and eloquent English before falling off their chairs the moment the studio red light went off. Leading the pack were a glorious pair, Roger Moffat and Bruce Wyndham. Fluff-it and Windbag had decades of experience between them, acres of charm and personality, and would have drunk Lake Windermere had it been alcoholic. They represented an era of broadcasting in which charisma, bullshit and experience, allied with a passion for the job, delivered an unmistakable sound to the airwaves. After midnight, it just got a little fuzzy round the edges.

Elsewhere, the institution was still rather stuffy, despite local radio and the disc-jockeys. However, it was confident and expanding, and our training lecturers continued to deliver firm strictures about standards, though none of them needed written guidelines, mission statements and corporate policies. Above all else, they concentrated on the fact that nearly all of us on the staff were under thirty, and that in the previous two years it had become clear that much of the audience for local radio was probably over fifty, maybe sixty, going on seventy. Getting us to tune into our listeners' wavelength was much more difficult than persuading them to find the right VHF band to listen to us. Time and again, it was hinted that the instinct to make pro-grammes which *we* would like might not be as successful as making programmes other people would like. It's an old lesson, but becomes ever more true, as the media business attracts the young and becomes an increasingly fashionable career. How satisfying to hear your friends discuss your programmes – and how unlikely; one of the embarrassments of a local radio meeting was trying to find anyone on the staff who'd actually gone home and listened to our own output.

So, charged with our responsibilities, we made for Bristol and another Grand Opening Day, this one to be headed by the founding father of local radio, Frank Gillard himself. True to the spirit of local radio, I had a good go at running over this charming and inspirational man just before he went on air – I being unfamiliar with our new radio car, and he being too much of gentleman to shout before I pinned him against the pillar of the front gate.

We were housed in one of the Victorian villas which made up the BBC stockade in Bristol – a ring of architectural splendour composed of a warren of interconnecting houses, totally unsuitable for broadcasting. Never mind, it was prestigious; this had been the BBC headquarters during the war. Also, every so often something either foul or dangerous went missing in the inner courtyard, due to the enthusiasm and incompetence of the weekly children's TV programme *Animal Magic*. Cries of: 'It's harmless – but don't annoy it' were a signal for two hours' mayhem as the production team were seen lurking round the car park armed with assorted snake-bags or warthog lassoes.

As usual, we were attempting far too much daily broadcasting for a tiny band of newcomers. Added to the usual local radio ingredients of the morning show, news, sport, phone-ins and record requests were the children's serial, access radio, competitions – and the live music request show. We felt the urge to be innovative, and it didn't seem enough to play records – so we'd acquired the services of Arthur and his Lady Friend, a splendid couple who'd honed their talents at a pub piano somewhere in Bristol's nether parts. Every Friday lunchtime, they ambled into the studio and challenged our listeners to call and ask for any tune whatsoever. Whether it was obscure jazz or a favourite hymn, Arthur would say 'Roight my lover,' and launch himself at the keyboard. He was never fazed – he possessed a thick pile of sheet music, which he never referred to – so we were impressed by the entire performance, though with two slight reservations: first, it was curious how 'Yellow Submarine' and

'Alexander's Ragtime Band' *and* 'In a Monastery Garden' sounded so alike; and second, we weren't quite sure what the Lady Friend's role was.

Again trying to improve upon the tired old theme of requests, we introduced devious competitions. Adrian, our frenetic freelance DJ (local radio not daring to have such a creature on the staff), took to cycling round Bristol to note down the numbers of public telephone boxes, which he'd ring during his Saturday morning show, poised to play a record to be identified by the hapless occupant. Much impromptu radio then took place, featuring enraged Bristolians trying to get through to their grannies and finding themselves on air being asked if she liked the Rolling Stones.

The whole business of freewheeling pop music shows was a worry to the cautious local radio management. Showing more enterprise than the whole of Radio One, our boss David Waine announced to a startled staff one morning that we'd hired Kenny Everett. Ken, the most original and talented DJ on the airwaves, had just been fired – again – by a terrified BBC controller in London unable to appreciate that genius needs to be on the longest piece of corporate string possible. We were agog at the thought that he was heading for Radio Bristol, and muggins was told to 'be his producer'.

Three days later, this skinny, bearded and slightly manic elf appeared about an hour before he was due on air, with a mammoth box of records and tapes.

'I'm your producer,' I said helpfully, rather overawed. He shrugged, said, 'Please yourself,' and disappeared into the studio.

Apart from getting him tea every so often, my role was non-existent, for he lived in a marvellous magical music world of his own. Attacking the radio operations desk as if it were a stove with ten pots boiling on it, he was consumed with energy, twining his way round the microphone, waving arms, flapping elbows, and delivering thoughts, jokes and unexpected, cleverly edited snippets of fantasy. I just sat there and watched. Years later, I caught myself saying at a rather trendy party, 'Ah, well, as Kenny Everett's producer . . .'. It would have been more accurate to say that I had been his tea-lady.

Part of our remit was to involve as many people as possible in making our programmes, opening up the rather secretive world of recording, interviewing and tape-editing to 'the Great General Public'. A steady stream of keen individuals knocked at the door and asked if they could help. We hired a motley crew, each producer acquiring a posse of helpers and dogsbodies – and gifted discoveries: my wonderful gang consisted of an admiral's wife, an out-of work actor (the pre-Baldrick Tony Robinson), an opera singer studying to be a probation officer, a greengrocer-cum-theatre-critic-cum-bookmaker who used to take me racing, a model (the pre-Green Goddess Diana Moran), an Austrian countess who did the gardening spot, an American intellectual who'd worked in US network TV, a nice young man who I believe became an arms dealer, a completely original cook who couldn't spell 'recipe', two intelligent women with three eyes and three legs between them who never once mentioned disability, and a brilliant interviewer called Sandra who minxed her way into the station by verbally seducing Michael Buerk live on air on Bristol Downs. They were paid – on results only – about two pounds a week, but only when we were feeling flush.

They streamed in and out of the station, full of ideas and local knowledge and carrying tape-recorders which they had only just learned to use. They learned to edit tape – I was a graphic instructor, wielding sticky tape and razor blade to such effect that Mary, the admiral's wife, arrived on her second visit bearing a large first aid kit. All their efforts were headed towards the ten-thirty mid-morning show called *Womanwise* – known to me as *Womanwise And Not The Knitting Hour*. Later we added two hour-long documentaries to the weekly output – a ludicrous workload, but we were nothing if not keen.

It was a producer's dream – even though we had virtually no budget. The airwaves were there to be filled, and we went in all directions. I started to lift up the social carpet and have a look at some of the problems affecting ordinary lives; it was the early seventies, and change was in the air on abortion, divorce and employment, along with industrial unrest and terrorism. I wasn't alone in making these programmes, but merely part of a general movement in the media to keep abreast of change, and lose some of the establishment subservience which still hung about quite a lot of broadcasting. I felt my own ignorance keenly, growing aware of the way in which most of us can live our lives without deviating from the path which seems comfortable and familiar. I trained myself to stare at a street of houses and be nosy about what went on inside – what did a sheet hung up instead of curtains indicate? Why did half the country garden fanatically while others tolerated a wilderness of mud and tin cans and broken gates? If prostitutes operated in City Road on a Wednesday afternoon in broad daylight, who were their clients? (Turned out to be businessmen glad of half-day closing in south Wales, according to my research involving two hours on the pavement and seven possible clients.)

I grew more and more fascinated with the complexity of social issues: heading in almost the opposite direction to most journalism, I felt that it was nearly impossible to make a programme about one social issue without finding half a dozen other problems knocking on the door. Spend days investigating a homeless family slung out into the street for non-payment of rent, and discover, by a roundabout route, that the younger son set fire to their last two homes, apparently because his father, repeatedly imprisoned, beat him up whenever he came out. Interview a desperate couple trying to get their severely disabled daughter into a mainstream school, and elicit the fact – in an aside – that their determination and devotion had driven their other daughter from home to a life on the streets. Realise that officialdom was a mixture of overworked, underpaid, decent folk, indistinguishable initially from lazy, indifferent inadequates.

I learned that a crusade could destroy those who were merely trying to keep a system afloat, and that inaccurate research could let crooks off the hook. Charging into a local housing department full of righteous indignation about homelessness, I found three families with fourteen small children among them conducting a sit-in round the housing officer's desk, the parents brandishing bread-knives and the children tearing up the contents of the filing cabinets. Interviewing a special needs official about complaints regarding the running of a unit for those who were then called educationally subnormal children, I departed with a reassuring and credible account of his efforts – only to see him in court six months later on child sex-abuse charges.

I learned the hard way that it was total irresponsibility to put out material on the radio without having the greatest faith in it, and ensuring that it was accurate, fair and honest. I looked at the headlines which the newsroom dealt in upstairs, and then started looking for the real story, muddled and complicated, with virtue and vice living together under the same roof. I grew increasingly averse to a black-and-white view of life. In other words, I started to grow up, probably a bit later than many others.

I felt a burning desire to reveal and uncover and put right – but also to get it right.

I spent hour upon hour listening to strangers unburden themselves and complain and accuse and confess. This was a time when people found the arrival of someone with a tape-recorder quite novel, and there was little of the grandstanding and showing off and parading of public confession that have now become commonplace. Local radio was the *vox populi*, and with an open mind and a sharp ear, you could detect the true pulse of daily life.

And there were times when things should be left unsaid. Guilelessly, people spoke of their intimate secrets, unaware of the way they were damaging themselves. Sometimes revelations were made which would have harmed and hurt both the speaker and others, if made public – and for no good reason. And sometimes a juicy little snippet of information begged to dance on the public stage, just for the hell of it.

One quiet afternoon, the newsroom interviewed Bernadette Devlin, probably then the most notorious MP in the House of Commons. In her mid-twenties, a hate-figure to many because of her support for the nationalist cause in Northern Ireland, she had little going for her – she was young, a woman, articulate, and a thorn in the side of much of the House. She was due on the regional TV programme, but not for an hour, so I was asked to take her to the canteen for a cup of coffee.

'Would you like some toast – or biscuits?' I asked.

'Love some,' she said over-eagerly.

'Are you hungry – shall I get the girls to rustle up a plate of eggs?'

'Yes please.'

'Sausages, beans, the works?'

'Oh, thanks.'

She sat there in a white polo-neck sweater under a shocking pink pinafore dress, looking a bit like a tube of toothpaste, and shovelled in every morsel. Without a moment's reflection, I said:

'Eating for two's not that wise, you know.'

She dropped her fork and blurted: 'Oh God, how d'you know – who told you?'

'Dunno,' I said, 'just instinct, I suppose.'

Her confidence was gone and she cringed down into the canteen chair. An unmarried Roman Catholic woman in a public job, she was only too well aware of the horrendous implications of her situation becoming known: the joy it would give her enemies – and some of her chauvinistic supporters.

'Are you going to tell?' she asked.

'I've no intention,' I said. 'This is your private business, and it's for you to do the telling.'

Some twenty-odd years later, we passed in Broadcasting House in Belfast.

'It was you, wasn't it?' she said. 'You never told.'

'No,' I said. 'How's the daughter?'

'You should know,' she said; and indeed, the young woman whose earliest days I'd instinctively discerned in Bristol was at that time in gaol, awaiting extradition to Germany to be questioned on terrorist charges.

Our programmes were hardly an array of award-winning radio, but we began to build an audience – and tried to put out something which asked people to think. Homelessness, vagrants, prisoners' wives, adoption, mental illness in children, the conditions in psychiatric hospitals, alcoholism, abortion – the boss remarked that entering the station after half-past ten during *Womanwise* meant encountering a sense of outrage, accompanied by discussion of very intimate women's bits.

Some weeks, I could hardly believe that such a field had been opened up for us to roam in. In the spirit of the times, we felt we could use our little local radio catapult and topple giants, as long as we hit our target fair and square. David was a liberal and far-sighted manager, refraining from interference wherever possible. Programme discussions took place on the stairs thus:

'So, what's on next week?'

'Incest.'

'Christ, Kate.'

(Long pause.)

'Do you know what you're . . . ?'

'Yes, I know what I'm doing, and I'm prepared to stand by every word . . .'

(Short pause.)

'I look forward to hearing it.'

Our workload was ludicrous, but we were all having a good deal of fun, fuelled twice a day in the BBC Club by a fashionable seventies intake of several lager and limes finished off with a couple of gin and tonics. We worked an average fourteen-hour day, so needed to keep our spirits up, and drink helped – as did the thumping sounds which emanated from the Unattended Studio, where much intimate attending-to went on. We also sang, an eccentricity that drove the station manager nuts. At about four in the afternoon, the sports, arts, religion and documentary production office – as the downstairs front-room slum was known – occasionally climbed collectively on to the desks and sang 'Oh God Our Help In Ages Past'. Well, it made us feel better, and it kept other irritating members of staff from bringing in their trivial problems: they thought we were all a bit mad. We varied the repertoire a bit, and colleagues learned that 'Onward Christian Soldiers' was a good sign, and the strains of 'Eternal Father Strong To Save' meant that deadlines were being missed and that no one was in a mood to discuss doing an extra shift.

Having to churn out such a mass of tape and interviews and scripts meant a daily problem with the deadlines, especially for my mid-morning programme, scheduled to begin at ten-thirty. Initially, I had most of the material edited and the script written the night before. After a while I got fed up with burning the midnight oil and never seeing the boyfriend, and couldn't face another toasted cheese sandwich from the Club bar for dinner. So I managed a decent social life and then came in at seven in the morning and typed away. Even this system came under pressure as I found myself hammering at the typewriter keys while the programme's signature tune was being announced. Eventually I threw in the towel, cantered into the studio carrying the typewriter, and wrote the opening words of the script as the sig tune was playing. I learned to type in between recorded items like a concert pianist on heat. And I could compose scripts with just seconds to go before the red light went on. There cannot have been a better training for my later job in television news, for writing under pressure is at its core.

It was all going swimmingly until my appendix decided, one Sunday afternoon, it wanted nothing to do with local radio, and I headed into hospital for an emergency operation. A little rest for the wicked? No way. At eight-thirty the next morning, half an hour before I was due in theatre, Sarah Pitt, my assistant producer, appeared as I was loaded on to a trolley. Notebook in hand, she said, 'OK, I've found the tapes for this morning, now how about a script?'

Alongside the serious stuff we did out-and-about programmes, on the lines of a venerable BBC warhorse, *Down Your Way*. I'd also acquired the farming programme again, entirely according to the Corporation's tradition of considering you an expert on something you've done once. I adored it this time round, taking myself out into the West Country and the Dorset vales, the Somerset Levels and the bare hills of Wiltshire. And all I had to do was carry the tape-recorder, for I'd found a real expert in Richard Maslen, who discussed Mervyn Peake's novels and brucellosis in sheep with equal authority as we drove round the Mendips and the Quantocks.

The farming programme's yearly highlight was the Bath and West Agricultural Show at Shepton Mallet, only slightly marred by the arrival of the entire radio station and a small tent, plus Arthur and his Piano and his Lady Friend. Local radio had every intention of proving it went out and about, and if this meant pushing a piano over half a mile of showground at six in the morning, then having Arthur's sheet music eaten by representatives of the British Goat Society, this was what local broadcasting was all about.

One of the reasons the farming programme had come my way was no doubt the fact that several of us had decided in a fit of madness to live on a farm. Bristol was then full of ancient Georgian properties, and the passion for renovation was in its infancy. Some of my colleagues lived, or rather camped, in rotting splendour in gracious crescents. Four of us decided to opt for half a farmhouse a couple of miles beyond the Clifton suspension bridge. The farm looked glorious in summer sunshine and boasted an Aga. We spent the next year offering dinner to every likely man we encountered in order to have someone to sort out the bloody Aga, remove huge spiders from the bath and keep us warm. It was cheap, though – BBC salaries weren't generous – and we kept the rent down by volunteering my services as part-time pig-farrower-in-chief.

The arts programme also fell to me, meaning that I spent hours sitting through amateur theatricals, wondering what law permitted *The Desert Song* to be attempted by a cast of small fat Weston-super-Mare residents in striped dressing-gowns. And then there was the weekend political programme, which meant chasing an MP – any MP – down from Westminster and begging them for an interview, driving miles to Saturday morning surgeries and rendezvous in supermarkets and football grounds. It also meant several encounters with Tony Benn, a man who always asked in advance how long the interview was to be, and when you replied, 'Oh, three and a half minutes – say,' froze you rigid by ending his last sentence with a look at his watch and the words, 'Two minutes twenty-nine seconds, will that do?' But nothing ever goes to waste: trying to corner Tom King, a Somerset MP, when he was defence minister nearly twenty years later, I delivered the *coup de grâce* as other reporters elbowed for precedence: 'Come on, it's me, we used to meet in a lay-by near Chippenham.'

As if we didn't have enough to do, the radio station was keen to produce 'specials' – half an hour on any known subject in the universe, as long as it had a Bristol connection. The arrival of a Royal Navy warship at Avonmouth docks one weekend resulted in a conversation with Mary, the admiral's wife. Lady Hogg wanted to know why we weren't doing a 'special', and I muttered that I knew nothing of boats, except for 15,000 ton cargo vessels built in Sunderland, which HMS *Thing* did not resemble.

'It's HMS *Norfolk*, and she's a ship, not a boat,' said Mary with an instructive gleam in her eye. Little did I know that I was about to start on a path which I could never have envisaged then.

Mary persisted: 'And what are you going to do when HMS *Bristol* comes alongside?'

'There isn't one, is there?' I tried.

'There certainly is,' said Mary. 'I launched her.'

Thus we embarked on a wonderful task, with Mary sailing full steam ahead, interviewing the men fitting out the destroyer at Swan Hunter's on Tyneside, and later going to sea to tell the story of the *Bristol* and her six predecessors. Hitherto, I had never really met the navy; now, helplessly mixing business with pleasure, I found myself lurking on docksides the length of the British Isles, not entirely in a broadcasting research capacity. I never thought that one day I'd see naval ships in action, that I'd need to know about the weapons systems and the defence capabilities, and that I'd lie on the deck of a carrier while fighters and bombers took off over me. I was in local radio – and not even in the newsroom.

I was, however, a sports reporter – but only because there were never quite enough reporters to cover the ambitious efforts of a Saturday afternoon, so anyone with a pair of legs and eyes was dragooned into the wonderful world of footy and rugger and cricket and everything else (though the Angling programme was self-sufficient, rich in strange men hooked on bream and roach). When it came to doling out the Saturday soccer matches, I was clearly not Division One material – I was firmly Minor League. My favourites were Welton Rovers, whose ground I initially failed to find; they came from Midsomer Norton, there being no such place as Welton. On the day they were due to play Mangotsfield United, I had a bit of trouble with the radio car, and again turned up after kick-off. I unravelled various bits of cable and stuck on a pair of headphones; looking up, I heard a few shouts of excitement – first goal. Rather too quickly, the sports presenter back in the studio decided that a visit to the Welton–Mangotsfield clash was due; I stared at the huddle of shirts, reckoned that Mangotsfield were one up, and gave the joyful news to the world in a neat forty-five seconds.

One of the features of Minor League was that you could park the car right on the sidelines, and what there was of a crowd then formed round you, giving a nice bit of atmosphere. A few lads sidled up, including a small bespectacled know-all clutching a soccer magazine and a radio. He stared at me and said very thoughtfully: 'Some stupid cow's just said that Mangotsfield's scored. 'Snot true.'

'Go away,' I hissed, then realised that the radio car's telescopic aerial was playing its usual trick of voluntarily collapsing. I rootled about in the mechanical mess, only to hear another shout from the field. The tiny crowd had wandered off to the halfway line, and there was no one to ask. Yet again, the headphones squawked, and I decided to hedge my bets: 'One all,' I said. The small boy with radio walked past in silence, holding his thumb down.

Nothing much happened after that until, as I was packing up the car while the lads trooped off the field, the ref came over for a word.

'Great game,' I said brightly.

'Yes,' he said, 'it's not often we get four goals in a match like this.'

Four? I fled.

The whole area seemed unbelievably softer and richer than the north-east. The nineteenth century's industrial scars were hardly visible here, and Bristol had a confidence and affluence that were new to me. It also had a social life in which the radio station joined with panache; we partied and learned the joys of eating out – a novelty for most of us in the early seventies. I joined two amateur operatic societies as a rather off-key chorus member, knowing full well there was more fun behind the scenery than the audience would ever know. Rather like local radio, in fact, where everyone found the energy to enjoy themselves unstintingly off air, the main rule being that any thumping sounds should never reach a microphone that was on.

A genuine *broadcasting* rumpus was always welcome, though – and this is where 'access' programmes triumphed. We advertised on air for the public to come forward and 'do your own thing'.

Thought by our masters in London to be a tentative step towards drawing shy amateurs on air to make their own programmes, this initiative, we soon discovered, made us easy meat for loony groups and determined lobbyists. Friday nights were enlivened by the sound of anti-hunt protestors and pro-life campaigners disputing with a mild-mannered producer, who became an expert on the law of libel and the need to convince participants that May They Roast In Hell was not a particularly endearing programme title.

The other kind of access which we apparently offered was to the world's frustrated tellers of tales. Little did any of us know that every other household nurtured a resentful and desperate creature whose life centred on closely typed sheets of dog-eared A4, packaged in a brown envelope which had been re-labelled thirty times. The short-story writer.

One innocent afternoon, a presenter mused on air that it would be nice to hear the odd story or two at teatime. The next week saw a complaint from the BBC post room, submerged in old manilla envelopes. We parcelled out the offerings among various producers, less than certain that genius and talent was about to burst out and grab the Nobel Prize for Literature. We were right; the word Dire danced in front of us. Shaggy dog stories, meanderings down ye olde rural byways, and It Was a Dark and Stormy Night . . . We read and read, and then composed a gentle letter, kindly thanking for having sent, but regretting . . . and got a sackful of acid-laden missives by return. The only producer spared this unpleasant correspondence was a colleague who solved the problem of a loose floorboard in the downstairs office by replacing it with eighty-five unread short stories. They'll make a great find when the place gets demolished.

Radio Bristol's concern to bring back children's radio led to a couple of hours of anarchy on Saturday morning, when a large number of children and a foul-mouthed mynah bird took over the studio. The mynah was a star, and held the title for several firsts on air, mainly other words beginning with 'f'. The producer, a talented writer – Ken Blakeson, who went on to deliver prize-winning drama – decided that the children deserved to hear a real serial, so he set to, pouring out extraordinary tales of medieval adventure and science fiction. Having no repertory company to draw on, he could be seen corralling the staff on Fridays, waving a sheet of paper in front of them and shouting – 'It'll only take a minute, you're a crazed assassin, just go into Studio Two and sound angry, determined and mad in an eighteenth-century sort of way.' One Friday, I was absorbed in a particularly difficult meeting with a group of Wages for Housework activists, trying to look thoughtful and businesslike, when I saw a script being waved round the door. The feminists looked round, unamused, to see Ken in a frenzy of programme-deadline arm-waving: 'Look,' he pleaded, 'it's only two pages and you're a hideous thing from Planet Pluto.'

As a former member of the National Youth Theatre, I was good at theatrical pique – though with no reason whatsoever, for in three summer seasons with the NYT as a teenager, I'd only ever made it to Assistant to the Assistant Wardrobe Mistress and Member of Shakespearean Crowd. My Wardrobe efforts centred on darning tights – a challenging task, as most of the boys were wearing them at the time. As Crowd Member in various productions, I thought I could Rhubarb Rhubarb with the best of them, and was mildly puzzled why my talents were ignored in favour of the likes of a nice but perfectly normal girl from London. I mean, what did this Helen Mirren have? However, I did carry away from the NYT an abiding love of theatre and a string of absurdly romantic theatrical interludes, leading to the habit of squawking, 'I went out with James Bond!' embarrassingly loudly in cinemas whenever Timothy Dalton appeared on screen.

None of this cut much ice with Ken and his plays on Radio Bristol – as shown when he delivered his pièce de résistance: the decision to stage a Passion Play for Easter, updated as if reported by modern broadcasters, and full of contemporary dialogue. *On The Hill*, it was to be called. To add even more spice, the excellent

Blue Notes Jazz Band, with morning show presenter Roger on soprano saxophone, contributed linking music. Ken stalked the station, trying to cast the play suitably. There was a bit of an argument about the main part, as to whether it should go to Ken himself – delivering updated sacred words in a strong Yorkshire accent – or to Frank Topping, the religious affairs producer, who had once been in *Coronation Street*. Ken, being the author, won. The newsroom produced centurion Michael Buerk, and the news editor, who had a standing rule that Ken's serials only included him if he got to play kings or prime ministers, agreed to be Pontius Pilate. The rest of the producers were rabble and Pharisees; no problem. The resulting production, daring in its time, was well received, and to our amazement the BBC in London made interested noises. Eventually, it was transmitted on Radio Three.

At the age of six, I had failed to be Snow White in my prep school play, ending up as the wicked witch; so there were no surprises when I copped Mary Magdalene. Thus it is that, though I have only ever uttered four words on Radio Three in my three decades with the BBC, they were memorable ones: 'Wanna nice time, dearie?'

FIVE

A motley crew

Television reporters have to like company. The screen may show an image of a solitary figure standing amid the noise and fury of some disaster, but a couple of feet away is a cameraman – or these days, occasionally, a camerawoman.

This is sometimes forgotten by the 'duck and dive' school of reporters, who bounce energetically up and down. Their 'I'm just dodging the bullets' performance is being recorded by an immensely pissed-off cameraman, stoically pointing at the antics of the frontline star, and not moving an inch.

So, you are a team. Or that's the theory. For the first few years that I worked in television, I got the impression that they were the team, and I was the opposing side.

It all began rather charmingly. I went to regional television, entirely by mistake, and ended up walking out of the door on the first day in Plymouth, heading for my story about sheltered accommodation, with a rather nice man following me.

'I'm Colin,' he said.

'Hello, I'm Kate – I'm just off to the old folk's place in Tavistock.'

'Yeah, I'm coming with you.'

I stared at him. Why on earth should he be coming along? I'd spent years doing interviews for local radio on my own, and I couldn't fathom why I should have someone trailing along with me. He did not look like a trainee – more like someone who'd been around the Beeb for twenty years. I'd heard that regional radio – a rather strange left-over bit of broadcasting that still functioned in Plymouth, chirpily entitled Morning Sou'west – could be a tad old-fashioned, but did it really need two people to carry a tape-recorder the size of a dictionary?

Colin looked a bit baffled, and shifted an enormous bit of technical gear on to the other shoulder.

'That's a camera,' said I.

This observation didn't go down well. Colin may have been used to filming all manner of regional loonies and eccentrics, but working with them was beyond the call of duty.

'It *is* a camera,' he said, in the manner of a man weighing up the possibilities: Idiot? Editor's floozie? Member of public with delusions of TV talent? He took a deep breath, and said: 'I find a camera very useful for taking television pictures.'

We were still not on the same wavelength.

After over seven years of local radio, I had not quite grasped that I'd hopped over the radio barrier into the strange field of telly. No one had quite spelled it out to me. In Bristol, I'd been told they'd 'got a bit of a gap' in Plymouth, and been sent down the A38. It had also been indicated that, after doing the Bristol Flower Show on Radio Bristol for the fifth time, I was running a little short on things to ask the champion gladioli grower – the same fanatic who won every year.

So here I was, willing and able to help prop up regional radio, with this odd man who was now holding open his car door, and indicating that he – and another man with a lot of equipment strung round his neck – was offering me a lift.

Somewhere on the way to Tavistock, I gathered that I was going to have to do something terrible: appear on television.

I'd only done fun bits before, joke TV: Bristol's region had always run out of money halfway through the financial year, and the cheapest programme they could mount was a quiz. In order to do it at rock-bottom cost, they advertised for members of the public to be on the teams. In order to do it for absolutely nothing at all, they hired myself and Derek Jones, a veteran radio presenter, to be team captains. I did several series, and thus grew to know that a dish of curled sandwiches and a glass of Bulgarian wine, after the programme, constituted TV high life in Bristol.

It was not viewed as a career move by the rest of Radio Bristol. The regional TV newsroom did its best to ignore the local radio newsroom; my colleague, Michael Buerk, failed even to get an audition with them. We lived in a twilight world of not-grown-up BBC.

I'd spent a short time with the Outside Broadcast Department, and for a time thought that if TV beckoned in any form, it should be with this rather jolly outfit that dealt with Sport, Religion and Events. (It also did circuses, but we didn't have any in the south-west region.) Learning the ropes as a trainee director, I thought the world of television seemed complex and time-consuming; there was a large technical crew which added up to a small invasion force when we descended on unsuspecting villages to do *Songs of Praise*. The crew were traditionalists to a man; 'wimmin' were meant to be fluffy programme secretaries – the nice girls who passed your outrageous Expenses forms, including all kinds of Hotel Accommodation, while you'd all been camping in a field, *and* charged the BBC for the tents. A woman lurking around the OB scanner van was viewed suspiciously. Especially one who kept asking what specific jobs were done by various crew members. For it quickly dawned on me that there was a lengthy tradition that certain posts were filled by chaps who apparently didn't do *anything*, but were referred to as 'the Gaffer' and 'Old Charlie' and so on. They did fill in Expenses forms though.

The crew had an engaging side which outweighed the skirmishes with Administration: come the recording of *Songs of Praise*, they all slipped out of the overalls in which they'd been lugging cables and building camera platforms and appeared in immaculate navy-blue suits. They'd then shepherd excited choirs and congregations around the TV equipment and into church, handing out hymn-sheets, being staggeringly polite, and dispensing titbits of discreet but thrilling television gossip to the elderly ladies in their best hats. 'Such gentlemen,' cooed the ladies, 'just what you'd expect from the BBC.'

Out in the van sat the director and vision-mixers, huddled in the dark and staring at a row of screens, trying to figure out what might go wrong. Almost anything, it transpired, especially if vicars were involved. For, far from being a harmonious meadow of saintly charity, Religious Programmes were a battleground of ungodly ambitions. In order that a full congregation be achieved for *Songs of Praise* – no TV producer likes an empty church – neighbouring parishes were invited to participate. It was like inviting Attila the Hun and his horde to a tea-party given by Genghis Khan. Choirs suddenly mush-roomed in membership, and unseemly jostling took place in the pews during rehearsals. I knew the score, having seen my family's Methodist church in Sunderland do battle three times with the worthy battalions of the local C of E (the Methodists always won – they sang louder). Organists threw fits of conniption, flower arranging turned into a competitive sport, and vicars acquired a faraway gleam in the eye when told that they could 'say a few words' at the programme's close. That gleam encompassed a dream of addressing several million people instead of the usual faithful few.

'Two minutes maximum,' the vicars were told politely but firmly.

'Of course, of course,' they would intone, as they headed to their studies to pen the words which would grip an unsuspecting nation in its Sunday evening armchair.

Wise to the ways of vicars, and mindful of the occasion when one had stretched two minutes into eight, it was the director's duty to station the floor manager in such a position that the vicar was kept under control – and within his allotted time. We all used to thank God fervently for our floor manager, Mr Sluggett.

Mr S. had no rival when it came to slithering noiselessly up the pulpit stairs on his stomach and seizing a ranting vicar's ankles – a ploy which never failed to stop the most enthusiastic cleric in mid-flow. Every church should have a Mr Sluggett; sermons would be shorter.

One small point about *Songs of Praise*, in stark defiance of all BBC witterings about 'range of musical favourites' and 'inclusive breadth of styles of worship', i.e. lots of new hymns, with odd bursts of guitar or gospel, and new tunes to much-loved favourites: the audience knows what it likes. It likes a certain number of hymns. Eight, to be precise.

The oddities of BBC budgeting meant that the crew who recorded *Songs of Praise* on Friday or Saturday evening had to produce a live *Morning Service* as well on Sunday, whether the vicar liked it or not and regardless of the crew's hangover. Just for the record, an Act of Worship *has* to be transmitted live, at the behest of Lord Reith. It was one of his strictures, and it's never been challenged. If you're wondering why *Songs of Praise* got away with being recorded, it's because the BBC sneakily reclassified it as Light Entertainment.

Morning Service was a great way to learn about TV directing. In exquisite settings throughout Devon and Cornwall, in tiny dark Romanesque chapels, naves glowing with Victorian stained glass, or softly sunshiny Georgian model churches, events as time-honoured and ancient as Sunday worship slid gently out of control. For 'the first time in forty years', the churchwarden lost the key. On one occasion the crucifer, a gentle elderly soul whose ability to carry the very heavy cross we had questioned, surprised us by making it all the way down the aisle, only to forget to lower the cross as he approached the rood screen. Sitting outside in the OB van, the first hint of trouble was a screen showing the choir bunching up in front of Camera 2, rather like a crowded tube train. Camera 1, meanwhile, was tracing a pair of legs bicycling helplessly as the cross remained hooked over the screen, crucifer hanging on grimly, swinging silently.

At least the choir stayed for the rest of the service. Not so a month later, when the lusty singing of a particularly muscular Cornish choir suddenly stopped dead in Hymn Number Three, Verse Four. Those of us in the van outside peered at our screens, as the choir left their stalls at a brisk and unecclesiastical trot. We'd failed (a) to hear the alarm klaxon at the village fire station; (b) to ascertain earlier that the Auxiliary Fire Brigade all belonged to the choir; and (c) to realise that it was the BBC generator outside our van that was ablaze.

Even if the programme went perfectly, it had to be sent electronically to the nearest transmitter, problems with which led aeons ago to the most ancient BBC technical excuse that exists: 'Well, it's all right *leaving me* . . .' implying that engineering buggeration always occurs way down the line and it's not your fault that a bulldozer hit the cable, or God delivered an electrical storm in defiance of the BBC weather forecast, or the tide went out. The tide? Somewhere in the mysteries of Engineering Department there was the explanation as to why TV Outside Broadcast pictures fade when the tide goes out. Mine was not to reason why, mine was to go out and buy a set of tide timetables, and suggest to vicars that *Morning Service* should be shifted to coincide with high tide.

OBs were fun, although much of the time was passed in acute frenzy, on a diet of pub grub – supplemented by the crew with bacon sandwiches into which an entire pig had been levered. There was an extraordinary thrill in arriving anywhere to be greeted with excitement: the BBC is here. It was a royal visit minus royalty: lots of preparations, a sense of occasion, and a very definite reminder that your visit wouldn't be forgotten – for whatever reason. People remembered in detail the last time 'those telly people were here', sometimes with dark mutterings, and you were expected to come up to certain expectations. Whatever happened, the local pub takings were usually spectacular.

In the seventies, broadcasting from a small village church in Devon with a number of neatly dressed women in hats and a sprinkling of families scattered among newly polished pews, knowing that an equally modest number of viewers were joining you, nevertheless constituted part of Public Service. As well as highlighting the nation's special events, there was still a place for everyday life, including all kinds of minority activities.

As light relief to Religious Programmes, the occasional Event came our way, into which category fell general elections. Apart from getting the outside broadcast scanner vehicle (that's the big important one) stuck at the bottom of a cliff at Westward Ho! – no problem, I said, I know who to call, I've lured the army to stranger places – most of the 1974 campaigns sailed along in a whirlwind of sparse meetings and pointless rallies. We were faced with one big challenge: to uproot the entire OB unit from central Barnstaple after the polls closed on election night in order to secure the earliest interview with the Liberal party leader Jeremy Thorpe at his home in the village of Chittlehamholt.

Somehow the lumbering caravan of overweight vehicles wormed its way down the Devon lanes in the wee hours, and the crew set to work dragging cables and cameras silently into the garden. Another camera was carried up a hillside to what I imagined to be the perfect spot for a dawn panorama of glorious Devon. Might have been, but mist as thick as a chemical cloud appeared instead of the sun. As usual, the manic team in London in charge of election night – and the morning-after programme – were shrieking dementedly down the line well before dawn, desperate for anything to transmit. They clearly anticipated a glorious landscape, in which honey-gold South Devons and little Ruby Reds mooed past on their way to milking, accompanied by picturesque locals in smocks conversing knowledgeably about politics.

I stared at our screens, all an identical shade of black.

'Got nothing for you yet,' I said, 'all dark.'

'Why?' came the reply from TV Centre.

'Lack of sun.'

'Can't you do anything?'

'Like what? Spin earth faster on axis? Move OB from Chittlehamholt to central Africa pronto?'

This had the desired effect of getting rid of London for a good hour while we waited for sunrise, which duly took place to no great effect, our screens becoming an identical shade of mist-grey.

Suddenly, the intercoms from London were going full tilt, with the alarming information that they definitely needed 'a long scene-set from Devon, reporter in vision, lots of pix'. David Lomax, our excellent current affairs man, affable, competent and unassuming, dressed in country tweeds (in total contrast to the news reporter lurking in the Thorpe garden, bedecked in bouffant hair and pastel shirt), volunteered to stand in front of the camera on the hillside.

The noise emanating into the van from London indicated that the morning-after programme was in a morning-after state – guests not arrived, OBs in technical overdrive, presenters frayed. I stared at the monitor screens, thinking that David was taking his time to get to the camera position. Just as London yelled, 'Coming to you in five', a dark shape emerged on to Camera 2's screen.

'Stand by, cue David!' I shouted, and Mr Lomax's voice drifted lyrically out of the mist. He delivered a lengthy peroration on Liberals, landscape and local lore – the sort of thing which is very acceptable just after dawn, but exceptional when you can see nothing and are standing up to your hocks in a soggy cow-patted field. When he'd finished, London thankfully stood us down for half an hour, and I stared gratefully at the misty blob on the screen, telling him he could come in now. The blob didn't move. After a bit, I told him again he very definitely deserved a gigantic crew bacon sandwich, and he could leave the field.

'I'm here,' said a voice in the van doorway.

To this day, I can claim the dubious prize of having been the only assistant director to transmit a tree as a vital part of an election programme.

*

In view of this chequered history, it's not surprising that I had a rather diffident view of appearing in front of a camera, so that finding myself faced with the prospect of being a TV reporter did not fire me with joy. And the idea of having anything to do with News was even more alarming.

My entire experience of News up to now had been as a substitute, and as a last, desperate measure. In local radio I was the farming producer, the arts producer, the weekend political programme producer, the twice-a-week documentary producer, the three-times-a-week mid-morning magazine producer – and God, when we're really desperate, the football reporter (Minor League only, no away matches). What I was not, was a news reporter.

Apart from anything else, the newsroom at Radio Bristol was a female-free zone. It was dominated by Brian.

Brian Roberts was a charmer. Six foot four, always wore a smart suit, with pocket handkerchief, and had dark golden hair carefully arranged. He was exaggeratedly but genuinely gentlemanly to women – as long as they kept out of his newsroom. It wasn't that he disliked them in there. He just couldn't see what they were for. You might just as well have dressed as a chorus girl and fishnet-stockinged your way round the teleprinters; you weren't going to be taken seriously, so you might as well get noticed.

Reporting aside, I'd had the occasional brush with news. The Welsh-language protestors occasionally took to daubing rude but thankfully very Welsh words on our buildings; Northern Ireland was beginning to rumble, and we used to get regular IRA bomb threats. There was none of the health and safety stuff which now fills volumes of Corporation guidelines: whoever took the call usually delivered a feisty insult back down the phone – and if an argument followed, there was no need to get particularly alarmed. Every so often though, things sounded more sinister, so we'd have a hasty conflab, usually based on the weather. No one in their right mind was going to evacuate the building in order to stand out in the cold and wet; if it was a nice day, however, we'd all take a little stroll in the sun while the police truffled round the building. After several false alarms involving difficult encounters with the security-conscious Avon Constabulary, we developed a middle way: we opened the ops room window and threw out a microphone and various essential pieces of equipment, and then sat in the car park and went on broadcasting while the police 'searched' our offices – a cursory riffle through the mountainous waste-heaps of scripts and tape. They were unamused when we booby-trapped filing cabinets with pomegranates trailing a piece of string and felt-tipped OIRISH BOM.

On the odd occasion, I was sent out to reinforce the reporting strength, when there was absolutely no one else left to send. I was not an outstanding success, and for many months had to endure shame while my first big fire story was recounted. I thought I'd done quite well, but I'd overlooked the infelicity of standing in front of a massive warehouse ablaze to the cost of several hundred thousand pounds while saying from the radio car, 'Well, as you join me, it's burning merrily . . .'

The newsroom functioned in its own world, resounding to journalese – words such as 'copy' and 'par' and 'lineage', none of which I understood. Thus, when snoozing through a recorded interview programme in the studio, I was unprepared for Richard Talbot from the newsroom to burst in, demanding to give a flash. Up until then, I'd thought him very reserved and well-behaved for a journalist, and we had quite an embarrassing exchange before he got on air to announce that the government at Stormont was being suspended. Aha – a *news* flash. I went another notch down in the newsroom's estimation.

I could never quite grasp the air of urgency with which the news was surrounded: we'd not had a lot of news on Radio Durham, mainly because someone had forgotten to give us a budget to pay for it. So the thrusting outfit in Bristol that hurtled through studio doors and scraped the radio car's shanks was a source of fascination to me. You couldn't fault them for devotion to duty. The lunchtime programme, *West to One* (well, if London had *The World at One*...), was a typhoon of essential information served up by at least four reporters and presided over by Brian; I'd sit at the control desk in the studio and watch them, winding down the sound level when it came to the sports news, when all of them inexplicably used to shout. One day Michael Buerk was about to launch into a major story when he made a very strange sound. Looking across to the news table, I saw that Brian and the others were getting up and flapping their hands: the table was a sea of blood. It's amazing what a nose can deliver. As a hapless Michael dripped towards the door, Brian picked up the sodden script and proceeded to read it, incidentally covering the rather blood-averse sports producer, who came over rather faint. Nothing was ever allowed to impede the imperious flow of news – except on the day a nice man called Mr Richard Titball came in to be interviewed, and insisted on air that he be called Dick, then proceeded to describe British Rail's problem with frozen points. By the time he'd finished, three of the news producers had crawled out of the studio overcome with grubby hysteria, and I had to make a strangulated announcement to the effect that We have a technical problem so here's a little music.

So here I was, in Plymouth, and on the telly, and in news. I was extremely frightened. I bluffed my way through my first interview at the old folk's home and, with a lot of help, managed to write a script to fit the pictures that had been cut by the film editor. I hadn't a clue about any of the techniques which might be required, and I felt a fraud. That evening, I was told I'd be going to a rabbit farm the next day, to report on the growing exports of rabbit meat to northern France. I was aware that television reporting had something called a 'Piece to Camera' – the moment when the reporter pops up in vision and delivers a flawless speech. I thought I'd better write it in advance, and learn it, although I knew next to nothing about rabbits.

Next morning, with the patient Colin, I toured the farm, interviewed the proprietor and took lots of shots of fluffy bunnies. P to C, said Colin finally, and I got out my script.

'All that?' said Colin. 'You sure?'

I delivered my magnum opus – almost to the end – then got in a muddle. Tried again, and then again. Colin looked around rather despondently, and said, 'Here, take this, and try and look more relaxed.'

He handed me a huge buck rabbit, which kicked like a horse. I grasped ears and back legs, and launched yet again into my speech. Several goes later, I finally got to the last word – and looked triumphantly at Colin.

'Finished,' I said.

'Yep,' said Colin, 'so's the rabbit.' A limp lump of white fur hung in my arms, pink eyes bulging like marbles, squeezed half to death by a stressed reporter.

We got several complaints about the story: some about my vice-like grip on the rabbit, but mostly about children having seen the item and being overcome with horror at the suggestion that their pet could end up on a French dinner-plate. Bunny-killer, said one letter.

Not a good start.

Still, I persevered, conscious that television was what everyone wanted to do – except me. I learned what is sometimes called the 'grammar of television'. It's the antidote to the fond conceit that what happens on screen is natural, uncontrived and unstructured, and the idea that the camera does not alter people's behaviour. Admittedly, news reporting comes closer to reality than much of the action on the box, but even so, reports have to be thought out and constructed so that they make a watchable item. Real life is filleted and compressed, and reduced to a short, pithy – and explanatory – essay which complements selected pictures. Compare this to *real* real life – say, a story about trouble in a city centre – drink and crime and violence perhaps. A reporter and camera crew spend one, perhaps two whole nights lurking in the shopping precinct. Sod's law will ordain that it's the quietest weekend for years. They return the following weekend, and with considerable difficulty – drunks, harassed police officers, incomprehensible scuffles and brawls – they get some action on camera. The reporter researches statistics, and interviews a policeman, a local shopkeeper, the chairman of the chamber of commerce. There are also a couple of not-quite-usable vox pops with lads in the precinct – full of four-letter words and playing up to the camera. After editing, the result should be a workman-like two and a half minutes, a story which gives several sides to a complex picture, and is interesting to watch. *Real* reality is what you see on the surveillance camera: ten hours of incomprehensible footage, in which blurred and anonymous figures dash about.

Reporting is a distillation, and a selection. The camera and the reporter choose, select and edit continuously. The whole process is one of choice and decision-making – even when events unfold around you, beyond your control. The camera looks in one direction at any one moment, and it's far less observant than the human eye. Vital images, significant events can happen – indeed, have a knack of happening – while you're concentrating on a tricky shot in the opposite direction. At a riot, a demonstration, a political rally, this is how the unexpected – that which becomes news – usually begins: well away from the main event, and not on camera. Grasping what may become a significant event, while mayhem breaks out around you, is a matter of hard experience and not a little luck. I've lost count of the times when I've spotted something out of the corner of my eye, and yelped to the cameraman to swing round and start shooting in the opposite direction. That's why it's so important to be a team; the reporter acts as an extra pair of ears and eyes, watches out for the cameraman's back in dangerous circumstances, and keeps scanning the scene while the camera looks steadily and carefully at individual images.

You try to sort out the significant from the merely interesting or odd. If twenty thousand people march past to demonstrate about a serious matter, then the one man in the crowd dressed as a banana does not warrant particular attention, unless this is a protest mounted by the Banana Protection League. Often it's tempting to go for the peculiar or the sensational, but if you've only got a couple of minutes in which to tell your story, fairness has to rule.

And you have only got a minute or two. Heaven knows how these conventions come about, but most of the world's events are meant to be compressed into about four hundred words, or as it was put years ago: a TV news item is an animated postcard home.

I set to work to find out how the postcard is composed. From archaeological finds to dahlia competitions, I followed the camera and tried to work out how to tell a story without every viewer turning off in irritation or boredom. I learned not to walk in front of the camera's lens while filming was going on, mainly from our Cornish crew, very tall John and his diminutive wife Olive. John carried the camera, and Olive carried the sound equipment, the tripod, the spares bag, the lighting gear, the stepladders and lunch. I was regarded as superfluous to the operation, being merely 'words', so went unnoticed for most of the shooting, until I happened to walk into shot. Watching an irate cameraman pursuing his reporter at a gallop round the quayside at Charlestown shouting Stupid Woman is not the best way to encourage the nervous harbourmaster to relax before his interview. ·

I learned that interviewing on television is a more complicated business than on radio. Radio tape can be chopped up into tiny bits and rearranged, or electronically moved about. Coughs and Y'knows can be tidied out, and questions misunderstood or unanswered can be removed. Telly involved yards of film and the difficulties of marrying sound and picture; the whole affair had to be less casual, more of a performance, in order to get a decent sequence from an interview. And the camera was not as humane as the human eye: people whom you thought were regular of face and feature when you met them sprouted wall eyes and snaggle teeth under the cold eye of the lens. Personal quirks leaped on to the screen, and I began to develop an awareness of Devon farmers who spat during interviews and Penzance housewives with very loose dentures.

I also began to see that the camera cleans up life like an electronic duster: a pile of rubbish, foetid and rotting, merely looked like a jumble of objects. A ruined building, dripping and smoky after a fire, came out on screen as a striking silhouette of timbers. A filthy house, squatted in for months by a group of travellers, looked merely untidy. I'd always thought that television gave a true representation, but now noticed that a filter is ever-present, which takes the edge off reality. Later I grew immensely frustrated as I witnessed wartime scenes of destruction, knowing that only part of the impact felt by humans at the scene could ever reach the viewer at home.

Television was also altogether more cumbersome than radio. For the wireless, a reporter nipped about with a tape-recorder like a large handbag, able to chase down streets and elbow through crowds, with luck, recording all the way. Try doing that with some of the more traditional television crews.

'I'll be ready when I'm ready,' intoned from deep in the boot of the camera car as the police convoy races past with the prisoner.

'There's no rush, cricket's a slow game,' as the film camera lens is being cleaned lovingly with a tiny paintbrush while the county's England cap is caught at silly-mid-on for a duck.

'Explosion, oh *that's* what it was?' as a new magazine of film is being loaded laboriously into the camera.

The sight of a reporter banging head against wall silently was part and parcel of television news.

And then there was the business of appearing.

Some people take to it like ducks to water, gliding in front of the lens confident and engaging. The rest of us can only try, try again. I'm an average performer – the record of retakes for a piece to camera was logged at twenty-three by some cruel creature in

Television Centre, and my name's not involved. However, starting with the rabbit in Plymouth, I realised that this was something that didn't come entirely naturally, and I was going to have to work on it.

I knew one shouldn't be too ambitious, for the film editors in Plymouth kept several cans of out-takes for their Christmas party show, and they immortalised a parade of reporters talking to cameras while falling in slurry pits, walking into lamp-posts and being bitten by various animals, as well as strolling down piers whose length they had badly miscalculated. No, keep it simple: stand still, and talk as if to one person, rather than addressing a public meeting.

My mistakes were kindly thrown away, and somehow I managed to get stories of more or less acceptable quality on to the regional programme. There had been no doubting my role, though, as Cyril Wilkinson, the editor, had smilingly intoned: 'Well, you're the girl, aren't you? You get the nice soft stuff.' He wasn't being unpleasant, just acting on convention, and it was incontrovertibly true that I'd never really worked in News before. So I trekked about doing the Missing Parakeet and the Nudist Beach and the New Drainage Scheme for Dartmoor stories. But it didn't take me long to realise that while I was straining to find something illuminating to say about drainage, the boys were tapping out scripts about murder and sinking yachts and dockyard strikes with much less angst than I was. So what was hard about Hard News, I wondered? In Plymouth with BBC South West, I got little chance to find out; even when the country was racked with drought in the summer of 1976, the boys were out with standpipes and mud-cracked reservoirs and I was in studio in a bath-tub in a bikini, advising on how to get washed with just one bucket of water.

Then came the chance to apply for a job as staff reporter BBC South. I was successful and headed for Southampton – where I immediately discovered that not only were 'hard' news stories not coming my way, they were unlikely to, as the news editor heartily disliked them. I soon found myself wearing a mob cap and frilly petticoat and being chased around a village in Dorset by the local vicar in aid of a hitherto obscure tradition called Randy Pole Day.

Then I was dispatched to Brighton to – as the editor put it – 'put Brighton on the map'. I was puzzled by this mission, as Brighton did not seem a shy town in need of special attention. I was informed that I was expected to deliver regular 'live' reports from 'our special facility' in Brighton. This facility turned out to be a basement room in a high-rise block of flats, shared with a set of washing machines. On the roof was a transmitter, ready to beam the signal directly to Southampton – except when the tide was out. Yet again, it transpired, one of the more exciting aspects of my broadcasting job was its dependency on the book of tide tables. Every time the waves receded from Brighton's pebbles, the transmitter's signal receded as well. I found that planning to coincide regular news reports with phases of the moon wasn't the most efficient of systems.

Still, I thought I'd got a feel for this strange television world, and had an inkling that there must be more to TV news than rabbits and randy poles.

SIX

Under siege

As a reporter working for the national newsroom, I sat in a small and tatty room on the sixth floor of Television Centre, pounding out scripts on horrible grey typewriters which had been modified to dull their clacking sound. It was like bashing a cushion. We – about fifteen souls who did duty according to a shift system which theoretically delivered three days off after four days on – possessed two not-so-easy chairs and a TV set that worked when given the standard BBC repair treatment for any piece of equipment: a whack on the top. The low chairs were for the reporters who found themselves working their ninth day in a row. We looked out on to a miserable stretch of Shepherd's Bush in west London. A shepherd would have found only a few blades of grass in a muddy park behind the Victorian straggle of Wormwood Scrubs prison. Any sheep would have been swiftly acquired and dispatched by the enterprising inhabitants of the nearby White City housing estate.

Once upon a time, a grand exhibition had been built on the site where we now resided in an unlovely glass and concrete doughnut – and the world had flocked to see Britain's innovations and glories of the early twentieth century, using the imposing new underground terminals, all art deco and pride. A few local residents had memories of pavilions and a wonderful boating lake; now the area was not entirely desirable, and the Blue Peter Garden merely suspiciously soggy. We TV people were pitied by the grandees in Broadcasting House three miles away in the heart of the capital.

The newsroom itself was a shabby sprawl, light years removed from any idea of style or the world of entertainment, lacking even the filthy glamour of Fleet Street. At weekends, it was not unknown for the crews and reporters to fetch in a Chinese takeaway and spread it messily among the typewriters. This tradition ended when Angela Rippon was seen reading a new-fangled 'direct from the newsroom' bulletin perched on a desk one Sunday lunchtime, to the sound of 'Any spare ribs left?' and a backdrop of waving forks.

It was a down-at-heel place, full of cigarette smoke and located wrongly for easy access to studios and film cutting rooms. As a result, a lot of running about and shouting went on – the idea that electronic communication might work internally is so ludicrous in the BBC as not to merit a mention. Whenever a 'graphic' – a map or diagram – was needed for the bulletin a reporter went into a slum next to the newsroom and rummaged among the heaps of paper and pots of glue to unearth a 'graphics artist', who would inform the intruder morosely that 'art' wasn't made in a day, never mind in two hours before the *Nine O'Clock News*.

Downstairs, film was developed and cut. The developing process was known as Soup and the worst words a reporter could ever hear, after a day spent gathering unique footage, were 'S'gone down in Soup.' Film processing, although hardly a novel science, appeared to be a mysterious experiment in the BBC which frequently went wrong. Blank, Fogged and Buggered were Soup's main achievements with celluloid.

If the film survived Soup, it was rushed into the cutting room, where reporter and film editor viewed the results as the film juddered through a table-top editing machine. The reporter then wrote a script, recording it in yet another studio, and the whole lot was chopped and stitched together, usually very much up against deadline. If it looked as if the process wasn't going to be finished before the news began, the reporter took a few timings from the film and galloped into the studio to 'second voice' – a frightening method where the reporter watched the pictures come up on a little monitor in the corner of the studio and read out bursts of script as little green cue-lights winked. All of this live, and fraught with anxiety, not least because the studio was quite dark in the corners, and full of lurking equipment. Falling over monitors and shouting Bugger used to annoy Angela Rippon, especially if she was in mid-pronunciation. Viewers at home would merely think that it was all the more exciting.

There were a number of back-up departments which were a luxury after my time in the regions. There was 'Newsinf' – a small reference library, a classic old-fashioned and reliable bit of the Beeb, staffed by trained librarians who met hysterical reporters on the threshold yelling: 'Reggie Maudling's just died and I've got his obit to do in fifteen minutes and I can't think of anything other than that scandal . . .' and minutes later served up cuttings and information and dates. They also kept copies of old scripts, invaluable in moments of desperation, when you'd spent half an hour in the cutting room looking at film of minor royals looking bored at chrysanthemums at the Chelsea Flower Show, and couldn't think of anything polite or accurate to say. Newsinf came to the rescue, digging out last year's script written in bravura style by my colleague Brian Hanrahan. I merely changed a royal name here and there.

It all seems stone-age now, but it worked surprisingly well. The speed and drive and professional expertise in the building were second to none, and the determination to get the latest story on screen gripped bulletin editors like a fever. Very, very rarely was there any thought of referring a story 'up' – that is, consulting the top banana, the news editor. Reference to anyone else, such as the director-general, would have been thought ridiculous; there was confidence and conviction in newsroom decisions –

and if you got it wrong, then there was an immediate inquest. Accidental errors received a public bawling-out. Wilful or lazy mistakes marked you for a limited life in the newsroom, followed by posting to Feature Production in the regions, or a job in Special Projects – so special, they never happened: a highly efficient BBC oubliette, from which no one ever returned.

TV Centre was an exciting place. Programmes I'd watched as a child were still being made. You met the *Blue Peter* dog in the lift on Mondays, and Thursdays saw an influx of older blokes into the bar as a fresh load of totty from *Top of the Pops* jigged in to grab their chance of stardom. The cast of the police series *Z Cars* also drank there – very much in character – and every so often the News garage went out of bounds as it served once again as the set for a ghastly alien wasteland in *Dr Who*. The building was a factory of television; not an arty-farty creative salon, but an industrial powerhouse, full of noisy, slightly eccentric and gifted people. One evening a colleague pointed with awe to a gaunt but intriguing man who'd been imitating the Leaning Tower of Pisa for ten minutes, his arm rigid against a bar-room pillar. He's brilliant, he's the producer of *The Morecambe and Wise Show*, said my colleague, as the pillar slid elegantly to the ground and remained there, out cold, unbothered by the other drinkers.

The TV News department repaired regularly to the BBC Club; lunchtime boozing was relatively frequent, and inquests after the *Nine O'Clock News* were always held under the influence. This rarely dimmed the sharpness of the exchanges. News was an area of cut and thrust and blunt opinions. Senior editors nudged around the reporters and sub-editors like ancient rhinoceros, seeking a victim to stick on the horn of their journalistic judgement. High praise from them about a story rested in the words 'All right, I suppose.'

The sheer pace of work carried us along. In the mid-seventies, Northern Ireland sucked resources out of the London newsroom, and terrorist incidents nearer home were a 24-hour threat. The staple diet was that of any news organisation – industrial trouble, race riots, demonstrations, disasters, politics, murder and social unrest, sport and royals – never mind the Diary: the relentless regular trek to the Chelsea Flower Show, Miss World, Crufts, pools winners slurping champagne, the Notting Hill Carnival, drama productions objected to by Mrs Mary Whitehouse, and funerals.

There was little or no specialisation for the reporters – expertise could be assumed because you were the only reporter left in the room to send. In the morning you stood for three hours watching a whale being freighted into a plane at Heathrow; in the afternoon you switched your attention to quizzing the Duke of Westminster about estate management. Instead of bed, you enjoyed four hours being insulted outside an ambulance station during a rather bitter dispute, and then gobbled breakfast before driving to Yeovil to film a bomb factory. I loved it.

Life opened up, revealed corners and oddities and secrets and surprises. And with it came the privilege of being able to ask questions, wangle your way into official buildings, sit through eccentric court cases, do everything from chasing a Colorado beetle through an allotment in Hastings to being throttled by a print-worker in the print-room of the *Daily Telegraph*. I felt hugely lucky, for I possessed not one day's training as a journalist, couldn't do a word of shorthand, and was female – all major drawbacks.

I'd also been hired in slightly eccentric circumstances. The BBC ran a system of interview boards for all posts, inherited from the Civil Service: grim endurance tests in which usually four men sat behind an impressive table and looked disapproving while you gibbered on your too-small chair. It was a system wonderfully summed up in a cartoon – by one of the reporters – pinned for years to the newsroom wall, in which recognisable senior people glare at a victim while asking: 'Can you think of any single reason why we should give you the job we've already fixed for someone else?'

Most members of staff remembered their boards as a form of legally sanctioned torture. In Bristol, the interviews were held in a grand room which had three identical doors along one wall. Nervous candidates never noticed which one they'd come in by, and a ritual regularly took place at the end of the interview. Shattered candidate needs to make instant decision and appear the confident, well-informed applicant worthy of the job, so strides purposefully to middle door – thereby ending up in broom cupboard. After a short pause, in which it becomes obvious that the candidate has decided that death in a cupboard is preferable to ignominy, the board get up and announce very loudly that they are going outside for coffee. They were, after all, gentlemen.

The only man I ever knew who liked job interviews was the programme organiser on Radio Durham, Geoff Lally. He made a hobby of them, recalling a particularly enjoyable morning in Portland Place in London when a body hurtled past the second-floor interview-room window. He attempted to draw the Four Suits' attention to this matter, but they held him firmly in check, and told him to 'just answer our questions like a good chap'.

I didn't get a board for a post with the national newsroom. I'd been mouldering in Brighton as a branch-line reporter for BBC South, but had been working weekends in the London newsroom (talent was not the employment criterion, they were always desperate at weekends). Before breakfast on a fateful Friday in Brighton, I was rung by a neighbour who had dodgy friends who did interesting things which he found difficult to be candid about, though sex and the antique trade seemed to figure.

'You want to get up the road, gal,' he giggled. 'Loss goin' on.'

Indeed there was, and one of the corpses was still visible hanging oddly over the fire escape on the third floor.

Cheeping with excitement, I rang my cameraman, a not-very-handy twenty-two miles away. An hour later, by which time the crowd on the pavement had grown, and theories were as numerous as the cops, Ian the cameraman arrived, complete with entourage: sound recordist, boyfriend and Samoyed dog. We filmed bodies being removed and a splendid altercation between the Sussex Constabulary and what turned out to be members of the Metropolitan Police, well off their turf, but for some reason feeling proprietorial about the stiffs. I'd found a real murder – double, no less – and I went in search of a phone box.

The Southampton news editor was not of the traditional cut. His hobby was church bell-ringing and he thought news vulgar.

'Where have you been?' he rasped at me. 'You're late.'

I ignored the warning tone and delivered a machine-gun burst of murder story, adding, 'And we've got great pictures.'

After a short silence, he picked up where he'd left off: 'You're late,' he said, 'and all the ladies in Ditchling Memorial Hall have been kept waiting for two hours to show you their Embroidery Exhibition.'

He fired me – carefully, of course. I was just non-personed, labelled 'unsuitable' to reporting.

That night, the home editor called from London to ask if I'd do a weekend shift. I came clean and said I was probably no longer the staff reporter for BBC South.

'Well then,' he said, 'you'd better come tomorrow and stay.'

So a little bubble of insecurity lurked just under my surface for a good long time in the national newsroom. However, I was buoyed up by the energy which bowled around the place. Unlike Southampton, where the newsroom could have been mistaken for a funeral parlour – literally, for several of the district reporters and stringers whose phone numbers were listed on the walls had passed on some years previously – London was abuzz with enthusiasm. Editors actually wanted your stories for their bulletins – but only if they checked out. Unlike the regions, where, for economic reasons, every crew dispatched had to return with a contribution to the programme, however irrelevant, limp or desperate, national news editors wanted to hear from you on the spot whether the story 'had legs' – and they dropped it like a stone if it turned out to be a piece of gossip or a false alarm. It was exhilarating, I felt, to be free of the obligation to fill minutes of television with some stretched and embellished yarn which had insinuated itself on to the regional programme. To be honest, other regions were much more robust, but somehow Southampton seemed to exist on a diet of eccentrics in Wiltshire and musical travelogues round the South Downs. And the editor had already had occasion to lecture me about what he considered too frivolous a tone about the Druids who got lost on the way to Stonehenge one midsummer morning.

Journalistic considerations apart, being a female was also a source of diffidence. In the regions, it had been straightforward. In Plymouth, I had been told, 'You get the health stuff and the fashion and the kiddies . . . obviously, eh?' There'd been no embarrassment in the newsroom when this statement was delivered. Lucky to be in the newsroom, girlie. I might have been seven years in local radio producing politics and farming and social problems – but that was upstart local radio. This was regional telly, where convention was stronger and the image of announcerettes gushing next to a vase of flowers lingered. And in Southampton, the opportunity to do 'hard news' – the nitty-gritty of strikes and murders and so on – had been severely limited by the editor's determination to exclude real life from his vision of Hampshire and Sussex – as witness the abrupt end to my stint in his newsroom.

In London, the situation was not very clear. There had been mutterings that 'more women were needed' – and there had always been one or two female reporters around. What was exciting for me was that the men who assigned us to stories were all, without exception, completely unconcerned by gender politics. You merely represented a pair of legs to be dispatched as fast as possible to a breaking story; indeed, you were always expected to run out of the newsroom and down the corridor, as a sign of dedication. After years of mutterings from the men in local and regional newsrooms, the jokey put-downs whenever a woman turned in a great interview or an unexpected scoop,

Television Centre seemed a New Republic of Equality. And so it was – in some areas.

The last bastion of blokes and jokes about tits on the telly existed in the Crew Room. I wasn't quite ready for this, having spent a happy year working with a crew consisting of a delightful gay, the boyfriend, the sound recordist and the dog – at a time when these matters were not much spoken of in public, and where I occasionally had to soothe ruffled feathers, especially if we were filming in naval establishments and too much mincing went on. I thought I'd got it sorted, and I reckoned I was the tolerant sort. I'd been through an almost all-male university and adored every minute – women had to be raffled for some formal occasions, so scarce were we. Local radio had delivered a social life so heterosexually frantic that 'happy exhaustion' was regarded as a legitimate excuse for missing early shifts. And I could still remember being told on my first training course that pregnancy was not a total disaster for unmarried BBC ladies – the Corporation merely moved you discreetly to another BBC establishment – though two pregnancies were considered the limit. So I'd grown to see the BBC as a liberal outfit, one where tolerance was the norm, as long as you didn't frighten the horses. I found, too, that it was a lot safer to have a boyfriend well outside the Beeb – so avoiding the relentless exchange of intimate information which filled *longueurs* on pavements and stakeouts, as people recounted assignments with other members of staff underneath studio tables.

But I hadn't reckoned on the stubbornly neolithic Crew Room in London, which contained a fair number of beer guts and Old Hands.

Several were openly hostile, and I discovered just how deep this hostility went when, in my first month in London, a cameraman in his large crew car attempted to crush my small Ford Escort into a motorway barrier at 70 mph. In the ensuing minute, I chased after him as he two-fingered me, then drove him off the road. He never got over it, and refused ever to join me for a drink when on location; I made myself let these things go. Later, the same man had his little stash of child porno photos discovered at a customs inspection. Others complained that it wasn't right for a bird to go on foreign assignments. I suppose I was an embarrassment when they picked up tarts and then had rows about payment prior to the police being called to their bedroom down my corridor. On one particularly tough story, another crew member, who I already knew spread nastiness like his dandruff, called my room one night, ostensibly about 'something he'd heard about the story'. I went along to his room and pushed the door open, to find him stark naked and leering, and a bit drunk. I tweaked the key from his bedroom lock, dangled it enticingly, and as I tripped him in the doorway, locked his door, leaving him flat and nude in the corridor. Back in my room I sat shaking and furious all night, having flushed his keys down the loo at a third attempt; but yet again, decided that nothing said would be the best policy.

I had no rules to go by. Any fuss would rebound, and anyway, these were days when women were breaking new ground everywhere, grabbing opportunities, being given such wonderful chances – why wreck them? It would only have been seen as 'not being able to hack it'. So I reasoned. And anyway, there were a great number of cameramen who were terrific – kind and encouraging, fun, and protective without being patronising. Why rock the boat – possibly hole it – while the battle was still being fought?

So, by dint of some sly tactical planning, I began contriving to avoid certain crews. I had no problem when it reached me that the 'Old Hands' were avoiding me. They could put them up someone else's skirt.

This was in the mid-seventies, and the language and aspirations of feminism were an undertone to any discussion about 'appropriate' work for women. The BBC was in an odd position, for it had had impressive women in senior positions since the Second World War, when male engineers and technicians required for war service had been replaced by women; and, unlike in other professions, many of these women had resisted the push to return them to housework when the men came home. I met some of them, now heads of department, on my first local radio training course, and it was obvious that several had married the BBC – and found it a rewarding substitute. But their careers didn't fit our times, and we had no intention of sacrificing a large part of our lives on the career altar. Men seemed to 'have it all' – so we were at least going to give it a try. Even so, no one discussed these matters in the newsroom, which inevitably was predominantly male. Those of us who had discovered the world of news thought it too precious to complain about; the gift horse might bite every so often, but we weren't ready to yank its jaws open and see if it was still a male chauvinist pig on the inside.

And attitudes were changing. True, on some stories, a captain of industry or shop steward still talked only to the cameraman, out of sheer habit ignoring the 'secretary bird' who had clearly just happened along for the ride. And I was frequently addressed with a waspish leer and 'It'll be Missss Adie, I presume . . . ?' So what; the times they were a-changing, and they could only get better.

I was living in London by now, having given up commuting from Brighton with considerable regret. I'd lived in a wonderful Regency pad by the sea and had to exchange it initially for a crowded flat next to a six-lane highway in west London containing assorted BBC people and ruled by a cat called William. I was flat-hunting desperately and trying to work out how you convinced your neighbours you had a respectable job as you hurtled out at three in the morning and stayed in bed all day at the end of your shift. I made a point of saying to estate agents, 'I work at the BBC,' which seemed to alarm them less than if I said, 'I'm a journalist.' Anyway, I wasn't really sure if I *was* a journalist.

There was still a problem of confidence. I hadn't had any training as a journalist, and still made the most basic mistakes.

I forgot to write down names, ask conventional questions – are you married, age, and so on. Sent to Heathrow straight from home very early one morning to intercept an African diplomat, I'd been given only a sketchy idea of why he was flying in to London, except that he represented the Organisation of African Unity. My quickly laid plan to nab one of his party and discover a few facts before the interview was sabotaged when he swept majestically into Heathrow's then very tiny press room. An aide announced: 'Television first,' and placed two chairs opposite each other. I looked around, and ITN wasn't there among the rest of the pack.

'Begin,' announced the dignitary, plonking himself grandly in front of me.

In the circumstances I felt utterly unable to ask for a few basic facts, so I leaped into the dark: 'What do you wish from your visit to London?'

'To change planes,' he replied.

All seemed lost; but thankfully he added: 'I expect to gain much from my visit to the Secretary-General at the UN in New York.'

I felt I had something to go on, and looked at the piece of paper the crew had given me from the newsdesk, on which was written Ken Min Sec, suggesting the foreign minister of Kenya or possibly a Chinese Triad.

'Does Kenya want greater involvement in the negotiations?' I hazarded.

'I wouldn't know,' he replied, 'President Kenneth Kaunda has not consulted them.'

Christ, Ken for Kenneth, not Kenya. Now where was Kaunda president of? Zambia? Possibly – but was he *this* man's president?

'But your foreign policy may influence the talks,' I tried.

'I don't know,' he said, 'obviously, as I am not the foreign minister.'

I think I managed to get something from him before his aide abruptly cut me off, shouted, 'Next!' – found there were no takers – and the whole entourage swept out.

Back in the office, the news organiser asked, 'What did you get? By the way, what's his name?'

'Ah,' I said, 'there you have me.'

When sent on a story, I had no idea how my method of work compared to that of other reporters, and I was very unsure what it was that made my colleagues shout 'Great Story!' when a barmaid, a goat and a vicar were mentioned in the same sentence. As I'd never seen any other reporter at work, I'd no idea how they went about their business. Camera crews occasionally dropped the hint that I'd missed some of the essentials, but most left me to my own devices. So I made up my own rules as I went along.

Early on, I seemed to specialise in things that sank. A Greek freighter called the *Christos Bitos* got into trouble in the Irish Sea and a lengthy rescue operation was mounted. I was beginning to realise that national news could call on more resources than local radio, having taken an angry phone call demanding, 'Why haven't you got a helicopter yet?' I still remember the excitement of clambering into a naval Sea King at RAF Brawdy, and that first lurch into the air as the camera crew and I hung on to any dangly things we could grasp. The coast fell away, the sea skidded below us – *this* was flying, door open, wave-hopping in a thick fog, off to find a ship in distress. I had a gnawing feeling that life was about to be an adventure. I'd never considered that this might happen.

Why hadn't I ever sat and mapped out a career, or listed my ambitions? What ambitions? I'd never given it a thought; and here I was, part of a professional, slightly risky exercise, where a great deal depended on accuracy and experience. And I had to get things right, as well, for whatever journalism was, it wasn't a free ride. I can still see the *Christos Bitos* as she came into view: a half-sunk ship, her decks already awash, ripples of water sliding gently across her, but with people frantically working on the bridge to pump her holds. We circled at what I thought was a crazy angle, and I clutched at anything to avoid exiting the helicopter like a child on a slide. The cameraman was up at the door, kneeling, and through the clattering noise I gathered it was my job to hang on to him. The navy were preoccupied with lowering a large pump on to the stern of the vessel, and I realised that in these circumstances you work in parallel, avoiding any interference with their job, while at the same time ensuring you get the pictures you need. It's a delicate task – you are the strangers, the extra load, the people who may well be a problem if there's an emergency; yet you have a reason for being there, and you tenaciously get your filming done.

And there was a little problem with the pump. It turned out to be twice as heavy as anticipated, and the helicopter winchman was having difficulties as it swung wildly around the ship's superstructure. After a very tricky minute, it was released, and the helicopter did something that it wasn't exactly built for, a kind of backwards leap that not even a bird would attempt. The Sea King's crew went into a mode that I've since seen frequently, slightly grim-faced and sharp-eyed, with short barked instructions into their communications systems, and urgent simple signals for us to follow. We were flat on the floor, slithering, quite a lot of fuel had been jettisoned, and I appeared to have inhaled a cloud's worth of kerosene droplets. We were flying at a very odd angle for several seconds – indeed, I wasn't entirely sure we were flying.

As we puttered back to the air station, I peered out to see what looked like every emergency vehicle in west Wales gathered on the tarmac. The navy peered out at as well and smiled: 'RAF,' they said, 'panicking.'

I thought hard about the incident. Adventure is something that children read about; after childhood, it drops away as an option. Here I was, faced with the possibility that adventure might have re-entered my life – and I was unable to explain how or why this had happened. I did know, though, that if adventure and reporting went together, it was a slice of luck on my plate that I had never expected. And I loved it.

For the next few months, I became Mrs Ship Sinking, covering inquiries into the *Amoco Cadiz* disaster, several North Sea Oil incidents, and the Fastnet race getting blown off course. In January 1979 a series of blunders during the unloading of an oil tanker at Whiddy Island in Bantry Bay led to a massive explosion, which nearly took the town of Bantry with it. As we flew the length of Ireland's southern coast at dawn in a tiny aircraft, we saw a grey streak far in the distance. We were just south of Cork, and the smoke from the *Betelgeuse* was visible above the very tip of south-west Ireland. An hour later, down we spiralled to have a close look, having removed one of the door panels to film. Not quite believing my eyes, I nudged the pilot. He looked through the smoke and shook his head. 'I never thought to see the sea on fire,' he said.

And it was, in a huge ring – something out of a horror film.

Suddenly, the plane lurched, the pilot climbing hard. As Oggie Lomas, our cameraman, looked round to see why his great shot had been interrupted, the pilot said sharply that the temperature in the plane had rocketed to dangerous levels, so intense was the burning and boiling of the sea below.

We spent the day gathering interviews and fixing to get the film driven back to Dublin, along with my recorded script. In those days, southern Ireland was one of the more remote locations, and we were surprised to hear that the story made it on to that evening's news in London. In the meantime we had found lodgings in the town of Skibbereen, which has never felt remote as to its place in world history, being the home of the famed *Skibbereen Eagle*, a newspaper which greeted Russia's covetous moves on China in 1899 with the words: '*The Skibbereen Eagle* has its eye on the Tsar of Russia.'

By now, I had graduated to the occasional foreign trip. The very first was explained to me by the foreign editor as if to someone who was somewhat unfamiliar with Abroad.

'It'll be a nice easy introduction, Kate,' he assured me, 'absolutely nothing to be worried about.'

Nice of him. We nearly got killed.

As the BBC was going through one of its economy fits, we drove to Harwich to board our economy-class ferry to the Netherlands. The cameraman, Jim Taylor, known quite rightly as Gentleman Jim, and a veteran of world travel, was not impressed.

'This is not how I see an assignment for the BBC,' he said, as the Hook of Holland hove choppily into view. 'There's something not quite right about this.'

I privately agreed, for I was ready for the Heathrow experience, free drink and glamour in the sky and all that.

We had been sent to the Netherlands during an upsurge in cases of polio. They were all, for the moment, confined to members of a strict Protestant religious group, the *gereformierde kirke*. We interviewed the Dutch health minister, saw distressing sights of semi-paralysed children in hospital in Zwolle – it had been twenty years since such cases had been seen in Britain – and then headed for one of the small villages in the grey, flat north.

Standing across the narrow road from the undistinguished clapboard church, we filmed a few members of the black-clad congregation on their way to Sunday morning prayers. Straight out of a Rembrandt painting, the women wore long, full skirts and white starched bonnets. They looked extraordinarily other-worldly and meek, glancing at us only briefly

Needing a little more footage, we hung around until they reappeared after the service. We were concentrating on two women walking towards us, on the opposite side of the road, when with no warning one of the cars parked outside the church roared towards us. We threw ourselves over a small fence, Jim clutching the camera – with tripod attached – like a baby. I peered past a clump of grass to see the two black skirts rustle onwards, with not a glance in our direction, or at the deep rut driven through the grass verge obliterating the marks made by the tripod. A nice easy introduction to the delights of Foreign News.

Looking back, I realise I had never thought of danger in connection with reporting. The nearest I'd come to a nasty moment had involved a dustbin-men's strike in Plymouth, when, with mounds of rubbish on the streets, and an enraged group of women high on the sight of a rat, we got chased through several gardens. My cameraman was cornered in someone's kitchen, and severely belaboured with a saucepan. I felt very guilty, and resolved never again to abandon a cameraman – I was behind a line of washing, completely puzzled by the sharp downturn in civilised behaviour, and bemused by the thwanging sound from through the kitchen door. Other than this incident, and the usual argy-bargy on strike picket lines, I merely accepted that some elements of life were a bit rough, and not the sort of thing which either my family or my school had imagined me getting involved with. But, heck, if you learned not to answer back or join in, ran fast enough and could clear medium-height walls at one bound, then it all added up to the spice of life at the cost of just another pair of ruined high heels.

Dangerous or not, the pace of life was frenetic: weather stories, weeks in Northern Ireland, picket lines – and all the time, access through doors normally closed to the general public. Being a reporter is a constant nosing behind the scenes, a chance to hover briefly where only the privileged operate. Through the doors of the Foreign Office – to discover it is like a vast Victorian town hall, a very male building of tiled floors and leather seats, the walls crammed with portraits of those who have sent a gunboat to ensure Our Voice was heard in distant parts. Into the Royal Box in Covent Garden – inspect loo to see if the Andrex has a crest on it – sadly, no. Round the basement of the British Museum, into Gartree Prison, Dunfermline Abbey, Number Ten Downing Street, Regent's Park Mosque, the Oxford Union. It is also, of course, a way to stand on countless pavements waiting for sundry politicians, criminals, Bangladeshi activists and the Archbishop of Canterbury.

We had two main bulletins to service, the early evening one and the *Nine O'Clock News*. There was none of the round-the-clock broadcasting now considered the norm. 'We' were a very small team of reporters who ranged over every kind of story: none of us knew what lay in store for us in the next few hours, and we swallowed background information and basic facts as we dashed out the door to interrogate boxing promoters or the shadow chancellor of the exchequer. Those who would later sneer at this method, despising reporters as 'non-specialists with a clutch of newspaper cuttings', failed to understand that we brought to each story a journalist's methods, allied to curiosity and an effort to ask the questions our audience wanted answered. A contempt for basic and proven journalism betrays, at bottom, a contempt for the audience.

Clutching the cuttings about Sardinia ('Italian, relatively undeveloped except for grandiose up-market Costa Smeralda scheme in north-east, large sheep population'), I made several trips following the spate of kidnappings that passed for income generation on this Mediterranean island. A British family, the Schilds, had been taken, and it was some time before we realised that the Sardinians regarded the whole affair as business, to be settled with the right amount of dosh. Our very first night on the north-east coast resulted in a genuine BBC panic, when we discovered that the hotel we'd booked ourselves into late the previous night was the most expensive in Italy. How were we to know that little mud-washed cottages were a *faux naïf* attempt to give the very rich a sense of the simple life? We removed ourselves sadly the next morning, conscious that the words 'moderate' and 'reasonable' were the watchwords of the Expenses Department.

We roamed round northern Sardinia, among the stone-covered hills and up into the grim and unfriendly villages in the mountains. Bearded shepherds waved rifles angrily at us, and the shutters snapped shut as we came into the village square. The atmosphere of menace was palpable, for here came the foreigners interfering with the good old-fashioned system of raising money in a poor region; all around us were two-storey buildings with the walls of the top storey half-built, waiting for the next ransom to be stuffed under the door. Even so, what freedom we had. In 1980 the only phones which worked – sometimes – were in the main hotels. We'd book a call early morning, talk to the office, and know that until we came back with new information and pictures, there'd be no communication from Television Centre. It meant we chased the tale according to what we found on the ground, with no inter- ference from editors, no minute-by-minute calls on the mobile phone, no directions as to 'how we see it in London'. Reports reflected the priorities as seen in a foreign country, rather than a consensus view from a newsdesk in Shepherd's Bush.

Having struck up a good working relationship with the handsomest of *carabinieri* special forces colonels which involved fibbing to the crew about 'briefings over a spot of pasta', I was less than amused when we were suddenly sent to Yugoslavia to keep vigil over the expected death of President Tito, especially as the old partisan seemed in no hurry to depart this earth. For ten days we wandered around Belgrade, trying to shoot relevant stories and being arrested. This was my first-ever brush with the Yugoslav security system, and it was a nightmare, making the Russians look like dozy pussy-cats.

Having got press accreditation at the International Press Centre in Belgrade, we headed for the streets and within four minutes had to produce our newly acquired papers on the demand of a sour-faced policeman. After an hour of confusion in a police station, we were directed to another mammoth government building for 'accreditation'. Protesting that we'd done it already, we were sternly lectured by a woman who looked like a weasel in a badly-knitted twin-set.

'As well as this being Yugoslavia,' she spat, 'this is also Serbia,' and proceeded to start in on its history, most of which was completely unfamiliar to me, and seemed to involve a lot of glorious death. I wasn't to know that I'd be back ten years later, listening to the same history being declaimed as the bullets flew and the knives went in.

Mrs Weasel then embarked on a lengthy set of questions about our intentions, none of which she seemed to think honourable; indeed, the very idea of using a camera on the streets of Belgrade seemed one false passport short of espionage.

'Where do you want to film?'

I shrugged and waved my hand towards the window, outside which the city sat dark grey and rather glum.

'Where in Belgrade?' she demanded.

I realised things were not going well, so I pulled myself together and said: 'The centre, the significant buildings, the main streets.'

'Which ones?'

This was getting silly, but before I could remonstrate, Mrs W. had burrowed in her desk and was flapping a map at me.

'Show which streets,' she said.

We pored over the map and I put my finger on the largest-looking thoroughfares.

Mrs W. typed away, peering closely at the map. She then laboriously typed out our details in quadruplicate and produced a box of ink-pads and stamps, banging fiercely on every bit of flimsy paper. We got up to leave, and she darted to a cupboard, producing a huge pile of glossy illustrated volumes on Serbian landscape and culture which she handed to us, unsmiling.

'You to work can go,' she said.

Well . . . maybe.

Next morning found us in Josip Tito Allee, a broad sweep of official buildings, enlivened with those ugly plastic kiosks so beloved of communist states, usually a tasteful shade of luminous orange or rotten-grape purple. We took a few shots which we call GVs – which I think stands for General Views, though after several decades in the business I realise I don't actually know if that's true; anyway, it means basic wallpaper, street scenes, landscapes and so on – and then we focused on the Parliament Building in the distance. We'd decided to compile a short essay on the mood in the capital as Tito's era neared its end. After thirty seconds, the mood turned a bit nasty. Three policemen arrived and, having perused our papers, took us off to another police station. Here the head honcho waved the papers at me and thumped his desk, the statutory dead communist pot-plant jumped on its cracked saucer, and someone went looking for an interpreter. An unwilling-looking student lad arrived, and began to translate by saying: 'You are in big trouble so please not interrupt.'

When he got to the part about No Permit, I'd had enough, and challenged the uniform who was stubbing out his third cigarette on the expired plant. I pointed to the second line of our paper and jabbed at the words Josip Tito Allee. The policeman looked at me as if I was retarded, and pointed a nicotine-amber finger at a couple of words after Allee.

'So what's that mean?' I asked the student, who was getting more nervous.

'South side,' he said, 'of Josip Tito Allee. Do you stand on north side to film? Bad.'

The rest of the afternoon's arguments were illuminating in one respect; when asked what we had dared to let our camera film, I mentioned the Parliament in order to substantiate our case that we were proper journalists, intent on respectable business. The pot-plant got a severe juddering and finally fell over as our sins were repeated in loud Serbo-Croat. The *coup de grâce* was a question put with disbelief in the voice:

'You think you can go round taking a picture of our Parliament without permit? What if you stand in front of *your* Parliament Houses and do such a thing?' Even the student's voice was indignant.

The crew eased themselves in their chairs as they saw the afternoon stretch before them.

Bull by the horns, I decided.

'Right,' I said to the student, 'get him to understand this: Parliament Houses, Prime Minister's House, Queen's House at Buckingham Palace – our POLICE house at Scotland Yard – Done 'Em All, No Bloody Permit.'

The atmosphere shifted, and the policeman looked genuinely curious.

'What *do* you need a permit for?' he asked.

'Possibly a nuclear submarine in a dockyard, though not at sea.'

This was somewhat beyond the student's English, but he made fish movements, and the word nuclear produced total amazement in the cop.

'You mean,' he said, after some serious thought, 'that you journalists run around in your country filming WHAT YOU LIKE?'

'Pretty well.'

He was absolutely fascinated; he had obviously never conceived that society could function in such a manner. He also expressed contempt that the British allowed such 'disorderly' behaviour. Had I known more about the Yugoslav – and particularly the Serbian – official view of life, and the narrowness of their experience, I would not have been so surprised; for this little scene replayed again and again in my mind when the country fell apart over a decade later, and we were harassed and threatened by outraged police and military men whenever we produced cameras.

In Kosovo, nearly twenty years on, I came full circle, in the Serb heartland of Kosovo Polje. Soldiers of the Green Howards had just driven their armoured Warrior vehicles into this suburb of Pristina as part of the NATO move into the province. They were met with surly looks, quite a bit of trouble, and a very hostile gathering of policemen and militia members. We were taking pictures alongside the senior British officer as he approached the police station when a number of furious Serb police raced towards us – it was our camera that proved more provocative than the arrival of an occupying army. The Serbs screamed abuse and went for us; an unwise move when the British army is being purposeful. And I knew just what sort of thinking lay behind the Serbian fury.

Back in 1980, the BBC gave up waiting for Josip Broz Tito to expire, and told us to return to London. I was a little disappointed – I wanted to know more about how the country worked – but I obediently headed home to more humdrum affairs, being sent immediately to Knightsbridge the next shift to find where one of our sound-recordists had got to. He'd merely popped out to get a visa in the Iranian Embassy.

One of the features of Hammer Horror films used to be the graveyard scene, mist wreathing around the elaborate tombs. And they didn't have to build special sets – just head for north London, for behind a high wall just off the North Circular road is a privately run cemetery, chock-full of ornamental Victorian death. Mossy angels and shiny cherubs, sentiment dripping on the headstones, a Christianity of definite heaven.

At the far end is a nondescript patch of long grass, a certain distance from the ranks of tombs and seraphim. On 23 September 1980, five men were put into unmarked graves amid the grass, with a few murmurings from a Muslim cleric. So ended an attempt to make a political statement about a hitherto obscure area of Iran known as Arabistan – an attempt which became one of the most spectacular events to happen for many a year on the streets of London.

Six young men had gathered in Baghdad in Iraq – all exiles from Iran, and all wanting independence for their region in the south of the country. When they fetched up in London, they had a plan to enter the Iranian Embassy in Prince's Gate in Knightsbridge, and, by holding hostages, force the government of Iran to release ninety or so prisoners who had agitated for independence. They would have had no idea what their actions would lead to, and they apparently fully expected the ayatollahs in Iran to accede to their requests.

They did not expect to find a BBC sound recordist and a news organiser in the embassy, patiently waiting for visas, along with a diplomatic policeman, Trevor Locke.

The initial attack on a Wednesday afternoon, in which several shots were fired, left everyone confused, as the police hastily cordoned off the area – and we arrived.

There's nothing quite like the moment when the penny refuses to drop: something serious was going on in the embassy. Our colleagues Sim Harris and Chris Cramer were not back from getting visas for – er, a trip to Iran. Aha – it's possible – you don't mean – oh God, where's the nearest phone?

I think I made one of those calls which begins, 'Look, you're not going to believe this, but . . .'

By the time the penny *had* dropped, half the newsroom of the BBC was thundering down to Knightsbridge, and there was an enormous press crowd setting up next to the railings of Hyde Park. The media could hardly believe what was unfolding in front of them: a massive anti-terrorist operation in the heart of the capital, involving an embassy, weapons, hostages and a shadowy bunch of Arabs. In rolled the outside broadcast vans, the horde of photographers, the mass of reporters, the Americans, the Europeans, and, stuck in the back row due to their unfailing politeness, the Japanese press.

As the days unfolded, it was pure drama, a terrifying soap opera with all eyes glued to the embassy's front door. In went food: people signalling and scuttling. Out came a woman hostage, also Chris Cramer, ill with gastro-enteritis. There were alarms and inexplicable incidents – and all the time the cameras watched. The reporters were working a shift pattern, and the most junior got the night shifts. I spent hours squashed into one of the reporter's cars we'd managed to worm into the press pen formed on the road next to the Royal Geographical Society. We lived on sandwiches and hamburgers in growing squalor, and the lads answered the call of nature by hopping over the railings into Hyde Park. This didn't seem an option open to me, and the

RGS appeared to be permanently closed, so I went to the building next door and asked nicely. I felt very privileged peeing in solitary splendour in the Ladies at the Albert Hall.

There was no doubt that I was dwelling on the outcome of this siege more than the other reporters around me. I knew Chris and Sim very well, and with Sim still inside, I felt very tense. The actual reporting was pretty routine; the most important point to remember was not to speculate on the outcome, however tempting.

As the weekend came, there was growing trouble in the building, and the police were noticeably twitchier. I went home on Sunday, and was told that I'd be doing the 8.00 p.m. shift the following evening, Bank Holiday Monday. On that Monday, things hotted up; shots were heard, and a body was pushed out of the front door. Mid-afternoon, I was told the more senior correspondent on duty wanted to go off to a dinner party and thought the junior should get in early, so off I went to Prince's Gate. I turned up at just after six, to find that the other correspondent had already left. It was Bank Holiday evening, and the press pen looked like a seaside resort after a riot: deckchairs and piles of litter, technicians snoozing in Hyde Park, and knots of journalists gossiping and eating luke-warm takeaways. So often, it seems that the press inhabit a parallel world to the story being covered. We had no inkling of the horrible scene in the embassy, with tensions boiling over, guns held to hostages' heads and the smell of fear everywhere. With hindsight – and having sat through the trial of the surviving terrorist – it's easy to understand the sequence of events and the hostages' emotions. Standing a hundred and fifty yards away, staring at a building, I could only imagine, and imagination is not what's wanted on air.

When the first stun grenade explosion occurred, all my worry about Sim burst out, and I shrieked long and loud, nearly deafening Bill Nicol, my cameraman. My fear, all of it, came out – it was as if I was ridding myself of something from deep in my guts – and I needed to get rid of it, if I was going to start work. As black smoke billowed from a first-floor window, the police in front of us panicked and ran back and forth telling people to lie on the ground. I crabbed along the ground towards the OB van, and a microphone appeared snaking towards me. I seized it and went on air, ruining millions of people's evenings – the World Snooker Championships had reached crisis point on BBC1, and suddenly on came this woman wittering and a lot of smoke and men clambering across balconies and jumping through windows.

I stuck to telling what I could see, though my imagination was racing. This was the SAS – though how had I any proof of that? We could see nothing of what was going on inside, though I had a darker feeling than many of my colleagues at the time about military action. I remember thinking that I did not expect to see a line of Arabs with their hands in the air, walking out of the front door. I just described the scene, and kept going, realising this was a marathon but without a script. I kept saying to myself, keep it even, keep it cool, and stood rigid with concentration. The drama should be on screen, not in me. I had no idea that I was broadcasting to one of the largest audiences ever – and a good thing too.

Later, I was not surprised to find that just one Arab had evaded the SAS, by pretending to be a student, and exiting the building among the female hostages. His trial was an interesting exercise: it was detailed and dignified, the only omissions being the precise actions taken by the SAS – so that, for example, one of the terrorists had been virtually cut in half, so many bullets had hit him. That this kind of trial took place at all would have been a puzzle to the regimes of both countries at the root of the siege: Iran and Iraq. For 23-year-old Nejad, a poorly educated dock-worker from Khorramshah, to have a well-argued defence, and for the precise nature of what went on in the embassy to have been laid out for public scrutiny, you need a fair and independent judicial system. Both Iran and Iraq should have squirmed in embarrassment at such treatment.

Over the years, I've met people who were involved in the SAS rescue, and was having a long conversation one evening with General Sir Michael Rose about his supervision of the operation when we were interrupted by a loud explosion. 'You planned that,' I squeaked as I took cover. Rather unfair, I suppose, as the Serbs and Muslims were outside going hammer and tongs in Sarajevo. The particular point I had been raising with him was a long-felt twinge of guilt – that I'd somehow contributed to a gung-ho 'send in the SAS' attitude which grew more common in the eighties, undoubtedly because of the stunning impact of the embassy siege. However, the Regiment apparently don't harbour a grudge, and I'm rather relieved about that.

One surreal coincidence remains vivid. At one point in the siege I was approached by the police and asked if I would be willing to go into the embassy and conduct an interview, should the need arise – in fact, it had been mentioned by the terrorists more than once. I readily agreed, but for a very odd reason. Exactly six weeks before, I had been sent to a weekend seminar in a country house in Oxford, where there was to be a discussion on terrorism – a 'hypothetical', in which we role-played in a scenario dreamed up by a moderator. I should not have been present, but a senior correspondent with *Panorama* had been called away to sort out a mess in Northern Ireland. The gathering was breathtakingly impressive – judges, senior civil servants, Fleet Street editors and so on. Five of us – myself, a Home Office mandarin, my BBC editor, a deputy assistant commissioner at Scotland Yard, and a military man – were led through a hypothetical situation, where a diplomatic trade mission building in London was taken over by terrorists, who then threatened to shoot if their demands were not met, including talking to a TV reporter.

Six weeks later, all five of us were gathered at Prince's Gate – for real.

SEVEN

Almost the Falklands

War was something that happened in my parents' lives, and in history. I'd never given a thought to getting involved in one. Military history was a closed book to me, ditto the difference between artillery and fritillary.

I'd acquired a specialist portfolio as a reporter. What rot: I'd been cornered and told someone had to 'do the Common Market'.

'We're going big on Europe,' said the head of our department, 'we need more Euro-stuff, we ought to take a real interest in, perhaps, the German elections – and find out what really goes on in Brussels.'

Utter rubbish. We'd been leaned on by the BBC governors – a rare interference then, but engendering guilt in the newsroom, which found the EC absolutely tedious.

So in 1981 I became a Euro-commuter, spending days in the ghastly Berlaymont building in Brussels reporting incomprehensible diktats from the Commission, being patronised by triumphalist officials from very small countries, and wondering why the viewers of the *Six O'Clock News* were being subjected to regulations regarding New York-dressed poultry. Other things

European, though, were wonderful. I worked with the Robberechts brothers, two wonderfully gifted cameramen whose approach to television was a revelation: they operated from modern offices, experimented with every new piece of equipment, and were knowledgeable and entertaining. They also ate like Belgians – and evenings were long and fattening.

We spent days camped outside various chateaux during summit meetings, and lived in fear of having to interview Mrs Thatcher, mainly because none of us understood the intricacies of EC funding, and our diffident questions were lawnmowered as she raced over the ungrateful ground of Europe. ITN's Trevor Macdonald and I were waiting in line when she devoured a young reporter from independent radio, who'd had his daisy-head chopped off in the first answer so proceeded to what he thought was safer territory:

'It's Easter this weekend . . .'

'Yes?' said Mrs Thatcher, challengingly.

'Will you be taking a holiday?'

'Holiday? Holiday!' The reporter cringed. The Prime Minister looked as if she'd been asked whether she'd be spending a few days in a brothel. 'WHAT'S THE POINT OF A HOLIDAY?' she bellowed to anyone who cared to listen. Silence followed, and Trevor and I edged out of the room, unwilling to be masticated.

During yet another mind-boggling EC conference, with Lord Carrington leading the British charge, a frisson of gossip ran through the huge band of Euro-hacks: someone had invaded British territory somewhere . . . no one had the details, but every phone in Europe was ringing. We shoved our way unceremoniously to the door where we knew Peter Carrington was, and slid inside – only to coincide with the appearance of his press secretary from another room.

We then witnessed one of those odd moments of history.

'Foreign Secretary,' said the press secretary rather breathlessly, 'we've just heard that the Argentines have invaded South Georgia.'

A short pause.

'Oh fuck,' said the Foreign Secretary.

Later that morning, having got the only interview with Lord Carrington – an utter gent as well as good fun – we found ourselves jumped on by the rest of the European press. I recall how they all, with the exception of the French reporters, treated the invasion as something of a joke, a blow which the British would have to take on the chin. I hadn't got that impression, even in the few minutes we'd been with the Foreign Secretary, and said so. Amid smirks and disparaging remarks from the Germans, Italians and Spanish, three journalists from Paris nodded to me, and said, 'We know what you mean; if it were us, the Foreign Legion would be on its way, now.' A decade later, I met that same set of attitudes in Bosnia.

The BBC was busy getting out its atlas and finding South Georgia. No one had any maps of the Falklands. The foreign editor was summoned to be asked who our correspondent in Argentina was: 'Our South America correspondent who covers thirteen countries, you mean?' he replied, trying to remember where he was based. It turned out that the man was in the process of moving from Brazil to Argentina – but hadn't yet got a phone.

Mrs Thatcher was dispatching a task force, and, with much reluctance, had agreed to send a few journalists along. She'd been influenced by the myth from America that the media had been responsible for the inglorious outcome to the Vietnam War, and was later reported as saying: I will not have another Vietnam. A quick scan of the likely correspondents found two already stuck in war zones, one on leave, and muggins with violent food poisoning in Luxembourg; so Brian Hanrahan packed his knapsack and went off to the South Atlantic.

Knowing now what he faced, I'm not sure that I'd have risen to the challenge – I knew nothing of the military and less of war. However, I had an extraordinary few months on the fringe of it all, and I am still staggered by the way in which war fever gripped so many people, and took over every aspect of journalism. (War, by the way, produces an expandable BBC budget; in this, it resembles the army – also in the manner in which it cancels all leave and starts sending people in every direction with peremptory orders.)

We raced to Devonport to see the *Canberra* – becoming a troopship now; flew over the task force as it left the western approaches; flew to Brussels and Luxembourg for diplomatic meetings. We sat in Naples listening to several hundred British schoolchildren singing 'Rule Britannia' on deck as their requisitioned cruise-ship came alongside; 'Not only Mrs Thatcher is mad,' said Wim Robberechts, peering through the camera. We sped to Gibraltar to see submarines slipping off unannounced, and then crossed the Atlantic for more meetings at the UN in New York. All the time it was an effort not to be carried away by the palpable excitement, the thrill that military action engenders in so many people, the spice that shared apprehension produces in everyday life. And when so many people are willing that events take a particular course, the words you write as a reporter often have to have a bucket of cold realism poured on them before they're transmitted; your job is not to influence opinion, just to lay bare the facts.

It was a blur of politics and conviction; a life of endless hotel rooms, aircraft seats and plastic food. (There is no glamour whatsoever in running at full tilt through airports clutching boxes of equipment and knowing your supply of clean knickers has run out.) Of standing for hours outside glowing windows where deliberations are in progress, wondering if there's a loo within half a mile. Of phoning your family, friends and boyfriend in the early hours, unable to remember which country you're in and completely unclear as to where you're flying tomorrow. It's a stream of uncertainty, and horrifies those whose lives are buttressed by regular routine. I've lost count of the times I've been asked: 'And where are you going next?' only to encounter worried head-shakings when I say I don't know.

To my credit – in a very small way – I've only once woken up with not a clue where I was. It was a very worrying moment, as I stared at the furniture, the curtains, then out of the window at a blank stretch of sea. There were no clues. I crept downstairs and stared at a woman behind a small reception desk.

'Kippers?' she said. I wondered for a split second if this was a greeting, perhaps in Bulgarian.

'Kippers,' I repeated carefully.

'Local speciality'.

Obviously not Bulgaria. Full of relief, I gave in.

'Local meaning where?'

'Here.'

'Where's here?'

Turned out I was on the Isle of Arran. Just how can someone forget flying to Glasgow, getting lost in Glasgow and missing a ferry? Never mind that, just why *are* we on Arran? I pondered, heading for a delicious kipper.

With horror, in the middle of all the war frenzy, the BBC remembered they'd forgotten about the Pope. A year's meticulous preparations for coverage of his tour of Britain had been dumped in the wastepaper basket, and instead we were sent to ask him if he was actually going ahead with his visit – those cardinals in Rome thought to be Argentinian-sympathetic and all that? It was noticeable that the country had gone from Pope-anticipation to Pope-suspicion in a trice.

I hovered outside St Peter's in Rome at six-thirty in the morning, wondering with British reserve whether cameras were allowed near – only to realise that Italian television was crawling all over the building. Plonking a flowery hat on, I bumped straight into the Cardinal Archbishop of Westminster, Basil Hume, at the north door, who took one look and said, 'My dear, what a pretty hat – but there's absolutely no need for this When in Rome sort of thing. Hats off, you're British.'

He was one of the most endearing and impressive men to meet. His brother had been one of our family doctors in Sunderland, and he was more aware than most of the nuances of denomination in a Methodist town.

We pursued the Pope round the Vatican, and he gave a non-committal comment about the tour, standing in an aura of distraction, head on one side, then ambling off mid-question. I was far more interested in the terrifying medieval feel of the place. I could almost see posses of horsemen thundering round the dark and deep alleys, the spirit of intrigue lurking behind grandiose pillars, and the peculiar maleness everywhere – fussy young priests skittering around and fat cardinals with jewellery gliding like Daleks over the marble.

As news of the sinking of HMS *Coventry* reached us, we were planning to join the papal plane for London – an Alitalia special, leaving at six in the morning, on which a sumptuous breakfast was served, even to us hacks stuffed in the tail. We counted five bottles of Drambuie taken through the curtain, cardinal-wards. At Gatwick, such was the tension about terrorism and demonstrations, the papal 727 was directed to a remote area miles from the terminal. As we tried to tumble down the back steps to witness the traditional ground-kissing, we were stopped by a bespectacled constable who started shouting in Italian. Apparently the Sussex police had decided to give us a briefing, and tracked down the only Italian-speaking policeman in the county, not having realised that the press pack was almost exclusively British.

We managed to catch a few notes of 'Welcome John Paul' from a small party of schoolchildren, as the cardinals looked around in vain for the usual mass of people. This moment of bathos – sumptuous scarlet flapping and gold rings flashing in what appeared to be a builder's storage yard at the end of a runway – expressed an unspoken comment: This is Britain, no disrespect intended, but there's now a war on, so we have other things on our minds. What had been intended as one of the greater events of the decade became a sideshow. The crowds were substantial for religious events, but the rest of the country was too preoccupied to line the streets. Even the Reverend Ian Paisley, personal opponent of the Anti-Christ, crushing a small child against a barrier in Edinburgh as, lost in ancient bigotry, he shouted medieval insults, seemed a distraction.

The high moment was curiously English: on a glorious day in Canterbury, the sun on the roses in the private garden, perfect green backed by warm stone walls, we watched the Anglican Church parade in finery and then celebrate with tea on the lawn. The bevy of cardinals, again all scarlet and black and glittering crucifixes, appeared on a short flight of steps from the body of the cathedral. They looked splendid, but stiff and urban, aristos of the Vatican, and just a tad out of place among the laughter and tea-cups, with Mrs Rosalind Runcie presiding with spirit and charm.

The Pope had hardly departed when we went back to Rome, for President Reagan was coming on his first official visit to Europe, and in the fuss of impending war the BBC had forgotten to get us any official accreditation. This meant that as the President's limousines were clogging up the streets on the way in from the airport – thirteen in a line, with security men trotting next to them like flunkeys next to carriages – we were busy wheedling our way into the Quirinale Palace, where he was due to have lunch after visiting the Vatican. We had none of the plastic passes necessary, but such was the aggravation between the Italian police and the US secret servicemen that we kept being pushed further into the palace, past bickering guards. Rather embarrassed, we ended up with a large press corps in a small rooftop garden of formal miniature hedges divided by sharp white chippings, behind a line of dignitaries – including the elderly Italian President and the ever-elegant social big cheese Signora Agnelli, wearing a trillion lire worth of tangerine silk.

'Here he comes,' said a cameraman, and in the distance a tiny speck above the red roofs grew into an enormous shiny green helicopter, which hovered and pulsated above us, creating a huge and dangerous maelstrom of sharp stone chippings. As we all huddled on the ground, the President was carried away and the tangerine silk did a gazelle-like leap for the French windows. Bouncing down, engine still roaring, the helicopter disgorged half a dozen secret servicemen talking up their sleeves, and then it lurched off. The garden was a wreck, the welcome-party had all fled, and the press were in various states of minor injury, camera lenses scratched. As a second helicopter hove into view we ran for a tree, and cowered behind it to see more officials jump out, hurrying away with sinister briefcases.

By then, most of the press had given up, and CBS television and ourselves were left to witness the third helicopter rattle into view. It perched quietly down, and its rotors drooped. The door glided open and the leader of the free world stepped out with a thin woman apparently surgically attached to him. He looked hopefully round the garden and clearly didn't have the script for this scene. Then he spotted us, raised his arm and strode towards us, wife attached. They stopped four feet in front of us and he said, 'Hi.'

'Er, hi, Mr President,' said the CBS cameraman absent-mindedly from behind his camera, unaware that *he'd* been addressed.

Nothing happened.

I could not think of a single intelligent question to ask this grinning pair, who resembled waxworks. Mr Reagan clearly hadn't the slightest idea where he was – understandably, for he'd just spent fifteen minutes fast asleep during his audience with the Pope. Mrs Reagan had a fixed expression which looked surgically risky to alter.

We all stared at each other, and the CBS cameraman shrugged his shoulders, hugely embarrassed. 'Just a couple of old folks on their first trip to Europe,' he said to us. They must have heard every word, yet they moved not a muscle.

After a full minute, two demented Italian officials chased by the secret service burst out of the French windows and came to claim the President and Nancy. Interestingly, neither moved, then slowly Mr Reagan raised his arm again and said, 'Bye . . .'

Just how is it possible for a reporter to obtain an exclusive and intimate meeting with the American President and not ask him anything? Just like that, that's how.

Possibly fired with the thought that my interviewing skills were on the wane, I returned to London and was sent to Downing Street,

uniform in the Gulf War, 1991, with floppy hat (official issue) concealing pearl earrings ...ot at all official issue)

With my adoptive parents Maud and Wilfrid Adie at home in Sunderland, 1945

First time on TV – in a student quiz programme in Sweden – Newcastle University v. Uppsala University

Tennis-mad teenager at Ashbrooke Club in Sunderland (with schoolfriends Nancy Ainsworth, Christine Jones and Diana Dodds)

BBC Radio Durham – in the mini-
skirted late sixties – posing with a pile
of records, being the grandly titled
Station Assistant in charge of the
Record Library

BBC Radio Durham needed a piano, so I headed
for the local auction rooms; unfortunately, BBC
funds ran out during the bidding

The radio car – a disembowelled Hillman Hunter with a pole through the roof – the very
latest technology, but usually mistaken for a TV licence detector van

Presenting *Woman's Hour*, live from Mousehole in Cornwall

Radio Bristol's farming programme, at the Bath and West Show in Somerset

With Radio Bristol colleagues Michael Buerk and Roger Bennett at the station's twentieth-anniversary party

he Iranian Embassy Siege at Prince's Gate
London in 1980, amid the scaffolding and
uipment that grew daily to accommodate
e immense media corps

gular up-dates for TV News from
ince's Gate

the London television newsroom, about to
ad a late-night bulletin

With cameraman Chris Marlowe, using available transport on Prince Charles's tour of India in 1980

The delights of touring Upper Volta in central Africa in 1984

unting, filming and baling in Bangladesh during the floods, 1988

1ujahedin fighters on the outskirts of Jallalabad in the Afghan war with Russia in 1989, the
ble cleared of ammunition boxes, ready for a lengthy lunch

In the empty streets of Tripoli, after the American bombing raids on Libya, 1986

The plight of refugees in Rwanda, fleeing for the border with Zaire after the tribal massacres in 1994

In Sierra Leone during the British military intervention in 2000

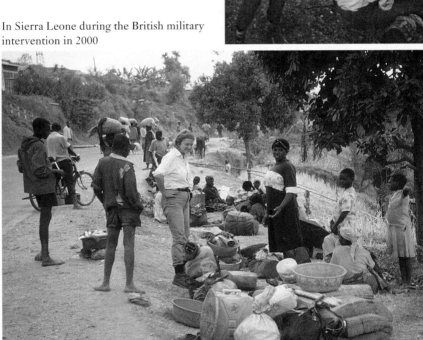

where Mrs Thatcher was about to hold an unexpected press conference. There was a mighty scrum outside Number Ten that evening, for much of the world's media were hanging about Whitehall. I burrowed through a forest of legs on wet tarmac, got right to the front, and squatted, microphone thrust above me.

Out strode Mrs T., clearly at full throttle. However, I did have a number of questions for her about the task force – I wasn't going to be caught out again, bereft of pertinent enquiry when faced with A Leader: Pope Next to Nothing, US President Zero, British Prime Minister . . . ? She was describing with warmth, not to say some heat, how British forces had retaken South Georgia, and when she paused for breath, I shot in a question:

'Prime Minister, can you confirm that the . . .'

Ignoring me, she launched into a blast of praise for the lads.

I tried again, got out two words, and she careered verbally through me.

Never say die. Once again:

'Mrs Thatcher, can you . . .'

This time, she put out a hand and very firmly pressed down on my head.

'Enough,' she trumpeted – 'just Rejoice, Rejoice.'

Did I make her say that? I've a lot to answer for.

I got on a plane to New York the next morning for more diplomatic meetings, returned the day after, and walked, glazed, into the office.

'Go to Uruguay,' said the foreign editor without looking up.

I trudged off down the corridor, thinking mainly about clean laundry and a rocky love life, until struck by two small thoughts, and went back to the newsroom.

'Why?' I asked. 'And where exactly is it?'

'Don't ask me, and here's an atlas,' he replied.

The journey was complicated by my having ten thousand dollars stuffed down my bra and knickers. The delicate arrangements for the BBC to operate in Argentina – all on Irish passports, grannies born in County Kerry suddenly having been discovered –

depended on quite a lot of unobtrusive cash payments. I rustled into JFK airport for the second time in a week, not daring to sit down, I crinkled so much. A colleague from radio, Geoff Wareham, met me in the transit lounge, and I pushed off his warm embrace.

'I'm loaded,' I hissed, 'and it's all illegal, and it'll come loose if you hug me.' We set off in a dignified manner for the plane to Montevideo, which I was just learning was the capital of Uruguay. Two days later, I tried to remember what people do in spy films when they have to hand over secret documents. Wear a trenchcoat? Red high heels and a fur coat? I felt inadequate as I lurked in the local market in a dull anorak, eyeing the slabs of scarlet meat on display. I snapped at a man whom I thought was persistently trying to interest me in several kilos of prime beef, when it dawned that I was busy rebutting a man who knew my name, and it was a safe bet there are no other Adies in Uruguay. I shifted the large packet of dollars into his hands, and he disappeared. The man behind the meat counter watched the exchange, and thoughtfully picked up his cleaver. Politics being what I vaguely knew it to be in Uruguay, I fled.

Some days later, the war arrived in front of our eyes. The horrific burning of the Royal Fleet Auxiliary *Sir Galahad*, with the Welsh Guards taking the brunt of the injuries as they tried to disembark in Bluff Cove, had meant that the badly injured were evacuated by hospital ship to the nearest friendly port – Montevideo.

As we stood by the dockside, I could not get my bearings. Uruguay was a mixture of the familiar European and the exotic South American, but had a sense of being removed both in time and culture from home. People looked as if they'd be at home in Paris or Madrid, and were distinctly un-American. However, they were puzzled by the intense British commitment to a group of islands which lay near their shores. And the war had hitherto seemed even more remote than it had been in the UK.

A ship came into view – not battleship-grey, but white, signalling her purpose for everyone to see, and for the first time

I felt that for us, the war was coming to call in all its reality. She approached very slowly, and we could just make out people standing at the rails. It was a very quiet arrival – the Uruguayans wanted no fuss from someone else's war – and the waters of the Plata were flat silver hiding the wreck of the German battleship *Graf Spee*, another reminder of another war.

The men leaning at the ship's rails did not wave. As they came nearer, we saw that their hands were hanging over the rails, encased in balloons of plastic bags, in which pinky-orange liquid sloshed. They were coming from a far, far battlefield, and were not yet home. Among those on board was a Welsh Guardsman, Simon Weston – horrendously burned, but even then, a stunning example of fortitude and good humour.

The ship travelled past us, a quiet and reproachful reminder of the fortunes of war, and its reality. We filmed the figures in the distance. We felt it wrong to go too near.

What had seemed an adventure in the South Atlantic was war, showing itself in its usual and frightening legacy.

Geoff and I got orders to move to Chile. Both of us were slightly bemused as to why, but we knew that the BBC has always operated on the 'it's only two inches away on my map' basis, and that someone in the newsroom was trying to work out where the nearest landfall to the Falklands was. We boarded a LanChile flight to Santiago, having been reassured that it did not call in at Buenos Aires across the Rio de la Plata estuary, otherwise, we – the enemy British – were going to be in big trouble with the Argentinians. Operating according to Sod's Law, the plane immediately headed there, with the pilot announcing that it was all due to 'war business' – but no need to worry, only a brief passport inspection in the terminal . . . Geoff and I decided on emergency measures, and I stuffed an airline pillow under my jumper and made a few moaning noises as we landed. We then convinced the air stewardess that extra movement might precipitate matters, and I couldn't possibly risk the rickety stairs and a draughty transit lounge – all too stressful. It worked, but I had to spend the lengthy flight over the Andes being asked innumerable solicitous questions about the *bambino*.

Santiago to Punta Arenas was an even odder flight. The pilot was adamant that Geoff's elegantly rolled umbrella constituted an offensive weapon, and overcome by 'worries about war business', insisted on it being secured in a special locker. The passengers were all loyal followers of the Chilean national football team, and as we gusted southwards above the spectacular Andes, the pilot put the World Cup Chile–Germany game on the intercom. When Chile scored, I genuinely thought we were going to die, as the plane rocked to their celebrations.

We'd reached what seemed like the ends of the earth – the Straits of Magellan, with wrecks from four centuries beached like giant whales' carcasses on the gritty shore. Punta Arenas was a town with a frontier atmosphere, all red corrugated roofs and a dreadful, never-ending gale which made conversation impossible in the street. Several journalists had been here since the start of the war, and the atmosphere among them was of Japanese soldiers who are on their own on Pacific islands and have no idea of whether the conflict is over or not. You couldn't get World Service radio, phoning the outside world was impossible most of the time, and the Cabo de Hornos Hotel served avocado and king prawns every other day, alternated with king prawns and avocado. Delicious initially, but after four weeks . . .

We were met at the airstrip by Peter, one of our most experienced cameramen, who was clearly itching to get to the action. He rabbited on and appeared to be involved in launching an invasion force of his own. Things sounded more than a little surreal, and as he drove us past a barn, while delivering a stream of information about the local coastguard, the weather conditions for sailing and favourable times to avoid enemy naval action, he slipped in the words: 'And that's our plane.'

I craned round and saw a peculiar shape hiding in the barn; I expect planes to have two wings.

'Twenty thousand dollars only,' Peter enthused. 'The only Catalina flying boat in South America, and she's ours.'

'You expect us to go to war in that?' I felt that something wasn't quite right.

'No problems, soon as the wing's fixed, and we could try going in from an Antarctic base as well.'

At the hotel, Peter handed me keys to the room recently vacated by fellow reporter Brian Barron, with a letter which Peter had opened.

'Welcome, you've got my room, good hunting,' it said.

I sat disconsolately on the thin mattress and wondered what on earth was up. The rest of the press seemed not in the usual spirits, and Brian is a great colleague, enormously helpful. I reread the note – my room, good hunting – and tore the place to bits. I found Brian's eleven-page epistle under the second mattress. 'Well done,' it began, 'they've all gone mad . . .'

The combination of frustration and isolation had been potent. We were nearest to the war, and yet we might have been in Croydon – though the penguins and cattle-sheds and shrieking wind proved otherwise. True, the SAS had made an unscripted appearance on the shore, and their helicopter had then been mysteriously engulfed in flames (Took *gallons* to get the bugger to burn, a naval pilot told me years later), but other than that, the war was far from us.

To this day, the notion of our wobbling over the horizon in an antique flying-boat sends shivers down my spine – but at the time, the Punta Arenas pack were willing to try anything.

So we spent our time plotting, despite being told by the extremely sociable naval base commander that he'd sink any journalist's craft that ventured out to sea.

So we discovered Chilean wine and read Bruce Chatwin's *In Patagonia*, in which he conjured with the country round us and distilled some of its bleak mystery into wonderful prose. We tried to keep in touch with events, but even with forty feet of wire strung across the hotel's roof we could hear only intermittent bursts from the BBC World Service. We stared out across the South Atlantic and wondered about the significance of Tumbledown and Goose Green, and knew that others might feel equally detached from home and hearty enthusiasm for warfare.

And we explored. I can still bring back the sights and horizons of a place so far south that the Andes mountains were but a blur to the north. In many ways, it was a daunting landscape, peopled by immigrants who spoke their grandparents' language as well as Spanish, so that you could use Italian to buy a jacket from a Neapolitan tailor and order a tea in Russian at the café opposite the town's pride and joy – a sculpture of sheep. But it exerts an odd hold. For years afterwards I bumped into people who at the mention of Punta Arenas grew instantly nostalgic; for a start, half the BBC's Natural History Unit in Bristol has tracked whales and Belgian hares and Darwin's adventures and a million penguins from this spot, where you could stand on a hill and see far to the east the grey of the Atlantic, and to the west the sun setting over the Pacific. Among the resilient and hospitable residents, the Macleod family took us to their ranch – and we went riding among their hundreds of thousands of sheep, while they pointed to a light in gloaming and said, 'Our nearest neighbour, a hundred miles to the north.' They were a fascinating family, highly educated and well-travelled, all speaking English with refined Edinburgh accents – and all born in Chile, the grandparents having left Scotland just after the turn of the century. Absolutely in tune with their magical land, its vast stretches and great silences, they were equally urbane when passing through Charlotte Square in Edinburgh over a decade later during the Festival, greeting me with the words, How good to see you, we're just having a short break from the ranch.

So the Falklands War mainly passed us by – except for one evening when a group of elderly people called at our hotel. They wanted to ask the 'visiting British' about the war, and over a long evening drinking pisco sours, they told us about their mixed feelings. They all had dim memories of the Falklands, for their parents had emigrated from Britain, and tried to settle in the islands. But after one or two seasons, battling with boggy land and howling winds, they decided that there was no realistic future there, and scraped together money for passage to Punta Arenas, where they'd prospered.

What was the war for? they wanted to know.

When thinking about reporting wars, I'd always – like anyone – pondered the effect that seeing violence at close hand might have. Do you get nightmares? Do images stay with you? Over the years I've grown aware that all kinds of incidents can have an unexpected impact, not just the set-pieces and the large-scale events.

In the summers of the early eighties, the bureau in Washington used to go quiet as the politicians left town, so London-based reporters were often sent to do a stint while the resident correspondents took their holidays. For all the razzmatazz of the USA, there didn't seem to be a great deal to do in July and August – and there was supposed to be a limit on the amount of wacky Americana that could be broadcast (Martin Bell had cornered the market in cowpat-throwing competitions). However, I found the lure of cactus-rustling irresistible, and spent a few happy days in Arizona with a formidable cactus-tracker called Mr Richard Countryman. He ranged about the range, shotgun in one hand and Environmental Regulations in the other, tracking those pesky critturs who were stealing his cacti, especially the great branched saguaro which feature in every Western, spiky arms held high against the horizon. For now they were beginning to feature in suburban front gardens – impressive twelve-foot-high totems, whose great beauty was their need to be watered only once every seven years. Mr Countryman was determined to bring to justice the varmints who carried off the glories of Arizona's landscape in their pick-up trucks late at night. He was also hot on the trail of the layabouts and do-nuthins from nearby Phoenix, who drove out into his desert and shot at his beloved saguaro for sport. He recounted with great satisfaction having come upon such a person recently, a drunken young man who'd drilled the cactus so full of holes that it had toppled over, and killed him.

Most of the reporting seemed to concentrate on crime stories – and here the liberal attitudes of the Americans towards the press were a revelation. Show a camera to a British judge and the usual response was 'contempt of court'; show one to an American judge, and they expected to be interviewed. The jury was supposed to be out of bounds – but only sort-of, and the lawyers were all TV stars. The greatest obstacle was the design of American courthouses – grand neoclassical edifices, with sweeping flights of steps down which the press pack hurtled backwards while interviewing their quarry. In the movies, it's all very nimble; in reality, the pack frequently has a nasty mishap and slides into a heap at the bottom in order to be walked over by rich attorneys.

However, it was the consequences of trials that were gaining public attention under President Reagan, and especially after they'd tarted up the death room at Huntsville. They'd added curtains and a glass window and a coat of white paint.

I've seen people killed violently, tripped over corpses, and attended more funerals than I've had hot dinners in war zones; but it was the unremitting ordinariness of the state penitentiary that got to me. The actor in the White House had fostered a climate in which a Hollywood-style easy answer to crime took hold. One American state after another either reintroduced or reactivated the death penalty: such a simple solution, and one which fitted the simple notions of the good guys in the white hats and the dastardly rest. But none of the fuss which attends the argument over capital punishment in Britain was to be heard in the USA. I raked the serious newspapers for debate, even the signalling of a major change coming over the justice system. Hardly a word. As state after state tweaked the electricity supply, got in the gas pellets or reached for the rifle, priority was given to the rising crime statistics. The moral arguments – never mind credible proof of deterrence – were missing or deemed irrelevant. A call to the American Civil

Liberties Union produced the first voice which seemed to chime with British sentiments. Concern, worry, and an impassioned set of beliefs. But it was just one voice.

So, off to Huntsville, Texas. Extraordinarily accommodating on the phone. None of the 'Ring the Home Office and wait a year' sort of treatment.

'You want to come and see us. OK. You want to talk about Death Row. No problem.' There was a moment or two while I took stock. Having had encounters with the British prison system, which quite often tried to deny its own very existence, I thought this was going a bit too fast. Last time I'd been on the phone to the Home Office Prisons Department, I couldn't get a disdainful official to admit that a riot was going on in Horfield Prison in Bristol.

'What proof do you have?' sneered the bureaucrat.

'How about the main wing?'

'What about it?'

'It's on fire.'

'And?'

'Well, there's the roof of the next building.'

'And?'

'There's a lot of blokes on it, chanting.'

'Means nothing,' he replied.

'There's a very large pile of furniture in the street,' I countered.

'Really?'

'It got there by sailing over the wall.'

'Tut tut,' he sighed.

'What do *you* think is going on?' I tried again.

'I suppose they're not very happy,' he said.

'Is that all you have to say?' I ventured, very precisely.

'Yes,' he answered. So I refused to back down when his department went berserk after I quoted him verbatim on the lunchtime news.

On the phone to the penitentiary, I realised they saw things differently in Texas.

If getting in and seeing Death Row was such a doddle, how about the human side?

'How about speaking to the governor?'

'Just give me a coupla days' warning, ma'am.' It was then that I found myself full of British reserve about further interviews.

'How about . . .' I paused. The other end of the line drawled into the gap easily.

'You want someone who's only a got a short time to go?' he volunteered.

Gulp.

'Yes please. If it's not too much trouble, not intruding you know . . .'

'Nope. We got lotsa them. They'll all talk, not much time to lose, see.'

The helpful official was called Mr Bird. He was the public relations officer for the Department of Correction. When I met him, I remarked that British gaols didn't have such employees. 'Oh,' he said, 'everything just goes fine and dandy in your prisons then?'

On a dry, hot morning, we walked through electronic gates set into high metal fences, our course monitored by the odd guy in sunglasses cradling a rifle. It was all very leisurely. None of those notices telling visitors what they mustn't get up to. Just a welcome brochure with the facts and figures of Texas's toughest correctional establishment, with the helpful addendum that they were about to become one of the first states to introduce execution by injection.

The inmates wore immaculate white overalls, though only one or two had white faces.

Mr Bird was relaxed. I was still full of rather polite reserve. I felt that discussing prisoners who were eyeing us indifferently, but within earshot, was behaving a bit as if we were in a zoo.

Mr Bird surveyed them as if staring at a company balance sheet.

'Gotta do two to get in here,' he said.

'Two what?' was my dim reaction.

'Homicides,' said Mr Bird. 'OK, murder to you folks.'

Tall men in white hefted brooms, and engaged in sweeping spotless paths between the coarse brown summer grass.

We went into a single-storey brick building with no distinguishing features. Mr Bird trotted ahead purposefully. We were in a corridor with a row of cells on one side, about ten in all. The men in them didn't bother to look up as we passed. I caught up with Mr Bird.

'Are these . . . ?' I still didn't seem to have my usual questioning habit to hand.

'Sure,' said Mr Bird. 'Every one. And the guy the far end, he'll be the next one to go.'

All said in the voice which had changed from accountant to tour guide. 'Want some statistics?' he enquired blandly.

I glanced into the cells with embarrassment as he rehearsed a litany of Texan crime and punishment figures. Each one was kept very neatly. Most of the men were perched on the end of their beds, staring at nothing in particular. One was reading. Mr Bird was well into the detail of the occupant of the end cell, apparently distinguished by the fact that his appeals – all seven years of them – seemed to have finally run out. The end-cell inhabitant was lying on his bed, staring at the ceiling.

'He's the next,' said our guide matter-of-factly and walked briskly through a door at the end of the corridor. The camera crew and I scuttled after him, and bumped into each other in the dark. Mr Bird could be heard scrabbling for a light switch. Something warned me not to scrabble helpfully with him, a caution vindicated a few seconds later as light illuminated the PR man entangled with the plastic drip lines leading to the stretcher on which The Next would shortly have his life ended.

The stretcher was brand new, on a trolley with shiny chrome wheels.

It was a very small room. I hadn't known what to expect, but whereas the penitentiary was vast and sprawling, this seemed a poky corner for such a significant act. The crew and I bumped into each other again, none of us knowing where to put ourselves.

We had a grunted exchange about getting some pictures. Mr Bird launched into guide-speak about Death Row. I began to feel very odd. Maybe I'd been expecting something sombre and daunting, grey stone walls and massive security. This was more like a tatty outbuilding of a run-down NHS hospital. And Mr Bird was describing its use in terms more appropriate to a hospital administrator explaining that operations are routine and nothing to get worked up about.

There was a kind of barrier about four feet in front of one wall, just a simple bar. I pointed to it and looked enquiring.

'Witnesses,' said Mr Bird. 'All have to stand behind it. Democracy, ma'am.'

He ticked off a long list of officials – legal, medical, administrative – adding, 'and two members of your distinguished profession. Mind you, we sometimes have trouble filling both places.'

I muttered that not every journalist might want to be in the actual room as someone was put to death seven feet away.

'That don't matter one bit,' said Mr Bird. 'The problem's the state insists two journalists *must* be here. Otherwise, procedures get delayed, and that ain't nice.'

I felt life becoming surreal. Envisaging a gaggle of people – seventeen seemed to be the rough number – squashed behind the barrier in this brick box.

Mr Bird was looking at me quizzically. 'Kinda hard to know what it's going to be like,' he said, helpfully.

'I can't imagine,' I said truthfully.

But Mr Bird had not quite got my drift, and launched into a precise description of death by injection, which the state of Texas had yet to implement, the law having only just been amended. He gave a workmanlike short lecture, pointing to the plastic drip lines leading from the stretcher through a small gap in the wall, next to a second doorway. He beckoned to us to follow, and in the gloom of an even smaller room showed us the drip bags hooked up ready: one for innocuous saline mixture, administered initially, the second for the lethal chemical. A little plastic valve joining the drip lines, to be tweaked by a medical orderly at a moment unspecified, to end a life.

'Yep, kinda hard to know what it's going to be like.' Mr Bird sounded professionally curious but unengaged, as if discussing a new recipe for pizza.

I groped for the doorway, collided again with the crew, who couldn't decide what could decently be filmed in close-up, in the half-dark. Something glinted in the back of the smaller room. I peered. Mr Bird, as ever, came to my aid.

'Well, ya never can tell,' he said. 'This new stuff might not work, so we've kept Ole Sparky just in case.'

I fled. I threw up all over the brown grass outside, watched by a number of indifferent white-clad black sweepers.

I'd have coped better with more drama. A sense of the solemnity of taking a man's life according to law. An air of tension, perhaps, or of dread. But all around was an acceptance of the ordinariness of execution. Just part of the system. Not so much a matter of life and death as just one of those things.

Back in Washington, the issue had attracted some interest. After all, state after state was reinstituting some form of death penalty, including Virginia, which hadn't executed anyone for forty years. A former policeman, a double killer, was to be the first to experience the new toughness on crime. When he'd first been convicted, the electric chair in Richmond, Va, was not in use. Having come to the end of ten years of appeals, he was to find the chair now ready for business again. But there was always an appeal to the Supreme Court – on yet another technicality, one that was to demand a judgement from nine judges.

The execution had been scheduled for Saturday. Being a weekend, there was great hope among the small number of anti-death-penalty campaigners that the Supreme Court could not be properly convened.

We journalists gathered in the basement of the Justice Department, one of those imposing marble edifices attesting to

American confidence. Outside, on a sweep of steps better than those which figure in courtroom movies, were camped the media circus, with live trucks and cables and lights.

The hours ticked by. Surely no one could gather up nine judges on a Saturday – they were probably not all even in Washington DC. That was indeed so, we learned by late afternoon.

'Well, that's it,' we said to each other – only to hear from a departmental official that modern technology had come to their aid, and their honours were going to be united via a conference call in order to deliberate together.

We hung around in the weekend-ghostly marble corridors, waiting for a decision. News came, early evening, that two judges could not be contacted, notwithstanding Ma Bell Telephones' best efforts.

The corridors felt a bit warmer. Surely, as the evening advanced, it was too late for sensible discussion, for a momentous decision? For at midnight, the legal authority for execution lapsed. When a date was set, it was that date only; otherwise the whole process had to be reauthorised.

At ten o'clock we were told the court was in session, by phone, having decided among themselves that they had a legal quorum.

The basement corridors echoed to the tiniest noise. Our band of a dozen correspondents stayed in a rather subdued huddle in one corner. At five to midnight, a justice official appeared at the far end of the corridor, running towards us. It was a jaw-dropping moment. Clacketing shoe-heels as she cantered nearer. The decision. Minutes to go. We all gasped to each other. This must be it – get ready with the words – 'Saved with seconds to go . . .'

The official stopped five yards from us. Couldn't speak clearly, breathless – and apologetic.

'They did for him,' she said. 'No reprieve.'

It was a mockery of all the movies; of misplaced optimism in drama. And all done by telephone, for the court called the state prison, and he went to the chair at one minute to midnight.

EIGHT

Northern Ireland perhaps

One of the joys of a BBC Radio Home Service childhood was the regional news. We lived in north-east England, so the BBC – naturally – gave us the daily doings of life in Belfast. (In explanation: BBC regions are the product of 1920s transmitter technology, and have nothing whatsoever to do with pious utterings about rich regional identity, and so on. And BBC Engineering is next to God, if not in charge of actual evolution.) Once a week, at teatime, a Voice of *Children's Hour* intoned mellifluously: 'And now over to our studio in Armagh.'

Another announcement followed, this one in a high-pitched squawk: 'Ay warnt to be an actorrrr . . .'

There followed a half-hour or so of Children's Drama, delivered in cut-glass Northern Irish voices. The downside was that I spent several childhood years believing that theatrical stardom could only be attained through fluency in ripe Ulster tones.

A quarter of a century later, while running down a street in Armagh as Woolworths was reduced to a heap of rubble, I wondered where the actorrrs were.

At least I knew how to pronounce the names. The sounds came flooding back when I was added to the host of London-based staff who'd been foisted on The Province (as we were not allowed to call it), since the start of the late-twentieth-century Troubles. But as I recalled the broadcasts of the fifties and surveyed what was happening now, in the seventies, there was no link other than the names. The old news bulletins had never indicated anything other than a rather distant part of the UK, linked to us by BBC Engineering, and full of agricultural shows, Harland and Wolff's shipyards, and lots of Ulster Culture. There hadn't been a hint, as far as I recalled, of any problems simmering just under the surface. Of gerrymandering in elections. Of the rigid, but to outsiders unseen, division between Catholic and Protestant.

By the mid-seventies, patterns of reporting the Troubles had been established. The violence was still daily, nightly. A kind of equilibrium had been established *vis-à-vis* the locals and the visiting BBC reporters. The Prods regarded the BBC as traitors, having assumed initially that support for unionism would be axiomatic over the water. The Catholics felt less acrimoniously about our role: we were fuckin' Brits, and destined for the flames of hell.

The first time I was addressed quite casually as a fuckin' Brit in the course of an interview, I was surprised. Wasn't everyone here British? Oh, ignorant, naïve, newly arrived woman. Time to go back to Broadcasting House in Belfast, and study the League Table of Permissible Words and Insulting Definitions.

Ulster; you thought that was where you were? Please, no. Annoys the nationalists.

You mean the Catholics.

No, not all Catholics are nationalists.

How about the Six Counties?

Tsk, tsk. Don't go wading around in political terms.

But there are six counties, and twenty-six in the South.

Yes, but there are Historic Connotations, and for heaven's sake don't talk about The South.

Why not? That's where it was, last time I looked at a map.

They're a nation now, for heaven's sake.

Ah, Eire.

No *no*, far too – er – Irish. They're The Republic of Ireland.

The people in the Bogside in Derry say they're Irish.

*London*derry please, you'll upset the Unionists.

You mean the Protestants?

Sort of, nearly.

But aren't they Irish, by dint of living on the island of Ireland?

Don't split hairs.

But we use the term 'Irish Republican Army'.

You may have noticed that we don't – quite. We call it the IRA. That avoids the unpleasantness of enunciating the words 'Irish' and 'Army' in a description which Many People regard as inaccurate.

So we can call them Provos, eh?

Certainly not, that's slang.

Provies, perhaps?

Another slang term, used, may we remind you, by the army.

Whose army?

Ours, but don't call them Our Army. Annoys lefties in Britain.

Lefties on the mainland?

Please – mainland is derogatory.

To whom? The people of Ireland the island, or the people located geographically Over the Border, or the people of the Bogside?

All of them.

So when a Provo bomb wounds a lot of people . . .

Careful; civilians are not wounded. They are *injured*. That makes the distinction between wounded soldiers of The Army, and injured members of the IRA, who, you'll remember, are not in an army.

So we call it a terrorist bomb, to be on the safe side?

Yes. But not on BBC World Service, who aren't happy with the disputed definition of terrorism.

Are we? I mean, this terrorist war has been going on for some y . . .

WAR? WHAT WAR? THERE IS NO WAR. WAR IS NOT A WORD THAT CAN BE MENTIONED.

Outside BH Belfast, the streets erupted, the houses blazed, the men with guns prowled.

I had much to learn.

And the first thing was that no one really wants to hear about the place, no matter what it's called. Even twenty-five years later, having been asked about every conceivable rat-hole and shooting-ground across the world, I find that questions about what goes on in Northern Ireland never arise. And not just with those who are across the water, on what appears to them to be the mainland. When I spoke at a smart charity luncheon a few years ago in a country hotel in County Antrim, there was a battery of enquiries about the Gulf, Libya, and so on. Then a charming behatted luncher got up to ask: How did I like my first visit to Northern Ireland?

'I've practically lived here,' I replied. 'In fact I know the back streets of west Belfast better than those of my home town.'

There was a polite silence.

'I've never been there,' said the behatted lady, in a voice which denoted volumes of opinion, and could have frozen the water in her glass. A little volley of questions batted up from around the room, all taking as their subject something at least a thousand miles away from the territory we were on.

And afterwards, there was genuine surprise that I knew the place well.

A blanket of indifference, woven of horror, irritation, impatience, dislike and despair, has been thrown over the province. Even TV audiences reacted in a singular manner, considering that news bulletins might well deliver unwanted and unpalatable items; a bulletin leading with the words: In Northern Ireland tonight . . . used to produce an immediate 20 per cent drop in viewers. But working there was unavoidable, if you were a reporter on shift at TV Centre in London in the mid-70s. And after the early surprises, and a swift learning curve (both involving a challenging amount of drink consumed after, during and before work), I began to look forward to stints 'over the water'.

The first day I drove in from the airport, having picked up a gloriously battered hire-car – the only sort available to journalists because of their poor record with car hijacks – I wound down the window as I approached a city lying in sunshine, were it not for the filthy coal-fire smoke topping it like a thick grey pie-crust. In the distance I heard a distinct small boom. Utterly in the grip of a self-imposed discipline not to react hastily in uncharted territory, I drove blithely on towards Broadcasting House. Faced with forbidding gates to the car park, I got out, and wandered off to see if the front entrance round the corner would tell me how to get in. Twenty yards along, I heard shouting. I turned round to see the gates opening and a scrabble of people trying to heave my wreck out of the way.

'I'm sorry,' I stuttered out, 'I've just come in from the airport.'

This compounded my culpability, as a car bearing a wild-looking camera crew nudged mine aside.

'Then you surely heard the fuckin' big bomb as you came in?'

I spent the next two hours trying to pretend I didn't exist – which wasn't hard in the Belfast newsroom: a wonderful evocation to the point of parody of all the filthy, ancient and demented newsrooms in any drama.

There was little light; the room had iron shutters on the window, which were a weathervane of the temperature on the streets. Most of the time on my first visit they were closed. What light there was was reduced to permanent dimness by chain-smoking journalists. The typewriters were antique, the tables a lattice of burn marks. Mercifully, the beer-sodden carpet was obscured with mounds of paper: crumpled-up scripts, reams of unread Northern Ireland Information Office handouts, loopy claims from various back-street factions, creative expenses claims, hundreds of yellowing newspapers;

piles of telephone directories, several torn in half by a violent correspondent of frustrated sex life unable to demonstrate normal communication. A woolly mammoth could have remained concealed in the mess for weeks. Then there were TV equipment, odd bits of clothing and a lot of bottles. There were also scanners for illegal monitoring of security communications, and, on the walls, huge, dog-eared maps coloured according to faith: green for Catholic, orange for Protestant. Broadcasting House dwelt in a godless grey area. It all added up to a splendid tip, with a real lived-in feeling. Out of it emerged some of the most efficient and carefully judged journalism, under the most trying conditions. But with unspoken compromises.

For a start, there were two sorts of journalists. The Home team knew the ground, knew their history, lived in the community. The Away team from London were baffled by the ground rules, felt nothing of the emotion which was fuelling events, and lived in hotels that had very short lives.

The Home team never left the story. From the office, they drove through streets full of incident, where ominous-looking armoured vehicles thundered past, guns poking out of the back doors. Roadblocks, official and otherwise, sprouted on familiar roads. Their children went to school in a city where children were as vulnerable as anyone else to the random bomber. Shopping involved being processed though metal gates, with bags frisked. High-street stores had security guards to peer into handbags. The route to a local pub could be blocked by white tape, beyond which a dinky remote-controlled bomb disposal robot would be jiggling its way to an innocent-looking car. Night sleep was punctured by the tireless efforts of the Belfast fire brigade.

No wonder the Home team retired to the BBC Club before heading home. There, they would find the Away team clamped to the bar counter.

One of our excuses, in the Away team, was that there was nothing else to do. The cinemas, the opera house, the restaurants –

all had been finished off by the bombers. The only public buildings relatively unscathed were churches. Even there, you ran the risk of encountering the Reverend Ian Paisley declaiming about sodomy and damnation and papists and Anti-Christs and anything else that didn't take his fancy, while pasty-faced little men thrust collection plates under your nose, with the words: 'A silent collection, if you don't mind.' (Notes, not coins, if you haven't come across this method of extraction before.)

The Away team also found themselves in a land which was not at all like – well, Britain.

Sunday mornings equated to life in Sunderland – which Belfast resembled, with its Victorian brickwork and shipyard attitudes – but to life in Sunderland in the early fifties. The streets were dead, and the churches attracted crowds of formally dressed families. The women were straight from my childhood: tight little hats on tight hairstyles; sensible winter coats, with the children scrubbed and uncomfortable in little-grown-ups' clothes. And all with an air of outraged disapproval as we journalists went about our business. Doing anything on the Lord's Day was not so much a sin, as a hanging offence. Nothing was open. Finding a Sunday newspaper was a challenge; finding somewhere to eat on a Sunday was a test of skill and cunning. An enterprising woman ran a kind of restaurant in her front room near the university. We all had to behave as if we were family, and money changed hands very discreetly. The alternative was the one Chinese establishment, where there was drink as well as food, as long as you knew how to order it. 'Tea, please,' produced a pot of red wine; 'Perhaps coffee?' a pot of white wine. You have to be extremely desperate to slurp wine out of tea-cups. Most Sundays, we were.

The rest of the week, Northern Ireland was a place which should have been familiar, but was more like a film set where the director jolts the audience by having horror burst into the mundane and the normal. Reporting it was relatively routine, though. The alerts and tip-offs came in by phone to the solid, motherly ladies who kept the newsroom going. I rarely saw one panic or give vent to anger as they passed on news of shootings and bombs and suspect cars and bodies found on wasteland.

At times, the sound of explosions rattled our windows, so we set off without questions asked, the smoke usually visible above roofs as the car shot out of the fortified courtyard. A knowledge of Belfast's web of terraced streets, the roads that were blocked off, and the religious affiliations of the drably dirty housing estates was essential. Being able to reverse a car fast was useful. Deciding who to stop for, a difficult one; the police were worth taking notice of, they carried guns. But men who suddenly appeared at traffic lights and headed for your vehicle waving something – this was in the days before squeegee-merchants – were to be avoided. Acceleration through a red light was preferable to lending your car to unidentified persons for an unspecified period. At night, we all ran red lights.

I found out the hard way that British soldiers also stopped traffic.

Sent off by the *Today* programme to cover the annual conference of the Royal Ulster Constabulary, I had assumed it would be a routine evening meeting with a conventional speech of support by a dutiful Secretary of State. I turned up at the tatty gothic of the Slieve Donard hotel in Newcastle, County Down, to discover a medal-bedecked phalanx of large policemen, and their overdressed wives, heading for the several bars. In which they stayed for hours. A Dinner Dance was proclaimed on the posters. Dinner and dancing seemed not on the minds of these redoubtable folk, so I went off for a wander outside. The gardens were a tad neglected, and I was studying the random assortment of bushes, when one of them got up and moved. A few minutes later, another, larger bush did a neat little skip and repositioned itself. I headed for the bar, becoming aware that security took many forms in County Down.

It was time to do a few interviews, before things took a turn for the unintelligible. Burly police paws pressed generous 'wee ones' on me, and my questions began to gin-up a bit. Well after half-past nine, the uproarious bar was invaded by an incandescent man who was clearly the chef. He announced to anyone who could hear above the din that 'there'd be burnt offerings or nuthin'' if the constabulary failed to reach the ballroom in five minutes.

The crowd heaved joyfully in the direction of food, at which point a senior police officer discovered the Secretary of State and his wife hovering in a corridor. Both were towed in, plonked down and regarded with the greatest good humour. A senior policeman's wife took it upon herself to regale Mrs Secretary of State with a set of ripe jokes, then hugged her vigorously after each punch line. Mrs S. of S. – a well-bred Home Counties person – maintained charm and politeness, while being grappled on to the tablecloth by the peroxide Valkyrie next to her. Her husband fared little better. At one point – certainly not the end of dinner, which seemed a long way off – he attempted to make his speech. He received roars of approval, somewhere into his second paragraph. The applause was sustained, and clearly signalled that two paragraphs would do.

I was sitting underneath the head table with several other hacks, in a vain attempt to hear what might have been said. We all concluded, thankfully, that there was no story.

Leaving ahead of the crowd, I staggered out, much the worse for wear. After a brisk walkabout, avoiding the bushes, I felt better. Anyway, there was no option but to head back to Belfast. I was on late shift; it would be my fault if I wasn't available to hurtle off to a heap of exploded rubble at three in the morning. I drove to the outskirts of Belfast stiff with determination and, in the dark, saw a red light waving in the road. Highly conscious that we'd just involuntarily lent a car to persons unknown a few days previously, I decided that a chat with the men in balaclavas was a bad idea this late at night, and speeded up.

What sixth sense made me stand on the brakes and hit the windscreen, I'm not sure. I peered out, dazed, at an entire unit of the British army.

A slightly irritated captain asked where I'd come from. 'Been with the police all night,' said I. 'Anyone else?' he enquired acidly. 'Secretary of State,' I tried, but had trouble with the word Secretary.

'I'm a reporter,' I said lamely.

'Ah,' said the captain. 'What's the story?'

I thought for a moment.

'What do you know about bushes that go creep, creep, creep?'

I swallowed most of their coffee supply, and was shepherded back into the city centre by a land rover, having had the system of red warning lights at military checkpoints drilled into me by a patient sergeant, and a briefing in which it was explained that most of the lansdcape in Northern Ireland, if poked, would grunt.

The sheer number of 'incidents' we dashed about covering beggars belief. And even then, we were alerted to only a fraction of what was going on.

We'd hurtle off, reporter in the back of the camera car, clutching notebook and hoping that we had enough clothing on to endure four hours standing in a wet street watching a suspect car, only to hear a muffled explosion in the distance, followed by sirens in the opposite direction, and a passer-by remarking, 'Youse haven't seen the corpse on the allotments, then?' This was before mobile phones, and our two-way radios worked only in a few favoured places.

We scampered from one grim event to another. At tense periods, there were regular riots. The crews and reporters used to gather in the newsroom in the early evening. We then allotted each other various insurrections. 'You take the Prods this evening – I had them all last night, and I'm fed up with biblical abuse.' 'I've had the Ballymurphy mob two nights running, and they're throwing dog dirt.' 'Why do I always have to do the Short

Strand crowd?' 'You're the only one who can swim, and they might decide to dip the BBC in the Lagan.'

In reality, it was hour after hour of both mischievous and evil-intentioned behaviour. There was a ritualistic quality to most riots: dustbin-lid banging by raucous housewives, grey with Valium, heralded the bigger showdowns. Hordes of children and young teenagers spelt mischief – but ensured that 'the boyos' were not yet on the street. The swooshing sound of a bottle meant that the rocks and stones and clods of earth and bricks and bits of wood were being augmented by the petrol bomb. The vile 'splosh' as it gained its target and ignited sent us running.

I didn't find it particularly frightening; I was so busy trying to sort out what was happening, where to go, how to get pictures, who was involved. What was much more upsetting was the reaction of local people. So much rage – the only time I've ever seen men frothing at the mouth with fury. Women screeching with hatred, their faces set in ugliness. Hostile, truculent children, mouthing catchphrases of prejudice. Nearly everyone pale and unhealthy, a mass of badly nourished bags of nerves. I grew fascinated with the misshapenness of so many of the protesters. Lanky youths with sticky-out ears, small stumpy men with skinny legs. Discontent put physical awkwardness in the spotlight – protestors were a gangling crowd who couldn't run properly, figures undernourished on bags of chips and booze and heavy smoking. They managed bursts of energy, but even the teenagers often paused for breath, the lads all triangular, their shoulders like coat-hangers tapering to tiny pelvises – a product of poor nutrition even in their mothers' wombs. There were times when there seemed to be a wilful presentation of poverty: 'Youse think we're shite,' they'd yell, 'youse think we look like shite as well, don'tcher? Well, we don't care.'

Women with ratty hair and cheap clothes, no tights and thin nylon cardies on a February evening, women gulping tranquillisers, at the end of their tether and only too aware that they looked a mess and had given up trying. It was something that few men – particularly reporters – seemed to notice; or if they did, they were puzzled and gave it no thought. Young soldiers from Aldershot, many from fairly tough backgrounds themselves, were hugely disparaging when in close contact with rioters or demonstrators, or when searching their homes. 'Slags,' they'd shout, 'ugly bints.' It all added to the nasty incidents where people forgot common humanity.

One day, on one of the West Belfast housing estates, after an attack on a post office in which a soldier had been injured, I crouched in a front garden opposite while four soldiers pushed their way inside a semi, searching for the gunmen thought to have taken refuge. They elbowed aside two yelling women in fluffy slippers on the threshold, and I heard the tramping of boots up the stairs. A minute or so later, there was a commotion, the sound of thumping and furniture barrelling about, with women screaming. Out the front door came two soldiers hauling a lad in a torn T-shirt, the third soldier pushing off the two women who were clawing him. From the shouts we gathered the lad was one of those being sought; he'd been found in the bathroom and tried to empty bleach into the soldier's faces – the offending blue bottle was poking out of a camouflage pocket. By now, the women had been joined on the pavement by neighbours, and the temperature was rising. I noticed a movement behind me, in the front room, and looked in. The fourth soldier was using his rifle butt to sweep every trinket and knick-knack off the mantelpiece, crunching cheap china under his boots. He saw me, gave me a sullen look, and smashed the remaining ornaments on a couple of shelves, before appearing at the front door and saying: 'They're dirty buggers in there, my mum would puke if she saw how this lot live,' and tramped off to join in the rumpus round the newly arrived police armoured pigs.

I couldn't bear to see the women return, and went up the road to join my crew filming the start of stone-throwing. It's incidents like these which stay with me, not the panoramic sweep of violence.

Sometimes the riots became lethal, sometimes surreal.

Crawling around the Markets area, a standard stone-throwing and occasional shooting ground very close to the city centre, one night in the early eighties, we got stuck next to a wall, with the army on one side, and a lot of shouting on the other. It was pitch dark and drizzling. Bernard Hesketh, a cameraman of huge experience and wonderful humanity – but prone to get stuck in well ahead of his diffident reporter – scuttled forwards as the army deployed, or at least ran around and did a lot of shouting. I crept across a cobbled back street and witnessed strange moving things. About fifty yards away, several five-foot-high rectangles of corrugated iron roofing were skittering nimbly across the lane. A hail of stones and bottles cannoned out from behind them every thirty seconds. Then a few petrol bombs. There were a lot of loud bangs. Plastic bullets. I looked behind, to see dark shapes of the army bearing down towards me, so hit the cobbles. After about ten minutes, I was still lying in a large puddle, soaked through and miserable, and missing my cameraman. I was wondering what life held for me, when a voice honed like a whippet who's had elocution lessons said into my right ear:

'I say, are you busy, by any chance, next Tuesday?'

I wondered if I'd possibly passed out and was having a weird dream.

'I'll probably be dead before then,' I countered, as a petrol bomb went splosh a few yards away.

'Pity,' said the voice, which belonged to a slight but elegant shape wriggled next to me in the gutter. 'We're having a bit of a do in the mess, and you're very welcome.'

I thought about this for some time, and formulated a reply, in order to be drowned out by a bellowing sergeant who stood on me while orchestrating a major onslaught on the corrugated iron dancers.

The charming captain rose from the gutter, whippet-like, and led the charge.

Ten years later, at the opening of the Bristol Cancer Help Centre, with Prince Charles wielding the ribbon scissors in a beautiful garden, his aide-de-camp sidled up.

'You never came to our do,' he said.

The entire reporting of Northern Ireland was a Sisyphean task, with us rolling the ball of news to the top of the hill, only to have most people desire never to hear it, and the rest not to believe that we had applied honest and well-intentioned principles in its compilation. Some mutt decided early on that all riots were started by the press, mainly by handing out five-pound notes to potential stone-throwers. This canard still pops up as a supposed concrete piece of evidence that the media are the source of all trouble. It's one of the folk-myths of late-twentieth-century television:

'Oh, I heard that reporters carry fivers and that there wouldn't have been a riot if they hadn't encouraged people to misbehave for their cameras.'

This expands into: 'There wouldn't have been half the Troubles if the cameras had been banned,' added to by Mrs Thatcher, in a rare moment of illogical stupidity, banging on about Terrorism and the Oxygen of Publicity, suggesting that people of evil intent only do it in order to get on screen. Tell that to Pol Pot.

Many much better placed and more experienced than me have charted and dissected the reporting of Northern Ireland over the decades. There's no doubt that purity and total honesty are lacking in all quarters. The closer to home a disturbing situation becomes, the more blurred the vision.

I worked for the BBC: pure establishment, fuckin' Brit, in the view of many people.

Disloyal, traitorous, letting the side down, lefty, gullible, in the view of others.

Compromised, compromising, censored and blinkered, according to yet others.

Trying hard, and failing sometimes, in our own view.

One Wednesday lunchtime, Bernard Hesketh and I were walking across a wasteland next to the Divis Flats in central Belfast. The Divis were notorious, never mind for being a bastion of republican sympathy, but also for being the only place in Europe to have experienced an outbreak of cholera in the late twentieth century. A source of satisfaction to the Paisleyites, who predicted plague next. It had been a twitchy week, with incidents piling up, and we were trekking back to our car – hoping it hadn't been acquired for active service with some unofficial outfit – having spent a couple of hours waiting for a bomb to be defused. As we passed the Divis, a man called to us out of a window on the third floor.

'Youse wanna see something,' he said, not as an invitation, but as a statement, threateningly meant.

'Such as?' I managed to reply, worry-feelers a-twitch.

'You'll see, wait.'

We were standing a few yards from a corner of the flats, and I stared over my shoulder across the mess of garbage to where there was a car on fire, about two hundred yards away. There was a glint next to it. Ah, so the police were aware of us, binoculars in use. After about thirty seconds, during which time Bernard and I had had a hurried exchange about the value or sense of hanging around, three men came quickly down one of the rubbish-strewn stairwells, wearing balaclavas and carrying rifles.

Oh fuck, was my only thought.

This is the kind of simple nightmare episode which can lead only to disaster.

The three posed about ridiculously in front of us, one carrying a weapon that would not have looked out of place in the Boer War. The other two were rather better equipped. I was wondering what to do, debating quickly whether we should film or perhaps walk away, when it dawned on me that Bernard had already been filming the entire scene. 'What the hell are you doing?' I hissed.

'Filming it, you silly woman,' he hissed back.

The little messenger from the third floor then tripped up to us, out of camera range, and said: 'Now don't make a mistake: what you're seein's the INLA. Not the Provies.'

It can only get worse, I thought. The dissident bunch who make the IRA look mainstream.

Within seconds, they were all gone, and Bernard and I had a hurried consultation, realising that the police had probably clocked us and the boyos. Just then the window above us came open again, and a voice shouted, 'Fuck off then.'

The session we went through back in the editor's office could have been smelled several miles away in Stormont: the stench of trouble brewing. The kind of trouble that could be kicked up by the RUC, the Northern Ireland Office and several hundred rampant backbenchers of all hues in Westminster, all alleging collusion and treachery.

Robin Walsh, a mercurial and gifted editor, decided that we would show the footage, justified by several contemporary incidents indicating that the INLA was making a bid for power in republican circles, and so growing confident enough to show off in central Belfast in broad daylight. I wrote a tight script, using all of Bernard's pictures, including the final shot of a window opening and something inaudible being shouted.

We transmitted it on the *Six O'Clock News*.

An hour and a half later, reports started to come in about a shooting in the Divis flats area. Calls came in that a known republican activist had been shot dead by the security forces. Both army and unofficial republicans acknowledged the death, and came up with a name. Even later, we learned that the shooting had taken place in a third-floor flat.

I could never get confirmation as to how the incident had been initiated. I wondered about our report on the *Six O'Clock News*, and pondered how far our responsibilities went.

Most of the time there was little occasion for reflection. One evening, having had three lively hours running back and forth in a riot in the Beechmount area, we heard of a shooting on the

Ballymurphy estate in West Belfast. Heading there, we found a couple of police armoured land rovers blocking our path. Trying to find out a single fact in these circumstances was a challenge; anyone on the street was either intent on trouble or busy dealing with it. The army and police land rovers were 'closed down', and knocking on their back door would not be welcomed. Away to our right, with most of the street lamps knocked out, we could discern some shapes moving along a garden fence. Then there was a hail of petrol bombs, a revolting firework display, with bottles sailing towards us in a continual and regular arc. Some kind of home-made contraption had been set up behind the fence, and the barrage was effective and scary. We couldn't see a ditch and we felt our way on to a muddy grass verge. Lying on the ground a few yards from the police vehicles, we could hear the cracklings of radio-talk. However, there was no one around to tell us what might happen.

We decided to stick it out, rather appreciating a static incident as opposed to doing a marathon round the Beechmount again.

The army arrived, generating an extraordinary amount of noise, shouting, boots scraping, rifles clattering. The petrol-bomb machine had stopped, clearly for a reload.

Soldiers moved ahead of us, figures moving and darting. Then the machine started up again. The soldiers were outlined for us by the series of short, flaring fires as every bottle hit the road and pavement. We were filming.

Suddenly, a larger fire whooshed into view. Ten yards in front of us, a soldier – a sergeant – spun round, alight. There was a series of shouts, and much running.

In those few seconds, I wondered if I should do something. I had nothing with which to douse the flames, but the soldier's yells were truly awful. I also knew that his mates were with him – and that we were unknown, unidentified figures who might be considered hostile if we suddenly rose from the ground and headed for him. I didn't formulate those thoughts in any detail at the time, but I knew we were useless in that situation.

After what seemed an age – just a few seconds – another soldier had got an extinguisher from one of the police vehicles, and the sergeant was on the ground, a hissing cloud rising around him.

From behind the fence there were screams of delight.

We put the pictures out just over an hour later on *Newsnight* – with few details, but some general background on the night's problems. I felt they illustrated honestly what happened regularly, but was rarely caught on camera.

Some days later, I was publicly berated by a backbench MP in the Commons for failing to give aid to a man in distress.

'Typical of the callous press, filming a man in agony … Typical of media bias and the media's sensationalist approach.'

There's no comeback to that sort of criticism, except to explain my motives, and the judgement on the ground at the time. But it cuts little ice with many people, who like to believe that the world is not a messy place, of grey areas, and fallibility, and chance.

The sheer volume of unpleasant incidents tugged at my ability to view people as human beings capable of love, kindness and tolerance. Every day, you reminded yourself that it was the combined elements of a complex situation that caused men to blow people to bits – not innate satanic character.

At a working men's club one afternoon, there'd been a shooting. We got there quickly, on a tip-off. The double-fronted Edwardian house was shuttered against bomb blasts. Inside, it was pitch dark. For some reason the electricity wasn't working, so we turned right from the hall, towards a figure with a match. It's a common notion that all such scenarios have someone who knows what's going on. Not so. If you stumble early on a murder, an explosion, there is just confusion and blundering. So now we blundered backwards into the front room, getting out of the way of a group of police pushing their way toward the match-flame. The camera light went on. We were standing in the murder, literally. Blood and brains were around our feet. The body was slumped half against the wall.

We all swore. The light went off, and we fled.

Outside, I walked straight down the path, stepping out of my rather elegant dark-blue mock-croc shoes which were slippery with brains.

We got back to BH. I did a cursory report.

Your own emotions surge and fizz and rage all the time as a reporter. The idea that you are an impervious embodiment of objectivity is only for the theorists. The very nature of journalism takes you to the unusual, or to the extremes of human behaviour. You can properly appreciate what you witness only if your intellect, observation and emotions are in play.

It's true that some stories are all about a string of facts, a description of circumstances. But most produce a reaction in the witness: from a flower show to a massacre, even if the reaction is boredom or indifference, it *is* a reaction, and can colour words, opinion, tone and judgement.

The textbook position is that reporters – especially those working for public service organisations – are 'objective'. This frequently refers to political stance, and is relatively easy to police. In the social area it becomes more complex, with the reporter's views on the way society is run often brought into play because of the revelatory nature of the press. If you learn of injustice, do you not reinforce the discovery with a sense that injustice ought not only to be exposed, but dealt with? And in stories where human nature is put to the test – life and death matters, terror, shock, cruelty; the meat and drink of the front page – then the reporter has a dilemma. To report a mere string of facts would not suffice. It would not do justice to those involved, or convey the full picture of what has happened. Reporting the emotions at the scene, conveying the feelings of individuals at the heart of the story, is essential. However, there's a very blurred area where a reporter has to gauge just how much he or she should shape the story with his or her own emotion; and that area is dominated by the people who pay the reporter, and also the audience; not by the ability of the reporter to *feel*.

All reporters work on the end of a piece of string which leads back to an editor or proprietor. Away with romantic ideas of the Hack Raging Against The World. Hacks have to eat. And they have to get on air, or published, too. Hacks are not prophets, nor are they missionaries. They might try, but they'll probably be fired. Journalism is not a branch of philanthropy. It used to be seen by the more high-minded practitioners as a kind of downmarket vocation It has become more and more a business.

That piece of string can be very short and thick, tugged so that the reporter-puppet is dancing to the head office tune. Or it can be a less visible, but strong line of understanding, representing mutual agreement about 'where the boundaries lie'. So when reporters appear to become more emotional, more 'involved', then permission has been given from the editor's office to turn on the feelings.

Perhaps it's in response to an audience which sees the world less in terms of ideologies, and more in terms of fascination with the individual. No president or monarch, in a country where the press is relatively free and democratic, can any longer hope to hide personal details behind grand office and title. As formalities and hierarchical traditions have receded, the demand to know more about the lives of others – their relationships, their opinions, their intimate details, all of which used to belong in a clearly defined 'private' area – has increased. Great dramas are seen more and more through the lives of a single person. And our interest in ourselves is all-consuming, producing 'how it will affect you' news. Or as the Americans neatly put it: 'All the news you can use.'

On top of this, the not-very-gentlemanly trade of journalism is now part of an immense international media business. In a very short time, even national newspapers have been transformed from traditional institutions with traceable roots to add-ons in someone's empire. The TV and radio stations have also found themselves jolted from their carefully nurtured, home-grown origins into a bleak and rapacious world where entertainment rules the roost, and several news editors in the USA have found themselves working for Mickey Mouse.

Down on the ground with the humble reporter, the string from the editor twitches, as the demands of the proprietor and the customer – at least, the profit-minded proprietor and the mass of customers – appear to alter. And if economic profitability and the biggest audience are deemed to rule the roost, then perhaps the performance of the reporter needs a little 'attention'. If the audience is interested in individuals, then the reporter's included in that game. Facts, please; but how do *you* feel, the one watching events on our behalf? A string of vivid adjectives, a catch in the voice, a shake of the head. It does not take long for the idea to catch on that reporting is bereft of authenticity if the reporter's heart fails to be in the story, preferably in view on the sleeve. Sentiment stirs the crowd.

It's a step towards the 'infotainment' world, where the pill of fact has to be sugared by a performance. Reporting – in particular on television – always had a narcissistic element, but now it's been encouraged to flower.

Back in the seventies, what I saw in Belfast on a daily basis could have been given a personal interpretation, with just a small loosening of the emotional strings. However, that was not the style. Nor would it have sat easily with the reactions of local people. They lived with these disgusting and frightening incidents all around them, and got on with life. A tragedy here, an outrage there; it would have been ludicrous to have had reporters pouring out their own sentiments while housewives swept up the glass and firemen mopped up the blood. A quarter of a century on, the blast in the small town of Omagh received much more sensitised treatment. The TV pictures were deliberately less graphic, but the emotional picture was much wider.

Remembrance, anniversaries and memorials – all these feature much more prominently today. A quarter of a century ago, the Belfast newsroom – and its audience – was much more dedicated to what it termed 'a good planting'.

'A funeral is a *public* occasion, and here, my friends, it is also a political one, so get out there and do your public duty. Try not to fall in any hole.' Robin Walsh reigned for many years as the rod of iron in the Belfast newsroom. He was a great editor. On this occasion he was addressing a little group of us, destined to spend a morning avoiding being seriously duffed up by men in sober suits in a cemetery. The Provos liked a good send-off. The Prods liked to think of it as an opportunity to pay their last respects, perhaps by hijacking the coffin. Dignity was not a word associated with such burials. The troublemakers went to their graves to the sounds of fist-fights and oaths. In death as in . . .

This particular interment had come about as the result of a sharp-eyed soldier spotting a bunch of masked and armed men about to get into a yellow cattle truck in the village of Keady. There was an intense fire-fight, and the Provos – with several injured – high-tailed it towards the border. They'd tried to hijack an ex-prison officer's car outside his bungalow and he'd potted at them with a shot-gun.

It was a Saturday, the weather was warm and pleasant, and I arrived in Keady mid-evening. We'd had a vague report about gunfire. Something had clearly happened. The streets were deserted. Bullet holes in pebbledash and garden wall attested to some action. And the doors we knocked on had produced spit and insult. We finally headed for a house where the meagre flowerbeds had been churned up by boots and the patch of scrawny lawn had odd bits of metal embedded. I had to bang on the door several times, before a stony-faced man in vest and baggy jeans answered. He was none too impressed by us. Keady was staunchly republican. He faced the camera determinedly.

'Shootin'? What shootin'?'

I pointed to a bullet hole in his window-frame.

'We was watchin' a John Wayne fillum. Obvious, isnit? That's what we heard.'

There's no point appealing to logic in this sort of interview. Anyway, the door was banged shut as the camera nipped backwards just in time. Logic was lost in a place where gunmen erected roadblocks in cul-de-sacs, and the reply to the question: What is your name? was: What was your meaning?

That might have been the end of the affair, except that overnight, it was rumoured that the Provo party had abandoned their car, and dumped at least one of their injured mates over the border in Monaghan. Nothing was confirmed, so it was time for a furious dash southwards, driven by our legendary cameraman, Cyril Cave. Cyril held the record for the Derry-to-Belfast run, an unofficial grand prix, staged regularly to get footage back from Londonderry for transmission to London. It was stated that other traffic, cyclists, police and wildlife all stayed indoors when Cyril was behind the wheel and on a mission. Roads in the border area and across into County Monaghan are better described as lanes. Not often do you get to do 101 mph down a lane.

Screaming to a halt outside a rural Garda station, Cyril told me to go look for the getaway car, reputedly found by the Irish police. It was Sunday morning and the station was closed. There were high walls round the yard at the back. Cyril gave me an 'I am a cameraperson, you are supposed to be the intrepid newshound' look, and I shinned up. A minute later, he was on my shoulders, and we had a battered yellow vehicle in the can, as some sort of evidence.

This was a period when cross-border cooperation was a hot issue, and no one was very honest about what went on, either side. The actual position of the border was open to interpretation as well. The answer to the question: Which country are we in? usually got the answer: Which would you like to be in?

As we fell down from the wall, we saw a Garda patrol car in the distance. We zoomed off.

'Hospital,' said Cyril. I thought the likelihood of a known Provo, who had several crimes to his credit, fetching up in a public hospital bed rather long odds. Cyril wisely suggested that bursting into the back bedrooms of every house in Monaghan was the other alternative. The old-fashioned set of buildings, neat little flower-beds scattered between its several buildings, looked very quiet. We presented ourselves at the front door, and rang the bell. After at least two more bell-ringings, and three or four minutes, a figure appeared in the gloom beyond the glass door. Glaring at us, the nun took some time to decide to open the door. Cyril, a gentleman, inclined his head and said, 'Good morning, Sister.' She didn't respond, and went on glaring. I'd rehearsed a polite enquiry, and began: 'We've heard reports that yesterday, a man with a bullet-wound . . .'

Without warning, the nun sprang at Cyril, who was raising his camera to his shoulder. Her nails scraped down his face.

Now, I was brought up in a highly prejudiced north-east English town, where Catholics were Romans, and nuns were weirdoes. School hockey matches against the Catholic Grammar were characterised by surreptitious swipes at any nun dumb enough to attempt refereeing (they were bound to find against the toffee-nosed Protestants, weren't they?). Then I'd grown up, and consigned religious prejudices to the toy-bin. On the other hand, I'd never learned to treat someone dressed as a medieval King Penguin as anything special. So, someone attacks my cameraman, I floor them. And I did.

Grabbing the bleeding Cyril, I gasped: 'He must be here – and she's so mad, I bet he's dead.'

Cottage hospitals are fairly orthodox in design. We scrambled round the corner of the main building, and I heaved open doors to the little row of outhouses. The first two yielded nothing, the third was dark and had a certain smell of chemicals. All of this frantic activity was driven by the knowledge that it was almost impossible to pin down any facts about terrorists – including their demise. Claims would undoubtedly be made for either a heroic martyrdom or even, possibly, an accident. All kinds of tales would be woven to conceal the bare reality of a young man, who'd already killed two people, who'd chanced too far.

In the dark, I called on a memory from student days. The most heinous crime you could commit in Newcastle's Royal Victoria Infirmary was to remove a Deceased to the mortuary without the Essential Label. All students who volunteered for holiday work in the RVI learned this as a mantra. I looked at the sheet on the slab and took a wild guess at one end. Tweaking it up, I got Cyril to focus on the large luggage label attached to a big toe. There was our man, name printed in large letters.

We left the hospital seconds later, and Cyril set the record for the Monaghan to Belfast Formula One trophy, which included at least one sheep vaulting a high fence in panic.

A nineteen-year-old lance corporal had dispatched the terrorist – the first man he'd ever killed. I next met him when he came back from the Iraqi desert in the Gulf War, famous as Andy McNab of *Bravo Two Zero*.

Several days later, after sizeable rows between police forces, politicians and relatives, the body returned across the border. This was the funeral we were attending.

On a perfect spring morning, the city of Armagh's two opposing cathedrals ignored each other against a blue sky. There was a medium-sized crowd outside the Catholic one. Close friends and family, and some large men, partners in crime. Our cameraman, Patsy Hill, a lovely man with an acutely honed sense of nervousness in the presence of thugs, was cursing gently, as various unfriendly faces turned away from his camera. We were invited into the cool interior and a warty-faced man offered me a prayer-book. I declined politely, and turned to Patsy. 'Bomber,' he whispered.

We retreated to the graveyard, and I tried to work out a useful, but discreet position, where we would see what was happening without offending London's sensitivities about just how far you could see a coffin enter a grave – the BBC had an incomprehensible set of rules about coffins, all clearly based on the author's memories of an unpleasantness at a family do.

Patsy found a very large tomb, and propped himself beside it.

The cortège wound among the lush green, heading for the newly dug grave, next to which was a huge mound of fine red earth. As the final preparations were made, an unholy buzz interrupted the birdsong. A giant military helicopter growled overhead, drowning any Last Words. The mourners started to look active, rather than passive. The priest raised his fist to the sky, and in doing so, took a step backwards.

Patsy said he missed the actual moment when the priest went in the hole.

We fled. A final glance back confirmed a struggling mass of earth-covered people, ensuring that their man was going to rest in an authentic atmosphere of hatred and anger.

As we ran, Patsy, out of breath, wheezed: 'Are the big men after us?'

I gasped: 'Dunno, I'm looking out for a nun.'

As I said, there was little time for reflection in Northern Ireland. We careered from the wreckage of a bomb explosion to Mr Paisley spouting bigotry in a chapel then to a bunch of rioters then to Mr Adams quietly oozing hypocrisy in the Sinn Fein offices. We drank a lot when we had a free moment, and BH Belfast had an atmosphere of manic jollity which overlaid real cameraderie when it was needed. There were also, always, unexpected pockets of help and friendship. Total strangers offered their hallways as refuge in the midst of riots. A family mourning the latest victim gave you sandwiches and let you use their phone. A policeman took you to meet his family, have dinner – sorry for someone so far from home for weeks on end. Cups of tea from housewives, a drink in the presbytery, a stream of jokes from soldiers crouched on street corners, a thermos of coffee from the woman who'd seen you standing in the rain for hours; endless small gestures which leavened the grim events, but seemed to leave a stronger memory. Reporters are birds of passage, but it's extraordinary how often you're taken on trust, invited in and made welcome.

Stuck in the memories of the nationalists in northern Ireland are the hunger strikes of the early eighties. A cracking example of how history is divided, as it is made. To the supporters of Bobby Sands, and the rest of the convicted criminals in the Maze prison on hunger strike, heroes were in the making and Irish history was being followed. A great sacrifice was under way, with a commitment and significance which they believed would make the world sit up and notice – and which would change the course of the Troubles.

To those in the opposing camp, the hunger strikers were a group of misguided self-glorifying thugs, all with long sentences to serve for their crimes, and all subject to their own gangland regime within prison walls.

To those over the water, it was baffling. Starving yourself to death seemed one of the stupider things to do, and hardly a moral act, especially when you had a conscience heavy with terrorist crimes.

The reporting took on the character of a surreal death watch. The press, encamped outside the Maze, a bleak and damp spot off the motorway south of Belfast, swapped black jokes. Bad taste ruled the day, and for those of us from outside the province, there was little sense of a drama unfolding.

The tedium was enlivened by Sunday marches up the Falls Road. Six miles of (usually rain-sodden) tramping past boarded-up shops and mean little houses, arguing with the cameraman about whether to take a shot of misspelled banners – you'd have thought they'd have mastered 'death' at least . . . and observing that the marching, or rather strolling, crowd, often several thousand strong, looked like a doctor's waiting-room on the move: pasty-faced, lank-haired young women, with pushchairs of mewling children. Skinny lads, with hunched bony shoulders and pipe-cleaner legs; middle-aged – or perhaps not, but older – women, in groups, all smoking during the six miles up the Falls, skin shiny with anti-depressants, and voices raucous; older men, more dignified, but with a tendency to scuttle if there was trouble. Few of the boyos – walking up the Falls with the TV cameras about wasn't their thing at all. An afternoon to view graffiti at leisure, and look in front rooms and eye little patches of hedge and grass – after all, most loyalist imagery insisted that Catholics lived like pigs, never planted a flower, and were generally mucky. As most loyalists had never walked, never mind strolled up the Falls, it was useful to tick off a few facts for mental ammunition, next time confronted with a bunch of bigots from the Protestant Shankill.

Mecca at the top end of the Falls Road was a litter-blown, flea-bitten 'shopping-centre', named The Busy Bee: a single-storey huddle of window grilles and broken bottles. The army had a habit of being around as a kind of Unwelcoming Party. And it was then that the grey snake of small people would be shown up in all their trailing dinginess. The army was full of pink-cheeked lads, squat and muscly, remarkable for an outfit fuelled on chips and beer. Next to the denizens of the Falls, they looked another race, and it struck me how much the place was living at survival level, stressed, washed out, and desperate – yet still very determined.

To us, the strangers, hunger strikes seemed a rather foreign habit, vaguely sanctioned by the gothic Catholicism of the South. Our lack of sympathy shocked even hardline loyalist journalists. 'There's history here,' they said: 'the Irish with a grievance used to take themselves to the threshold of the man who had wronged them, and sit there until reparation – or death – came.'

But medieval habits cut no ice with the British press corps. Indeed, this symbolic angle to the story rarely got a mention. Bog-trotting stuff.

The hard indifference and cold dislike with which Northern Ireland was seen by many was just being reflected in the wet and irritated journalists following the daily details of the hunger strike. It's no secret that although many who came to observe the Troubles were fascinated and passionate about what went on, a large number found the entire scene repellent. And there was much to disgust even the casual observer, never mind the hack who had to view shredded remains lying around after what would be termed 'yet another bomb'. Some reporters loathed going to Belfast, and found much to despise in what they saw. All around was a society rich in hatred and lies, with the least intelligent wielding the biggest sticks and getting themselves elevated to the level of spokesperson, if not politician. And underneath the stark acts of unforgiving terrorism was a murky river of organised crime, springing from the old tradition that war is good for business.

The cynicism and contempt for all things Ulster took a year or two to sink in in the local newsrooms. I'd watch the middle-aged copy-takers typing some dreadful details, their heads cocked to one side as their headphones hissed with atrocities. 'Poor souls. Dreadful. Oh my God,' they'd say quietly, biting their lips – regardless, of course, of which faction had been in action. However, they'd be watched by staff from London with stony faces, sighing with exasperation as yet another disgraceful line was added to the list of appalling outrages, and pretty indifferent to the individuals – because nearly the whole of the mainland took that view as well. Only the convention of regularly reporting what are considered major events has kept the story in news bulletins and on front pages; and it's a convention that has found little sympathy in most of Britain. Even then, the habit of some newspapers of printing a Northern Ireland edition concealed from many people in the province that what was plastered across the front pages of their miseries was more frequently relegated to a small inside paragraph in the edition of the paper being read in Scotland and the Home Counties. And, as I said, it took time for the attitudes of London-based journalists to impinge on those in Belfast. It wasn't until the late eighties that I heard a seasoned hack from Belfast round on a young reporter, fresh and confident from London, and scream: 'We know how much you despise us, but kindly keep your opinions for your smart friends in Chelsea!' The reporter flounced out, tweeting the word 'provincial'.

I have no idea where the best reporting came from: from those locals who were involved – in the closest way, their futures part of whatever happened in the news; or from the visiting vultures who came to see, were intrigued and interested, and attempted to understand what was going on; or from those who treated the entire place as a human sewer, using their cameras and pens like tongs to fish out bits of information – shorn of sympathy, but objective, in the coldest sense of the word.

The dustbin-lid-rattling which greeted Bobby Sands' death had been a long time coming. His last few days on hunger strike were a babble of statements, allegations and rumour. So high were feelings running that there were suggestions of murder, or neglect, or medical malpractice. A huge queue formed outside his mother's modest council house in South Belfast, as the coffin went on display. All Protestants looked away, not only in political disagreement, but in dislike of himself on public view. All Catholics, it seemed, were going for a look.

On the first evening, there was still a lot of argument swirling about as to whether his body showed signs of the alleged ill-treatment. So, deciding that the first rule of the book is see for yourself, I joined the queue, in headscarf and scruffy anorak. Religious hypocrisy is not my cup of tea, so my main concern was that I would be unable to make the sign of the cross – not so much for reasons of belief, but because I'd never done it, and wasn't sure exactly which way it went. The evening wore on, and luckily there wasn't much conversation in the queue – I just sniffed in answer to a few remarks.

The nearer I got to the house, the more I realised that this was territory marked by other animals. There wasn't a policeman for miles. Shifty lads slid this way and that. Grim men in dark suits chatted – women were ignored.

The front room was stuffy. I took a quick peek, and started to cough to cover my surprise. In his coffin, Mr Sands did not present a pale face of suffered humanity. He looked like a banana. Luminous yellow. I sniffled and coughed and looked hard. This was not the time and place to comment on the effects of hepatitis A and liver failure – nor the fact that the local embalmer had apparently used furniture varnish by the look of it. Thank God no one put a friendly arm round my shoulder at my supposed overcome state. I'd just learned what actors mean by corpsing.

The yellow image hung over me as we lurched through a lengthy riot in his honour. Again, depending on which side you were, it was an outpouring of grief and rage at the loss of a valiant foot-soldier in the cause, or it was an excuse for criminal damage in the name of a petty criminal and tool of the IRA.

When number two came round a week later, a ritual had already been established. Death, rumour, allegation, outrage, dustbin-lids, riot, and then funeral show. However, Francis Hughes had the benefit of a highly committed family, un-willing to let him go quietly. They were gathered at his bedside well after his demise in a small hospital to the south of Belfast, refusing to leave him. We were all gathered outside the gates, having been told that the family had negotiated with the police to have his body taken through the streets of West Belfast to his final resting place. Not quite so, we learned. The police were pointing out that West Belfast was nowhere near the route to the graveyard awaiting him in his home village of Bellaghy. Mr Hughes, they reckoned, was being sent on a final lap of honour through nationalist heartland, and they weren't having that.

Stalemate ensued, with our main effort directed at burrowing into the hospital, which had a stout police presence everywhere. I did moderately well, but unfortunately fell, rather than sneaked, out of a convenient tree I'd found by the wall. Returned forcibly to the press pack by the gate, I was trying to figure out another route, when the police pushed us back peremptorily, and ushered out a large car.

''Bye, doctor, thank you, doctor,' gushed the minion on the gate. A smart suit and striped shirt, stethoscope draped round neck, graciously acknowledged him, then turned to look at the waiting crowd of hacks. Later, my colleague Paul Burden of the *Today* programme said that the hassle in the hospital – and the lack of information even inside – had all been worth it just to see the look on my face as he cruised past me.

There hadn't been a lot to find out. Inside, the Hughes family was now conducting their sit-in in the hospital morgue. Outside, a crowd was growing as news of events filtered to a nearby Protestant housing estate.

Late in the afternoon, a large number of police vehicles arrived, and it was obvious that the body was about to begin its final journey. The atmosphere of respect and quiet which would accompany such matters in the rest of the United Kingdom was not apparent: the waiting crowd was jeering, and the police were revving engines. The cortège drew out, a hearse with armoured police vans at nose and tail.

The police seemed to have underestimated the welcome party, and the vehicles got only a couple of hundred yards out of the hospital gates before being submerged in very angry non-mourners. We fought our way towards the hearse and found a large RUC man stuck through the driver's window. Peter, my cameraman, crawled on to the bonnet to find that the driver, who did not want to follow the route chosen by the police, had stuffed the keys in his mouth, and the policeman was attempting to prise his jaws open. Around us, there was the sound of a riot brewing up, much encouraged by members of the deceased's family who were shouting their version of events and goading the arrivals from the housing estate. One of the relatives was a priest – I noticed the black shirt as he slugged my cameraman in the face. I thumped him back, not in any way motivated by Methodist/Church of England anti-popish motives, merely determined that no bastard gets away with assaulting my cameraman.

The crowd was by now getting well stuck in, and I was wondering whether we might end up being run over by the hearse, when a distraught pop-eyed man in a bobble hat and black anorak tugged at my sleeve and tried to tell me something. Peter was by now having more trouble with the grieving relatives, who seemed to be amateur prizefighters.

'The Pope!' yelled the little man in the anorak. 'The Pope!'

Wondering briefly if plonking a fist on to a Catholic priest was bringing instant retribution from higher authority, I shouted, 'What about the Pope then?'

'He's been shot!' he screamed, and started to bellow, 'The Pope's been shot!' at the brawling crowd. Feeling that one riot was enough and that any public-spirited citizen ought to be getting a grip on events, I got bobble-hat by the throat and yelled at him: 'Shut up! There's enough trouble already without you spreading lies.'

Chastened, he skulked off, and the crowd thankfully never learned until they went home that Mehmet Ali Agca had just fired his gun in St Peter's Square in Rome.

The police got the hearse to move, and we ran off to find our Volvo and give chase, soon catching up the long line of vehicles as it snaked down a road cleared of any other traffic. We hurtled past the waiting nationalist supporters who must have had a half-second in which to pay their last respects, and approached the city centre without losing any speed, cornering into the road past the City Hall by mounting the pavement and twanging a bus stop sign. I felt I was taking part in a northern version of the Monte Carlo grand prix, as the City Hall went by at 70 mph. There was a horrendous moment at the end of the street as we lurched left, just missed a Rover carrying CBS News, and overtook two police land rovers which were obviously not Formula One material. As we hit the multi-laned motorway heading north, Peter was half out of the passenger window filming, while I hung on to his belt.

I could just hear him as he screamed, 'Faster, faster, we're losing it!' And indeed we were, the hearse becoming a tiny pair of tail-lights in the distance. I looked at the speedometer, my foot flat on the floor. Mr Hughes may have begun his journey at a crawl, but he was heading for his grave at a hundred and fifteen miles per hour.

The chaos and emotion which pervaded nationalist funerals had their complete antithesis in the old-fashioned Presbyterian-influenced Protestant affairs. The streets through which an RUC victim of terrorism would be driven were a model of rectitude and reticence. Chillingly correct, I sometimes thought, as the silence descended on the pavements and all the curtains were drawn tight shut. Often, it was an all-male affair – in that, there was common ground with the Catholics; but on one occasion the stiff, dignified, masculine, expressionless ceremonial was terribly challenged by a desperate human being.

The coffin was in the church, brass handles gleaming, the service coming to a close. The press were up in the gallery, as uncomfortable as you ever feel at a stranger's funeral, redolent with the tragedy of a life lived in duty and cut short. There was no crying, the faces were impassive, granite-like, and the merest whiff of emotion would have been snuffed out in embarrass-ment. At the discreet signal to lift the coffin back on to its shiny brass bier, we prepared to leave, when we were struck rigid by a terrifying noise. Rising from the very bowels, growing from an animal roar to an ear-splitting and sustained but deep-throated scream, the widow gave vent to her suppressed grief. It was like a bolt of emotional lightning, and we were rigid with fear. Below us, the congregation stared ahead, giving away not the slightest tremor of empathy. Even as the woman, in neat winter coat, hat, gloves and handbag, clambered on to the coffin and lay spread-eagled on the polished wood, there was no movement in the church.

I felt physically sick, unable to do anything and unfamiliar with the noise that was still filling the vast space around us.

I could only think of an animal, trapped in unimaginable pain, and unable to do anything else than tell the wide world of its suffering.

And all in a church where no one made a move to end the misery.

I have heard the sound twice more since then, and it is a dreadful and particular sound which embodies the whole strength of a human being concentrated into grief. It is a humbling noise, the cry of the heart, and it is a terrible signalling of mortality.

And of all the memories that remain, again the most powerful is not of a major event, of thousands in rage or grief, of the ruined high street in Omagh or the gutted remains of the Droppin Well disco, but of a Christmas tree.

There was one house only on the gap-toothed Ligoniel road which leads up to the hills overlooking Belfast that had a Protestant family left in it. Other had been driven out, or left, unwilling to be a minority. We had a call to the newsroom of a shooting – no details, just a rough location, and the roads were quiet, speeding our arrival. The street was half-derelict, and no one was about except for a knot of people on the pavement – a couple of women, an elderly man. As we drove up, some army vehicles crept into view. The door was open to a modest Victorian terrace house, with a dim light in the front room. As the crew got the camera kit out of the car, the neighbours gestured silently inside. I went into the hall and looked through into the front room. A small boy, seven or eight perhaps, was standing by the fireplace. 'Me Daddy,' he said to me immediately, 'me Daddy won't get up.' Under the Christmas tree was a man's body, awkwardly splayed.

I felt absolutely useless and the wrong person in the wrong place, a gross intruder – and I looked round to see a young soldier standing in the doorway. Helmet and rifle and thick gloves and muffled against the cold, he looked reassuring and professional. He pulled his scarf away and turned out to be baby-faced and pink-cheeked. He stared at the boy and his father, horrified, and then looked at me hopefully: 'You'll deal with the lad, will you?' he asked.

I felt completely guilty. I was just a reporter, an intruder, the wrong person, and I was too close to a story. I pushed past him out into the hall and saw that the two women were still at the front gate. 'Please take the little boy out,' I asked them, and then grabbed the camera crew before they tried to come in.

You wonder what good reporting does, being at these events, a spectator, unable even to extend a reassuring arm because you feel such an intruder.

You go back to the office, with some pictures of a terraced house with a tiny hole in the front-room window made by the motorbike passenger's bullet, and type out a little list of facts: the only Protestant family who'd chosen to remain, the wife out working her nurse's night-shift, the name of the dead man.

You omit the Christmas tree and the little boy's words.

But I loved Northern Ireland. It was rare that I felt real fear; in the midst of mayhem there was always a drop of humanity. Having got hopelessly entwined in a privet hedge in the Lower Ormeau Road during a riot – never dive headfirst into a privet hedge for cover, it's pointless and embarrassing – I heard a window squeak open above me. Fine, I thought, instead of stones or petrol bombs it's going to be a bucket of boiling water out the window – quite a common sideshow in Belfast. A few moments' silence ensued.

'Would youse like a cup of tea?' said a voice.

NINE

Reptiles by appointment

Look, they've got one.

Suburban Sunderland (very conscious of its outward appearance: nice front gardens and no back alleys, washing-lines up Monday only please) was agog in 1953. Quietly agog, mind you. The very idea that you should hang around watching that H-shaped bit of metal being hoisted on to the chimney-stack would be indecent.

They've got a television.

Word was passed on Saturday mornings in the smart café in Binns, the dominant department store. Binns, synonymous with the phrases 'put it on the account' and 'I'll have it delivered', was the bedrock of civilisation in Sunderland, along with the Conservative Ladies' Tea Club and the annual Durham County Tennis Tournament. By these means were the shipyards and the coal-mines held at bay, along with two-thirds of the population who were being shifted by a determined Labour council, via the miracle of slum-clearance, to paradise on earth – the brave new world of the council housing estates on the rim of the town. Shifted, in other words, to sterile orange-bricky wastes bereft of shop and pub, away from the narrow, blue-grey slate and stone lanes which had their toes in the river mouth, and which, round the clanging yards and hooting sirens, heaved with life and lice (I sold a lot of nit-combs from behind the pharmacy counter).

The sirens howled round the town to waken the ungodly welders and platers and shipwrights and fitters, and get them into the yards at the earliest hour. The middle class shrugged with irritation at these wailing commands, hearing the four o'clock afternoon hoot as a sign of the yards' union-clogged indulgence. 'They're finished work now, I suppose,' sniffed many a suburban mother collecting her child from school. No thought was given to the hoot which had dug the men of Doxfords, and Austin and Pickersgill, out of their cottages before daybreak.

Sunderland was an odd town. At the turn of the century, while other northern cities had international reputations for industrial prowess and commensurately huge gothic town halls, Sunderland was famous for its football team, the 'Team of all the Talents', and for precipitating the introduction of outward-opening doors in public buildings. However, it apparently supported a workforce better-paid and more flush than anywhere else in the kingdom. It had invented a particular kind of urban housing, the 'Sunderland cottage'. Rows of single-storey but remarkably roomy dwellings, with two or even three bedrooms and a neat line of outhouses in the yard. Three doors: the wash-house, the coal-house and the nettie. Three identical doors: the curse of visitors, who were regularly found mucky and desperate for a pee among the nutty slack.

The centre of town had a clutch of municipally grand buildings, including the Victoria Hall where, in 1883, 183 children had been crushed to death against a bolted door while heading for free toys on the stage, so leading to national improvements to safety in theatres and music halls. Mention of this grim incident was rare; Sunderland seemed to want no part in such historic events.

Even as it basked in industrial affluence and laid claim to the proud boast of being 'The Biggest Shipbuilding Town in the World', the gentle decline had started. Sometime during the First

World War, while new ships were sliding down the ways into the Wear, cheered with flags and patriotism – for war means work – the sneaky Japanese pinched our shipbuilding title. A fact always met with scepticism in the town: 'The Japs, pet? No, they don't do ships. They'd never manage to hoy a big rivet doon the lonnen.' So I was lectured by the Boilermakers' shop steward during a particularly bloody-minded strike in the late sixties. Why anyone would want to measure skills by throwing rivets down a back alley beats me, but he was a man of rather fixed views, and the lads had been on strike for several weeks and were in no mood for discussion. Especially as I was a female standing in the doorway of their meeting-room in a gloomy pub, the moral equivalent of a tart loitering round a gents' public lavatory.

A century of gentle decline, with a stark statistic at each end. In 1900, Sunderland was paying the highest wages to working-class men in Britain. In 2000, Sunderland had the lowest average wages in England.

Mid-century, as a child and teenager, I spent a good deal of time behind the counter of Wilfrid's pharmacy in Southwick, an old part of the town on the north bank of the river, with the back yard opening directly on to Austin and Pickersgill's shipyard. It was a shop of alchemist's smells; elegant carboys filled with coloured liquid stood above the window displays, and row upon row of wooden drawers were packed with odd powders and liquorice root. There were marble slabs for scraping pink skin ointments into waxed boxes, and rows of green-ribbed 'poison' bottles. It had been a Victorian pharmacy – and still was, in many ways, from the disused gas mantles hanging from the ceiling to the enormous brass and maroon cash register. Two bentwood chairs were provided for those waiting for their prescriptions – nearly always women, a good number of whom appeared to have 'walked into doors', for heavy drinking was rooted in the male culture; only when the children were hurt could any of them be persuaded to go to hospital. Even then, they were fearful, expecting to be shamed in such an official building; so we kept small parcels, sold for just a few pence, of toothbrush, face-flannel, comb and shampoo – a novelty to most of these families. Men avoided the doctor, determined to stay at work, for jobs were hit-and-miss in the yards. Welders and platers seemed to get the worst injuries, but they were borne stoically, until the wound became so bad they'd creep quietly into the shop 'to have a word with the chemist'. As they rolled up their sleeves or trouser-legs, I saw and smelled my first cases of gangrene – and this was the 1950s.

I counted pills into shiny round cardboard boxes and made up gallons of a foul-smelling concoction known as a Police Bottle – Lord knows what was in it, but most of the population seemed to need a dose of it regularly, and as it tasted awful, it 'did me a Power of Good, pet'.

Through the back door, there was another odd sideline to the pharmaceutical business, a small building which had an indescribable chemical odour and which hummed a peculiar electric tune. Into this went a procession of Accumulators. I never understood this. I collected these huge, heavy glass jars from customers, and tried not to look at them too closely. They appeared to consist of a mixture of ink and very old pond. They had pot handles, and the odd wire – straight out of Frankenstein, to my young mind. You hooked them up to some weird system in the throbbing house, and then they reappeared, 'Charged'. I never saw what they did or where they lived in anyone's home. On learning they were storage batteries, I was no wiser: How did you connect the smelly glass brick to a torch?

We developed photographs as well: mounds of tiny black-and-white prints which showed families marshalled against the back-yard wall and chopped off in their prime; there must have been something odd in the Box Brownie viewfinder, because the average Southwick family appeared minus heads and lower legs. There were snaps, too, of summer days on the beach at Roker and Seaburn, children in woolly costumes and the working men all sitting on the sand in their suits.

I sold hairnets, denture powder and foot plasters and, on Friday nights, cheap make-up and Evening in Paris scent. The girls from the glassworks and ship components factories spent their week's wages in one go, preparing for their one night out dancing. They were horrified that at seventeen I wasn't 'courtin'' seriously, and at eighteen was still on the shelf. Many of them had two children at nineteen – 'settled'; but with no more nights out and no money for Yardley face powder and Toni perms. The only means of contraception available were the deadly hush-hush items which men slunk in to mutter for: 'Packet of Three and Nines' – known only by that term, long after they ceased to cost three shillings and ninepence.

Because I had the knack of deciphering doctors' writing, I did a fair amount of dispensing work and acquainted myself with the *British Pharmacopoeia* and the eccentricities of our local GPs, all of whom were respectable middle-class men and some of whom were drunks. A couple regularly tried to kill their patients with miswritten prescriptions. All pills and potions were elegantly presented in shiny white boxes, wrapped immaculately in rather expensive paper, and labelled. It looked clinical and impressive: medicine had to be taken seriously. Literally how it was to be taken was another matter. The shorthand Latin instructions from the doctor were translated and written on the labels, but I learned to pre-empt the panic which would appear if the items were popped straight in a bag. The number of customers who could not read was considerable. Before they were forced to acknowledge this, you had to quickly explain about the dosage, chat a little, and then repeat the instructions casually, while holding up fingers for numbers to reinforce the message. It was a gentle convention, understood by all, but not foolproof: I occasionally spent a frantic hour or two scrabbling through old prescriptions trying to find what particular overdose had occurred, while the hospital stomach-pumped a customer. Suicide was rare – mostly the dazed patient came round with the words: 'If two do me good, then surely ten'll do me better?'

The pharmacy was a place for gossip and advice, and a parade of the ills of poverty. Bad housing, dirt, ignorance and drink were the reasons people sought help. We used to say we hadn't seen a decent germ in years. I wondered again and again why we were dispensing panaceas and placebos and sticking plaster, when the causes of the bruises, bronchitis and depression were so obvious. However – and this is not hindsight through rose-tinted spectacles – there was rarely any open aggression or even bad manners: kindness and neighbourliness kept most households going.

On the work front, the town suffered decades of decline in the shipyards, coupled with a longing for the passing grandeur of heavy industry, its apprenticeships, traditions and pride in hard labour; there was also an acute sense that anything golden or desirable or lucky that made its way up the A1 from the soft south was snaffled by those buggers in rich Newcastle. Sunderland heaved with quiet disappointment – and hugged itself to itself, becoming the biggest village in England.

We didn't get many royal visits, either. The nearest thing to a glamorous visitor was usually a fat Greek ship-owner with a woman possibly his wife wearing unsuitable clothes – there's a lot of grease about during ship-launches, even on the posh platform ... But in 1953, when the new young queen was visiting the length and breadth of the realm, someone in Newcastle clearly forgot to put up the usual roadblocks to Sunderland.

My memories centre on a seven-hour endurance test – the sort of thing that would make our craven local newspaper report: Worth Every Minute Of The Wait, Ma'am! Clad in school uniform – long hairy grey overcoats and puddingy hats, in which we were referred to unkindly by the Grammar School lot as The Midget Russian Army On The March – we had been bussed to our allotted space on the pavement, expecting to stand dutifully in line for a few minutes and wave a flag while her gilded Coronation Coach trotted by. We knew all about the coach – we'd seen the recording of the Coronation on Our New Telly. But for reasons unknown – probably something to do with the Labour council organisers, who 'hated them snobs at the High' – we were placed high above the river mouth, on a nondescript stretch of road between the seafront and the back-slums of the shipyards. I cannot recall a single thing that we did during the wait, but know that it would consist of being told not to do it. Propriety and public image were strong at the High School.

Eventually, night having fallen, ditto rain, there was a distant murmur. And right in front of us, for a second – maybe two? – went this purring shiny car. Unlike ordinary cars, this one looked like a little living-room, gliding through the damp river air, all cosy and yellow-glowing. The Queen looked nice and warm too, but was looking the other way for my two seconds. We were hugely miffed that there were no white horses and all the other things that had attended the Coronation, but at least We'd Seen For Ourselves. We'd Been There. And all these years later, I still remember. Time and again, I remembered those two seconds while stuck on some godforsaken municipal forecourt or elbowing through a mass of staring-eyed anticipatory people on Royal Tours.

Court Correspondent: one of the BBC's grander titles, unceremoniously dumped on me, probably because I failed to think up any quick excuses not to do it. I'd managed to crawl out of the Europe job – the BBC had eventually forgotten that it was meant to be keen on Brussels, and the governors would be the last people on earth to notice what reporters were doing – so I was back in the correspondents' room and ripe for another stitch-up: royalty.

However, there was vagueness from the management about any special attributes of the job. I mused about clothes. Hats? Would I have to scamper around clutching a hat-box, just in case? This was swiftly countered by the memory of a senior editor years earlier who had advised: never use props. Never wave your hands. Never wear a hat. This is television, not a circus. Then there was the odd business of accreditation. Bizarre, for no other specialist post – defence, economics and so on – apparently needed such endorsement. And this was the early eighties – surely we were into a new era? After all, there was a young Princess of Wales who was a worldwide icon and pin-up, and we were a long way from the obsequious reticence of the Crawfie days. Or so I thought.

I was sent off to Buckingham Palace. There was a definite perk in driving my small and grubby BBC Ford Escort through the gates. This was living! Should I perhaps wave at the gawping tourists pressed against the railings like zoo inmates? Perhaps not. The courtyard was very big, and the gravel deep. I might trip up and immediately be sussed out as Very Non-Royal. So I scuttled towards the right-hand doorway with the tongue of crimson carpet poking out. Once inside, I was given no time to stare. A footman in what appeared to be a version of full evening dress led me down a corridor of quiet carpet and gliding people. I was delivered into the hands of a stout and brisk woman from the press office. She seemed to think I was late and a slight nuisance. 'Follow,' she said, and cantered off smartly. I blundered after, sticking neck to left and right, longing to see more, to catch a glimpse, to satisfy my nosiness. We heeled round a corner, and it quickly became clear that we were tracking lengthily through the less-royal areas; a floor below, and we were on stone flags, in store-room territory, weaving round odds and ends of furniture, as in an unused Victorian hotel. In some cranny dwelt a policeman with a sheaf of forms and a supply of plastic passes. I was photographed, convict-like, and handed the pass. A slightly breathless press office assistant then started on the return journey, thought again, and made a determined bolt for a different staircase. 'Can't waste time,' she barked, 'short cut.'

We emerged into white and gold and grandeur. A long gallery, stuffed with portraits and enormous vases and chandeliers. This is more like it, I thought, and stopped for a good stare.

Meanwhile, the formidable press officer had swerved to a halt, blocked by an imperious footman. A hissed altercation ensued – and hierarchy clearly played a part. Finally, the flunkey raised an imperious arm and pointed to the far end of the gallery. Very precisely he hissed: 'Persons Are Approaching.'

The press officer turned, charged, and hooked me into an alcove. 'Damn,' she said.

We were in an uncomfortable clinch behind a gigantic urn. 'What . . . ?' I squeaked.

A snuffling sound ensued, and a fat corgi inspected our ankles. Somewhere beyond the urn, Her Majesty went by.

I rightly concluded that not everything in this job was going to be logical, reasonable, or particularly normal.

I should have known, though. Two years previously, I had been assigned to a Royal Tour. Billed as 'semi-official', Prince Charles's first visit to India and Nepal was a mixture of ceremony and a bit of a jolly. The entire operation was attended by chaos and diarrhoea, but it was a fabulous way to see the subcontinent.

I was entranced; I could hardly believe that I was getting a free trip to exotic places – and seeing so much. The wonderment of being a reporter gripped hard; the actual business of reporting rather less so, for it soon transpired that film processing and telephones did not figure in the arrangements. So it quickly dawned on us that television news in London was not going to be receiving daily stories; possibly not weekly, either. However, this had to be balanced against the very minor editorial significance of the tour. The fourth member of our crew – we still lugged someone for 'lights' with us everywhere, regardless of all the footage being shot in broad daylight – took a very basic view of editorial priorities. 'Well,' he intoned on Day One, 'we've got bugger all to do unless he's eaten by a tiger.' True, but we persevered nevertheless, shooting film every minute of the day, and knackering ourselves in the process. Not the lighting technician, to be sure. He merely got a bit drunk and annoyed the locals with unfailing Cockney un-humour. And on the only occasion in Kathmandu when requested to provide some illumination for an interview, he sabotaged the electricity supply for a goodly part of the capital.

We set off in high spirits, a score of press, including Fleet Street's Royal Reptiles: experts on every aspect of royal life, except the facts. A characterful lot, and a joy to be with. We had a briefing from the royal press officer, the able and affable Michael Shea, a diplomat – and he needed to be, faced with us. His first briefing touched on a possible visit to a tiger sanctuary. The press were not invited, so po-faces all round, and a typical press/court exchange on the subject:

Tabloid Representative: Why can't we go?
Shea: It's a private visit.
T. R. Is it a big place?
Shea: It's the largest sanctuary in India.
T. R. So there's room for us, then?
Shea: That's not the point.
T. R.: How many tigers is he going to see?
Shea: We don't know.
T. R. Lots?
Shea: It's a sanctuary – he may not see one.
T. R. Then what's the point of going?

[*A short pause ensues.*]

T. R. What about lions then?
Shea: This is India.
T. R. So what?

A much smarter and quieter posse attended the Prince of Wales, including a doctor with a very large bag and the royal ADC, a highly fanciable Royal Marine. The female reporters mused on being rescued from sticky situations by the Marine, not realising that the medical bag would be much more relevant to our survival.

New to the Tour business, I hadn't expected it to be quite so frantic. The main aim seemed to be to get to places before Prince Charles, leave after him – then get to the next place before him again. An interesting concept, complicated by his posh car being given priority over our cavalcade of battered 1950s Ambassador vehicles, and the fact that there was little of the meticulous planning and protocol which usually ensured that a royal visit ran on rigid rails. This was, after all, 'semi-official'. As a result, we all semi-arrived at several locations; either late, or at rear entrances, or stuck in mammoth crowds – few of whose members had any idea why they were gathered, but were enjoying the excitement generated by a smart car, a demented straggle of yelping foreign press, and frequent interventions by lathi-wielding police. ('What's a lathi?' enquired a tabloid hack, barging his way through the first Delhi crowd we encountered. Down he went, whacked by a three-foot cane, as answer.)

On our very first event, the tour had gone a bit pear-shaped. What was intended to be the usual round of formalities – shake hands, sign book, murmur pleasantries, meet line of un-memorable people – had turned into a chirpy demonstration.

We had piled out of the ancient Ambassadors to find ourselves in a sea of noisy placard-wavers. With difficulty, we attempted to discover the thrust of the protest. The placards were intriguing: 'HRH – hands off our Vejjins'. Vejjins? What were they, and how had Prince Charles achieved this feat in the few short hours he'd been here? The crowd was in a good paroxysm of indignation. I tried to question a man leaping up and down frenziedly. 'You are a disgrace in the airport,' he bellowed at me.

Puzzled, we all heaved onwards towards a knot of steely-faced High Commission officials, all showing years of Foreign Office training by standing two yards from a riot and ignoring it. On being asked to explain the commotion, they smiled wanly, and delivered the kind of verbal head-patting reserved exclusively for sweaty journalists.

'Little misunderstanding,' they intoned. 'Nothing that affects the warmth of the welcome, you'll observe.'

We observed the heaving demo, a glorious dust-whirl of colour and placards and hoarse, pop-eyed protesters, now seriously engaged with the forces of law and order. The FO has its own prism through which it views Events.

As we ran for the line of waiting Ambassadors, with the royal party already off down the road, someone managed to drag along a local reporter only too eager to enlighten the ignorant visiting press. Details were gathered of headlines in all Indian papers regarding allegations that young Indian women had been subjected to virginity tests by the Immigration Service at Heathrow Airport.

Prince Charles's involvement was unclear.

Diplomats hate this sort of Event. They like royal tours to be smooth, featureless, and absolutely un-Event-full. Their boss is in line for a medium-weight gong at the successful conclusion of a Tour, and news of Events filtering back to the FO seems to land a considerable blot on the career prospects of junior officials, never mind putting the gong in jeopardy. So the party line is adhered to. According to them, the day went well. Riot, what riot? As for clarifying the heir to the throne's connection to Indian Vejjins, nothing could be gleaned.

I was beginning to learn that following royalty about involved a considerable shift in journalistic perspectives.

Aware that we'd actually come across something that resembled a story, I contemplated getting it back to London – only to discover that phone calls took several hours to set up, and that the film had to be sent in a can via Bangkok. Clearly it wasn't going to be bang up-to-date by the time it limped into London. A shipping agent arrived to arrange matters, bearing a wodge of forms and several rubber stamps; an ingratiating individual who implied that certain financial negotiations were necessary to prevent the film taking the scenic route home via Hawaii. And this was the standard state of affairs at the start of the eighties. A can of undeveloped negative made its way fitfully round the world. Often the journey was successful, only for a nosy customs person to prise open the can – Aha! Exposing a film that has just been transported several thousand miles is a cruel business. And yet it happened time and again.

Nothing daunted, we dispatched our first offering from Delhi to London, happily unaware that the rest of the subcontinent had quite a lot of phones, most of them serving as smart ornaments, unconnected to telephone exchanges. But we found a use for the lighting technician – who spent the rest of the tour traversing India looking for shipping agents.

The tour left Delhi and gathered pace. We were on a marvellous tourist jaunt, except that we scrambled from place to place at breakneck rate, always aiming to get the Arrival shot, which was a kind of *de rigueur* opening to royal stories in those days: car draws up, cutaway shot to building, car door opens, out gets royal, handshake, cutaway shot to flag-waving lot on pavement, royal rear recedes up red carpet. Absolutely conventional, and accompanied by an equally conventional script; I started to wonder if I should revert to the style which had served Pathé News for decades: 'The crowds were out – and so was the sun! As the royal visitor was given another warm welcome – and what's this? One small lad who'll not forget the day he nearly tripped up Royalty! No tea for you tonight, sonny!' And so on.

But I soon learned that the much more experienced royal press pack had ways of countering the tedium of un-Event-full touring. Not for them the excitement of a bull-rearing project at Baroda agricultural university, or the gripping intricacies of an aircraft tyre factory in Calcutta. They were intent on a couple of special projects, the sort of thing that *really* interested their readers about India – or at least, their editors in London.

They had plans. Under two headings: Turban and Crumpet.

As we lurched from Agra to Bombay to Pune to Calcutta, the hacks plotted – those in a fit state to do so, that was, for on day two the dreaded lurgy had reared its head. Every hour or so, at least one member of the party was a picture of intestinal desperation. Early on, a kind of truce was agreed, whereby the entire press cavalcade screeched to a halt while the desperate person cannoned out of an Ambassador into the nearest ditch for relief. And no one took any incriminating photographs. At a Punjabi farm educational project, the *Daily Telegraph*'s reporter and myself displayed female solidarity and ran from the Welcoming Ceremony in search of a loo. A concerned lecturer trotted with us, summoning students and apparently announcing our destination to everyone. He pointed to a barn-like building, open at window level on all sides. Inside, dead centre, was a hole. We approached, and the room grew dim. Every window had heads peering in. Necessity fought with modesty. The lecturer then entered the room and charmingly said that it had been the rector's express orders that no member of the royal party was to be left unattended. It was too late for discussion. Nature intervened as we howled to the assembled audience: We're not bloody royal.

Meanwhile, the Turban story was being pursued. Michael Shea became increasingly perplexed by questions relating to elephants, and whether there might be any hanging around in any of the villages on our schedule. A large package appeared in the back of one of the Ambassadors. One morning, this car sped on ahead. As we got to the village outskirts, we saw that there were two welcome parties. In the distance, shyly gathered next to the newly whitewashed houses, were clusters of scarlet and green saris, and officials in blindingly white shirts; in the foreground were the triumphant hacks, one unwrapping a huge saffron turban, another steadying a small ladder, behind which loomed a large elephant.

As we piled out, the royal party drove up.

The hacks, cameras ready, indicated that their tableau was not to be ignored. The elephant was craftily wedged across the road.

Prince Charles's head appeared out of the car window. 'Bastards,' he said.

Negotiations took place, with the tabloids adamant that no pictures were making it into their papers because 'there hadn't been anything Indian enough'. Thus the turban. Eventually, a village elder was prevailed upon to present the giant yellow symbol, and – goaded by the ecstatic hacks – it went briefly over the royal pate. The elephant proved a symbol too far, and it was led off, having earned its owner a hack's ransom.

I wondered why we were all here.

The tour swayed between inspections of worthy projects and bizarre 'photo-opportunities'. The palace wanted a trouble-free trip, generating positive feeling. The journalists from the serious end of the press struggled to put real meat on their stories, and not sound like an upmarket travel brochure. ITN and ourselves spent hours trying to contact another world in which telephones and television were not treated as exotica. The tabloids sat glazed through speeches about Anglo-Indian cooperation, roused only by the sight of a snake charmer, a monkey or yet another elephant. And still plotting.

The fragile relationship between palace and press seemed be based on mutual need and mutual recognition of difference, fuelled by awkwardness. The palace officials understood that the press were a necessary adjunct to royal public activities, yet we were clearly tolerated, and not quite trusted, rather than welcomed. The family, on the other hand, appeared to regard the press as a kind of omnipresent sub-species of wildlife, quite amusing to observe, occasionally dangerous, and better kept at a distance. The press knew the royals were occasionally good for a great story, but in between these lay a desert of dutiful tedium.

The styles of both press and palace were a demonstration of British class attitudes, mutual incomprehension and nervousness. The last arose from the quite obvious palace panic when a royal event went pear-shaped (the high-drama soap opera of the eighties had yet to appear), and also from the peculiar fear that lurked in the journalists that they might be thought to have 'transgressed' – been rather rude, commented too strongly or behaved improperly. This fear was supplied from the editors' desks, and originated high up the tree, in the office of the proprietor, the managing director, the director-general: the powerful press personage who either wanted a gong or harboured rumbling doubts about upsetting established views – not so much in The Establishment as in the hearts (rather than the minds) of the general public, the paying customers.

The result was an odd circus. Some of the hacks had already made small fortunes from 'exclusive' pictures and 'scoops', and therefore saw the royals as a goose whose golden eggs were multiplying as younger and more photogenic minors made their appearance. These dedicated – and rather rich – members of the press corps often got the real McCoy in terms of a scoop, after painstaking enquiry and lengthy stakeouts. They were the eagle-eyed, twitchy ones, never letting a royal out of their sight, a cash-register 'tching' warming their toes during eight hours in the Balmoral undergrowth. Others in the pack relied on inspired guesswork. And the rest did very well in the school of creative writing – well, if the palace wouldn't respond, why not 'make it sing, make it dance and make it up'?

Yet other hacks were present because their editors thought they *ought* to be there – though they weren't very sure what for, except that the tiger-eating scenario (death-watch job, in American terminology relating to their President) was always a possibility. Major incidents involving royals with not a camera within miles cause any editor sleepless nights.

What we were meant to do if the tiger never pounced was a conundrum, for the daily royal round was hardly the stuff of headlines. Some of the tabloids could still serve up gloopy 'looking radiant as she graciously' stuff, but most of us were stuck with observing tightly planned schedules which were tailored to exclude the odd, the dangerously interesting and, absolutely, the unexpected. Thus the press pack found itself glued to dull events which, under normal circumstances, pots of money wouldn't have dragged them out of bed for. Tiny incidents – royal hat nearly comes off, royal car door gets stuck, mayor's mistress in town-hall line-up, corgi trodden on – provoked animated debate among reporters as to whether it merited a 'splash', a column, a picture. Normal people would have suggested a wastepaper basket.

Radio reporters took cover in delivering lists of people to be presented, to be greeted, to be given awards, and padded items further with lots of historic bumph about when Queen Victoria had first visited and so on. Television crews gathered staggering amounts of footage of backs of heads going into buildings, red carpets, flag-waving, blurred police uniforms shoving at the lens – out of which a story did not present itself. It wasn't journalism as I'd begun to know it. I found myself wondering what our function was. Support system to the House of Windsor? Public representative of masses at exclusive dos? Constitutional observer of minutiae? Enemy of republic? Or person from the BBC expected not to rock the boat, but indicate decorously when royal train going off rails?

On a foreign tour, exotica usually filled in the gaps where there should have been journalism. Thank God for turbans, elephants and the threat of tigers. Even so, the palace was never far from a panic, because so much more could go wrong; and so, in order to soften up the press, they always invited its representatives to a grand drinks party at some point during the tour.

I'd never been to one of these occasions, but in India the seasoned members of the party said it was usually a standard mixture of very large gin and tonics and very small talk. In Delhi, the High Commission would be the host, and there would be a large number of Indian guests, all of whom would have fought very undiplomatically for the prized invitation. The seasoned hacks felt it was all a bit of a chore, and that the whole ritual could do with a bit of a stiffener itself.

I got my only suitable garden-party frock out of the suitcase, laid it on the bed in the dusty and down-at-heel Ashoka Hotel, and whizzed off to see Prince Charles shake hands with Mrs Gandhi. On returning, I spent ten minutes sprinting up and down the tall corridors of the Ashoka looking for my dress. Just in time, it was returned to the room, having been pounded on a stone and ironed like a board, and turned a good deal paler in colour since the morning. A group of us walked across the road the short distance to the High Commission, and were swallowed into an impressive mass of glittering saris and impossibly white shirts. We all felt rather dowdy, and went for a walk near the garden walls, clutching nice huge drinks. We'd had several when Michael Shea shooed us into the centre of the lawn. This was the informal chat bit, and the press were corralled. Mr Shea gave us the once-over with a practised eye, decided we were relatively sober, then realised that not all of us were present.

'Right, where's the *Sun* then?' he sighed. We all shrugged sheepishly, like schoolchildren denying all knowledge of a mate bunking off. Then, like little lambs, we were pushed determinedly towards HRH, who was being besieged by stout Indian dames. The subject of Vejjins had clearly surfaced again.

Shea swooped in. The palace quadrille is a sight to see. Pincer movements to get rid of embarrassing guests, discreet shoulder manoeuvres to exclude the argumentative, deft interventions to shunt the royal towards calmer waters.

ITN's Sue Lloyd Roberts was propelled into position. Prince Charles was a little flustered, having had a surfeit of Vejjin business. As is his wont, he initiated the conversation, and stared at Sue earnestly.

'Contraception,' he began, 'I do think it's so important, don't you?'

Nonplussed, she stared at him. Her cameraman made an effort to push the conversation somewhere else, anywhere else, but Prince Charles was off on a worried monologue about third world problems and poverty – completely unaware that he was addressing the only pregnant member of the tour party.

Then it was our turn – and we had an equally odd conversation, standing in a tropical garden in India. 'Covent Garden,' began Prince Charles, 'so *marvellous* the opera there.'

Recovering with yet more enormous G&Ts as the garden-party chatter rose to ever greater heights, we noticed another sound making its way through the din.

Thump. Thump.

Some white-jacketed servants headed for the perimeter wall, where there was a little-used set of large wooden gates.

Thump. Thump.

As the chatter subsided and the saris swivelled, glinting, towards the noise, the palace officials sensed Something Not According To Plan, and strode gatewards. Too late. Heaved open, the gates revealed the latecomers to the party. The *Sun*. Harry and Arthur, atop a large and tatty elephant borrowed from door-duty at the Ashoka Hotel. Its eye glinting knowingly, the beast swayed through the capital's *crème de la crème*, Harry and Arthur above and beyond the impact of their transport.

At the first glimpse of a trunk, the officials had deployed defence tactics, and were shepherding the prince away. This was the sort of thing the palace abhorred. This was why we weren't to be trusted.

Nearly two weeks in, and we were all less than acclimatised. The royal medical bag started to be eyed hungrily. Our initial enquiry was met with a candid admission. 'Sorry, you're not the priority. There's a bit of royal squitters.' Some days later, after a night in Bhubaneswar – all rooms with hot and cold running ants and inclusive hole-in-floor – the press party was exhibiting a nicely varied range of blotches, bites, sweaty parts and general malaise, exacerbated by the day before's noon tour of erotic carvings at Konaka followed by a very dodgy dinner. (Forty Soviet construction workers had got to the dining room ahead of us, and hoovered up the kitchen's contents; the manager kindly 'sent out to a tasty place' to feed us; at four in the morning the hotel was alive with horribly private noises.) The medical bag was spotted and requests turned into pleas. Some of us had got to the point where we weren't particularly fussy what medicine we swallowed.

The only healthy specimen was the Royal Marines officer. However, his fitness nearly caught him out. Enthusiastically taking up HRH's suggestion that an early-morning dip off the stunning coast would be a good idea, he supervised a happy half-hour spent splashing. As the prince went to towel off, the Marine headed towards a group of people who'd been waving vigorously from the beach. Somewhere in the gibbered information was the unmistakable word Shark. A rather reflective Royal Marine spent the day considering that he could have been responsible for creating England's first one-legged king.

In Bombay, the second plot surfaced. Operation Turban was joined by Operation Crumpet.

In the jolly world of Bollywood, an afternoon's visit to the studios sounded fun. We roamed around, marvelling at a film industry that was capable of rushing its stars from one production to another, picking up a page of script, shooting a take, and nipping off to the next set to assume a different character – perhaps four different films churning along simul-taneously. However, action of a particularly British kind was also being rehearsed. There had been discreet enquiries about the presence of pouting starlets. A fetching sari could be seen amid a little clutch of hacks; and as the presentation of various screen luminaries approached, the royal pack was manoeuvring. Forming two lines, the cameras pincered Prince Charles, who found himself chest to chest with a very pretty girl. Padmini planted a rather delicate kiss on his cheek, and the cameras flashed in perfect timing.

Just another little photo-opportunity, we surmised, neatly satisfying the editors' demands back home.

We weren't in town for the headlines next day. The scandal. The opprobrium. And the eventual charges against the girl of outraging public decency.

We moved on. A clash of cultures is a thing to dread on the royal tour.

At Agra there was another potential difficulty. Privileged, we had the Taj Mahal to ourselves. Being on a royal tour is super-tourist class. No queuing, the transport is always at the door, and a sense of purpose propels the journalists to the front of the crowd or the heart of the action. We stood in the marble enclosure while hundreds of disappointed visitors milled outside. Having taken the standard shots of Prince sees Taj, we had time to amble around. There was a story – the first complaints were being made about industrial pollution contaminating the shining marble. Leaning over the back balustrade, we watched vultures chomping on a large carcass. Good old-fashioned clean-up techniques. But along the river, the chimneys and hazy clouds of modernising India were easily visible.

However, getting to grips with real journalism was virtually impossible. The atmosphere of a tour is one of Candide-like innocence: everything is for the best. Complaint? Problem? Not the time to ask, nor are there the people on hand to question. And the whole operation is one of icing-sugar delicacy. Upsetting a government while a guest would be out of the question. Killer journalism would be, at the very least, bad taste. It was an exercise in suspended reporting.

Instead, we found ourselves heading towards one of the buildings near the gate, as Prince Charles had been spotted besieged by another press pack. The local press had finally argued their way in (they were usually included in the arrangements, but tended to turn up in staggering numbers, bearing ladders and flashguns which fried people within a yard's distance; so we weren't very generously disposed to our fellow professionals). I elbowed through the throng and gathered that all the questions were firmly about his marital prospects. England's eligible bachelor was looking a bit agonised. Michael Shea was prowling the pack perimeter like a hyena, but outnumbered. The Indian press is laudably persistent, and not backward in personal enquiry. They were down to the nitty-gritty, and sure enough, the word Vejjin was discernible. He looked hopefully towards us. My cameraman Chris and I shunted aside several photographers encumbered with enormous flashlights, and I shouted a couple of anodyne questions. We held the ring for a minute, and, as a pay-off, I repeated what an eager young Agra reporter had been hopelessly whispering in Charles's direction. 'Would there ever be a return visit?' As Prince Charles made an embarrassed but graceful reply involving a possible return with a wife, the Indians chattered their pleasure, and the tabloids leapt with glee at a juicy headline. And the prince made his escape.

A few yards from us was a marble bench. The recollection that an image of a woman sitting on it, alone, more than a decade later, should come to symbolise a marriage gone cold sends a little shiver down the spine.

We left Agra, the prince's retinue bearing an ever-growing heap of gifts, this time including a foot-high miniature Taj, complete with light-bulb inside. The hack tour veterans marked it down as 'another for the basement', averring that beneath Buck House was the equivalent of a kitsch arcade, whose labelled contents were whipped out on to a prominent plinth whenever the donor country paid an official visit. (The exception to this was possibly the goat stashed in Princess Anne's land rover by the grateful citizens of Upper Volta and rumoured to have turned into lunch.)

At this time, a visit to Mother Teresa in Calcutta was inevitable. Her orphanages and refuges had been much publicised. 'Decent photo-op for once,' said the hack pack, and started planning. Curious, for the royal family is famously non-sentimental. Proffer a child, a cuddly animal, a touching image of misfortune, and the response is a robust remark or a look which would freeze Satan's balls off. Undeterred, the details for the visit to Shishu Bavan and its abandoned children were picked over for the best angles and images. As the opportunity for spontaneity is ironed out of any royal tour by worried palace officials and diplomats, there's nothing left for it but to be creative. The smaller and the more pathetic the child the better – but cute-looking, of course. Tabloid sentimentality is hand-in-glove with realistic salesmanship. Something Mother T. was not entirely unaware of.

On the appointed morning, we contrived to arrive early for a recce. The reporters cornered various nuns to extract information on a likely little star, and the photographers scoured the wards for candidates. I dawdled outside the main gates of the well-fortified orphanage. It was a stunning scene of early-morning devastation. The poverty heaved and scuttled as ragged people were roused from the pavement by an advance party of policemen. Beggars were prodded and whacked and warned off. Two heaps of rags failed to move. Exasperated at having to deal with the nuisance of overnight public death, the police called several staring spindly teenagers to carry them off. The lads, clearly practised at the task, organised the corpses into a neat stiff bundle and set off over a wasteland of rubbish and stray goats. Where the waste was piled up into a large mound, they swung their bundles into it, and returned to wait for Mother Teresa's next VIP visitor.

Throughout the tour, the crowds never had a clue who they were watching. 'You've come to see Prince Charles?' we asked. The question usually elicited animated nodding and big smiles. But so did the question 'You've come to see Mickey Mouse?' For a mob gathered wherever there was the flashing police light, the shiny car in the slums or the signs of free public entertainment – though this never prevented examples of the 'enthusiastic crowds lined the route to welcome the prince' school of journalism.

Meanwhile, the police were busy shouting at a group of emaciated people pushing and shoving near a small door to the nuns' compound: the morning soup-line. They were scattered with difficulty, hunger drawing sinewy legs creeping back to the door despite regular thwacks from the swishing lathis.

At the appointed hour, the gates were drawn back, with the British pack neatly positioned for the best shots – a plan instantly threatened by the simultaneous arrival of the mammoth Calcutta press corps, who stood in front of us. In a trice, while welcomes were being exchanged, hands pressed together in traditional greetings, the compound became a heaving mass of competing cameras. This was not what the Brits had planned. They'd already sold the pictures to their editors in London. So, with a scraping sound, a ladder was dragged from behind a hut by two British reporters and turned into a long barrier, pinioning a large chunk of the Indian press against the wall. They writhed and wriggled and popped flashguns dementedly, but to no avail. The royal party headed indoors, and the tabloids got their calculated moments – though not quite as sugary or piquant as they'd hoped: Prince Charles, hands thrust deep in pockets, showed interest and concern for the little scraps of rescued humanity in their cots, but, true to training, didn't hug, didn't touch.

Mother Teresa looked indulgent, and patted everything in sight, including HRH. Standing some distance from her were a score or so of officials who hadn't figured in any of the printed arrangements, but who materialised at every stage of the tour. Well-dressed, well-rounded, they beamed with the pleasure of association with limelight and status. A portly gent eyed my rather rumpled summer dress caught up in the heavy camera tripod clutched under my arm, and consigned me to 'foreign minion' pigeon-hole.

'You will be one of the press-types, I suppose,' he said, staring past me. I said I was.

'Wasting your time, I'm thinking.'

I made an indistinct noise, wondering where this was going.

'Bloody woman,' he said, again staring past me, but with his eyes on the diminutive nun from Albania showing Prince Charles the contents of the soup cauldron.

'And?' I said.

'Comes here, goes hunting for the sweepings of the street, cannot understand that our poverty has a logic. Will not stop interfering in nature's way. See—' he pointed at the soup-line which had persevered past the police outside, 'they are nearly dead, but they get a little food, go out and scavenge and ask for more, so taking food away from stronger people. She keeps the no-hopers going. For what good?'

I thought for a bit, and had decided to avoid discursive mention of Christian values, when one of his group tapped my arm and said forcefully: 'This is the Indian view. We understand our poverty. It's you foreigners who like her.'

I was debating whether I should call Chris over and do a short interview. We'd already had a word with a couple of nuns, which consisted mostly of the word Mother and several giggles. I felt neutered.

Yet again, I was left musing on the weirdness of royal tours. The convention of what was expected: photo-opportunities, positive moments, ooh and ah. As a journalist, it was a kind of foggy walk. You made out the shapes of a story, but the fog of convention made it difficult to grasp. No one wanted a disputatious piece about the rights and wrongs of charity methods. The editors back home didn't rate a royal tour as significant enough to bear the weight of serious issues. And the palace employees would whinge for days in a hurt tone, indicating that some kind of Betrayal had taken place.

I began to get a notion of what emotions treason was founded upon.

Eventually, we collapsed on to a plane for Kathmandu. We had vague ideas that we might leave our diseases and bowel troubles behind, but sadly we were to be disappointed.

As the small plane taxied in a neat dance round the pi-dogs grilling on the runway, I rootled for my passport bearing the Nepalese visa. It was quite ornate.

"Snice,' said the senior correspondent for Britain's largest-selling daily, a man who rarely missed a trick on a tour. The sort of man who could squint into royal handbags.

'Well, you've got one too,' I replied.

'Haven't,' he said, 'what's it for?'

On learning it was a visa for Nepal, he looked puzzled, and called to his fount of all wisdom, his photographer, Arthur.

After a short discussion, both looked at me sceptically.

'Nepal,' I repeated. 'Visa. It is another country.'

'Nah.'

Fleet Street's finest glared at his photographer. 'They bleedin' never told us,' he said, clearly accusing the newsroom of Britain's largest-selling daily of wilfully concealing secret information from them.

'Are you sure, Kate?'

'Yes,' I said, 'we've all got visas.'

'Nah, not that. That it's another country, I mean.'

We soon got confirmation of that. Prince Charles's arrival – his private plane having hung back so that we could sort ourselves out in advance – was a merry muddle. The Nepalese had a very different approach to the press, compared to the Indians. They approached us at a run, or at least their security people did, attempting to dislodge us from our quickly organised plane-arrival position. As the smart red-and-white royal Anson made its approach against a background of unspeakable Himalayan grandeur, the pilot would have been able to make out next to the landing-strip the swirl of dust and arms and tripods and camera bags which denotes a little set-to between the police and the press. The royal party yet again managed that ineffable ignoring of noisy nearby unpleasantness, gliding past the grunts and thuds and flailing cameras without a glance – except the resident High Commissioner, who glared, and flapped a briefcase towards us as if trying to magic us into invisibility.

The rest of the trip was punctuated by intermittent mis-understandings, most revolving round the Nepalese view of their royal family as rather god-like – a view not shared by the visiting journalists, unimpressed with a princely trio of small fat brothers, forever surrounded by small fat guards; royalty whose ugly grey palace sucked all the remaining electricity from the light bulbs of their poverty-stricken population whenever a state function occurred. The incident at the war memorial – or whatever it was, we never got close enough to see – merely embarrassed the royal party yet again, and proved that the royal hacks were developing a technique for biffing small fat guards unused to opposition.

Nepal had not yet developed into a full-blown tourist destination, and the country was mainly a stopping-point on the hippie trail from Europe to Asia, symbolised by the sad little graveyard in the capital, under whose unmarked stones lay travellers who'd got stoned beyond physical endurance on Kathmandu Gold, said to be the best pot in the East. One of the press party nearly joined them, managing a two-and-a-half-day trip, rigid, on the floor of his hotel room. He came to his senses only fully when he was told that we'd heard on World Service radio that John Lennon had been shot, at which news he hurtled out of the hotel screaming, 'I've got to get there.' Spelling out that Lennon had died in New York, and we were in Kathmandu, failed to pacify him, and we began to wonder about the strength of Kathmandu Gold as he tore around the garden during a glorious sunset, arms out, making aeroplane noises.

We were scattered in varying accommodation – the modern hotel industry was only just laying its high-rise foundations, and the venerable Yak and Yeti was still crammed with hippies. One establishment of great style was run by Boris, a mesmerising Russian who'd been on the steps of the Imperial Naval Academy when the battleship *Aurora* had fired in 1917. He held us spellbound with lemon vodka and stories all through one night until dawn, a man whose life was lived to the full, crammed with adventure, charm and the unexpected. He'd been a naval cadet under the tsar, a ballet dancer, a black marketeer; he'd cooked for presidents and royalty, detailing his menus for the queen. And here he was in the Himalayas, running a hotel – and probably an intelligence service – in between vodka sessions. He was magical.

The staff of our hotel, the other side of town, were smilingly tolerant. They'd only been a hotel for a short time – we were staying in the ex-prime minister's ex-personal brothel. Very comfortable it was, too, with warm woolly blankets all the way from Witney on Slumberland beds with slithery eiderdowns. On the bedside table was a yellow telephone shaped like a – well, like something medical, with a dial underneath it. Clearly these had been flogged to the hoteliers in a job-lot from UK as *le dernier cri*. The room boy pointed it out with pride, while handing me my candlestick. The ex-brothel only got electricity occasionally, and certainly didn't have a phone line. However, it had wildlife. Halfway into the bath on the second evening, covered in cement dust from observing a Himalayan road-building programme, and clutching candlestick in the gloom, I heard shrieks coming from the corridor. Every door came open, and we watched Tim, a ginger-haired genius of a photographer, hare up and down, clutching only a towel, and yelling: 'Don't get in the bath. I've just done it and there were things in there with me.'

Grubbily, we headed off for a cultural event in a traditional building, about which we got the usual kind of warning from the diplomats that they'd like an incident-free evening. 'What's this place, then?' asked a hack, staring at the curlicued architecture. 'It's *traditional*,' emphasised the High Commission official. 'Called?' The official mumbled something. The hack persisted, suspicious. 'It's called Shital Niwas,' was the reply, followed by an eye-rolling appeal that we all observe cultural niceties. Not easy, as the Nepalese offered a curious mixture of drinks, which at some point in the evening became very mixed, with bootleg scotch, fruit juice and beer getting into each glass. There were incidents, the last one of which, I very dimly recall, involved reporter Paul Callan having a lengthy conversation with Prince Charles, in which Callan spoke in a more-than-passable imitation of HRH, and which ended with the exchange:

'Ay say, are you taking the piss?'

'Taking the piss? – Ay should say so.'

At which point, the redoubtable Royal Marine took charge, and everyone was ordered off to bed.

To cleanse the mind and spirit, never mind the guts – for we were still not particularly well – the last part of the tour, for the Prince at least, was a trek in the Himalayas. With enormous relief, we realised we didn't have to be Action People alongside him, and after a visit to a couple of Gurkha training centres staffed by charming, otherworldly soldiers out of Kipling, we had a couple of days to ourselves. We went to see the nine-year-old Living Goddess, a jewel-bedecked little girl, chosen to live an isolated life as a religious icon – still just a local curiosity, not yet the subject of foreign TV documentaries – and we took the flight 'over the roof of the world' – past Everest and K2. For all the hassles of a royal tour, I couldn't get over the fact that we were getting the best-ever visit one could wish for, hanging on the coat-tails of privilege.

On the final leg, we flew to Pokhara, and stood in a scented landscape in the foothills of the Himalayas as the little party of trekkers approached us. We'd arranged that this should be one of the rare formal TV interviews. A slight awkwardness always hangs over these occasions, as the camera and sound are fiddled with and the reporter tries to think up a reasonable set of questions, preferably not kicking off with Had a Nice Time Then? It was early morning, and the light was difficult, Chris kept moving the camera around, and HRH tried not to end up squinting at us. I kept things fairly anodyne – no, let's be honest: I couldn't actually think of anything significant, searching or resonant to ask. But thank goodness, he launched into a lyrical little reflection on the trek, and I sighed with relief, only to realise that either he was growing taller, or I was shrinking. Unwilling to interrupt the flow, which was shaping up to a very useful insert to the last story on the tour, I looked down. I appeared to be standing in a bog. And sinking fast. By the time he stopped staring longingly towards the mountains in his reminiscences, I was in up to my calves.

'Are you – er – ?' he said.

'Yes,' I hissed, 'but keep talking.'

Royal tours are very odd.

We headed home. I collapsed in Delhi airport, and was carried on board a Japanese 747 by Chris. It wasn't our flight, but our connection from Kathmandu had been delayed for seventeen hours. I had advanced amoebic dysentery and my life was saved by a determined BBC cameraman, unfazed by airport officials, police and aircrew.

Still, I thought the tour was great.

Two years later, having been given the grand title of Court Correspondent, I found myself lumbered.

Every day into the newsroom came The Royal Diary: lists – from various branches of The Firm – of the public engagements of greater and lesser Windsors. Most of it was a mind-boggle of tedium, and at the very least you had to admire people who smiled and looked interested when confronted by an endless stream of health centres, school extensions, libraries, bridges and other municipal glories. Shake hands, say how pleased you are to be there, and tweak a tasselled cord to reveal a plaque telling you what you've just done. Events enlivened only by glimpsing engravers' mis-spelling '. . . opened by HRH The Princess Margarot . . .' and hearing the little velvet curtains swish closed before the photographers could refocus. Or by observing Princess Alexandra at a ground-breaking ceremony for a new sports centre, unveiling a brass plaque set into a tasteful arrangement of boulders, only for her departure to be delayed as she chatted to young athletes – considerate behaviour rewarded by the arrival of the bulldozer, and the clunk and the clang as plaque and boulders alike succumbed to its hungry jaws.

Watching royals was not as interesting as watching people watching royals. On the whole, your quarry did its duty; the event went with clockwork precision, five-minute regal loo-breaks included; and the story was a nightmare to write for the *Six O'Clock News*: Princess not poisoned by killer marmalade in Dundee factory. However, those who had waited – perhaps a lifetime – for that little moment in which they could say for evermore that they had met the Queen occasionally took leave from reality. The standard formula at most engagements was for the press party to observe the arrival, then be herded through

Receiving an honorary degree at Newcastle University

UNIVERSITY OF NEWCASTLE UPON TYNE

At Buckingham Palace to receive the OBE with my sister, Dianora Bond, and my mother Babe Dunnet

Flying with the Royal Navy at Culdrose in a 'teeny-weeny' – a Gazelle

With the RAF in Germany, after a stomach-challenging flight in a Harrier

Above the mountains of northern Iraq, on an RAF aid flight to Kurdish refugees, perched on the tailgate for the best view . . .

Flying in to Sarajevo in 1994 in an ancient ex-Soviet freighter carrying UK aid; seats, seat-belts, in-flight catering and life-jackets not provided. Plane, crew and passengers fuelled by vodka

On Prime Minister Margaret Thatcher's whistlestop tour of Africa in 1989 – one week, one continent: if this is Thursday, it must be Malawi

Bangladesh. Always take an orange box to stand on, advised an old hand – cameras attract crowds

With the Archbishop of Canterbury's envoy, Terry Waite, and ITN's Brent Sadler on one of the many shuttles to and from Libya during hostage negotiations in the mid-eighties

A reminder in Egypt that, however serious the story, somebody or something always walks into shot unannounced

Overlooking Tiananmen Square in Beijing, China, the day after the Chinese army moved against students demonstrating in the Square

With cameraman, Eric Thirer, deciding to travel to Xian to gauge reaction outside Beijing

Filming in a helicopter above the wreck of the ferry *Herald of Free Enterprise* just off Zeebrugge in 1987, with cameraman Wim Robberechts

Princess Diana's funeral: we'd spotted the Royal Family coming out of a side gate to Buckingham Palace – unannounced – and had to push a truck into position and hoist up the camera moments before the coffin went by, just managing to catch one of the most poignant images of the day

Armed with tickling sticks, and fund-raising for the Clatterbridge cancer charity in the Wirral, with Ken Dodd, 1996

side doors and staff entrances to the next photo-op. Like a genteel version of Dodgem Cars, we looped round buildings and gardens until we careered into the royal party coming the other way, always getting the speeches, and always missing the refreshments. However, along the way, we encountered excitement, glazed eyes and breathless amazement:

'She actually said she'd eaten marmalade before!'

'Can you imagine, he asked if we'd been waiting long!'

'We've got a photo of her – I was just six inches away!'

The police had a particular line in odd comment: 'You can't do that, royalty's coming.' In fact, this view was found in any official who felt that his meticulous planning was under threat from a bunch of scruffy and truculent journalists. Years previously, having spent three freezing hours hanging around Bath railway station for BBC Radio Bristol's morning show waiting for the Queen to arrive, I calculated that a visit to the loo had become the priority. I spied the correct door halfway down the platform and headed for it, only to find the way barred by an outraged station guard.

'Where are you going?' he demanded, and when I pointed to the sign on the door, he looked positively incandescent.

'Can't,' he said.

'Got to,' I replied.

'But it's . . .' he gasped.

'Going to,' I squeaked.

'But it's forbidden when THEY are in the station,' he shouted, as I successfully lunged through the door.

Sitting, relieved, I regretted failing to shout back that I thought it was when the bloody *train* was in the station . . .

Even more unsettling, in a way, was the gentle suffusion of happiness evident in rows of faces behind barriers. 'I saw her, I saw her.' Staid, prosaic citizens looked gently pole-axed, hugging their special moment to themselves. The Princess of Wales had this effect on all occasions. At her first-ever public speech, naming a lifeboat in Barmouth, her walkabout was accompanied by a curious mixture of blurted endearments and gobsmacked inarticulacy. The prince, on the other side of the street, was just beginning to come to terms with the effect his wife had on people. I found myself next to him, and nodded my head in her direction; he shrugged with that quizzical half-smile. He was clearly not entirely sure what kind of curious mass chemistry had been ignited.

Just over the boundary of harmless happiness lay besotted bum-licking. Far more than stark demands for a democratic republic, putting paid to medals and tiaras and garden parties and the Royal Variety Show (the latter *definitely* a republican vote-winner), the crawling and fawning was the real enemy of a modern monarchy. It was everywhere. I never understood the verb To Simper until I stood two yards from the royal family. The body language of those wishing for a word, or being presented, was a comedy of slightly hunched shoulders and heads inclined to one side, accompanied by a nose-wrinkling smirk. An ability To Shimmer was another verb which sprang to mind, as perfectly normal human bodies tried to imitate aspen trees, flattening themselves backwards into walls as royals passed by. Extra loud barks of laughter were also common to this behaviour. My God, the Family must be funny, judging by the shaking shoulders and nodding heads.

None of this was confined to any particular class or group in British society, and it extended to BBC senior editors, one of whom I observed following the Yorks around at a drinks party, nervously shifting chairs which one supposes might have caused them some unknown distress, and propelling meeker members of the newsroom Yorkwards, blocking the way of the noisier hacks who'd discovered the BBC was serving real champagne instead of the usual transmitter fuel.

And all of this backed up by a long tradition of treacle in the media. To which I contributed. Not a lot – and I have my excuses – but *mea culpa*.

Daily news reporting didn't present too many problems – just stick to the boring facts, and keep it short. It was the 'tour specials' where I came undone. For ruthless budgetary reasons, the expense of following a tour began to be offset by delivering a half-hour or even hour-long programme to the network. This was the stuff of nightmares. A dish to be served with no meat whatsoever. Whatever bits of the journey had been amusing or unusual, or had got out of the control of palace officials, had usually been missed on camera. Wonderful bits of gossip and salacious titbits about the royal party and merry incidents involving drunken reporters, unspeakable scenes in hotel rooms, and rows between everyone due to frustration, drink and dysentery were inadmissible in a Sunday afternoon transmission aimed at complementing tea and crumpets. As the tour drew to a close, there was the looming sight of several dozen video cassettes containing arrivals, greetings, etc., etc. piled on a hotel bedroom table, and being viewed by a picture editor with a face set in misery.

Gordon, our producer, a man of great experience and matchless optimism, would try to soothe our worries.

'There's lots in here,' he'd say, 'great stuff, really colourful.'

'You're lying,' we'd reply.

Fortified by several bottles of wine, we'd spend hours stringing together the disparate visits to war memorials, machine-tool factories and cattle shows. Anything remotely involving music was plastered into the edit. Then came the nasty moment when I had to write the linking commentary. You'd think I was composing *Seven Pillars of Wisdom* or *War and Peace*, scribbling line upon line, then crossing it all out, going for a walk, looking desperately at Gordon and saying, 'Is there no more music you can shove in?'

Eventually, inevitably, I fell back into the syrup: 'At the end of another stimulating day in this fascinating land, their Highnesses were clearly delighted to blah blah blah . . .'

Professional weakness, made so much worse when people wrote in afterwards to say how much they'd loved the programmes.

Thankfully, the national newsroom in London was only interested in major events, or in following a particular royal who was already in the news, usually for all the wrong reasons. The royals goofed, you pursued. But every so often there was a slow news day, and you were cornered into collecting your rota pass which – nominally – prevented you being shoved around too much by the police, and allowed you to join the huddle of hacks on royal watch, usually in a roped-off pen half the necessary size, and at the wrong angle for seeing anything useful. The chief joy of these occasions was the gossip. In the first month, I drank deeply of the experienced hacks' knowledge of the House of Windsor. It was a specialised area of journalism in which verified fact and witnessed evidence had only visiting roles. Proof of any story was constituted through consensus. If two or more hacks decided that a royal had done something, the story got legs and ran in the papers.

They all had 'sources' – 'highly placed insiders', as they were referred to in print. I hovered on the fringe of muttered asseverations about Him and Her and You Know Who, my ears flapping happily, and noting that chambermaids, whom I'd hitherto not realised were 'highly placed', were a valuable crop which had been cultivated assiduously. The gossip was truly wonderful; I'd had no idea They led such interesting lives. There was a cod-scientific approach to the specimens beneath the gaze of the lens, coupled with a concern not to upset the petri dish lest these fine generators of acres of newsprint and miles of video should cease to wriggle publicly. Every appearance, every movement was scrutinised minutely.

'He's pulling at his ear again – think he's getting no sleep?'

'Seen that hat before – could run my piece on palace economies.'

'She's staring at us – d'you think she saw my story on gin versus scotch?'

I listened to the lore of the Royal Crested Hacks and felt inadequate. Even if I knew how to cultivate chambermaids – which I didn't – ninety-eight per cent of the information gleaned would be of no use to a BBC news bulletin. For the Corporation was ambivalent in its attitudes. On the one hand, I'd been give the job with a stern lecture that 'real journalism' was what was wanted; on the other, I immediately learned that anything which remotely hinted at pertinent but hitherto unrevealed information was to be held at the end of a long bargepole until investigated by sundry senior editors. Whether they were checking with chambermaids was unclear, but unlikely.

ITN's correspondent – the delightful Tony Carthew, gifted with felicitous phrases such as 'The Queen Mother in yet another variation of Paddington Bear's hat' – and myself were therefore slightly out of step with the rest of the pack. We were stuck with the formal round of events, unable to report candidly on some of the underlying realities because we could never get confirmation of stories. The occasional murmured 'guidance' from a press officer was the only official source, and even that, on occasion, was later denied. The BBC in particular exhibited nervousness, which to this day causes royal stories to be treated, at the very least, in a different tone from the rest of its journalism. I had been spared full-time consignment to the court beat, having negotiated to keep myself available for general reporting duties between royal jaunts, and although this kept my sanity, it pointed up the suspension of judgement that was inherent in the royal-watching. And there were always the Tours.

There was only one tiny drawback to going on a royal tour. I never found out *why* they took place. They seemed to be a kind of horizontal mountaineering. 'Her Majesty is going to Canada because it's *there*.'

Months of planning, every day the itinerary plotted to the last detail (Royal Party to move to Dais, Posy received, Open Land Rover to be ready, Posy to be placed on Land Rover front passenger seat), every location recce'd, all reception lines and guest lists checked. A tour is a logistics iceberg, seven-eighths of submerged palace and diplomatic sweat, one-eighth visible serene hat and gloved hand.

Before we all set off, there would be a briefing in Buckingham Palace, and we'd scan through the printed details, desperately hoping for more than the formal round and the thunderously mundane. However, time and again we learned that everyone got their oar in during preparations to ensure that the risky, the unusual and, God forbid, the unexpected were planned out of existence.

In Canada, after an especially non-riotous morning in a large brick shed masquerading as a community centre in the middle of nowhere, I asked one of the Canadian officials why Her Majesty wasn't going down the nearby silver mine.

'She's been there,' he replied. 'Three times.'

'There's the fish-hatchery then?' I'd conscientiously read the brochures on the bus journey.

'She's seen it.'

'The ski-lift?'

'What would she do?'

'Well, how about the Ukrainian settlement and its cultural stuff?'

'You think she's Ukrainian?'

We spent hours in mini-buses, hours on planes, hours on pavements, observing the plod of the traditional tour, and growing uncomfortably aware that we should have been reporting an undercurrent of apathy beneath flags and state protocol. Phrases such as cheering crowds and enthusiastic well-wishers were not inaccurate, but closer inspection easily revealed the elderly, British-rooted nature of those behind the police barriers. And the country was hardly alight with the kind of adulation which had greeted a young monarch seeing her Commonwealth after the Coronation all those years ago. But as ever, the journalistic noses had taken a severe rubbing in the mud early in the trip, and the relationship between palace and press was brittle, causing normal reporting habits to be blunted. A Toronto journalist, Caitlin Kelly – niece of veteran BBC radio stars Bernard Braden and Barbara Kelly – had written a perfectly reasonable article after having followed the first week of the tour. She described the Queen as dowdy, wearing clothes one's grandmother would be ashamed to be seen in in public. Indeed, when we'd been at the airport for the Arrival Shot, the experienced Crested Reptiles had remarked, 'Why is she wearing that old thing?' – a suit clearly dragged out of the back of the capacious wardrobe, with an odd hemline and just a wee bit tight. This had been followed by other none-too-fresh-looking creations. Be that as it may, the wrath which the article provoked in the palace party indicated a treasonable offence having been perpetrated. The papers back in the UK picked up the story immediately, and demanded that their hacks on the spot confirm that some crazed half-blind Canadian had dared to question royal taste. The hacks squirmed. Caitlin was a personable and intelligent reporter, who'd only pointed out the obvious.

One of the invisible traces which reined in the conventional reporting of royals had been kicked over. And, as the clothes saga rumbled on, it became clear that any other hint that all was not sweetness and light on the tour would get a hostile reaction, both from palace officials and from the editors back home. It was like being in school, with your loyalty questioned, and the threat of privileges being withdrawn. I knew just what kind of reaction I could expect from my lot in London – if you could have heard them above the strains of the national anthem.

Even so, there was no evidence that a tour did harm; to the contrary, most of the events brought pleasure to those attending, satisfaction to small towns and thrills to those who shook hands, and confirmed that civilised behaviour supports a thousand causes and charities and enterprises. Admittedly there were silly bits of protocol, clichéd formal speeches without passion, and upheaval and security beyond justification. Worthiness and duty were on show – but who is to say that such matters are to be consigned to history?

The only nagging doubt was that the serious underlying questions were never addressed. What was the tour *for*? What did anyone mean by it being declared 'successful'? When an Italian Canadian eyed the Queen going walkabout among a mostly indifferent crowd in Little Italy in Toronto, why were tour officials horrified when the signora asked: 'Wassa that woman doing here?'

Musing on the ramifications of constitutional constipation took up only a small amount of the royal hacks' time. Interestingly, the only tabloid reporter who knocked off shrill headlines *and* gave serious thought to what the future held was the man from the *Star*. Tall, with slightly owlish glasses, he'd ponder on the unspoken problems which these tours papered over, asking if I thought he was barking up the right tree. I told him I thought he was; a decade and a book later Andrew Morton shook that tree with great consequences.

But to be perfectly honest, most of us were having too interesting a time to brood. Tours were fun – so long as you had stamina, a good supply of pills and an ability to find a loo without being left behind as the motorcade left town. And you had to hand it to the royals: you'd never want their job. The repetitiveness, the politeness needed, the small-talk, the ghastly pushy local politicians, the tedious banquets, the dreary ceremonies. The knowledge that someone is waiting for you to put just one foot wrong . . . us, actually.

In 1983, slumped in the back of the royal Airbus after a ten-hour flight from Kenya to Bangladesh, I stared out as we taxied towards a red carpet at Dhaka airport. It was nearly midnight locally. Cameras were scrambled for, bits of clothing located, until one of the reporters found his close-printed tour guide which announced that it was 'an unofficial welcome, with a small low-level delegation, prior to Presidential welcome tomorrow'. We got ready for an efficient getaway, only to notice the line formed along the red carpet. As the Queen and Prince Philip descended from the aircraft, we counted 136 eager Bangladeshis, each waiting to give them a low-key unofficial welcome. 'Sometimes,' said an admiring hack watching the prolonged handshakes, 'I know why Princess Margaret behaves as she does.'

It was a lengthy tour, Kenya, Bangladesh and India, culminating in the Commonwealth Heads of Government Conference.

The Queen attacked it with briskness, undoubtedly fuelled by the intention to arrive in Delhi Totally in Charge and Fancy You Being Here Mrs Thatcher.

Kenya had gone smoothly, though not quite according to the plans of the sentimental wing of the press brigade. On the itinerary was the famous hunting-lodge at Treetops, where in 1952, as Princess Elizabeth, she'd learned of her father's death. The hacks had already committed thousands of words to print in advance of what they saw as 'one of the most poignant moments for the Queen – ever', before we trekked across a rather barren landscape to view a small watering hole overshadowed by the treehouse. After heated negotiations with the press secretary, one reporter, one photographer, and two TV cameras sneaked discreetly up on to the viewing platform high in the tree to witness this momentous and emotional occasion.

The *Daily Mail* edged quietly towards the royal couple, ear on a stalk, notebook ready.

Prince Philip was leaning over the rail, laughing. 'Serves them damn well right,' he announced. Below, our press colleagues were imitating a herd of unhappy but speedy wildebeest, legging it from the waterhole as a bad-tempered water-buffalo rocked towards them.

There was then a silence. The *Daily Mail* tried to be invisible, craning nearer for Her Majesty's memory to be poignantly awakened.

'Did we come here?'

Her words hung crisply in the warm air.

Prince Philip didn't reply. Then he scanned the waterhole area again, clearly hoping to spy a few buffalo-trampled remains.

'They've chopped down all the bloody trees,' he said.

Your average sentimental softies, the royals ain't. Whether it's inbred or just training is a moot point. However, it is very occasionally possible to have a stab at being royal oneself.

We had just completed a marathon through Gambia and Upper Volta, led by Princess Anne as President of the Save the

Children Fund. Sand, sandflies and a slightly tense atmosphere dominated the trip. The photographers were immersed in a serious game of trying to get a single picture which included a child and the princess within less than three feet of each other, and the princess was winning. Her private secretary and I had had a few words about our filming her meeting the President of Upper Volta, Captain Thomas Sankhara. Political sensitivities were surfacing. What was the need for us to take these pictures? The journalist normally buried in me during royal tours surfaced briefly. 'Murder,' I replied; 'African military rulers have a short shelf-life – the pictures will come in handy for the obituary.' And so they did, not a long time later.

After the princess's aircraft took off in a cloud of sand from the wonderfully named town of Gorom Gorom, we headed back to the capital Ougadougou for a night in a smart French hotel, an obscene building rising above a wasteland of wretched poverty, where the only vehicles were those belonging to aid agencies, and where the vultures flapped at the hotel's double-glazing, which was preventing them from reaching the only plump people in town. I'd reckoned that a rail journey might prove a more interesting way to start the homeward journey south to the coast – especially as Air Volta was having a bit of a problem with its left-hand engine when we'd last flown upcountry in its entire fleet a few days earlier. The rail tickets were bought the next morning, with our anxious enquiries about the train leaving on time that afternoon being met with the ultimate reply: 'When can you get here?'

Perhaps that was where the little problem was born.

We boarded *The Antelope* at four – and it moved off immediately: a wonderful survivor of French colonial days, faded blue paint and threadbare interior, staffed by impeccable ancient waiters. Dinner was simple, but served with elaborate care and attentiveness, the can of cola brought on a frayed laundered napkin on a bent metal tray, *s'il vous plaît* with a little bow and a smile. The barrenness – horrible evidence of the desertification of sub-Saharan Africa – swished by. Again and again we'd heard middle-aged Voltaic villagers recall growing up in a dense green landscape; now the country was literally blowing away into sand. In our bare couchette compartment, the sheets detergent-stiff but paper-thin, we went to sleep, aware that *The Antelope* behaved as its namesake, speeding along the rails in an undulating lope.

That is, until the border town of Dangouadoudou. Or possibly Wangolodoudou. We were asleep as our compartment door was slid back by officials, and we peered out at the platform, where we could dimly make out men in uniform. We hunted in the dark for passports, but these didn't seem to be what was wanted, and the officials disappeared. The train was silent, motionless. Just dropping off to sleep again, I heard Bill Nicol, our cameraman, come in from the corridor and say in an expressionless voice:

'I think you'd better come out here.'

Christ, I thought, we're in the middle of an African coup. Then he added, 'Take your time, and get a clean shirt, this train's not going anywhere until . . .'

Until what? I burrowed around, half-dressed, and emerged into the corridor. Lined up on the platform under dim orange lighting were about eight soldiers. Their captain snapped them to attention.

'Oh no,' I said.

'Well,' said Bill, 'if you don't, we'll be here for ever.'

I raised the right hand, palm inwards, and described the little circle which denotes The Gracious Wave. The captain saluted, and the train drew gently out of the station.

Royal tours are fun.

TEN

Alarums and excursions

Never having dreamed of becoming a reporter, I had no plans, no great desires, no burning ambitions. It seems odd now, especially as journalism has become fashionable and there are thousands of media students mapping out their careers and wondering whether to get their teeth fixed. Nor did I consider that my work was heading in a particular direction; the daily round was still something of a surprise, and we reporters were rarely *chosen* for an assignment – instead, a story came up, and got tossed to the hounds.

It was Arthur Scargill, I believe, who put an end to my spell of full-time royal duty. By 1985 the miners' strike was absorbing a large chunk of the newsroom's resources, and I was one of the pack of reporters watching grown men thumping each other at dawn on picket lines. Some days the miners won, some days the police won; the journalists were permanent losers, because our presence was deeply resented by everyone. However, it wasn't the bitter shenanigans at the pithead which had impinged on my job so much as a rather more restrained altercation between the Queen and a journalist in the newsroom of *The Times*.

Her Majesty was visiting the newspaper on the occasion of its bicentenary, examining the hacks tapping away industriously and followed by a shoal of nervous executives clearly praying to the Almighty that normal journalistic behaviour would not mar their great day. Then the Queen stopped to peer over the shoulder of a particularly preoccupied typist. She addressed him, twice, and slowly he got to his feet. We watched from a distance, our cameras having been made less than welcome by the newspaper's press officers. A pantomime then ensued, as the hack and the Queen embarked on a lively exchange which we could not hear, but which had all the marks of something going rather pear-shaped. The hack had squared his shoulders and was jabbing a finger vigorously in the air. His monarch had taken up an equally determined pose, and finally jabbed her own gloved finger at him. The posse of executives a yard away were showing signs of silent collective hysteria. Then the Queen walked off very smartly – and the management team tripped imploringly in pursuit, passing the reporter with looks that spelled 'Kill'.

During the following confusing five minutes, the *Times* hack was niftily whisked on to a fire escape by a BBC radio reporter while the TV cameras had a scrum with assorted press officers. It emerged that in reply to the Queen's enquiry as to the nature of the hack's fevered typing, he had eventually made a remark to the effect that there was a strike on, or hadn't she noticed? The subsequent exchange was crisp and opinionated, and apparently involved HM remarking very forcefully that it was 'all about one man now'.

I listened to the radio tape and clattered down the fire escape to the TV van parked outside, writing the story of royal comment on (presumably) Arthur Scargill with just fifteen minutes to go to the start of the one o'clock news. I called the newsroom to warn them the visit had actually produced a story – to be met not with eager anticipation, but by voices shot through with apprehension and not a little panic. I'd heard it before: that peculiar noise made by perfectly intelligent people who have a curious trigger inside them which appears to be attached to the words Treasonable Offence. Logic, reason and common sense are swept aside by the possibility of *lèse-majesté*, and the Corporation is found a-cringe.

Could I possibly rewrite the story without reference to the miners' strike?

At five to one I threw in the Royal Towel.

Later that day I had a civilised conversation with Michael Shea, the Queen's press secretary, who was totally unruffled by the incident – as was his boss, he intimated. 'Just what gets into the BBC at times?' he said.

'Ermine-trimmed funk,' I replied – and returned to a quieter life on the picket line.

I began to realise that in among the pay disputes and pools winners, the stories with a darker hue were occupying more time, and were also a more satisfying challenge. We're in the business of bad news not because we're ghouls, but because we're realists. Ignore what is happening in the world, and it will arrive on your doorstep with an unwelcome present. Take no notice of accident, crime and deprivation – and they will never be avoided or remedied in the future.

The nature of fear had begun to interest me – not in an academic manner; just the effect it had, not least on me. It never ceases to amaze me that I'm asked if I've ever felt frightened, for I've now reached a point when I recognise in myself different types – and grades – of fear.

Curiously, there seems to be an assumption that reporters gad about the world wrapped in a protective layer of press armour; that they are somehow immune from the hurly-burly, that the maddened crowd will sweep down the boulevard intent on revolution, suddenly to swerve aside – Pardon us, we see you're journalists – and leave you be. That the sniper squints around the hills and sees the camera crew walking into the enemy village – and puts the safety catch on, saying: Aha, but it's the press, they are not fair game.

Oh yes, we are. And it's been getting worse, as television has spread around the globe, and has come to be seen by the most primitive gun-toting angry man as part of the action. It's true that journalists have always aroused suspicion, especially in conflicts, but now the TV camera has come to represent a participant.

I would never have set off on any assignment if I'd been so seized by fear that it occupied my waking thoughts and ruled every decision. Knowledge – more to the point, acknowledgement – of what may lie ahead is essential; but letting the imagination run wild does not help. Few reporters ever view a scene which has not occurred a thousand times in history, and one of the most redundant phrases ever uttered by a journalist must be: I have never seen anything like this before in my life. It may well be the truth at the time – but a million others will have seen such things, merely lacking a camera or a tape-recorder, or never having had the chance to tell. The more I saw of contemporary violence, the more I went to the history books, for nothing was new under the sun.

Talking about these matters is never simple. I found that friends listened, but didn't quite follow what I was banging on about. Trying to explain it to family was an even more hopeless task. After four years in the national newsroom, and then all through the eighties, I realised that people found my job rather odd. I went back to the north-east every few months, driving up the A1 in my newly issued official reporter's car – an incredibly boring Ford Escort which had replaced my treasured sports beast. I'd graduated from MG Midget to MGB GT to TR7, only to discover that reporting meant parking near riots; so I'd reluctantly acquired the Escort and anonymity. This puzzled those at home – clearly I was going nowhere in the BBC in my little runabout. I also found that most people assumed that reporting for the BBC should be a round of glamorous locations filled with charming people, and absolutely no one had a clue why I seemed to relish the idea of going to Northern Ireland.

Northern Ireland taught me one of the simpler aspects of fear: that threats issued in your own language are far more frightening than anything delivered in a foreign language by people who look different. Surreal moments occur in Zaïrean police stations and Arab back alleys, when the journalists look at each other and say:

'That finger across the throat stuff – do they really mean it?'

'Er, maybe, but they're all jabbering away and it might just be their way of asking for quiet . . .'

Going into your bedroom at the Europa Hotel in Belfast, having just got off the plane from London, to find the phone ringing and a voice saying 'We know you're here . . .' is a different matter, and it took me a couple of visits before I'd reply tartly, 'That's good, now how about a bit of room service, with yourself minced up on a plate?' before banging down the receiver and heading quickly for the bar.

Threats, insults and obscenities strike home much more when spoken on your own territory, though I have to say that Britain has been the only place which goes in for spitting, a feature of the miners' strike. What also strike home are the various objects with which rioters equip themselves. Berlin has the kind of small cobblestones invented for a good confrontation with the forces of law and order – though you'd be advised not to head straight for police lines, as they have terrifying water-cannon capable of jetting people through plate-glass windows. It makes for great pictures – theoretically, I should say, for £20,000 cameras are not waterproof. Belgium makes a virtue out of flour-bags and tomatoes, courtesy of farmers' protests; the Belgian police once replied to these relatively benign missiles by charging their horses through rush-hour traffic and vaulting them over car-bonnets. Great pictures, again – well, would have been, but we were running for our lives. Danish football fans patriotically hurl Carlsberg bottles – having drunk the contents; whereas the English fans realise too late that they've been served with lager in cans.

In Warrenpoint in County Down, a group of Northern Irish protesters rounded a corner unexpectedly, and the sky was thick with objects as we sought cover. For a foolish moment I stared into the air, then fell flat on my back with the world gone dark. For a few seconds, supine, I reviewed the possibilities, while the crowd thundered past. Been shot? Blind for life? Face blown away? Strange – the rest of me seemed to be functioning, and I could hear the riot growing in volume as the protesters met the RUC at the bottom of the hill. I could also hear my cameraman shouting: 'Get up, you silly bitch, it's all going on, and you're just lying there.'

I sat up, dazed.

'I've been hit,' I said pathetically, waiting for a shred of sympathy. ''Course you have,' he said, 'by a potato.'

We learned to be nimble, keeping out of the way when tempers frayed. Never mixing it with demonstrators and protesters, avoiding any remark or comment that a group of highly charged people will take up and use against you. You avoid iron railings, shop windows and bridges – crowds are both blind and mean-spirited at times. Carrying a two-way radio is a red rag to a bull – you're immediately ranged with authority, and anyway they never worked properly in a riot. You park camera cars and links vehicles in discreet positions – a point completely lost on BBC Engineering, who in 1981 memorably positioned a large BBC van full of expensive equipment midway between the cops and the Brixton rioters, and wondered why both lots vented their spleen on it. Above all, you don't take sides. It may be that you're forced to work behind one lot, such is the animosity of the opposition; but in theory, you should try to get round to the other. However, theory goes to the dogs when you get bottled or arrested.

The theory also goes that if both sides are equally hostile to the press, you've somehow got it right, though this can have its downside, as in the disturbances outside Rupert Murdoch's newspaper plant at Wapping. The print-workers traditionally reserved a special contempt for journalists, whom they regarded as the poncing layabout part of their industry. At the same time, the Metropolitan Police were in a Stuff the Press mood – that was the phrase I heard as I took a printer's swipe on the ear one Saturday night, followed by a posse of men in blue bending me backwards over a railing and going for my ribs. A sore ear and two cracked ribs later in Charing Cross Hospital, a nurse enquired, 'Who did it?'

'Both sides,' I said.

'That's all right then,' she said, and swished off.

No old hand sets off towards a major disturbance with anything other than apprehension, and a terrific set of legs for running away.

One of the curiosities of rioting is the extent to which it's fun, a devilish observation which I nonetheless hold to. Large numbers of people who manage to keep out of real trouble and avoid injury can have the time of their lives. The exhilarating mood as the crowd gets going, the sense of shared purpose, of cocking a snook rather than doing real damage, the excitement of a chase and the childish glee at an overturned car and a smashed shop window, all conspire to provide a great day out. There is frequently a near-carnival atmosphere before a small incident ignites real violence and sours the atmosphere. For over an hour in Brixton, in the second of a summer of riots in 1981, we were entertained by a succession of speeches, songs, and finally a man dancing precariously on top of a traffic bollard, stark naked. Applause and laughter, intertwined with a sense of mischief – no more – were enough initially to express the social frustrations. All crowds have a character; and if you read it right, then the energy need not boil over into viciousness. Crowds with a common purpose, especially a serious one, discipline themselves, for at the outset they merely want to kick up a fuss and be noticed. I'm not belittling the mayhem which usually occurs, nor the true distress and damage that can be done, but time and again it's obvious to those standing to one side that it is possible to avoid the battle-lines being drawn, if only we all care to keep our nerve – and temper – and sacrifice a window or two.

In Northern Ireland there even seemed to be an unspoken set of rules, which had come about after years of street troubles. There was a deeply dishonourable understanding involving everyone – the army, the RUC, the rioters of both sides, and the press. We didn't film close-ups, or identify individuals; we avoided pinpointing prominent individuals – generals or terrorists; and we usually knew when a street rumble was turning into a dangerous fight: the age of the rioters changed, children and young teenagers melting back into their houses at an invisible signal, while the lean and shadowy 'boyos' took the stage. At times, riots resembled ritual tribal outings. However, I have never subscribed to the idea that the cameras were the cause; not once did I witness a disturbance that was anything other than an eruption of deeply felt bigotry, an emotion imbibed with mother's milk, and ready to flow at the least provocation; a camera was an irrelevance.

Riots also end quite mysteriously. We were running round the Short Strand one evening, with bottles and bricks and baton rounds and bits of furniture sailing overhead, when everything came to a sudden halt. We were nonplussed as the streets emptied, leaving a smouldering car and the usual heap of debris. Our sound recordist, a Belfast lad, was packing up and heading for the car. 'How do you know it's over?' I asked.

'Kick-off's in five minutes,' he said, 'Rangers are going to get beat.'

I learned to follow the fortunes of Glasgow's football teams – each with sectarian fans in Belfast – and work out when we could depend on a night off.

The appearance of a gun amid the stones and bottles changes everything. Then there is no mischief, just determination. In Beirut, it appeared that everyone was armed, for the civil war in the 1980s involved everyone. We had a number of brave – and paternalistic – drivers who worked for the foreign television companies, and who undertook to drive our video over the Chouf mountains for transmission from Syria, the Lebanese TV stations having succumbed to sustained fire. On my first morning in the city, I was getting my bearings at five o'clock by peering over the bedroom windowsill in the Commodore Hotel, watching a tank rattle past. There was no indication whether it was on its way to war or to a filling station, so I went back to checking that I'd got all my baggage from the airport.

Our arrival on the local MEA airline, one wing down, the other skywards, had been a bit rushed. As the Ferris wheel signalling happier times in the city went past the cabin window at an odd angle, the chief steward, who'd earlier been handing out business cards for his family's restaurants in West Beirut ('wonderful cuisine, forget the war'), made an announcement:

'Ladies and gentlemen, we are on final approach to Beirut airport. As there is a little activity involving rockets near the terminal building, please be so kind as to leave your hand baggage behind. It will be delivered later. When the aircraft touches down it will taxi very near to the terminal. Please make your way to the door at the front of the aircraft, then run like fuck.'

The baggage had been delivered, and I thought the airline impressive.

One of the drivers knocked at my door well before breakfast, and said I ought to have a look at the city before things got busy. (He didn't say what sort of busy.) We hurtled off into a glorious morning, with Beirut embarking on a frenetic show of normality amid chaos. Shopkeepers polished what windows they had, and swept round wrecked cars and barricades. Vegetables and fruit were being hefted in sacks through holes in walls to make elegant displays, and restaurants were splashing water on the pavement. In the distance, there was the odd crackle of small-arms fire.

'All very usual,' said Mohammed, 'but trouble later, so you must be prepared.' He bounced his bullet-scarred Mercedes through narrow alleys and stopped in front of what looked like an enormous hardware shop. The proprietor beetled out – the driver's cousin, as ever in the Middle East – and orange juice and cola were summoned. It was only then that I realised it wasn't pot and pans hanging from the rafters, but a huge array of rifles, pistols, ammo belts and God knows what else.

'You need a gun,' said Mohammed bluntly.

'I do not.'

'Just a little one,' he wheedled.

There followed a complicated conversation, in which it was clear that Mohammed genuinely had my best interests at heart, rather than a sale for his cousin. I ran out of excuses, the idea that journalists were unarmed being regarded as laughable in a city where the local press were active members of various militias. I decided to try another tack, to prove how risible the whole situation was.

'Have you got a tank?'

Mohammed's cousin looked skywards, arched his brows, and said:

'What sort you want – Russian – American – or perhaps I could do you a British?'

Mohammed had good reason to be concerned. The streets erupted that afternoon, and one of the militia groups had a dreadful argument with our hotel management, demanding to use the empty swimming pool as a defensive position.

It was an instructive conflict: the Israelis bombed, the Americans shelled, and the locals were at other's throats. We shifted about the city with difficulty. I had no knowledge whatsoever of weapons and their capabilities. I hadn't a clue how far a rifle bullet could go, and I had no understanding of the basic techniques of guerrilla warfare. I couldn't exactly put a finger on which part of my education should have included this stuff, and I wasn't quite sure where you acquired it.

One lunchtime, at no discernible signal, our part of West Beirut began to fall quiet. We had been conducting an interview in the hotel, and I strolled across the lobby to see people scuttling indoors and shopkeepers pulling down steel shutters. The traffic vanished, and about four streets away a tank mysteriously trundled over an intersection. There was the odd pop of gunfire in the distance, and then all hell broke loose in the hotel lobby. I disappeared into a phone booth, and other guests hit the floor as several young men raced through the building. Two of them then started a nasty fight next to the reception desk – and right outside there was a noisy spray of automatic fire.

This is the moment when you do not look for your cameraman and decide on the best camera position, or make an assessment of the scenario and plan a course of action. You sit, foetal-curled, on the floor of the phone booth, shit-scared and swearing, with your gaze darting from one noise to another. And events do not explain themselves – nothing makes sense as gunmen scream and posture, and the fight gets joined by another young man, and through the glass front doors you can see men crouched and firing down the street. Get caught in real action, and you get very little sense of what's happening, and very little footage – if any.

As quickly as it started, it was over, with no information as to what had sparked it all off. The firing moved away, but the streets remained empty. And the swimming-pool militia unit had reappeared and were busy counting ammunition.

After an hour I wondered if we should get our interview edited in the building across the side street, an alley all of four yards wide. If the story was to make it out to Syria that evening, then I had to start work now. I stood at the side door, listening hard. Little bunches of rat-a-tats came from streets maybe half a mile away. But the very occasional single shot came straight down the alley.

I clutched the video cassette and could not make a decision. It would take just one second – maybe two – to dash across. I stood for at least twenty minutes and just one bullet whizzed past. I could neither find the right logic to work out the risk, nor summon the impulse to go like a greyhound out of the trap.

Eventually an American colleague, Rick Davies of the US network NBC, saw me, and I told him I couldn't decide what to do. 'Here,' he said casually, 'I'll take it,' and ran across without incident. I couldn't even follow him. Such a trivial problem – and I had to admit to myself that I couldn't find the guts to act.

Two days later another afternoon of mayhem started up. This time Chris Marlowe and I were in the street outside, filming, as a car suddenly tried to turn out of the main street down the alley and stopped right in the middle of the crossroads. The air was loud with shots; peering out from the back seat of the car were two elderly women. We saw immediately that the driver, who'd been taking his wife and sister on a shopping run, had been hit in the head by a bullet. I don't know how long it was before the two women were pulled out of the car, one screaming and trying to get over into the front seat and shake the old man, the other rigid – all stout tangled legs and hanging on to her large handbag. Brute force was the only answer, I decided, for persuasion would not be heard above the racket and both were demented with terror. All the while, Chris filmed, as gunmen scooted like rats hither and thither. Very unceremoniously, I delivered one old lady in a heap into a clump of arms in the hotel entrance and made a lunge for the second one, who was about to wander off. I shunted her to the doorway, and fell flat on the road as something went bang loud and near. I then found myself like a fish on a slab, unable to move, and feeling glassy-eyed. The world moved off, distanced itself a bit, and the sound level went down. Maybe twenty seconds later, I gradually realised that lying flat on the pavement six yards away was my colleague Rick from NBC. He was bellowing at me – and at first I couldn't focus on what he wanted, for I felt very detached, and frozen to the spot. He flapped his hands, and I tried to concentrate – to hear him shouting: 'Come on, crawl to daddy – just crawl over here, you can do it.'

Ah, I thought, OK, not a bad idea, just crawl, well – why not? And I edged towards him, so that when I was in grabbing distance, I was thrown to safety like a large old trout. I rolled over, sat up, and the entire world came back with a roar – the shooting, the screaming, the noise of gunmen yelling – and then we noticed Chris standing in the middle of the road coolly still filming the car. Rick and I headed for him, to find he was immovable, so we just heaved him up like a shop window model and carried him rigid into the hotel.

Fear does odd things to you, and being in possession of all your senses is not guaranteed; bits of your brain keep working – but not always the useful parts.

The very sophistication and élan which Beirut displayed, even while in the grip of violence, could be deceptive for newcomers. On the first evening I decided to admire the view, and stood on the balcony entranced with the mountains in the distance, the sprawl of the ochre-yellow city at sunset, the restaurants shunting out menu-signs in defiance of war – only to give a little squeak when what seemed like a large insect took advantage of my wearing shorts. On my shin was a dark runnel of blood, and I felt bruised. Lying next to my shoe was a small bullet, a ricochet partly blunted. Standing staring at sunsets is a very daft thing to do in a war zone.

Our correspondent in the city was Jim Muir, whom I'd first encountered when he was a rugby-playing boy at Sedbergh School in Cumbria, and I'd been cheering on a boyfriend who didn't have Jim's wiry athletic build. In Beirut, he'd acquired some of the local insouciance, announcing one morning that we had a lunch invitation from some friends of his. As a jeepful of gun-waving militia overtook us, our driver undertook a rally-course round the back streets. 'Hang on,' said Jim, and was out of the car like a ferret. I lay on the back seat, wondering why we had stopped in a fire-zone outside a flower shop. For flowers, of course; Jim dived back into the car with a marvellous bouquet in spotted cellophane, exquisitely prinked with ribbon by the girl behind the counter – on the floor behind the counter. We had delicious food with an urbane and cultivated Lebanese family, who, as the afternoon wore on to the chorus of gunfire, suggested

Scrabble – in English, their third language – at which they soundly beat us.

Scrabble passed the time well enough on many a morning when the street fighting intensified, though during one game a rocket-propelled grenade bit a chunk off our balcony. We both rose into the air involuntarily and flew several feet to crash against the wall. The explosion made my ears sing – but every cloud has, as they say, a silver lining; for at least it made me have a hearing test when I returned home, to discover that the BBC had for years been employing a woman to record studio sound who was congenitally partially deaf in both ears. Ah well – at least I hadn't deceived them, though years before someone had remarked to me that amateur lip-reading isn't something that everyone goes in for.

Everything about Beirut at that time was madness faced with iron determination to conduct life according to some civilised rules. The shops, the banks, the money-changers chattering into radios, the restaurants touting for business, the hotel blithely serving breakfast in its coffee shop amid an inch of solidified fire-extinguisher foam on everything (Ah, madam, just a small fire – whole kitchen gone, but why wake our guests?), while heavily armed men slid around the street corners and tanks were more frequent than buses. A young gunman who appeared to have clout in our district – and whose Beiruti appreciation of elegant dressing led him to be known in our office as Designer-Guerrilla – often used to inform us of likely difficulties: 'small shootings after dinner maybe'. I went off him when he arrived one morning and insisted on shaking hands, passing me a grenade with the pin partly loose. I handed it back with as much dignity as someone can manage whose intestines have just knotted and sunk, saying 'Please, no presents.'

I then went shopping – it's always good therapy – and I was just turning into the main street and peering at the kind of diamanté-studded cocktail-dress tart-wear that represents 'the little black dress' in Arab culture, when the AK-47s started off yet again. One thing I have learned is that it's only in films that it's possible to tell where the stuff is coming from – or who it's aimed at. Under most circumstances it's anyone's guess, so dropping to the floor seems the least worst idea. On the pavement, I spotted three men waving frantically to me from a shop doorway, so I crabbed towards them, the thick metal shutters of the shop dropping behind me as I went in. All three fussed around me, offered coffee and fresh *confiseries*, and apologised for their fellow citizens' intemperate behaviour. Charming strangers, who calmed me down in the gloom of their shuttered emporium. Thus I found myself stuck – and in heaven – in Beirut's largest shoe shop. Three full hours of battle raged outside while I went through every pair of shoes in the basement. Finally, when the coast was clear, I staggered back to the hotel with three boxes of elegant shoes. The other journalists looked up from the bar enquiringly: 'Front line,' I said, 'heavy retail action.'

There's no doubt that some periods are lived through in a high state of tension – with every detail of a street scene swept in a glance, with distant or unusual sounds sending instant warning signals – and at the end of the day, you're knackered. You're capable of bursts of speed and of manhandling each other and the camera gear over walls and gates and through windows without giving it a second thought. You devour food rather than eat it, conscious of the pleasure such a simple action delivers, and aware that energy has to be sustained. You drink anything, but you would draw the line at Ovaltine. You become acquainted with fear and your own limitations. And you bless florists and shoe salesmen, who mark out a path of sanity in the storm.

You become conscious of life being snuffed out. Because, in our culture, we spend so little time now with the dead, life as a reporter brings a number of surprises in that direction. From the deathbed of Little Nell to the Hollywood hero who delivers a gracious speech before the head nods gently to one side, we are familiar with a fictional panorama of exits and of Kensington Gore-splattered bodies that rarely equates with reality.

The first man I ever saw mortally injured was a brawny reveller in a Ukrainian bar. On a student visit to the Soviet Union in the days when tourists were still a relatively unknown species of dangerous bacteria, we were entranced by the fun and the music and the genuine attempt of our student hosts to welcome us. Not that we didn't notice that communist buildings appeared to be held together by cockroaches holding hands, and that the travel system was truculent, with the Intourist agents spouting tedious propaganda. But the students were eager and rather shy, and the girls kept tweaking my Marks and Spencer woollies and biting their lips with silent envy (I gave them all away, and they were carried off being stroked by the Tanyas and Natashas as if of the finest cashmere). They took us on picnics and to bars instead of the official receptions (easy to arrange, for the official buses never turned up), and one night we drank and sang in a kind of woodland hunting lodge until a fight took place. From under a table, I saw a man slowly falling backwards. A huge set of antlers had been wrenched from the wall and the crown antler was embedded in his chest.

Bizarre, horrible and unexpected. At the time I hadn't reckoned that I'd ever have to contemplate violent death again.

In Turkey, when I was still in the early stages of working for the national newsroom, I was in the crowd of press drinking coffee opposite the Egyptian Embassy in Ankara, when some shots and a commotion caused us to turn round. Some days before, Palestinian terrorists had taken over the building and were holding hostages, having shot a guard as they burst into the building. Now the usual cordons and lines of police surrounded the building; we were allowed to congregate at a café opposite – from where we now saw a man dropped from an upstairs window, headfirst.

Witnessing murder is a dreadful experience, and it evokes a certain amount of guilt. The silence which followed contained everyone's horror, and our helplessness. And the body lay there, untended, a sorry heap which it seemed impertinent to call attention to when we filmed it.

The local media, who are a tough bunch – and need to be, considering the authorities' views on human rights – looked on grimly, and predicted that the army would be along soon. Sure enough, within an hour a slightly sinister but charismatic officer strolled up the road, carrying a megaphone. He addressed the embassy building briefly and then came to talk to us.

'What did you say to them?' we asked.

'I keep it simple,' he said. 'I tell them, one shot from you, then one shot from us.'

We weren't especially impressed, until we saw behind him the biggest bloody tank ever lumbering up the road to park itself at the embassy's front gate. Not big on negotiation, the Turks.

Films and TV series are full of scenes where people have guns pointed at them. They rarely convey the helpless, gut-dropping sensation that occurs in reality – a feeling that clogs the senses and also acts as a severe deterrent to intelligent interviewing. The Palestinian leader, Yasser Arafat, moved his headquarters to Tunisia in the early eighties, and agreed to an interview with the BBC – via a complicated series of messages, because of his well-placed fear that the Israelis would eventually pay him a visit with their air force. We scuttled around Tunis to odd rendezvous and eventually found ourselves, late at night, outside a modest suburban villa with what seemed like a clutch of jumpy garden gnomes bobbing around in the bushes. The fortified front door was unbarred laboriously from within. A blackness lay beyond, and, as I hesitated on the threshold, I realised that one of the garden gnomes was right behind me and had a gun barrel tickling my spine.

We were urged inside and I pawed my way in the dark, gathering at the last moment that I'd reached some stairs, presumably leading to a cellar. The garden gnome gave me a shove, and I juddered down several steps, stopping as I heard voices and movement right in front of me. I got another push with the gun barrel and came up against something softish but solid, which smelled strongly human. An undignified wriggling took place in inky darkness as the person below me tried silently to push upstairs. A tense exchange in Arabic got a dim light switched on and I found Mr Arafat's nose buried in my cleavage.

His bodyguards, jamming him against me, decided – for reasons unclear to me – that the interview should go ahead in situ. As he detached himself like a cork from a bottle, neither of us was in quite the right frame of mind for political analysis; and besides, the garden gnome spent the whole conversation jabbing his gun repeatedly in my back. So I kept things very brief – and very polite.

In Afghanistan in the late eighties, life was under threat not only from fighting, but from the earth below and the sky above. In bitter weather, dressed as Afghans, we had made it up through the Khyber Pass and were en route for Jalalabad, a city still engaged in fighting the Russians. We'd been assured by the group of fighters guiding us that the route was safe, but none of us believed a word, and as we threaded our way on a narrow mud path through patchy snow, a dark scarlet and fawn mess straddled our path, still steaming. A mine buried under the route had dispatched the camel in the party in front of us. We didn't know whether it was safer to tread through the remains, or chance the ground to the side, but as we stopped, several of the fighters danced and stamped over the untested ground, shrieking that their God would protect them. They made an unpalatable sight, cocky and stupid I thought, rather than, as they imagined, brave and fearless. Their whoops seemed childish in an ancient landscape, with imposing forts and an echo of history in the high passes.

We trekked past smugglers and arms dealers – a male-only scene; except for the journey as a refugee into Pakistan, the rural women rarely ventured out, and many were never allowed to. We stayed the night in a modest farmhouse, where the men lounged on garish nylon cushions and ate piles of rice and lamb while squatted round a plastic tablecloth decorated with teddy bears. Awkwardly, they asked if I would join them, a suggestion which plainly disgusted the host. Anyway, I had decided to see beyond the curtained doorway through which the women were pushing these plates out. Their quarters were more sparse than the rest of the house, and there was a legion of children. The women jumped when shouted at from the other room, and scuttled, pushing more plates through. When the plates came back, all smeared rice and chewed bones, it took me a moment to realise that this was going to be our dinner.

With not a word of common language between us, I spent most of the evening in frantic sign language; however, the women were squeaking with excitement to see a real live foreign female. I fished in my bag to see how we could make contact: the contents of my make-up pouch yielded foundation, mascara and eyeshadow. The mascara brush was passed round with little yips of delight, and they all experimented. They produced an intriguing array of small round tins holding thick powders, and I got a lot dabbed around my eyes. I found a set of photographs, and they pored over the pictures of family and friends and stared at the clothes – but I realised that explaining why I was now dressed in the tunic and trousers of a male Afghan was beyond any descriptive pantomime.

We established I had no children; they were silent with horror and embarrassment. Nor were they quite sure of my reaction when one of the younger women used a lot of fingers to proclaim her twelve-strong brood. But it was the way they watched through the plastic curtain strips as I went back to my crew – bare-headed, and talking to them as equals – that left me with a sense of sadness. They were not the cushioned houris of the harem, but second-class possessions who lived in a lesser world, all pregnancy and gnawed lamb bones.

It is not difficult to believe the suggestion that more women than men were killed during the Afghan war with the Soviet

Union. The men were able to take to the hills with their weapons, while the women had been ordered to stay – as ever – indoors; and the helicopter gunships overhead were oblivious of the primitive prejudices which ruled the women's lives.

The next day we travelled on, and were nearing Jalalabad when we saw our road was covered with tree branches and splintered wood. The Afghans said: 'A storm.' We said: 'Bombing.' They shrugged: 'Who cares? Allah is great.' At a nearby set of farm buildings there was a large group of *mujahedin* fighters, all in high spirits, gapped teeth grinning and rifles waving. Yes, the Russian planes had been overhead – but high, so high that they couldn't be seen, so what was the danger? The gunmen milled around in the open, while the boss invited us to lunch.

As we walked over to some logs set in a square, I saw a large pit to one side. This had been a Russian military post, it transpired, and they'd dug some basic defences. What we were doing in a place known to the enemy I couldn't figure out, but my crew and I were none too easy about it. Nevertheless, lunch was coming – Afghan priorities are rigid. Two large sacks were handed round, from which filthy hands tore pieces of flat bread, and whole roast chickens appeared. Mid-nibble, there was the unmistakable sound of distant military aircraft, and without thinking, I and my crew flung ourselves in the pit. Our discomfort was added to by contemptuous laughter and greasy and befeathered chickens lobbed in after us. Suddenly, there were two explosions behind the farm buildings, and mud and stones rained down. Two Afghans disappeared to the Gardens of Paradise – literally; all that remained of them were a few shreds of scorched cotton which fluttered around above the blackened earth. Their demise was treated as inevitable by their fate-ridden brothers-in-arms, who cackled and called on Allah again. I thought them hellishly dangerous to be with.

When we returned down the Khyber Pass to the frontier town of Peshawar, we reached our hotel filthy and disgusting, still nervous of walking on soft ground and occasionally scanning the sky. As we lugged boxes of equipment from our vehicle, there was a tittering and whispering behind us, and we turned round to be caught in the flashlight pops of a dozen Japanese tourists. They were all dressed in sunshine-yellow Hawaiian shirts and hissing *mujahedin* at us. Tourism gets everywhere these days.

But so does death. And a reporter's job inevitably brings you into close association with injury and hospitals, casualty clearing stations, makeshift clinics and graveyards.

What is the worst thing you've ever seen?

Such a common question, and one I don't answer. There are degrees of horror and awfulness and despair which can only be measured in personal contemplation, and are not for classi-fication. I will only say that, for me, the simple sight of an individual event has always been more telling than the wider scene of horror. But I never walked into Belsen in 1945, so my experience is limited and a matter of chance.

And do you not get used to dreadful sights – become indifferent?

Well, if you do, you should cease to be a reporter, for it is only through constant consideration of and reaction to what you witness that you are able to communicate in a way which reaches your audience – with humanity, but not with sentimentality. Caring about what you see is a step or two away from sticking your heart on your sleeve and delivering your own emotion as part of your report. Journalism goes through fashions, naturally, and at the end of the twentieth century, with fifty years of peace behind us in the United Kingdom, there has been greater scope for a more sensitised attitude to tragedy and death. When few people ever view a corpse, except neatly laid out – and even that becomes rarer – the shock of seeing a dead person seems harder to handle. Where life is cheap, and there is no money for a decent burial, it is commonplace to see the dead lying abandoned for a little time; not through indifference, but because of poverty and the frequency of early death. And in war, whatever the best of intentions, burying the dead is not a priority when other lives are at stake. So you trip over the dead while reporting, a very shocking thing to do. And you observe people grieving – sometimes unbearable in its intensity, and none too dignified. That too – the lack of restraint – can be shocking to our own culture. In Turin in northern Italy, the families of those crushed to death in the Heysel football stadium in Brussels in 1985 ran towards the military aircraft that brought back the bodies from Belgium, and clambered over the plane's tailgate as it was lowered. They threw themselves on the coffins and screamed and howled, and some of the women tore their hair – a phrase I'd read a hundred times but never seen happen. The men beat upon the coffins, and the older women fell on the ground and twitched and rolled. A young Italian air force officer turned to us aghast, both embarrassed and disgusted. 'Calabrians,' he said, 'from the south.' What we were seeing was an older and rural way of life which much of modern Europe has either forgotten or does not recognise. Through our TV camera lens it looked even more bizarre, for the tense communal feeling among the country people as they waited for the plane was absent; now there were just violent figures in black, flailing among the dead.

Shocking as life or death can be, news reporting is but a mirror to reality, and to distort it through either exaggeration or sanitisation is not proper journalism. However, we do censor (to use a blunt word to express the at times blunt excisions which are made): frequently, in British television news, responding to culture and a grey area of what is deemed 'tolerable' or 'acceptable' to the audience. The simpler rules cover close-ups of the dead and dying, nearness to suffering and trauma, but the way the rules are interpreted depends very much on the spirit of the times. A diffident management wishes for a quiet life, commercial pressures push for sensationalism, and lack of experience leads to bad judgement. Over the years, a reporter observes all of these in operation, and curses the creatures blowing this way and that back in the office. The first set of decisions, though, lie with the camera and the reporter on the spot. And there have been very few times when I've thought we should not record a scene – even if not for transmission, then for historical evidence.

Even so, there are stories in which the camera is an intruder and times when 'the historic imperative' doesn't seem justified. During a visit to Delhi during a Commonwealth heads of government meeting in 1983, the Queen was to invest Mother Teresa with the Order of Merit. For an illustration of the nun's work we were taken to an old people's home in the city – a building surrounded with high walls crowded with shuffling vultures. Inside, the sisters were welcoming but somewhat coy. As they showed us around the clean and spartan wards, there was a lot of giggling and knowingness. Eventually, one of the younger nuns couldn't help herself.

'You must see our wolf-lady!' she piped, as the gaggle of sisters yipped and hiccuped with excitement.

At the far end of a ward, something bolted under an iron bedstead. Two nuns set off in pursuit, and we followed more tentatively. Suddenly, a bundle with thin muscled legs rolled across the floor, shook itself and then bounded round the linoleum. The sisters made high, sharp calling sounds. The bundle jerked round, and two beady eyes in a wizened face darted to and fro.

'See!' cried a nun. 'Our very own wolf-lady, straight from the jungle' – and she stretched out a hand. A brown curled paw reached up tentatively.

We were mesmerised. I kept thinking of lurid stories in the Sunday tabloids, or the freak section of American supermarket newspapers.

Unconcernedly, the nuns chattered on about the day a couple of American missionaries had brought in their 'rescued child'. The story was characteristically vague, but seemed to originate in a remote village in one of the southern Indian tribal areas, where fundamentalist zeal to 'save' all humanity had led the pair to track down the 'jungle lady' of village gossip.

No child she. According to those who had medically examined her, she was at least sixty, and had lived in the wild since she was a very small girl, having no discernible language apart from easily recognisable animal sounds. For months, the nuns had been trying to wean her off her diet of raw meat – but with little success.

As she scampered round, moving with extraordinary athleticism and making strange noises, the nuns were trying to persuade us to film her. My reaction was based entirely on emotion, because I couldn't formulate arguments based on reason, but I had no hesitation in saying that we were going to do no such thing. The sisters were disappointed; perhaps they were less aware than most of the exploitative forces unleashed by publicity.

One small cultural point. Horrors abroad are not meant to be treated according to a different set of values. But they sometimes are – with the result that death or suffering in foreigners is viewed with a touch more equanimity than if the sufferers were our compatriots – especially if people *look* foreign. My superficial test of this was honed on royal tours, especially in Africa, when we got to airports crowded with thousands of dancers, all ready to give Her Majesty a 'unique cultural experience' – one she's had several hundred times. A good number of these celebrations involve non-white women moving very energetically, dressed only in skirts. This is described as A Warm Traditional Welcome in the British press. Should Her Majesty ever go to Newcastle and be greeted at the airport by several hundred Geordies moving energetically, dressed only in skirts, the British press would describe this as The End Of Civilisation As We Know It.

Caring about what you see may well be the key to good reporting, for it means you look closer, and you look to find out Why. The much-bruited idea that we are all damaged by grim experience is countered surely by the idea that we are all changed by experience, but not necessarily for the worse. One of the most joyous and life-affirming men I ever met was Leonard Wilson, then Bishop of Birmingham. He had been the chaplain in Changi gaol in Singapore, after the Japanese overran the colony in the Second World War. The brutalities and deprivations he endured – while sustaining other prisoners – were later followed by his baptising and forgiving several of his gaolers. In a lengthy, wine- and laughter-filled evening in Bristol in the early seventies, he talked of many things, and I asked him whether Changi had changed him. He thought for some time, and then told me what he had never told his own family, or made public: that he had gone off to the First World War as a thirteen-year-old, lying to the recruiting sergeant, and seen hell on earth in the trenches. His subsequent life had been one of helping others, but laced with a zest for living – so Changi was just another challenge.

But seeing death – or knowing too much about it – is for most of us more than just a challenge; witnessing terrorism and killing is not what anyone would sanely desire. Usually – and thankfully perhaps – the camera arrives too late, but you occasionally happen upon foul deeds – as they are being committed.

In Sri Lanka, tootling down a winding coast road, beguiled by palm trees and twinkling ocean, Eric Thirer, Fred Scott and myself were contemplating a quiet evening at a beach guest-house, cold beer and fresh fish and a few hours away from the civil war and terrorism which were racking the island. We had a driver who was tackling the curving road very decorously, and as we rounded one bend, a weird tableau presented itself. Before us were about seven or eight armed men some in uniform, busy and urgent, some darting into the undergrowth – a couple straddling the road and two or three on the beach next to a fierce bonfire. In a second, we glimpsed someone manhandled violently away into the trees. At the sound of our jeep, they all froze for an instant – dark, tensed figures against the setting sun. Almost every day on the island people disappeared – 'insurgents' murmured the authorities, as yet another body turned up on the sea-shore, charred to a cinder.

We screamed at the driver, and bent to press his foot on the accelerator. As we went past the silent figures, the beach bonfire licked and flamed unusually, and the faces we saw were unmistakably and assuredly those of men caught in the act of killing.

Sometimes the very atmosphere can communicate evil. On a snowy day in Romania, as Nicolae Ceauşescu's regime was crumbling, Wim Robberechts and I were shown into the warm office of the commander of a Bucharest police station. We wanted a brief interview about the rumoured fate of 'Ceauşescu suporters' and had been tipped off that this commander had information. His assistant said he'd be with us in a short while: he was 'downstairs, working'.

When he arrived, he was a large unremarkable man with the inscrutable manner of any Communist policeman, but brisk and proper. We interviewed him and got a formalised set of answers which gave nothing away. However, as soon as he said his final words, we fled, gathering up our equipment without a word to each other and racing out of the building into lightly swirling snow. We stood and stared stupidly at each other, then yelped in unison: 'the temperature – the cold . . .'

As the police chief had come in, the temperature in the room fell like a stone; not as if a door had opened, but as if we'd been transported instantly to a freezing plateau. It wasn't a natural cold, of snowy winter or an icy draught, but a presence of brooding, chilling fear-full evil. Neither Wim nor I are superstitious: but both of us knew that the police chief had been 'working downstairs', in the cells, and had brought death up with him.

Funerals are a complex ritual, in which much of one's culture is on display. As a child, I attended a distant step-relative's dour Bethesda Baptist service and sat through an interminable sermon, in which said relative was described as a 'caring and valued member of the congregation, generous and Christian'. As we headed for the ham tea, I asked, 'Who was that man talking about, 'cos wasn't she the mean person who was rich and never gave any presents, and was always nasty when we went for tea?' Shush, child. I learned that funerals can be social occasions where lies are permitted. They are also, of course, necessary rites of passage, even though the ritual may not be familiar.

After the terrible fire at Bradford Football Ground in 1985, when so many youngsters died, there was a string of funerals – I think I remember going briefly to seventeen in one week, and therefore to a variety of religious denominations. Having been christened Methodist, attended a Presbyterian Sunday School, gone to a school run by the Church Schools Company and been confirmed into the Anglican Church; having had a Baptist, a Congregationalist, a Methodist and a Roman Catholic in the family, as well as a cousin who went Independent Methodist (very independent, no discernible clergy, do your own sermons), and murmurings that a great-grandmother had looked *very* Jewish, I'd done the rounds of different pews. What I was totally unprepared for in Bradford, even though I knew that my experience was that of millions of fifties children – if rather pick'n'mix – was church after church into which came noisy schoolchildren shouting What's this then? What's a church? Why should we shush? What happens here? Why can't I sit where I like? Many were dressed in party clothes, all bright shirts and spangles, skimpy satin disco skirts and rude T-shirts. Some teenagers squashed up in a pew gossiping loudly asked me why I wasn't 'dressed up'; they said their old nans had told them 'to wear their best' – so here they were in their glad rags. They sat through the service in blank amazement, as if attending a tribal ritual in a far country – which, in effect, they were. They squirmed and chattered. The religious background which I've had many an occasion to question, to search in, to ask for answers, to disagree with, was unknown to them. And so traditional funerals were inexplicable. However, new rituals were arriving; for both in Bradford and later at Hillsborough, mountains of flowers, with toys and teddy-bears, started to show the movement away from eternal verities to instant shrines.

Other faiths, other cultures, provide a reporter with alternative pictures of death. There was the terrorist bombing of Bologna railway station in 1980, with a sea of red communist flags outside the glorious cathedral, as politics and protest ruled the day – enlivened even further when the municipal official in charge admitted that he'd somehow 'mislaid a coffin'. The quite terrible incomprehension of a family in Somerset as one of the first soldiers to be killed in the Troubles in Northern Ireland was laid in a village graveyard with full military honours – and no one having the slightest idea how many times this scene was going to be repeated. The Belfast funeral where the corpse was the subject of a sectarian tug-of-war. The bulldozer moving briskly back and forth as the victims of a mudslide in the Dolomites in 1985 were consigned to a mass grave. You cannot but pause and reflect, while the camera records, and you know that you have to deliver words to an audience which will not fathom the depth of feeling or even guess that vengeance and outrage are often present at the graveside.

An Armenian family once welcomed me to a wondrous funeral. We were above the town of Spitak which had been almost flattened by a catastrophic earthquake. In the shadow of Mount Ararat a biblical cull had taken place, perhaps thirty thousand people, maybe seventy thousand; the collapsing machinery of the Soviet Union in 1988 never managed to establish how many died, though I remember seeing an entire football pitch totally covered with rows of bodies. Above the town was one of the graveyards, with dark mottled marble headstones, to which were affixed photographs of stern party officials.

We followed the family party of a dozen people as they threaded between the graves, carrying baskets and parcels. Grandfather was already in his grave – the actual burial was of little consequence – for now, the real goodbye was to take place, and the funeral cake had been baked. A red-and-white checked tablecloth was spread over the new mound, and plates and glasses dug out of baskets. Goodies of every kind appeared – in the midst of confusion and social collapse, nothing had been stinted, and the wine bottles were propped against the headstone. We were invited to join in, and grandfather was recalled and gossiped about and all their favourite stories about him retailed. The funeral cake was produced – a Coliseum of dark brown chocolate, into which only the best flour and eggs had gone, and topped with a chocolate cross. It was delicious. As we finished the last crumbs, one of the uncles got up and made a short speech, full of affection and thanks to God for a life well lived. The toast was made by the family, including the children, half the wine-glass drunk and the remaining half tossed on to the grave. With everything cleared away, they all walked chattering to the cemetery gate, and·turned and waved goodbye to grandfather. It was beautiful.

You cry a lot in this job – but not on camera, for that is intrusive and thrusts your emotion in the viewers' face, inhibiting them from deciding for themselves what they wish to feel. Words, not emotion, are the reporter's medium.

ELEVEN

Magic carpet

'I suppose your driver takes you there – does he carry your bags as well?'

The idea that news stories happen according to when we reporters are ready to go is quite widespread. The reality is that the first remark from anyone at the scene of crime, the bombed village or the earthquake is: 'You should have been here yesterday . . .'

Being late, in the wrong place, or possibly the wrong country – You think it doesn't happen? You don't know the BBC – it is not only possible, but more than probable. The media have no special magic carpet to whisk them round the world, and to be present at the start of a story is a piece of rare luck, rather than splendid planning.

So. To begin with, are you ready, a news greyhound straining in the slips, packed and ready to go?

Um, sort of – er, sometimes.

I have a hazy memory of being assigned to the Solidarity crisis in Poland, when General Jaruselski took power in 1981, by finding the phone ringing underneath the sofa at midnight during a very good pre-Christmas party. Luckily, the crew was there as well – or not luckily, as the case may be, for none of us was exactly in Go Condition.

'Get to Poland, the military's taken over.'

'Fine. Right. Turn the music down, will someone? Right. Go to where? Why Walsall? Not Walsall? Ah, Warsaw – sure? What's happening? You don't know. Fine. Who's the crew? Yes of course I know where the cameraman is – he's behind the sofa – could anyone go and see if Ray's in the land of the living? Are we OK to travel? Are we ever? Are you absolutely sure you don't want us to go to Walsall?'

We staggered through Heathrow airport at dawn and set off on an adventure which saw us eventually in Copenhagen, boarding a ferry to Poland. As the gangway was being removed, three-quarters of the crew jumped ship, which gave a small clue to public opinion about the new regime. However, the band stayed on board and insisted on serenading us, the only passengers, as we headed overnight for the northern Polish port of Świnoujście.

At early light, as the ferry crept home, we sneaked pictures of the military occupying the port and warships gliding menacingly past. Once alongside, we immediately got arrested on the usual grounds of being foreign, being journalists and being unwelcome. The pug-faced major in charge of us could also have added 'being wrongly dressed'. None of us had realised that snow would be on the ground, for there hadn't been a lot of planning and preparation as we'd left the party in London; we'd mainly congratulated ourselves on not going to Walsall by mistake. I stared at my pointy spike-heeled shoes welded to the ice as we spent hours standing on the quayside looking at soldiers who were all much more sensibly clad than ourselves. More frustratingly, all the pictures we'd have given our eye-teeth to acquire were happening in front of us: military vehicles swarming with newly deployed troops, soldiers fanning out to gain control of vantage points, gates and roads, and small gunboats churning past aggressively; sour-faced dockyard workers slouching past uniformed men with guns. It began to snow lightly. No one seemed to have the slightest idea what to do with us, until Ray unaccountably dug in his pocket and produced his happy-snap camera. Perhaps he thought he'd record our last moments before we froze to death? Before he could immortalise us, the major pounced. Luckily he didn't have a spare firing-squad on hand, so with much yelling and gestures, we were shunted to another ferry and the captain instructed to deport us to Sweden. The oddest moment occurred at journey's end, as we went down the gangway at Ystad: a TV crew was filming us, and, seeing us shunted off the ferry by nervous sailors, in our unsuitable thin clothes and with meagre belongings, assumed that we were 'a few lucky Poles who managed to escape . . .' We had to come clean. The office doesn't like you appearing on ITN News.

I was by now well into the rhythm of reporting, but trying to ensure that the BBC didn't eat up my life. It was all too easy to surrender to full-time devotion to the job – and I'd no intention of that. Somewhere amid the shifts and the foreign trips and the unexpected phone calls, I lived a life. I fitted in sailing, singing, average cooking, above-average shopping, theatre, desultory attempts at skiing, antique hunting, and a horde of friends who tolerated my odd hours.

The BBC, the IRA, the miners' union, and sundry other interfering organisations attempted to sabotage normality; but with an effort, dinner, weekends away and an existence which doesn't include explosions and demonstrations can just about be achieved. And if you don't touch base with life as it's lived by just about everyone else, then how can you judge disruption and disarray when it occurs? I've never felt that dramatic choices are inevitable; you just need a certain amount of determination and a habit of taking your diary everywhere and staying in touch in the weirdest places – and non-stop energy.

As for work, most assignments were a combination of panic, improvisation and hard slog. Foreign news assignment editors were a peculiar breed of genius. They were skilled at worming seats on aircraft out of unknown airlines, remembering arcane facts about visas, border-posts, yellow fever jabs, time zones, the name of the president's wife and whether you needed a mosquito net. They also managed to find a stash of dollars or deutschmarks at short notice, and wished you luck with genuine concern in their voice. Only one of the foreign editors gave mild cause for concern, a charming man who would brief you thoughtfully before departure, his finger running over the *Times Atlas* while trying to find the whereabouts of the country you were heading for.

The home news editors – UK and Ireland – had an equally impressive store of information and contacts, ranging from the frequency of bus services in Glasgow to helpful assistant chief constables, details of hotels in Killarney serving dinner after nine o'clock, and advice about avoiding certain regional newsrooms run by drunks.

These editors were your link with sanity at times, and all of them worked their socks off for you.

You, on the other hand, were the person meant to head towards a story like a speeding bullet, not stopping on the way for food, fuel or sleep.

At least you weren't encumbered with luggage. I flew to Belgium in 1987 for the Zeebrugge ferry disaster, because I was in the newsroom that evening as the first newsflash came through, dressed in a smart light coat and high heels, after a long lunch with friends on a day off. Somewhere on day three, our field producer Brenda Griffiths, dealing with technical transmissions, Belgian policemen, accommodation for a huge BBC team and a hundred other things, waved a bag at me: 'Knickers,' she said, 'I did a bit of girly shopping for you.'

I've never felt confident enough to pack a bag in advance, ever since turning up in Tenerife in the Canary Islands in 1985 to find it was already 90 degrees in the early morning, and I was wearing a ski anorak and snow boots, having been diverted from a coach crash in northern Germany the previous day. It wasn't that I was ignorant of the climate, for we'd all been on the island just two weeks previously in search of gentlemen thought to be connected to the Brinks-Mat gold bullion robbery. And it wasn't only the clothes we got wrong – though they were a major problem; standing on a tourist beach carrying a large TV camera and wearing snowboots is not the best way to conduct a discreet pursuit of people wanted by the police in connection with their enquiries. It just wasn't our sort of story.

The Brinks-Mat robbery spawned years of investigation, several trials and a lot of rumour. A huge amount of gold bullion was involved, and so was a large cast of interesting individuals, none of whom you were likely to meet at your local Rotary Club. On our first visit to Tenerife, we went straight to a large hotel on the south coast at Playa de las Americas, described in the tourist brochure as 'a former simple fishing village', which doesn't prepare you for the skyline of a poor man's New York, and cut-price catering *à la* Clacton. We were seeking John Palmer, a Birmingham jeweller whose name had figured prominently in the police investigations into the robbery. While he was on holiday in Tenerife, his home in Bath had been raided by the police, who'd discovered a metal smelter in his back garden.

Investigative journalism is a specialist trade, particularly where crime is concerned. You need a contacts book full of people with names like 'Fred the Ferret' and 'Crowbar Jim', while your evenings off should be spent in pubs where you can't tell the difference between the local CID and the gangsters. A certain matey approach should be cultivated, allied with the ability not to offend those whose full-time occupation is frightening the wits out of their fellow citizens. I have none of these attributes.

In Tenerife, I wasn't sure how to go about locating a man the police were also looking for. With great embarrassment, I eventually got a tour company to tell me which hotel Mr Palmer's family had booked into, and later that morning we tiptoed into the reception of one of the tower-block hotels. Unlike the movies, where smooth men murmur information across the reception desk to insouciant hacks, we were told by an irritated member of staff to stand in the queue behind a mass of complaining holidaymakers with delinquent children. Twenty minutes later and halfway towards the counter amid a blizzard of whingeing, one of the two fierce holiday reps busy refusing refunds and denying the very existence of food poisoning in the world of package tours, shouted: 'What you want – you people with camera?'

I approached and said as quietly as possible: 'Do you by any chance have a Mr Palmer staying here?'

'Pommer – Mister Pommer. ANYONE HERE SEE A MISTER POMMER?' The entire reception area was addressed in the sort of voice used for rounding up drunks when the flight home is on final boarding.

We cringed, and were just about to beat a retreat when a well-built man walked up to us and said: 'Who wants to see Mr Palmer?'

'We do,' I squeaked.

'Which one?' he said.

That floored me. I hadn't expected to be dealing with a tribe of Palmers.

'The – er one – who – er . . .'

'I'm his dad,' said the man. 'You'll be wanting to talk to him about the gold? Follow me, he's by the pool.'

Confused, three minutes later, we found ourselves the main attraction amid oiled and sizzling sun-worshippers, all of whom flopped off their loungers for a better view of our encounter.

Mr Palmer junior was charming. Most people would probably heave a TV crew into the turquoise pool if interrupted on their hols by journalists asking about bullion robberies. He, however, seemed unfazed, unabashed, so I began the interview by asking his reaction to the police raid. He was indignant, he said, in fact very upset – he'd heard that the police had sedated his two rottweilers – 'a couple of old soppies' – and he was thinking of suing the chief constable. 'But Mr Palmer,' I persisted, conscious that the poolside audience was agog by now, 'the police found a gold smelter in your back garden.'

'Yes?' he said reasonably.

'Well, Mr Palmer, why do you have a gold smelter in your back garden?'

'Why not, Kate? Doesn't everyone have one?'

Interviews are terminated in many ways – but some come to an end because your crew are laughing so much.

Having felt we didn't exactly cover ourselves with glory on that first visit, we returned to the island to follow up developments a fortnight later – in snowboots, feeling rather diffident. This time London had failed to get us any accommodation ('It's a holiday place – lots of rooms, surely?') and we ended up in a back street in Santa Cruz. The room I was allotted had no lock on the door, and when I dumped my baggage on the bed, three legs gave way. I thought I'd have a word with the crew next door. The landing gave on to an inner courtyard, and I found the lads staring across it at the floor below. A man was playing the cello, wearing a pair of smart shoes and nothing else. From other rooms, there was the sound of strenuous activity.

A brothel with classical cabaret – that's a new one, we said, as we headed out to find something to eat. And that was just for starters. We never knew whether the phone calls we'd made about the story prior to arriving had anything to do with it, but after dinner, on the fringes of a local fiesta, we were set upon by seven transvestites in orange wigs and green satin frocks. The three of us survived with a few bruises – the transvestites lost a lot of their bottle if you pulled their wigs off – but the incident added to the feeling that Tenerife was not our scene, and that messing with gold bullion heists had consequences.

I did have a large supply of sticking plaster and aspirins – but that was the extent of any emergency pack that we carried in the mid-1980s. I'd always travelled with a very small bag, from the very first trip I made abroad, worried that a large suitcase would suggest to the all-male crews that a woman needed to bring the kitchen sink along – only to discover that it's men who can't pack and therefore tote immense amounts of luggage.

Women stuff shoes with make-up bottles and squeeze underwear into corners; men sit forcefully on cases. I've eyed vast amounts of opened luggage over the years in hotel rooms, and can attest to the fact that only men insist on packing shoe-trees and hangers, that they have not mastered the art of folding anything, and always have a bag of dirty washing at the end of the trip which is mysteriously extra to what they brought. Mind you, if they *don't* behave like this, then they're a bit of a worry.

My clothes were all workaday. Riots and bomb wreckage do not lend themselves to elegant outfits; dry-cleaners tend not to do business during civil wars, and rubble, broken glass and shrapnel play havoc with decent high heels. Even so, when I consider that most women who get the chance to appear on television will spend days rootling through the wardrobe, then go off round the shops, calling in at the hairdresser's, finally agonising in front of a mirror with every pot of paint and powder applied twice – I have had to live with a sense of guilt for many years. I got a very tart letter from a viewer after a boisterous stint on the Israeli–Lebanese border and in Beirut: Why couldn't my hairdresser there have done something about my appearance?

I imagine she could, but she wasn't keen to leave a busy salon in London and crawl around Lebanon with a hairdryer. Hairdressers are funny that way. Producing a hairbrush in front of a cameraman poised to record your image is the equivalent of holding up a large sign saying 'I may be some time – an hour or so, just talk among yourselves while the bullets fly by and I get things all a little more bouffant.' News cameramen are totally intolerant of preening, going so far as to record your image in a completely bird's-nest-surmounting-whey-face mode, obsessed only with the composition within the frame and the possibility of getting a bullet in the backside. A small hand-mirror and a very tiny hairbrush get stuffed into the pocket of my jeans, to be whipped out for about five seconds – otherwise there's a bit of a scene, and your image is composed with a lamp-post growing out of the top of your head, and a cameraman grumbling about vanity. It's a world away from normal television, which involves half an hour with the make-up ladies, and every blemish hidden. News is an unforgiving medium. In Bosnia, with no electricity, no water, and nights spent in the bath wrapped in a sleeping bag to minimise shrapnel exposure, life came to the point where I used to wonder if I dared appear on screen, asking the cameraman: Is the dirt too obvious? And a piece of advice: even if you know you're due on air in a short time, never put mascara on in a dark cellar during a mortar attack; the audience is puzzled by a report from a panda.

Wearing clothes that grab the attention is wonderful on game shows and showbiz interviews, but if you insist on eye-catching garb, then you end up having your clothes discussed and your reports ignored. It'll happen anyway if you're a woman, with most viewers observing you lying on the deck of an operational aircraft carrier with jets streaking by and wondering why your shirt looks a bit crumpled. Better, I suppose, than being known as 'that one with the sparkly jewellery' or 'her with the frilly blouses'. And if the shirt is really too grubby and covered in land-rover oil or odd spatterings of blood, there is always the last resort: cameramen have those large suitcases, so their clean shirt supply is endless; getting it off them in the middle of a street is the tricky part.

Nevertheless, as British television in the new century begins to turn itself into an entertainment-dominated medium, consigning serious programmes to late nights or specialist channels, news programmes are pressured into changing their style. Style in itself becomes a dominant argument, coupled with anxiety that the audience should not be offended or upset too much by eccentric-looking individuals, lest the ratings suffer. It used to be joked that American television network editors devoted much time to devising 'dress codes' and hiring 'grooming consultants'. The joke is no longer relevant, as their British counterparts have copied them. It's in no way a beauty parade, more a show of inoffensiveness, a bland gallery of conventionally acceptable people, who will perform well under trying conditions and always take their hair-spray with them. Perhaps it's a reflection of improved appearances generally, for there's no doubt that the younger generation today has cleaner hair and better complexions than my youthful contemporaries. This is coupled with the inevitable fact that the audience on the whole – and understandably – prefers beauties to beasts. However, in the competitive world of the media, certain norms arise in the minds of editors and producers, and they project a world on screen which reflects their image of a successful specialist industry, rather than the wider world. In America there are vast numbers of the population who can hardly get through a doorway, so great is their devotion to triple helpings with extra gravy and no exercise. These people never, never become TV reporters.

Regardless of looks, what about travelling essentials? First, never forget your toothbrush. Life can descend to the lowest level, the bombers may have blown up the power station, there's no running water, and last night's food consisted of an unknown burnt animal that died needlessly, but if you get out the medicinal bottle of scotch (essential number two), and wield the toothbrush, life will feel better. Everyone will sniff the air at breakfast time, assuming you've been at the booze a trifle early, but you will nevertheless feel superior and feel perkier. Number three is the torch, because next time you find yourself in a modern hotel, observe that modern architects don't believe in windows anywhere near corridors and stairwells, and in all crises, truth may be the first casualty, but electricity is the second. Playing Sardines is not what you really want to do if you're in fear of your life or your hotel is on fire. Understandably, most people have much better things to do with their time than to muse upon the benefits of electricity. However, it was fascinating in Bosnia to notice that most of us regularly went to the bathroom wherever we were staying, and spent at least ten seconds wondering why water didn't come out of the taps. In high-rise buildings, we sometimes went automatically to stand in front of the lifts, until the penny dropped. Woken by gunfire in the middle of the night, you reach for the bedside lamp out of habit, and unless you're a neatness freak, it is impossible to locate a full set of clothing in total darkness, never mind in the right order; there is nothing quite like finding your bra once you've got everything else on.

Right through the seventies and eighties, we never used to pack flak jackets, helmets or trauma kits. It never occurred to us that journalists should use them; we had no desire to be identified with the military – any military. Occasionally, in very hot situations, you heard that these things might be borrowed – and I remember the BBC once sending 'protective gear' over to Northern Ireland during a riotous period. The clothing must have been lead-lined, for the reporter who tried on the jacket fell to his knees and was unable to get up. The best protection appeared to be 'stand behind the cameraman' – for if you stood in front, both he *and* the rioters would hit you.

Not until the Gulf War did I wear any sort of flak jacket – and very odd I found it. However, it was merely a precursor of what was to come. For in former Yugoslavia, to our immense dismay initially, the full kit arrived: armoured land rovers, heavy-duty bullet-proof vests and helmets. I'd never have dreamed that we would end up wearing this armour, but life has changed as the world has become awash with more (and more lethal) weapons, and the press – television in particular – is seen by combatants as part of the action.

So, for many years, it was just a shoulder bag and one small suitcase – toothbrush in each, just in case, and spare make-up as well; shirts you can borrow, but the lads are no good in the mascara department.

Nevertheless, they used to compensate by carrying a ton of equipment. Turning up at Heathrow airport at short notice, in a rush and a little vague about the airline and the flight time, you were guided to the right check-in desk by the sight of a mountain of boxes and bags and tripod case and mini-steps and Lord knows what else. Camera crews on the move resemble house-removals gone astray. And this is the brave new world of video, for when we said goodbye to film in the early eighties and espoused the wonderful immediacy of the video world, I genuinely believed that the new gear would be flexible and lightweight. But the first time I saw ABC News piling into Istanbul airport with the new-fangled kit, I began to wonder. A heap of large yellow metal-reinforced boxes was blocking the passenger exit, while a producer tried to persuade a gang of taxi drivers to help. Eventually someone's cousin turned up driving a vegetable lorry, and the marvellous new electronics were hurled among the rotting greens and squashed pomegranates. There's something in TV equipment which enables it to breed quietly, so that more boxes come home than ever left. Except, of course, the box of 'essential spare parts', which will fly off from Heathrow never to be seen again.

I mention the mountain of kit, because I've helped move it a lot. Reporters are partly tolerated by crews because of their ability to disappear through that plastic curtain which separates the Arrivals hall from the baggage handlers. We've all stood there, waiting interminably in Baggage Claim while the conveyor belt grinds round for the umpteenth time bearing one sad unclaimed suitcase, and wondered what was going on beyond the flapping strips of plastic – well, reporters don't wonder; they're encouraged by their crew to go for a crawl – 'come on, you're smaller than us, get in there' – and you discover what it's like to scramble through the hole on a conveyor belt moving the wrong way. It's a challenge, especially when you find a crowd of Libyan police helping themselves to your baggage on the other side. You can try remonstrating – but cantering on all fours on a moving conveyor belt is not a dominant position, and you revert to yelling abuse as you are carried back into Arrivals.

Tales of flights from hell are the stock-in-trade of journalists, contrary to the perceived view that we have a magic carpet which wafts the press from home to story. I used to watch airline adverts wondering what sort of work you had to do in order to swan through airports and stroll on board a flying living-room, only to be sated with champagne and tit-bits by ministering minions.

On the other hand, as long as you bag a space on the floor of a Hercules C-130 military transport plane and a box of ammunition doesn't fall on you, you can get quite a good night's kip. You are merely grateful that the plane has a competent crew and fuel. It's a bit of a bore to have to weave among 747s taxiing on the apron at Cairo airport trying to flag down the kerosene tanker and offer the driver crispy US dollars to divert the fuel nozzle into a chartered aircraft. It's the old language problem, of course: 'You say you want aircraft, you got it, nice plane; you say nothing about fuel . . .'

And you count your blessings when airborne. If the pilot takes off from Cairo and seems to be intent on flying at rooftop level all the way, taking the odd washing-line hostage, you should merely nod in approval when he says, 'Old habit – I fighter pilot in last war with Israel, safer this way.'

If the pilot is sober, that's a plus – not always available beyond the Urals – and if he hangs on to the controls on descent while wrestling with a dog which belongs to the woman who's in the twelve-strong standing-room-only group in the aisle on the way to Tbilisi in Georgia, be thankful that the dog thinks it's a game and hasn't yet bitten him.

If the crew of the Turkish DC-10 airliner invite you into the cockpit, be grateful when they offer you lunch and a bottle of wine while locking the door behind you and producing a pistol. Their intentions are perfectly honourable – they merely explain that the returning *Gastarbeiter* – the Turkish workers en route home from Germany – are likely to get very difficult when they find out they get no lunch, and although sixteen carving knives were removed before they boarded, some are bound to have got through. Still, as there are two fridges and a lot of TV sets piled high in the aisles, no one's going to move around much.

To most people, flying is a thrill, associated with drinks and nibbles at thirty thousand feet and a pleasant destination. I seem to have done much of mine hanging out of a helicopter, squawking warnings of approaching electric pylons and then squeaking as we duck under power lines. It's a privilege to be allowed to hop aboard military transport – even if Biggles and his chums up front tend to regard TV crews as rather dim livestock heading voluntarily for the abbatoir. The professionalism of Royal Navy pilots under fire is a joy to behold, though beholding is difficult when in foetal position on the floor, waiting for bullets to drill upwards into one's fleshier parts. Old hands flying into Sarajevo in the early nineties used solemnly to remove helmets and sit on them as the all-too-active runway came into view. A bullet in the buttocks is not only painful; it also ranks as Funniest Medical Joke Ever, as hospital staff in the Bosnian town of Mostar once demonstrated to us as they fell about while some poor housewife twitched in pain and nurses and orderlies queued up for the show.

If the navy flies with style – 'OK, TV people, rotors turning, wheels up – Nigel, be a good chap and don't stand on that missile to film, we might just fire it' – the army has its own nonchalance in the face of naval cool. While crouched in the corner of a lumbering Sea King chopper on a hedge-clipping flight into Bihać in central Bosnia, whooshes and crumps and bangs all around, my contemplation of death in a minced heap of metal was punctured by General Rupert Smith's biro jabbing my flak jacket. As the helicopter lurched and bucked through gunfire, General Smith was wrestling with a ten-letter anagram in his *Daily Telegraph* crossword.

Finding yourself with the SAS on board is like discovering that the school bus has been taken over by Martians: quiet, watchful creatures, each with a personalised array of unrecognisable weaponry, and clearly on a mission where TV reporters are surplus to requirements – except when one of them wants to use a large machine gun to return hostile fire and uses you as a wedge to jam open the helicopter door.

The RAF regard TV crews as an amusing diversion on routine flights. On the Kurdestan border, dozing in a Chinook helicopter – a kind of horizontal flying banana with windmill sails stuck to it – I was woken by a crewman yelling above the din.

Would I like to see the view?

Yes, I said.

Silly me. The RAF's idea of a good view is obtained by sitting on the edge of the lowered tailgate at the back of the banana, with your feet dangling a thousand feet above the mountains.

On the ground, you drive yourself. For some reason American TV crews can't do this, and their rufty-tufty image is dented by being chauffeured to war. We British are made of sterner stuff, and I hate to think of the miles we've covered in every conceivable vehicle. Only in odd circumstances do we get driven. Trying to find a way to Armenia to cover the earthquake in 1988, after the authorities in Moscow had blocked all attempts to go through Russia, we – BBC and NBC TV – headed for Turkey. In the north-east corner, at the border with Georgia, Turkish border guards refused to let us take our hire-car across the frontier, so we were the first people ever to walk across that NATO border into the old Soviet Union. It was a lonely walk, watched by two groups of armed men, and we then sat apprehensively in the Soviet border post and had a confusing conversation with officials, who made a lot of phone calls. We apologised for not having Georgian visas.

'Who wants them?' seemed to be the reply. 'Our vice-president wishes to meet you, and we are preparing a banquet.'

Perhaps this was an elaborate way of saying Welcome to the Gulag – we had no way of knowing as we were herded into an army van and taken into town. But instead of the anticipated stretch in an unpleasant gaol, an army of strangers met us outside the dilapidated seafront Intourist hotel and gave us an overwhelming welcome.

Two hours later, the most sumptuous array of food was revealed to us in the peeling reception room, and we were being hugged and jabbered at by half the town. Our hosts were excited – a British and an American TV crew! – and they popped open bottles and announced a formal welcome to the Republic of Adzharskaya. Somewhere amid the din and the toasts and the mounds of blinis it occurred to me that I had never heard of this republic, but by then I was being addressed by its vice-president who was insisting I tell Prime Minister Margaret Thatcher that Adzharskaya wanted to join the Common Market, just as soon as those wretched Russians went home. I apparently made a speech, but thankfully everyone was beyond political acuteness and just sent for more bottles. As the evening wore on, we made desperate attempts to convince our hosts that we had no intention of turning into a trade delegation and had to get to Armenia – which was several hundred miles away, and we didn't have any transport. An Intourist lady took me aside and assured me that everything was in hand.

'We get you coach,' she said.

'Perhaps a minibus would be better,' I suggested.

She looked exasperated.

'Minibus made in Russia, is rubbish. You want nice coach made in Hungary. Sixty-eight seats. And driver who want to go find family in Armenia – so no hijack to Abkhazia.'

I was not thinking very straight, and had no idea why coach drivers wanted to go to yet another republic whose whereabouts eluded me; however, it had dawned that a coach was going to be expensive, and I had limited cash on me.

'Can't afford a coach,' I said, thinking to call an Intourist bluff, 'unless you take American Express.'

'That nicely will do.'

And so we set off, full of Adzhari hospitality, while I snoozed through Georgia, wondering if the EU might ever stretch this far. But all the signs were appearing that the old edifice of the Soviet Union had cracks, and Adzharskaya might yet have its day.

Yet more cracks appeared as we reached Armenia by means of a lengthy tunnel pouring rivers of water from its roof and littered with debris. The earthquake had had a great time with rotten Soviet building – and the area around the towns of Leninakan and Spitak testified to half a century's shoddy construction. A long, low cloud of brick and cement dust hung in the air as we picked our way among mounds of bricks – all that was left of several thousand houses in Spitak. Most people were plonked by the roadside in the open, still sitting in a daze – several days after the initial tremor. Children wandered about scavenging, and one or two men were poking disconsolately into the ruins with no obvious intention. There were no discernible roads in the town centre, so newly arriving Soviet army trucks were crunching over household possessions, makeshift shelters and half-starved pets. Contrary to all communist imagery, there was chaos. The immense edifice of the USSR looked pretty scabby close-up. The school said it all: a four- or five-storey building, it was difficult to tell, which had concertina'd down on its crumbly concrete self, with all of its pupils inside.

As we walked through the ruins in the early morning chill, we saw a wisp of smoke curling up from an iron plate laid over a small fire. A middle-aged woman in stout boots and mittens was energetically trying to feed the fire with bits of paper rubbish, while a pale boy and a girl looked on, and an elderly rheumy-eyed man shivered behind them. All their eyes were riveted on the plate, on which sizzled a tiny heap of chopped-up potato. We trained the camera on their faces, as they watched an egg being broken on to the feast. The three onlookers were clearly seeing their first modest meal in days. As we drew back, the mixture was deftly divided in two by the woman, using a bit of cardboard, sliding the yellowy lumps on to it.

With a gesture born of natural habit, she turned and offered it to us.

We were stunned with embarrassment that kindness to strangers extends this far.

We worked for hours among the ruins, ending up interviewing an elderly woman who couldn't find any of her family. She sat in dignity on her one remaining chair in the open air, every so often reaching out to touch the few possessions she'd unearthed – a vase, a coat-hanger, some clothes – and saying gently that as time passed, maybe, perhaps, God willing, her son or daughter-in-law just might appear. As we left, I said to the crew that I'd better find a loo, having wondered for some hours where you go in a flattened city-scape. Behind me, there was a scrape of a chair, as the woman guessed what I was looking for. She picked up what appeared to be a long skirt from her precious bundle, and motioned me to follow her, whereupon it was spread like a curtain for me to duck behind discreetly. Then she gave me a little hug, and returned to sit thoughtfully in her chair.

Our coach driver, who was keen to get to the capital, Yerevan, to look for his family, had been hearing gossip that the main road was damaged, so he heroically headed over the mountain which lay in our way. We lurched over moss and gravel and past stunning scenery of gaunt rocks and thin rapier-like trees and huddling villages, and got lost. At a village announced by a grandiose graveyard of massive wrought-iron bird-cage contrivances above each plot, we were unceremoniously dragged off the bus for a bout of feverish hospitality. Shunted into a warm front room, stepping over the freshly severed bullock's head in the porch, we were joined in minutes by virtually the whole village. Cheese and cakes and cured meat and sweets rained into the room, passed in from every house. Villainous-looking bottles of pale liquid clinked on to the laden table. Had the village been damaged by the earthquake? Yes, but what of it? It was so much more exciting to greet strangers.

They were agog when we told them we were from Britain; not for the first time that day, people cried with gratitude and asked repeatedly why a faraway country – from the 'unfriendly' West – should care a whit about them. We tried to explain that it was normal to offer other countries help in a disaster – and it seemed a novelty to them. Not for the first time, we found large numbers of people who either didn't know or wouldn't speak

Russian, in defiance of the Soviet claim that every citizen had a common language.

We set off to take pictures of the damage to their community, for their pride and joy, some communal cow-byres, had shuddered apart. The bottles and cakes followed us, as if we might be in need of sustenance every three minutes. I asked about the ornate graveyard, and several people launched into a complicated description of village religious history. Liz Rembowska, our interpreter, said they were saying – and giggling about – something she didn't understand. 'They're all saying they've got "flame" people.'

We'd come across Zoroastrians, whose eternal flame flickered in a small recess at the back of their cottages. Officially, the most ancient religion on earth did not function in Armenia; but in this as in so many other ways, the Soviet surface merely papered thinly over reality. Back in the hospitality room, alarmingly, more bottles and hot pies were appearing, and we tried to make our excuses – we still had to find a way of sending our story to London. A man pushed through the scrum in the room to express his gratitude to the British, and Liz dutifully translated until he began to address his thanks personally to me. There was a bit of a pause, and I thought I'd recognised the odd word in his Armenian involving the sound 'Tacha' . . . Liz and I had a quick conflab – just how did we explain that I wasn't Mrs Thatcher?

Having failed to send our story via the traditional route from the TV station in Yerevan – 'It's Wednesday. Wednesday there's no electricity' – we headed for the airport, to see if we could ship the tape to Moscow.

The airport, which should have been the focal point of relief efforts, had had three major accidents in as many days – no one could cope with an emergency, and the air traffic control system imploded. The runway remained partially blocked for days as the ancient Soviet habit of never admitting accidents took precedence over reality. I watched as a group of Austrian search-and-rescue dog-handlers unloaded their own plane and argued with an official who clearly wanted to be paid for letting them do their own work. The terminal building was a cross between a refugee camp and a madhouse. Armenian officialdom slugged it out with Russian bureaucrats. Shady figures slouched round trying to con incoming aid teams with offers of transport and accommodation (neither of which existed). Firemen, doctors and aid workers milled around unable to find anyone in charge. Miserable families camped everywhere in the hope of non-existent flights.

I sat down next to a man in a smart overcoat and fur hat, who spoke excellent English and was a university academic from the capital, Yerevan. 'They'll try anything,' he said gnomically, waving at the scene of confusion in front of us. I didn't understand.

'Who'll try anything?'

'The Azeris.'

What on earth had the citizens of neighbouring Azerbaijan to do with this? I wondered.

'They caused it.'

'Caused what?'

'The earthquake, of course. They set off a nuclear explosion beneath our country in order to further their war aims.'

I heard this canard frequently, and from educated people. The entire country had fallen apart, and the almighty Soviet Union seemed for once unable either to conceal the mess or to keep foreigners out. For the first time, a major international aid effort was under way which the communists were unable or disinclined to stop. In came rescue teams with state-of-the-art equipment, communications systems and confidence. Next to them, the Soviet military effort was woefully incompetent – and appeared to have a major language problem. Teams of almond-eyed young soldiers stood about, baffled when addressed in Russian or Armenian. They'd been trucked in from the distant eastern republics, only to be met with suspicion and taunts of 'Mongolian'. We'd also driven past ravines in which a dozen mangled army vehicles had met their end; the famed Red Army didn't have enough trained drivers in the east. In the nearby city of Leninakan, high-rise tenements had collapsed, and thousands sat on the immense piles of rubble, sleeping under cardboard and newspaper. We were seeing the roots of the Soviet system losing purchase, as the rest of Europe surged into the capitalist nineties, but we did not guess at the swift changes which were on the horizon.

In the weeks that followed, when most of the emergency international volunteers had left, the great Soviet Empire decided to make a massive gesture and create a new residential city on the outskirts of Leninakan. They promised elegant apartments and sweeping vistas, one of the largest investment projects in the empire. Nine years later I went to see it.

The promise had been translated into spectacular beginnings: foundations dug across acres of bleak heath, drainage pipes partly in place, gouged earth and steel reinforcing rods creating a remarkable landscape of skeletal building, surrounded by giant cranes. And that was that; for history had swerved past Armenia's need for a new city, taking with it all the imported material from other Soviet republics and cutting off the money for construction. For the USSR was no more – and one day the workers all went home to their own countries, leaving Leninakan with just a few blocks of spacious apartments with ornate balconies – half finished – in which a lucky few families were camping. The rest, more than 20,000 of them, were in metal transport containers, temporary accommodation, for nearly a decade.

The chance to return to the scene where you remember momentous events is a rare one. News is a bird of passage, and alights only for a brief moment. There's a school of thought which suggests that a regular activity of any news organisation should be to go back to stories for another look. It never quite works out, given the demands of contemporary news. And, to be candid, it's quite a test of a reporter's attitudes. For all stories carry with them a sense of occasion, wrapped tightly in a particular emotion or atmosphere – and that is rarely present second time round. And you wonder what happened to those who were kind to you.

You also wonder, when the American Express bill turns up, what happened to the coach you bought.

Travel is one of the delights of the job, even though there's little glamour attached, and comfort is not an optional extra. I've always pressed my nose to the glass as the countryside rolls by, and once, across the Channel as a student, I remember waking on the carriage floor to scramble to see each town where the train stopped. I come from the generation which wasn't prevented by war from crossing to the continent, and which in the sixties envisaged a new and cheap version of the Grand Tour sustained by sausage, bread and cheese and beer. I met hundreds of fellow students from Europe and North America trying out the new-found freedom to roam. We saw everywhere the effects of warfare, and we were excited about where postwar life was leading. We were curious and incurably optimistic – and, hundreds of thousands of miles later, I still am.

TWELVE

Ills and spills

In among the joys of travel is the discovery of the strength of the human intestine. You'll eat anything when you're really hungry – even a fussy creature like me will. Camel meat? Delicious. Dog? Never, it wasn't, just don't tell me. Any reporter who claims to have iron guts is lying. There lurk in the world truly wondrous tit-bits accompanied by minuscule germs that can blow your major organs away. That is, if the planet's creepie-crawlies haven't feasted on you beforehand.

Nepal had been my first encounter with killer diseases, and although no woman objects to losing a few pounds, shedding a stone in five days leads you to think you're going to disappear down the bath plug-hole by next Tuesday. You try to remember rules about not eating unwashed salad, drinking the water or scoffing tepid bowls of anonymous bits from roadside vendors, only to find that life's too complicated and anyway you're ravenous.

And even if you pay through the nose to the mafia who are running the most expensive hotel in town, you can't guarantee that the kitchen isn't run by a viral consortium. In Georgia, the newly built flashy hotel in Tbilisi delivered exquisite delicacies to its guests, while ordinary citizens endured shortages of milk and butter and meat. In this newly emergent independent republic in 1991, with a number of tanks prowling the main street due to republican birth-pangs, it seemed churlish to suspect there might be a few hygiene problems, and anyway, I'd just come from Libya, where Dead Salad was a speciality of Tripoli's main hotel.

I began feeling ill on the third day, after a wondrous afternoon listening to plainchant in the old cathedral, so I thought a bottle of local lager in the evening would be preferable to dodgy water. I didn't hear my liver crying out in fear as it fought to cope with alcohol. A week later, I was still just about upright, but things were feeling very nasty inside as we headed home through Moscow. That evening, I felt unable to join the crew for a last night out in the capital, and happened to walk past the bathroom mirror. A lemon stared back; with two banana eyeballs.

One of the rules of the game is to avoid treatment in countries which are having economic crises – your innards may be worth trading or the hospitals staffed entirely by students. I rang the BBC Moscow bureau and they said they would find a reputable doctor via the embassy. Half an hour later, a brisk Australian woman turned up and shrieked, 'Christ! You've got hepatitis,' as I opened the door. 'I know that,' I said. 'I just want you to keep me going until I get to London.'

This didn't seem to register. She continued: 'Do you know what they do here to people with hep? They put them in these filthy isolation hospitals with other infectious diseases – for a minimum of two months. Then you die.'

Grim determination took over, and I asked for some tablets to keep me from passing out in the airport the next day. She seemed to crack again and said she thought my case ought to be reported . . .

'If I go to hospital I'll make sure you come with me,' I suggested, and this seemed to do the trick, producing some pills and a hurried goodbye and good luck.

I hit the airport with more make-up than a Japanese geisha and a pair of sunglasses on a dark day. Several men made salacious hopeful overtures and I wondered if I should try the technique again when feeling better.

At least it was an identifiable illness; what most journalists dread is that odd feeling that something's wrong, but no one believes you. Kurdestan incubated a number of these delightful surprises. A land – but with its people spilling over several borders – curtained by fabulous mountains that embrace their people whenever the Kurds are again under attack. 'The mountains are our friends,' they found themselves saying yet again in 1991 as thousands straggled up the hillsides, terrified lest Iraq's Saddam Hussein should catch up with them and perhaps use them once more to test the efficacy of chemical warfare.

With the Gulf War dust still settling, there'd been panic in northern Iraq that Saddam would take easy vengeance on a familiar target, and while the West was pondering the ruins of Kuwait to the south of Iraq, the Kurds were collecting their belongings and fleeing into the hills far to the north. Gradually, this relatively unexpected consequence of a Western victory in the Gulf brought a posse of press to the borders of Turkey and Iran, wondering if a venture into the territory ruled by the man we'd just waged war against was a wise idea.

We were camped on the rooftop of a house in Cizre in eastern Turkey, a town that went in for a mildly Wild West lifestyle supported by medieval plumbing. The first hotel we'd tried turned out to be an all-night tavern already vacated by ITN, who'd found a fat rat asleep in the hand-basin. Hotel Rat was the only one in town, so we were sharing a fourth-floor roof with our American colleagues from NBC, with the landlord's rows of washing strung between us. It was idyllic: stars above us and the smell of hot bread wafting up just after daybreak. At ground level it was open sewers and streets jammed with rickety carts laden with several tons of green corn pulled by women in baggy trousers. The men sat on tiny stools at the innumerable coffee shops, glued there all day long.

Back in the capitals of western Europe there was much talk of relieving the plight of the several hundred thousand Kurds stuck in the higher mountains. The logistics were formidable, and the legal position of anyone crossing into Iraq was debatable. Nevertheless, we decided the border held no terrors for us and fetched up at what we'd thought would be a quiet frontier hut. Instead we found an immense modern truck compound, jam-packed with international routiers, and queues of irate drivers and aid workers and UN personnel arguing with fierce Turkish border guards. The Portakabin at the centre of the throng was a vicious free-for-all, besieged by hundreds, with a lucky few dozen confronting an implacable row of Turkish officials who took the view that Iraq was Closed.

On the second day of trying we noticed some vehicles heading across the border, so we heaved forward and got into the Portakabin, only to witness an American medical team nose-to-nose with the Turks, all scarlet with anger. Matters were brought to a head by an American military doctor drawing his revolver and demanding that he 'get to Iraq and save some lives', otherwise he'd shoot someone. The Turks backed off for a brief period, in which we concocted a tale about a day-trip to the Iraqi border town of Zakho, without mentioning our small convoy of white open-top jeeps piled high with camping equipment and cooking pots.

Once inside Iraq we whizzed along quiet roads through emerald valleys and shimmering scarlet poppy fields. The villages beyond Zakho were empty; there was only birdsong when we stopped to ford pebbly rivers. It was almost a paradise on earth, except that it was a landscape which had been blown through by fear – invisible but all-pervasive.

Eventually we fetched up in the hilltop town of Al Amadiya, a clutch of white houses at the summit of a corkscrew road, commanding an unforgettable view towards both the mountains at the Iranian and Turkish borders, and the ridges of jagged hills south to Baghdad.

We didn't have the town entirely to ourselves – a number of disconsolate Iraqis dawdled about; but the majority had heeded the warnings of Western military powers to withdraw southwards and the remainder seemed indifferent to our presence. We set up in the disused fire-station house, scrubbed it out and dragged a few ancient metal beds from next door. Joe Paley, the radio correspondent, pitched a tent on the lawn and Nigel Bateson, our cameraman, chose the roof. Producer Brenda Griffiths and I eyed the local insects marching across the floor, and pitched sleeping bags on to the beds in a bare concrete storeroom, along with Brian Smith, our editor, and Tony Fallshaw, our other cameraman.

Within a day, 45 Commando of the Royal Marines moved into the school round the corner, and one would have thought we were set for a straightforward reporting assignment. That is, if it hadn't been for the accidents. One of the more spectacular was Brian going up in a ball of flame as Nigel's improvised barbecue got out of hand. This was after Tony had had a major catastrophe with a jeep and a fast-travelling sheep. Someone almost fell off the roof in the middle of the night after much Turkish Buzbag wine. Brian then got attacked by the world's biggest insect which nibbled him and blew up his arm to three times its usual size. And a howling orange dust storm resulted in a flying tree – an entire tree – knocking me out for several minutes – followed by an incident with an axe as the tree was ritually sacrificed. Brenda's regular sprint to the Marines round the corner resulted in them moving their medical unit nearer to us.

Luckily we had avoided driving over a hundred miles a day to transmit our stories, for the transmission dish was back over the border in Turkey; we piggy-backed our tapes into the RM helicopter which was making regular runs back and forth. We also sent a shopping list for food to the engineers at the dish, and the Marines added items like 'more bandages for BBC', so we added crates of Buzbag wine to the list to keep everyone happy. We even attempted a formal 'dinner party' one Saturday night, with Tony and Nigel preparing a feast which was to centre round a roast lamb. Brenda had made contact with a local Christian priest who promised 'the right animal' and she drove off on Saturday morning to collect it. To her horror, dinner was bleating loudly as it was shoved into her jeep; nor did it look very lambish – more goatish. When the Marines offered to dispatch it, Brenda intervened, to be told that 'they'd put a little blindfold over its eyes if it would make her feel better'.

'It's not that I'm worried about,' she said. 'You appear to be going to machine-gun it, and we don't want mince.'

The priority was to reach the Kurds huddled on the ridgeline that divided Iraq from Turkey. As we headed upwards, the mountain streams ran yellow and filthy and we passed cars and belongings, abandoned as people had trekked ever higher every day. As we climbed nearer the border we saw, stretched across saddles of flatter land in the cold air and patchy snow, a multitude in misery, spread over miles of churned and litter-strewn mud puddled with urine. A truly biblical sight – except for the dense line of people who were pressed against a very high modern wire fence which snaked along the mountain tops, behind which the empty hillsides of Turkey dropped away, patrolled by gruff soldiers.

It took every ounce of concentration to find words which described these scenes; most phrases seemed too trite. Among the listless refugees bustled teams from the aid agencies, some focused and practical, others flapping around unable to contribute much intelligent help. Médecins Sans Frontières, the most ruthless and unsentimental – and efficient – were digging trenches to be filled with disinfectant; dirt and disease spread more quickly than hunger. As we crawled into the plastic lean-tos which afforded some shelter from the sharp wind, it was inevitable that hands were held and shoulders hugged. We crawled out with fleas and scabies. But everything is relative; we're fortunate that we have robust constitutions and the benefit of knowing that if something really nasty happens, we'll somehow get ourselves to a proper medical facility. And we can only wonder at the resilience of those who are forced to endure conditions that lay us low after a few days.

We spent weeks in Al Amadiya, encountering the unexpected every day. Driving past Saddam Hussein's 'Summer Palace', a well-fortified set of buildings on the road to the waterfall where we filled up twice daily, I slowed up as I passed the main gateway and peered down the drive. There was usually no one about, but that evening a young man in smart uniform suddenly appeared, carrying his rifle casually by his side, and he called out to me.

I don't speak Arabic and was quickly calculating the odds of being ritually sacrificed on Saddam's front doorstep. Oh well, I thought, and stopped. The young man came to stand next to me, good-looking and very correct, and I had that odd feeling we were being watched. Was I about to become a Political Incident? Bother.

'Salaam aleikum,' I tried.

'Salaam aleikum,' he replied, and handed me the rose he'd held behind his back.

Later there was a strained exchange with the Royal Marines, who'd had a finely judged moment as they lay in their concealed positions on the hillside above the palace, fingers on triggers, wondering just what Adie was getting herself into.

You can get yourself into trouble all too easily – and then lots of other people have to get you out of it. It's unfair knowingly to put yourself in danger without calculating the bother you're going to cause. When I first started travelling in the Middle East, there was always the fuss and unpleasant attention which a woman attracts if she's on her own. Talking about this in a bar in Cairo one night and giving vent to my irritation, I was given a sharp lesson by a very experienced American correspondent.

'I've been raped twice,' she said, 'and it's the worst thing ever.' She then described the circumstances, which were slightly banal and the result of very tiny lapses in awareness. She also outlined the consequences, not the least of which was the altered attitude of those colleagues who knew – even when they were wholly sympathetic. 'You don't win,' she said, 'attitudes haven't changed *that* much.'

Time and again I found myself choosing between the desire to head off on my own to demonstrate independence and confidence – and the possible consequences. When others expect you to demonstrate modern thinking and principled independence, there's a fine line of compromise: I didn't become a shrinking violet, never out by myself, but I made calculations in certain cultures and situations, and opted to play safe. Battlefields and war zones see most of the usual restrictions on decent behaviour suspended, so nothing can be taken for granted. And even the most benign Arab souk or African village has both men and women who don't or won't understand the rights of women. So innumerable cameramen have kindly endured shopping expeditions and healthy walks, and occasionally announced that I'm married to them – arrest and detention are particularly tricky times, but if you make enough fuss, you get to share a cell with your instant husband – in relatively greater safety . . .

Another day in Kurdestan, we saw a gathering of cars in a usually deserted spot by a river, and stopped to find a little congregation of Assyrian Christians who'd bravely driven up from Baghdad. They were celebrating one of their feast days – from a panoply of saints I had only vaguely heard of – and joyfully invited Brenda and Nigel and me to join them for wine and cakes; and these were the people we'd just bombed for several months. They discussed the war circumspectly and with many sighs – discretion everywhere being a sign of survival in a dictatorship – but they left us with gentle blessings and a wish that one day we'd come peacefully to Baghdad.

The landscape was deceptive in many ways. There was trouble in the towns just to the south where Iraqi troops still remained, and every so often we came across abandoned children wandering in empty villages, barefoot and defiant. We occasionally encountered fractious and jumpy bands of Kurdish fighters, and weird specimens of American 'Special Forces', all rather pudgy and bespectacled and unfriendly, who clearly knew bugger-all about anything Kurdish but acted as if they were in their own Midwest back yard.

Halfway through the trip, I was asked by London to peel off and look for a freelance crew who'd disappeared several weeks earlier on their way into Iraq over the mountains from Turkey.

Rosanna and Nick della Casa and Charles Maxwell had offered to film for us, and they'd disappeared. The signs were not good, for the mountain passes were bandit-ridden and the border region they'd been heading for had seen quite a bit of sporadic Iraqi action against Kurdish militia groups. I set off to follow up various 'sightings' which had filtered out of the area, and found myself turning over the remains of a little battle by a river: stiff and decomposing corpses whom no one was around to bury, lying in a field of tall wild flowers pock-marked with shell-holes. In villages nearby there were stories of a tall blonde foreigner – possibly Rosanna – but the dates didn't fit. We flew over the mountains for a scary little encounter in a Turkish village, and a sniff of the real story appeared, backed up later by 40 Commando who found some clues at a camping site high in the mountains – a woman's comb, a shoe and a diary.

Much later, a Turkish guide was arrested. He'd offered to lead the group over the border, then got angry when his request for extra money was refused. All three died. They were independent and courageous people, but there is always a major element of chance in such surroundings.

Towards the end of the assignment I began to feel faintly ill, but considering the number of accidents we'd managed, and a diet rather heavy on goat, and concussion from a tree, everyone thought I was perfectly normal; so we left Kurdestan with memories and bruises and I went straight to the Hospital for Tropical Diseases in London – where a very excited specialist announced after three days of blood-sampling that I was only the thirteenth person in Britain to have contracted tick-borne Congo–Crimea haemorrhagic fever. I can only assume the tick walked a long way.

No one should moan on about rotten food and gyppy tummies when there's so much hunger in the world, least of all well-rounded reporters. To have the temerity to take pictures of swollen bellies and stick-thin legs while a few sacks of flour are being dropped among thousands takes a particular form of professional hardness. You justify your actions with the hope that your pictures will stir hearts many thousands of miles away and elicit more aid, or perhaps embarrass a particular government into doing more for its own poor – for there are rarely thin government ministers or hungry generals. However, the images you transmit to the world are simplistic, for there is usually a complex web of interests involved: villagers going hungry in order to send the only available food to their soldier sons and husbands on the front line; the desperate Hutu refugees on the borders of Rwanda and Zaïre begging for food and medicine – every one of them complicit in the massacres of their Tutsi neighbours; warlords keeping their own people on minimum rations in order to evoke sympathy from foreign powers, Sarajevo not excepted; changes in climate and the environment which mean that traditional homelands are no longer viable, and the people cannot stay put if they want to survive; some aid agencies which are as self-justifying as any other business.

And though the images are those which grab the viewer's attention, there are limits to the newsdesk's tolerance. A prone, unmoving body under a heap of rags in Africa once led an editor to enquire from London: 'Is that a dead person? We can't have that on the *Six O'Clock News*.'

'Just alive,' we replied, 'with probably only a few hours to go.'

'That's OK then. Just checking. Can't have dead people when there could be children watching.'

An interesting collection of diseases with which to bore doctors at parties is one thing. Keeping your vital limbs attached to yourself is another. No one should underestimate the problems that are increasing as journalism becomes an ever larger industry, and governments and armies and bandits and gangsters grow more aware of press power.

Even in the eighties it was quite common to come upon national presidents who were naïve about interviews and soldiers who were wholly ignorant of the reach of the media. But most have now cottoned on; and, where they can't deploy public relations and propaganda to effect, they turn on the journalists themselves. The figures for injuries and deaths among media personnel worldwide – an incomplete and patchy record, admittedly – sees a decade-on-decade increase.

To begin with, weapons are ever more sophisticated; but, more importantly, they're becoming cheaper and more readily available. Gone are the days when gunmen in jungles or deserts or European cities had to be content with ancient rifles that had seen action in the First World War. A globalised arms trade, a richer world and the end of the Soviet Union have all led to easier deals which secure copious lethal weaponry with little effort and only modest outlay.

A young frontier officer with the Pakistani army described to me how the fact that Americans had armed *mujahedin* fighters to cross the border to take on the Russians in Afghanistan had changed life in his district: now there were often surplus weapons, a result of small groups deciding that they preferred to sell part of their American consignment to the horde of arms dealers who lurked in the local bazaars. Guns were traded internationally, but a number always trickled back into the local villages. The Pakistani captain was responsible for two villages where there had been a running feud of ancient proportions over land ownership; the crux was a small patch worth very little, but with significance as the site of a former mosque. Every two or three years in living memory, there'd been a bit of a set-to, with much shouting leading to stone-throwing, followed by a few shots on either side and everyone running home satisfied. The previous year all that had changed with the appearance of efficient semi-automatic weapons. In a few seconds, there were bodies everywhere, and the villagers had retreated into mute isolation – plotting long-term revenge, feared the captain.

Added to the proliferation of cheap guns is a growing dislike of the presence of well-fed, well-equipped foreigners who appear to operate disdainfully amid the miseries of war and pestilence: the 'bunch of vultures', always concentrating on the grim side of life, always looking for trouble. In the nineties 'the presence of the international media' nearly always meant Western countries having their cameras and photographers viewing a third world problem; Western people standing on a barren, windswept plain amid the dying, wearing their stout but fashionable boots and applying lip-salve.

I grew up without any knowledge of military ordnance. There was a red-painted sea-mine on the promenade in Sunderland, its beautifully polished brass 'horns' giving no indication of its former life – it had become a collecting-box for maritime charities. Those bits of bombs in the sideboard at home were objects of curiosity, but I had no idea of explosions and shrapnel. And not a clue about bullets and their trajectories.

Northern Ireland taught me something about explosions: cars hurled into the air, with an unmistakable whoomph; incendiary devices (fire-bombs; the security services have their own arcane language) crump-whooshing upwards through a building; odd things going thump in fields – IRA home-made mortars hitting rabbits and any other unintended target. So I thought I knew a bit about bombs. Not so. Sitting in the departure lounge at Rome airport waiting to board a flight for Cairo in 1981, we heard a weird rumbling in the ceiling above us, followed by the cracking and roaring of a fire. Bits of ceiling confetti'd down, and as we stared, large chunks of masonry started crashing around us. We lay on the floor, having an argument: Couldn't be a bomb. 'Course not, just because we're twitchy reporters. Big fire though. Funny smell as well. But it isn't a bomb, of course. All around us several hundred people ran hither and thither in blind panic, screaming 'bomba, bomba'. Quite right too. Bloody great bomb planted by the PLO in the office of the El Al airline. And as usual, when you're at the heart of the story, you're the last ones to wake up to what's happening and start taking pictures.

Perhaps we just weren't in the right mood. We'd spent days flitting around the Mediterranean like mosquitoes pretending that we were on a very serious assignment. In actual fact we were chasing the newly married Prince Charles and Lady Diana, but heaven help us if we admitted this, for the BBC was maintaining po-faced propriety and denying that it would ever stoop to such a grubby level. It had publicly announced in the run-up to the wedding that it would be covering the departure of the couple on the Royal Yacht at Gibraltar, and That was That.

That is, until we learned that ITN was hiring a plane to do meticulous low-level searches of the Mediterranean, and nearly everyone in Fleet Street was being deployed on the honeymoon hunt. The BBC is a tad naïve at times.

My colleague Chris Morris bid an elegant and tasteful adieu to the Yacht as it slid past the Rock to destinations unknown, and in London the foreign editor held an emergency meeting while staring at his atlas and making wild guesses. As a result, I and my crew were destined for Tunisia; mainly because someone in the newsroom remembered that Prince Charles had once met President Bourguiba. Why he should want to take his new wife to see an elderly Tunisian was not spelled out. The first plane leaving for Tunis was a jam-packed charter from Luton, so I was shovelled into the jump-seat in the cockpit and told that my crew would get the next scheduled flight that day. In Tunis I borrowed the phone on the Air France desk and made contact with London on a bad line.

'Have got to Tunisia,' I bellowed.

'Sardinia,' crackled a voice.

'NO, TUNISIA.'

'NO, GO SARDINIA CREW THERE.'

At times, it's wise not to reason why, so I asked the nice man at Air France to point me towards a plane for Italy; he had a word with a friend and I spent the next two hours on a jump-seat to Rome. Heading for the Alisarda airline in Rome airport, I was passed by several Fleet Street hacks getting off the plane I was boarding for the island. We stared at each other with mutual suspicion, but said nothing. Much later, whiling away the many hours in Egypt by the Suez Canal, waiting for the first glimpse of the elusive Royal Yacht, the assembled press corps calculated that we'd been spread across eighteen different locations on the first two nights of the honeymoon, all ridiculously certain of exclusive pictures, and the only time the ship had been spotted was when a photographer crested a hill on a remote Greek island, to see HMY *Britannia* steaming off towards the blue horizon.

At least the PLO's effort in Rome had given us only a few bruises. Beirut, Afghanistan, Chad, Iraq and Sri Lanka delivered more serious stuff, where there were few rules and you learned to calculate risk. There was no set text; observation, luck and experience were the only methods, coupled with good advice from wise old hands – which doesn't include know-all army-barmy wannabees who burble on about When I was in the SAS and turn out to be Walter Mitty. And there is absolutely nothing in any textbook about how to defend yourself against desperate hospital staff in Panama, under siege from General Noriega's army, who are dropping syringes from the top floor on to anyone seen crawling towards the front door.

It was in the Balkans where it all grew very grim. A curiously small-scale war with large-scale awfulness, where the search for facts was one of the minor aspects of life, and where survival became a priority. I'd had my first lesson in Balkan facts during the Croat–Serb conflict, beginning in the small village of Tenja, just south of the Croat town of Osijek, in 1991. On a dull July afternoon we'd crouched behind farm buildings as the unmistakable sound of tank fire thumped among the pretty trees screening a long wiggle of cottages and smallholdings. Up to that point, we'd seen the odd tank or two manoeuvring; indeed, my cameraman Nigel Bateson and I had spent nearly an hour up a walnut tree the day before sneaking pictures of a Serb armoured unit ruining a cornfield with monstrous tracks. But apart from unpleasant encounters with motley groups of young men who were undoubtedly spoiling for a fight, Yugoslavia still seemed to be nowhere near a civil war. However, the sounds from Tenja were much more ominous, and not one of the journalists watching distant puffs of oily black smoke followed by the leaping tongues of house fires wanted to go near to investigate.

I'd seen tanks in action in Afghanistan, Iran and Iraq – but there the landscape had been barren, the tanks like giant toys playing in a suitably empty sandpit. In a European setting it seemed – shockingly – much more shocking. There were two cows grazing in the meadow in front of us, tail-swishing away the mosquitoes which infest the sluggish river meanderings. Neat strips of garden ran from the back of the village houses, stuffed with patches of fat cabbages and ripening sweetcorn, dotted with plum trees for the autumn's brew of slivovic. A pert church tower proclaimed the Croat end of the village until – crump – it developed a large hole.

We stared at eachother. No one was quite sure about the niceties of observing a tank attack. So we wandered round to the back of our rather obvious shiny red Volvo and delved for flak jackets in the boot, embarrassed to put them on in the suburbs of a Habsburgian town full of stout buildings, a theatre and a cathedral. The jackets were new-fangled bits of equipment, weighted with heavy square plates and seemingly not made for the human frame. In the first few weeks we had been shy about wearing them – they looked far too 'warry', and we were journalists, not combatants. We also took ages to get them on.

The crumps grew more regular, accompanied by the chatter of automatic rifles – and birdsong and distant hurrahs from a town football match in Osijek. We all felt a bit uncomfortable, dressed like navy-blue armadillos, having opted to film smoky clouds above lime trees half a mile away, rather than – than what?

Hollywood films have journalists crabbing towards close vantage points which show them precisely who is shooting whom, while villagers who always speak comprehensible English explain how it all started. We were all far too appalled to move any nearer, and, as a rather dramatic sunset ensued, against which brilliant

291

flames reared up through blackened rafters – on the end of a long lens – we crept away rather shamefaced and not a little frightened, to deliver our offerings to London.

The next morning we returned and sat in the Volvo on the approach road to Tenja. We still hadn't a clue what was going on, but at least the village was silent. We decided to risk a walk and crunched over broken glass, past family cars magicked by fire into ginger skeletons. Like a music-hall act, Nigel, Susannah, our interpreter, and I all jumped into the air and gasped theatrically as an elderly woman suddenly clanged into view, wielding a broom somewhat pointlessly over what had been her garden and was now several square yards of dented cooking pots, soggy lumps of clothing and every possible knick-knack and memento which makes up a long life. Mixed in were uprooted geraniums and a budding, bent prize sunflower. Someone had had a fine time hurling Ilonka's belongings out of her house – removing the door for easier action – and didn't seem actually to have paused to pick over the spoils. It was a scene to be repeated thousands of times in the next few years: the ridding of all the signs which mark territory and claim residence, shortly to be known as ethnic cleansing. For Ilonka's son and daughter-in-law had fled that morning, with their children. She was too old, too resigned to go.

We picked our way along what was still a picture-book street, most houses still undamaged, but many of them with the slither of singed paper and underwear and odd shoes and smashed orange lustre china oozing below broken windows. We fell over odd bits of unidentifiable metal and averted our eyes from two dead dogs. A taste of war that was to grow into a diet of mess and misery for years.

But what were the facts? Ilonka had raved on about 'thousands of Croats giving the Serbs a good hiding'. But she was the only remaining Croat, and ahead of us were a bunch of hulking blokes, all auditioning for an armed Serbian version of *Fiddler on the Roof*: huge beards, big boots, hearty slaps on the back and much waving of slivovic bottles. Barring our path was a very large man, dressed rather like a pirate, a rakish bandanna round his wiry bush of hair – which merged with his black beard. His chest was criss-crossed with two bandoliers winking bullets. He had a revolver stuffed in his belt, what looked like a butcher's knife in his boot, and he was cradling an enormous rifle. He introduced himself as Nikolai and spoke passable English. Not waiting for too many formalities to turn sour, we turned the camera on him and asked him his connection to the village. Was he a soldier?

'No,' he bellowed. 'I am village librarian.'

Christ, I thought, what do the less intellectual look like?

I ploughed on, determined to track down a few facts about yesterday's events.

'What happened here yesterday?' I asked.

Nikolai drew a deep breath, and launched in: 'In 1943, the Croats came into our village and killed . . .'

Five minutes later, he'd reached a complicated bit of early 1944 and I interrupted, in order to receive a second lecture on foreigners' ignorance of glorious Serb history, and foreign responsibility for their present-day woes.

It was an object lesson, and I heard it over the years from Croats, Serbs, Bosnians and Kosovans. Everything grew out of history – the theft of a cow, the burning of a village, the driving out of hundreds of thousands from what they had always thought of as home. The events of yesterday – the previous twenty-four hours, such a vital element in my journalistic tradition – were but a recent drop in the mighty historical flow. How could you possibly talk of a few hours when centuries were clamouring to be heard?

A small seed of panic was sown in my mind: just how did you pin down what had just happened? Television news is a promiscuous medium, alighting briefly on a few verified facts – hopeless where eight centuries of disputed history are concerned. And believe me, everything was disputed.

I then made the mistake of telling Nikolai that the fighting in Tenja was the limit of my enquiries, and – again, not for the last time in the Balkans – found that pooh-poohing history in favour of journalism earned me a rifle muzzle against the throat.

Susannah did well – there was a lot of incomprehensible shouting – and a couple of nasty minutes later we managed to retreat, hanging on to lives and camera tape.

By the time all factions really got going the next spring, that scene was being repeated on a daily basis, its key ingredients distorted history, exaggeration about current events, and a deep-rooted sense of grievance which heaped the cause of all misfortune upon 'foreigners'. And foreigners like us were fair game – culpable propagandists who refused to understand and sympathise with the 'right cause'; we were therefore ranged in the shooting-gallery, with the word PRESS on our vehicles marking the target.

Two months later, Croatia and Serbia were infinitely more dangerous places to be, with anger and unpleasant surprises erupting from picture-book villages, each house with a traditional V-shaped rack of golden-orange sweetcorn cobs stored for winter, and purple plums promising many bottles of home brew. There was one local tradition, though, that weirdly presaged the trouble that was stirring. For autumn comes to Bosnia with a scream, amid laughter and clinking glasses. In the villages, a plume of smoke rises from the orchards. Children scuttle about eagerly, carrying pans and trays. A grandma stirs a witch's cauldron under the trees, and the men get on with men's business: bottles in hand in a circle, watching the struggling, screeching pig.

Pig-sticking I liked to avoid. Not just for the slithering death of the huge animal, trotters drumming, but because of the air of medieval joyfulness. Such a party. The whole family gathered, the townies come home to granny to witness tradition – and to get a nice bag of chitterlings. And ghastly things bubbling in the cauldron.

I used to feel snobbishly foreign. Such peasants. And I wanted to think that violent acts in the farmyard might be linked to violence across the landscape.

osed in front of an armoured Land Rover in Bosnia in 1993, waiting to go live into *Breakfast with Frost*, and just prior to scuttling for cover because of sniper fire

One of the day-long trips through the mountains in Bosnia in a lumbering armoured 'beast'

A typical parking problem in our Bosnian front drive – full of British Army armour

How to help out a Bosnian neighbour

A mine exploding under a Warrior armoured vehicle twenty yards in front of our land rover (our windscreen-wiper is on the left). There were ten mines hidden under rubble strewn across the main road to Zenica in central Bosnia

Kosovo, 1999 – an Albanian street-trader shot in the chest by a sniper in Pristina; terrified of the Serb-run hospital, he wanted us with him to ensure fair treatment

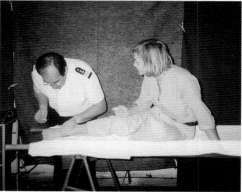

The field hospital under the telephone exchange in Sarajevo – with a French Naval surgeon fishing for bullet and shrapnel bits

The journalists with the British Army being briefed in the desert in Saudi Arabia

The CO of 7th Armoured Brigade 'The Desert Rats', Brigadier Patrick Cordingley, wisely not taking tactical advice from the press

Prime Minister John Major visiting the troops

By helicopter for the last few miles to Kuwait, ducking under pylon cables, flying over bombed front line positions

First morning in Kuwait, having spent the night in a freshly dug grave; still very attached to floppy hat

'We can't start yet ...
Kate Adie isn't here..'

The Basra Road, just north of Kuwait City, with tanks still 'cooking off' as we walked through hundreds of vehicles caught while fleeing north to Iraq

Editing in an army tent in the desert in Oman in 2001

On HMS *Illustrious* in Oman, 2001, with producer Anthony Massey and cameraman Simon Cumbers, as British forces backed up the US attacks on Afghanistan

Martha Gelhorn in London, in her eighties and still reporting

The family: Babe and Bill Dunnet, and Alastair, Dianora and Catriona

As a post-Second World War child, I'd hear the stories about War Pigs: the illegal porkers kept in unlikely places to supplement British rations. Born of expediency, they were, I presumed, dispatched by the local butcher, quick and quietly. Then I read a description of rural life in the Midlands, of pigs being slaughtered with ceremony and celebration equal to anything in the Balkans, in the area which is now the garden to my cottage.

In the twenties my small village 'stuck' a hundred pigs every winter. The villagers applauded the housewife who went forward to receive 'first meat', the belly-bit. The writer James Buchan, who later became a news reporter for the BBC in Glasgow, recalls his town-bred mother's distaste at the scene in my village. However, he later accepted the importance of the pig for a family's winter: the salted meat, the uses found for every bit from trotter to tail. I've looked for more recollections of pig-killing, but have failed to find anyone describe from living memory what must have been one of the commonest sights in the English countryside up to the Second World War. Still, so much for my snobbery and my assumption that the nineteenth-century industrial revolution in Britain had put away medieval tradition, entitling me to sniff at the medieval Balkans.

And yet. And yet. Eight years of observing life in turmoil in former Yugoslavia has left me with a lurking suspicion that familiarity with blood and screaming – even of a mere pig – takes the edge off humane attitudes.

Four of us were looking at a large hole in a church tower in a village near the Croatian town of Sid: Nigel Bateson and Mark Macauley, a very experienced team, myself and Susannah our interpreter. We'd for once had a leisurely lunch, and were wondering whether we should do a little filming to justify it. Tank rounds through church towers were becoming the starting signal for major local difficulties, and the Serbian army base just up the road had been out for a bit of practice. As we filmed in what was a perfectly peaceful rural idyll, a local family insisted on inviting us to their home to describe what had happened, and press yet another lunch upon us. Bottles of brandy and giant blocks of cheese and a delicatessen's worth of salami and ham were urged on us in their modern kitchen. The sitting-room attested to typical affluence: over-stuffed sofas, lots of electrical goodies, and large glass-fronted cabinets bearing cut glass and ornate china. As they inveighed against the damage done to their Catholic church by those 'Orthodox brigands', we nibbled cheese and sipped brandy, knowing we were in for a lengthy bout of hospitality.

We heard something rattle in the far distance, followed by a loud crump. The rattles grew insistently nearer, and our lunch party suddenly turned itself into a firing party. The women grabbed the children and headed for the cellar, and the men dived under the kitchen sink to produce several well-cared-for semi-automatic rifles. We cowered under the kitchen table and wondered what on earth was happening; what had turned our friendly bourgeois family into an assault team?

The kitchen window at the side of the house had been wedged open, and short bursts of gunfire were being delivered into the main street. Amid shouts of triumph, Susannah asked what was going on.

'We've just killed the postman. He's been coming to our house for fourteen years – but he's a Serb, of course.'

A neighbour arrived to say that Serbian troops had tried to bring a military convoy through the village and been ambushed by local Croat lads who'd thrown grenades into trucks crammed with soldiers. The Serbs had had to leave their dead and had now retreated.

We decided to get out, picked up our kit and tiptoed out of the back door, dodging sunflowers and large rose bushes. The street had gone quiet again and we weighed our chances: the village was sleepy in sunshine, but about a quarter of a mile away at the other end of the houses there was smouldering wreckage.

Feeling rather exposed, we dashed across the road into a garden with several large trees, only to hear more small-arms fire and an odd rumbly-squeaky sound. Nigel squinted from behind a tree and started to film: 'Tanks on the way,' he said.

The rumbling grew louder and I panicked, running to the courtyard at the rear of the garden and realising there was a line of outhouses and no back way out. I turned round in order to find Nigel bearing down on me, yelling, 'They've got machine guns firing at the houses all the way.' The kitchen door was locked and we all went at it like a slapstick team in a comedy sketch – One, Two, Three: Bang! We fell on the floor inside and seconds later saw puffs of white powder skedaddle round the outhouse walls, bullets zizzing into the soft plaster.

Two tanks went past and we lay on the floor for a goodly time. Completely at a loss as to what constituted intelligent action, we sat under yet another kitchen table – it seemed comforting – and had a fruitless conversation. Having scraped up enough courage to venture out into the yard, we barrelled back as a horrendous whoosh went overhead, culminating in a deafening explosion. This time we scoured the kitchen floor for a cellar trap-door. There wasn't one. A second whoosh saw us under the table and clutching each other. Tank fire is especially creepy – if you're right underneath there seems to be a milli-second of whirring as if the shell is vibrating anger on its way to you.

The sun set but the tanks didn't let up, and it sounded as if one was coming nearer. Nigel wondered if they'd try the machine-gun trick again, and we all rushed upstairs at the thought, only for the next shell to clip the eaves of the roof and detonate the house next door in a yellow glow that lit up the whole street. Completely unnerved, we crashed down to the kitchen again, and went back under the cosy table. It was only at this point that we became aware of a very odd cheeping sound next to us. Torchlight revealed several hundred fluffy lemony chicks corralled in a makeshift pen. The next eight hours were spent listening to whirr–whoomph–cheepcheepcheep until none of us felt sane. There were one or two moments when I thought This is it and many when I couldn't think at all because my brain was a void filled with fear.

In the early hours it went quiet; even the chicks shut up. We needed to get out – we had no other thought, and in the pale dawn we crept out of the kitchen door to be confronted by a dozen silent copper hens perched on the fence between yard and garden. They eyed us with what seemed like undiluted accusation, as if we were responsible for the worst night of their lives. No eggs for you, they seemed to say.

Peering down the road, it looked disconcertingly normal. We saw an elderly man come out of a gate a hundred yards away. We waved. He waved back and walked across the road. We set off in his direction, remembering that our car was some distance down a side road over the way. We soon saw the previous day's wreckage – three burned-out army trucks and an abandoned armoured personnel carrier. Then, again, there was an inexplicable set of shouts and yells and a group of young men ran out in front of us. They gestured for us to follow them into a driveway and round the rear of a large house where the drive sloped down to a large garage door in the basement. By now, the familiar sound of random small-arms fire had started up again.

In the gloom of the garage it became miserably clear that we'd met up with the young warriors who'd started the whole shebang in the first place, full of bravado and ready for more combat. I shrank on to the garage workbench as belts of ammunition were dragged out of boxes and shiny-eyed young men in black knitted beanie-hats smoked and fiddled with their rifles. Nigel and Mark were trying to guess the lie of the land from the garage door. Susannah was saying nothing – as would any Serb from Belgrade finding herself in a Croat HQ. The gunfire increased and a number of the lads darted out of the garage, firing randomly. I tried to get a better seat on the bench, and pushed at the object in my way, which instantly revealed itself as a large corpse.

I hurtled forward, having had enough and full of idiot energy. We cantered through an orchard with the Croats shouting for us to stay and watch the action, and proceeded to attack at full pelt an obstacle course of vegetable patches, pigsties, fences and flowerbeds. At some point we were going to have to cross the road, so I volunteered to go first and probably did an Olympic best. Susannah was close on my heels, followed by Mark. Nigel paused as a vicious volley went down the centre of the road. Then he started off, and in the few seconds it took him to cross I heard bullets whistle through the beech hedge next to me. He was running towards me, so I closed my eyes. He thundered past – he's a mountain of a man and takes several yards to stop.

By now we were none of us quite rational. We spent two hours in a cellar into which we were shown by a quiet housewife who was serenely doing Sunday morning chores despite the clatter of warfare. She apologised for not being able to make coffee – the electricity had gone off; but a bottle of pale home-brewed slivovic arrived, and for once it delivered exactly the right raw jolt to pulverise our senses.

Emboldened, we searched for our car, to find it sporting several bullet holes. An old man was leaning against his garden wall and shouting at us not to go over the fields – 'Minar, minar.' Bugger mines, we said, and jolted the Volvo over a mile of ploughed earth towards the next village, where the doors of the church were flung wide and the sound of Catholic mass mingled with the drone of a Serb fighter plane overhead. We felt wholly disorientated. And we had precisely seventeen seconds of tape to illustrate what we'd been through. I'd also got about seventeen hundred blotches all over me: the chicks had announced their presence, now the fleas were announcing theirs. I spent the next few days feeling very strange and unable to distinguish between shock and the fear that plague might still be around. But there was also the sneaking feeling that daily small skirmishes were leading us into cross-fire and killing much more regularly.

And so Croatian and Serbian troubles slid into Bosnia.

Civil war is domestic violence writ large: the bread-knife and the fear at the top of the stairs. All your neighbours become a suspect family, and no one will intervene. You shriek amid familiar surroundings and no one takes much notice. You appeal to the authorities – and they're rather embarrassed. And when the uniforms finally arrive they never understand the intensity of what's going on. Nor can they have a solution.

Civil wars are nasty, vindictive, and redolent of vendetta and revenge. Memories are vivid – for the events take place in and around the home. The local shop is burned out, the bakery becomes an ammunition store, the farm machinery plant an arms factory. Names of the dead are recognised – the people along the street. Also the names of those who did the killing.

The conflict is called a war, but has no rules of war, for everything is legitimised in the name of survival. You shoot your neighbour, the doctor, the postman. You kill cattle and burn houses full of useful belongings, just because they belong to the wrong people. And a Red Cross is meaningless – because there is talk of ambulances ferrying arms and fighters to the other side. Besides, your people do it too.

Superstition rears its medieval head, for there is faith in the past and your struggle is rooted in past injustices. So bodies are not left untouched, and even graves not left quiet.

And you never wish to live next to your neighbour again. The foreigners call it ethnic cleansing. But you fear their bread knife, in the middle of the night.

And the foreigners never quite understand. However, if the foreigners come over your threshold, they too might just get the bread knife in them.

When I was twelve, I had refused to be a Girl Guide. I thought the uniform awful, and there seemed to be little point in winning badges for sewing. Anyway, it had filtered through that the Guides went camping – not in some wild and wonderful wilderness, but in a dog-poo-strewn field off one of Sunderland's municipal parks. Hardly a big bold adventure. But then, I didn't want one.

The idea of wet grass, insects and eating luke-warm baked beans out of a sardine-tin never appealed. Camping – no thanks. I was a soft little creature. I liked clean sheets and food on the table, preferably cooked by someone else. I haven't changed.

So facing up to Bosnian domesticity presented a challenge. While Sarajevo started to shrivel into a siege, the rest of central Bosnia curdled around it. Trouble crackled across the bleak hills and the dark forests. In the valleys there were substantial modern houses – usually part-built and awaiting more remittance money from *Gastarbeiter* away in Germany – and plump-looking farms. Everyone had a few cattle or pigs, a patch of sweetcorn maybe, tomatoes and cabbages, and, of course, an orchard of plum trees for slivovic.

There was little of the exotic Bosnia seen by the writer Rebecca West on her travels in the late thirties. The quaint and the characterful had been erased. Intricate carved balconies, half-timbered white-washed cottages, touches of Ottoman exoticism – all had gone. 'Who wants something old? Yuk.' Modern rural Bosnians sniffed at the idea. The middle-aged generation, skilled carpenters and handymen, had been to Germany. They'd also worked in the Gulf, and seen family dwellings that suited their way of life: lots of space to take in the in-laws, nice modern kitchens and bathrooms. So they'd returned and pulled down the picturesque and the cute, and the admittedly smelly and insanitary. Instead, in the words of a young British soldier to his colonel on his first tour of the Lasva valley: 'How come we're saving the lives of a bunch of people who live in bloody mansions, sir?'

Lots of rooms, a big freezer full of family pig, a heavy carved sofa with a cream hairy skin of the world's largest sheep-cum-goat thrown over it. A glass-fronted cabinet where an orange lustre coffee set twinkled on crocheted doilies next to the brass coffee-grinder. And a very large telly and an even larger hi-fi system. Life in the Lasva valley and all around it was by no means behind the times. There were satellite dishes perched in gardens, and microwave ovens in the fitted kitchens.

I mention this because so many of the pictures which subsequently came to symbolise Bosnia were of rural village people, many of them elderly, the women in headscarves and their baggy divided skirts, the men gnarled and toothless under their dome-like hats. The impression given was of medieval folk cut off from western Europe. But these tended to be the inhabitants of the more remote hilltop villages which were ruthlessly emptied at the beginning of hostilities to gain strategic positions. And once petrol became scarce – so much of it being gobbled up for military purposes – the smart cars and tractors couldn't be used, so the ancient horses and carts were pressed into service. The cameras loved these scenes: the depressed peasants herded along country roads behind clip-clopping skinny beasts. For the received (but not much acknowledged) TV wisdom is that it is not quite so embarrassing to journalist or viewer when the suffering group looks a bit different from us. The camera can zoom in and look at the miserable faces: under thick headscarves, in funny flowered trouser-skirts, they're not the people you're going to meet in Marks and Spencer. There's no doubt that the less the resemblance to the life we know, the easier it is to intrude and to inspect.

However, much of the Lasva valley, which lies to the west of Sarajevo within shell-hearing distance on quiet summer days, gave the impression of prosperity and relatively affluent European life. The grocery shops stocked most of the goods to be found in any town in countries to the west – along with a phenomenal array of jam and a fearsome amount of sugary home-made spreads. This was one reason why dental jokes were the stock-in-trade of every British soldier – stopping and checking people at roadblocks could be made less tedious by holding tooth-counting competitions. We made a careful note never to call on a Bosnian dentist; we felt they'd be frightened by a full set of teeth.

Our first domestic base in central Bosnia was in Kiseljak. We'd recce'd the valley a week or so earlier, and reckoned that a rented house in the little town of Vitez at the other end of the valley would be most suitable; but another BBC team had a producer who'd also been scouting, a man more familiar with the *Good Hotel Guide* than war zones; he'd seen the sign Hotel in Kiseljak – a good eighteen miles from our preferred base – and unloaded a large amount of money at the front desk. He appeared to be unaware that war does things to hotels; either they're destroyed or looted, or, if they're still standing, they're occupied by lots of men in uniform who are certainly not porters. Others still standing but sparsely occupied tend to be on front lines, and not everyone fancies a crawl to bed under sniper fire.

Having discovered that there was nothing even resembling a hotel in Vitez, he'd plumped for Kiseljak, which boasted the Hotel Continental on a grand sign painted the length of the first-floor balcony. The ground floor consisted of a bar full of Croat drinkers, mostly uniformed, a pool table and a back room which doubled as the laundry. Upstairs was a large sitting-room with a hairy sofa and a very large TV and several tiny bedrooms. The landlady, Janja, was a staggeringly competent and resourceful woman who installed us but didn't mention the problem of damp. Kiseljak flu was persistent and debilitating. Nevertheless, she produced vast amounts of nutritious bean soup that could have fed an army. Considering the Croats in the front bar, it probably did. She also had access to a secret hoard of frozen chicken and trout which we never located – and it was better not to ask anyway, for Kiseljak was the hub of voracious black-marketeering. All through the war it traded and prospered, leeching off the needs of nearby Sarajevo and the huge through traffic of UN personnel; it also served as a mafia headquarters to some of the more organised thugs and businessmen who had a very good war indeed. There were only ever two notable explosions in the town over the years. One night the sole pizzeria in the wartime valley spread its ham and tomato paste over a very wide area due to a 'business difference of opinion'. And there was also the mother of all bangs down by the river, reported to be a local fighter off on a little business expedition who happened upon a mine. Hard to tell what used to go on in Kiseljak; business came first, and no one was at all inclined to be open and honest.

Janja did her best by us, feeding and providing for a crowd of journalists who were vague about how long they were staying, tramped filthy boots all over her hotel, and took only cursory notice of her lengthy rants that 'Musselmen are coming to kill us tonight . . .' We also fed her dog. Discovered as a cowering, scrawny wretch in the kennel next to our newly erected satellite dish, it was fattened into a sleek and amiable beast, the only Alsatian in Bosnia whose rations regularly came in by armoured land rover. If there were complaints that food was desperately scarce just a few miles away in Sarajevo, the counter-argument was that that was no excuse for tolerating neglect on your doorstep.

Life in the valley was getting more difficult well before we arrived. Shops were being boarded up and many had been abandoned and looted. The fields were often too quiet, the cattle kept indoors. All the routes to central Bosnia were either blocked or the subject of fighting. We made our journeys from the coastal town of Split up to Kiseljak like explorers setting off for the unknown.

We were already using armoured vehicles. Expensive and unwieldy up-armoured land rovers, they were nevertheless necessary. We carried equipment, food, water and personal gear loaded to the roof, and squashed ourselves in the tiny remaining space. I discovered that driving Miss Piggy, our first and most amenable brute, was like steering a rhinoceros. Miss Piggy had a mind of her own, and over thirty-five miles an hour she developed a certain unstoppability. On the other hand, if you do demolish a barn outside Gromiliak one fine and frosty morning, Miss Piggy will emerge phoenix-like from the flying timber and hay and continue as if nothing had happened. Not for nothing was she armoured.

The trip from Split was usually a nightmare. Having turned off the coastal metalled roads, there was a choice of rat-runs through the mountains. Old logging trails were the most favoured.

We heaved over bog and mud, along streams, across fields. We slithered our four tons into trees, prayed and sweated as we crept along the edge of sheer drops into the huge lake at Prozor, and spent a lot of time digging. Nigel, Martin Bell and I thanked God for the army in the Gulf; up until that time of my life I had never understood the importance of a shovel, and now I never went anywhere in Bosnia without one. Miss Piggy frequently embedded herself in farmyards, as if yearning for kinship. We dug and pushed and swore. Once back on the road, there was other traffic, too. At the most remote part of a forest track, the trees would crack and rustle and a huge bus would bear down upon us. Hurling Miss Piggy into a ditch secured survival, as the Tuzla to Frankfurt coach thundered past through the mud and bracken. War or no war, the northern town of Tuzla ran a regular service to ensure an income of remittance money from faraway Germany. The coach would be packed to the gills, the faces at the grimy windows tense and fearful. Travelling though Bosnia was no fun run for anyone.

Roadblocks, drunken soldiers, belligerent police, the odd wild boar a-leaping. Mud and muddle as various checkpoints changed hands, and every so often a stretch of road where Miss Piggy played sitting duck to a known Active Unit: it could be a distant mortar position, with a sharp-eyed lad bored rigid by lack of juicy targets, or a dozy thug eager to assert his new-found importance as a fighter for his people. Either way, there were bits of the journey which occasioned an intake of breath in Miss Piggy, a mutter between Nigel and myself as to tactics ('Bugger it, go for it'), and a heavy silence inside the armour as the engine raced and we ran the firing-range. Feeling just like a plastic duck.

We didn't exactly get used to being shot at. It just used to happen a lot, that's all.

By now we were carrying impressive medical packs, fearful that our Gulf army training was going to come in useful. A standard morning run up the Lasva valley along a delightful road winding through villages prinked with dinky minarets or squat churches used to be a catalogue of sniper incidents, odd mortar booms and roadblock confrontations. It made the Northern Line look very easy.

A drive through the valley looking more closely revealed a landscape suffering a horrible disease. Blackened buildings spotted the green fields. The fields grew coarse with neglect. People skittered indoors, or hugged walls as they walked. The local hoods roared around in far-too-shiny cars, four camouflage-clad young men wearing expressions of grim, sneering confidence.

It wasn't an ordinary battlefield. It was as if someone had decided to play a lethal board game and failed to produce a set of rules. However, break an invisible rule, and you got blown off the board.

Trying to report the progress of the conflict was a near-impossibility. None of the usual sources of information existed: there were no local newspapers, the radio and TV stations that functioned were a cesspit of rumour and propaganda. Local militia commanders, with one or two honourable exceptions, exaggerated their activities. They spoke of their troops as if they were in command of trained and disciplined battalions conducting strategic warfare. In reality, small bands roamed the countryside and horrific acts were committed which would have disgraced any responsible military commander. And it soon became obvious that much of the 'fighting' took place in the imagination. On the ground, there'd be heavy shelling from the distance on to a relatively unprotected target. When damage and terror had done their work and the inhabitants had fled, the 'victorious' troops would wait until they thought the coast was clear, then swagger in to claim their prize. Time and again we discovered that the claims for 'heavy street fighting' and 'hand-to-hand combat' were not just false, but inconceivable for most of the fighters we encountered. And everywhere gossip and rumour were taken for hard fact by everyone.

North of the valley were a group of '*mujahedin*' fighters, the rag-tag band of Islamic enthusiasts who'd headed for Bosnia to further their beliefs and impose them – by force – on anyone they encountered. They particularly terrified the local Bosnian Muslims, whose mild brand of religion – ham-eating, beer-drinking – hadn't encountered woman-hating, intolerant militant Islam before. We had hair-raising scrapes with them, finding ourselves screamed at by hyped-up Sudanese and Saudis, who threatened and cursed and lashed out, possibly because they could find no soulmates in the land they had come to 'liberate'. They vented their spleen in a monastery at Guca Gora, when they defecated on the altar and smeared the walls with Arabic graffiti.

Attempting to report all this, we found ourselves bogged down in the minutiae of everyday small-scale violence, while claims were made for widespread military manoeuvres. And over and above the whole sorry mess, there was the political scheming of all parties and the flawed moves of the United Nations.

As the conflict wore on, the roads became clogged first with white-painted UN vehicles, then with NATO's. Huge convoys, the hardware of modern peacekeeping trundling around. Our first lesson ('armour bites') involved flinging ourselves off-road as far as possible while some teenager in uniform from Catterick in charge of thirty-five tons of Warrior armoured vehicle revelled in the joy of having left his dad's battered Allegro behind for ever. Woe betide anyone who thought a Warrior gave way. One Lasva valley militia commander, admittedly drunk, took on a Warrior in a game of chicken with his trusty Lada Niva, Yugoslavia's all-purpose car, only about three moving parts and cheap. Nobody had ever road-tested a Warrior *over* a Lada before, though the results were interesting. The roof had to be pincered off what resembled a sardine tin, and inside lay a rather puzzled commander, track marks to right and left of him. The rest of us were more wary, because army transport is a weird animal. It doesn't stop for the usual reasons, such as old ladies, a cup of tea, or things exploding very nearby – it merely grinds on according to some pre-arranged formula, and doesn't notice Other Traffic.

RTAs – army-speak for Road Traffic Accidents – became a nightmare; and although it would seem logical that you should concentrate on your driving when someone's shooting at you, you don't. We slid into ditches, managed to turn armoured land rovers completely upside down, demolished small landmarks (I claimed a bridge and a barn). Also, local drivers developed a penchant for deliberately crashing into us in order to lobby for compensation. This took various forms, including a drunk and his mate slamming head-first into us in broad daylight at a crossroads in Kiseljak in full view of Dutch UN troops guarding their building opposite. My door was wrenched open and I found myself one foot from a very excitable man breathing alcohol you could set light to. He was also holding a large knife to my throat. All 'trained negotiators' emphasise the need to maintain contact and keep calm. Fine, except that the drunk was rampant-drunk, didn't speak my language and was enjoying himself. A small crowd gathered, curious, but with that Bosnian indifference to matters which don't concern their immediate family. The Dutch soldiers on the pavement opposite stared at the ground and stamped their feet and fulfilled their UN mandate to the letter: don't interfere in things you don't understand. Pretend it's not happening. Perhaps it will go away.

The cavalry arrived in the form of a gallant British Gurkha captain, Peter Bullock, who tackled the drunk, sorted his mate as well, shifted the bent car off our bumpers, got rid of the crowd and then stared long and hard at the Dutch, who looked only mildly sheepish and went back to dreaming of their UN hardship payments.

After some months the logging trails throughout Bosnia were thick with white military monsters and we wondered if they'd afford us some kind of protection. However, we soon learned that huge white monsters with small sitting ducks marked PRESS tagged on their tails merely presented a little more sport for the local hoodlums.

We wondered if we'd attract less attention if we painted our vehicles another colour. But what? Not blue – the Serb police colour; not camouflage green and black – we didn't want to join the war; how about yellow? Well, as Geoff Cox, one of our producers in Tuzla would testify, driving the *only* yellow vehicle in town, nay in Bosnia, having had an argument with a very malicious policeman, is a distinct disadvantage during the ensuing gun-toting chase. ITN, rather by default, acquired a pink armoured vehicle. 'No, it's peony,' said their embarrassed cameraman. It wasn't long before the local Croats decided that pink – or peony – was cute and hijacked it. There was then the added embarrassment of having it whizz past the press on some nefarious deed, with the addition of a large machine gun on its roof to offset its wimpy pinkiness.

Should we paint 'BBC' on the vehicles? Again, no consensus: Bosnians of all shades claimed that we were weren't telling the truth, but reserved their main dislike for CNN. As most people couldn't have seen anything but the occasional rebroadcast story on local news – if that, given the constant power cuts – we didn't feel we could do anything about our image. And we'd already lost a cameraman to a Serb tank round – young Tuna Tunavic, a fearless Croat who'd been driving near front lines in central Bosnia when a Serb commander ordered his men to open fire, for, as he remarked casually afterwards: 'Everyone knows the foreign press are spies, especially the BBC.'

Vehicles offered no great protection, and out in the fresh air the odds were worse. War had had the odd bonus of cleaning up rivers and banishing pollution – there was no functioning industry – but it meant the smell of burning homes carried across the fields ever more pungently. And every hamlet and copse presented a potential risk. There were few delineated front lines. True, the British army had stacks of maps pinned to its walls with thick black lines running over hill and dale, but that was the disciplined military trying to make sense of a pack of straggling militias. In reality there was the possibility of encountering every sort of armed creature in every field and copse, from relatively organised fighters to local vigilantes and criminal gangs. One of the routes out of Vitez was patrolled for years by a highly efficient bunch of crooks known as the Fishhead Gang. They tended to pounce near a fish-farm deep in the woods south of the town, and they may or may not have had allegiance to some political causes, but they had quite a profitable war and found journalists easy prey. Such saleable cameras. Such nice anoraks. And this useful box of food – Please, what this Pot Noodle?

And going through the sunlit hamlets there was always the chance of a mine. We developed twitchiness about them. 'Don't reverse the bloody vehicle over the verge.' 'Watch your feet – keep on the road.' 'Can you see any tracks in front of us – they've put those green dinner-plate things down again and I'm not sure if they're the real thing or not.'

One wet afternoon, cameraman Brian Hulls and I were driving between two Warrior fighting vehicles on a main road north of the steel town of Zenica, not far from Vitez. A few yards in front of us, the leading Warrior slowed. Even through the considerable thickness of our own armoured land rover I thought I heard gunfire and, sure enough, as I edged open the door an inch, there were pinging sounds off the Warrior. The huge white beast was edging gingerly round what seemed, through the slanting rain, to be a considerable rock-fall. A heap of stones were in a cascade from the cliff next to us, strewn across the road and entangled in retaining wire. Knowing we were under fire I asked Brian to roll, his camera fixed on the Warrior now crunching its giant tracks over the stones. The explosion that followed stunned us both. The huge vehicle leapt in the air, and flailed off a lengthy chunk of track. We were rigid with fright. We knew all of the people in the back of the Warrior.

We sat helplessly, for we had no radio contact with military vehicles, and opening the door and standing around didn't seem a good idea in range of people pinging bullets at us from across the fields. The rear door of the Warrior swung very slowly open, and

Colonel Alasdair Duncan appeared. Thoughtfully, he began to chart a track across the rubble, using aluminium food containers burrowed from the innards of the Warrior. As he carefully stepped from one to the other, we froze. I wondered if the army knew there'd been sniper fire. The huge vehicles, when driven closed down, don't hear little bullets bouncing off them. I twitched back into business, accelerated and stuck our vehicle between the open fields and the colonel, then reversed alongside him as he headed for the rear Warrior. He clearly thought I was nuts.

I lurched across Brian who, bless him, was still filming, and screamed out of his door, 'We're under fire' – or words to that effect, with some added emphasis. 'Thank you,' said Alasdair, in that cheery way men have when they're in charge of a situation and encounter an unhinged female, and strode onwards.

I slumped back and started to speculate: if that Warrior had gone right round the stones, the next vehic . . .

'Shut up,' said Brian.

Ignorance can be a blessing. You have less imagination. Time and again, I realised in retrospect that what might have lain ahead, had I suspected it, would have scared the living daylights out of me, and might have led to my having a lot of second thoughts about venturing out and about.

Even leafy lanes could be unpleasant places. Crawling one hot and insect-infested morning after a Scimitar armoured vehicle – a kind of tiny tank – just a mile off the main road from Vitez to Zenica, we found ourselves staring for the umpteenth time at the rear end of an army vehicle with not a clue what was going on. I stared out of the side window. A nice summer day, and the land rover was turning into a sauna. Thick greenery from a tall tree right next to us offered an inviting spot in the shade, so I pushed open my door just a bit to let in some air, only for a soldier outside to heave open the passenger door with a yell: 'Shut your bloody door!' The yell was the sort that soldiers can produce when they're reducing people to rabbit-like obedience. I stared back, a truly alarmed bunny. Outside, men crawled around the lead vehicle, produced various tools, and barked efficiently. Someone gestured to the tree four feet away from my door. Stuck on its side was a sort of green box, dulled and stained, sprouting a wire. We all rolled gently on down the track.

Some months later, a sharp-eyed corporal was handed his medal for noticing the trip-wire of the claymore mine, strung across a thickly grassed lane. He was driving the Scimitar in front of us and 'just spotted it'.

Mines, pot-shots, stray mortars, mad *mujahedin* and lunatic driving: it's no surprise that just a month 'in theatre' began to see us feeling a little frayed. The stories we were sending home were a lengthy catalogue of violence and destruction. We lost count of the villages we'd come across with milk-pans on the stove and breakfast half-eaten, as yet another bout of ethnic cleansing had interrupted ordinary life. That 'ordinary life' had degenerated to the extent that psychiatric hospitals were shelled, the patients pointing helplessly at the sky as another round tore in.

Set-piece 'battles' were rare; instead, small groups murdered each other and ran. Ordinary pedestrians were shot in front of the village store. Grannies had their throats cut in their beds and hospital patients were blown to bits by shrapnel. It was a dirty, mean and vicious conflict, and as the months went by the audience at home grew tired of it: not out of inhumanity, but from a combination of irritation, despair and distance. 'A plague on all their houses' was the reaction to attempts to explain the complexity of Balkan hatred.

From the very beginning of trouble in the Balkans, it became clear that the only way to report it properly was by maintaining a permanent presence – enormously difficult for most organisations; even the BBC blanched when it saw how much it cost to have just one crew in Sarajevo, and one in central Bosnia, knowing that our efforts would not have the audience asking for more.

The lack of basic facilities drained us. We ended up with ingrained dirt and wearing mucky clothes, however hard we tried to keep clean. We got the little problems that come with dirt –

and I met my first bed bug. A diet with almost no fresh fruit or vegetables, combined with copious amounts of 'local wine' decanted from heaven knows where, left most of us feeling slightly seedy. We had domestic accidents aplenty – one of my colleagues jumping with fright one night at the sound of an explosion and delivering his boiling coffee over my neck; feet that foolishly wore trainers and then stood on bits of bomb wreckage; fingers that had arguments with the doors of armoured cars; and numerous people looking for latrines in the dark and unexpectedly finding other large holes.

We became dog-tired and inured to mornings starting horribly early with a chirpy voice from the *Today* programme on the satellite phone demanding a reaction to events which have apparently happened forty miles away, involving a warlord you've never heard of, all while you were in the land of nod. Willing as ever, you mumble, 'Sure, just don't expect too much detail,' and lie back to wait for your cue, while a political discussion drones down the phone. Suddenly you jump – that horrible, twitchy jump which means you've had a little snooze – and notice a phone lying next to you on the pillow. Brain confused, you grab it, and – put it this way, only luck prevents you from addressing the Great and the Good of Britain mid-cornflake with the words HELLO I DON'T CARE WHO YOU ARE DO YOU REALISE I'M IN BED?

Somewhere in all this there was a faint memory that television involved not only surviving but *appearing*, at least for the reporter. Hair: no water for last two days leading to distinctive ruffled bird's-nest style. Make-up: needed to cover grey complexion and various scars from encounters with Miss Piggy's door. Clothes: well, they can't smell you back in UK, can they?

But we'd come to do a job. Journalism is not a grand crusade, and anyway, it's about other people. And all the time we journalists can opt out and go home – even when besieged in Sarajevo.

Sarajevo was a kind of madhouse – and, like all such institutions, looked normal enough on the outside and contained large numbers of people who passed for perfectly sane at first sight. Closer inspection revealed a large city in which lunacy reigned and where those in charge frequently lost their grip. Some time before fighting broke out I'd visited it briefly and stayed in what I reckoned was a prize-winningly ugly hotel, so it was inevitable that it would be my home for months at a time over the next few years. Not that the Holiday Inn didn't have character under its chrome-yellow and purple decor. The top five floors had been trashed, one side was out of bounds because it faced the Serbs a few hundred yards away, there were few windows with glass, and the management behaved as if nothing was wrong, taking wheelbarrows of deutschmarks from the foreign press for the privilege of having a bathroom with no water and dodging sniper fire to get to the bar in reception.

It had its moments. As shelling grew in intensity, various dining-room areas became glass-littered and open to the four winds. We retreated to a semi-underground room, a gloomy place of wine-stained tablecloths and mournful waiters who attempted to keep up standards in splodged shirts and fraying jackets and sad little bow ties. The food was either stringy, gristly, lumpy or bony – no one asked exactly *what* it was. We dined in flak-jackets, our sleeping-bags close at hand, conscious that our bedrooms might just disappear during dinner. One evening, slurping the 'war-soup', a tepid concoction enriched with stolen UNHCR rice, a thunderous explosion brought down plaster and wood and rocked the foundations. We sat for a minute, wondering what had taken the hit, only for a door to open and the chef to appear covered in grey dust and solemnly announce that 'Dinner will be a little late due to the destruction of the kitchen.'

There was food in the city, but in quantity and quality alike it depended on money and connections. While steak was quietly consumed by warlords and apparatchiks and black-marketeers, the majority of the population grew lean and grey-skinned on rice and sawdusty bread and aid rations which had been relieved of their protein by local officials for distribution among the front-line fighters.

In the summer of 1992 we underwent the worst six weeks of relentless bombardment, and didn't expect to survive. Near-misses became the subject of desultory remarks over a drink: the tank shell which flattened me as it whooshed over; the bullet which nicked Robert Fox's ear ('Never heard it, too busy getting the *Daily Telegraph*'s Beast to do more than forty.' The Beast, a much-battered blue armoured land rover, turned out to be drilled with bullet holes). Then there was the huge artillery round which missed our makeshift office under the concrete ramp to the PTT (post, telegraph, telephone) building and clanged noisily down the fire escape to lie in front of us, fat and menacing, occasioning a brief discussion as to whether there was such a thing as a Bomb Disposal Unit in Sarajevo. What was the point? Anything unexploded got commandeered and reused. Witness the shell which half-exploded in the hotel room next to us: before we could take pictures of the wreckage, the local Bosnian militia were in there with dustpan and brush, scooping up the rest of the explosive and lugging the jagged shell off to their arms factory, conveniently located in the art college next door until a careless spark sent everything sky-high a year later.

Early morning used to reveal all kinds of shrapnel and anti-aircraft rounds and sniper bullets littering the area round the 'office'. And the journey from hotel to PTT building was a twice-daily hysteria rally – three and a half miles of back streets and rat-runs parallel with Sniper Alley, the out-of-bounds main road. Life was nasty and determined. Our producer Anthony Massey and I used to set off at dusk from the PTT building with the intention that nothing would stop us, be it incoming mortars, snipers, craters, bits of crashing building, or people in London who had just asked us 'not to travel if it wasn't safe'.

It wasn't safe for anyone; the hospitals attested to that, wild places at times, with scores of injured arriving after each immense impact, fetching up as bloody lumps in the back of vans and pick-up trucks and even on hand-carts. There were times when it was imperative to forget you were a reporter and take over the business of triage – it needed someone fit and unengaged to sort out the torso wounds from those with just cuts and bruises. The emergency staff could only be described as heroic, working often without electricity, never mind the permanent shortage of vital supplies. The hospitals themselves came under fire, though in the spirit of Balkan warfare, it wasn't surprising to find the city's largest artillery piece living in the basement of the general hospital.

It was hard to discern a pattern of war or a path of politics, never mind pin down facts. We reacted to the larger incidents as best we could and followed daily life to reflect people's mood. We saw the mundane and the bizarre. There was endless trouble with aid convoys and UN administration, the initial deployment of Egyptians and Ukrainians and conscripted French troops adding to the city's chaos: the Ukrainians were led by a delightful drunk colonel, the Egyptians were led by a lounge lizard general and the French swiftly replaced their conscript battalion with the Foreign Legion, who were terrifying. Throughout Bosnia, the UN was a hopelessly non-joined-up operation, with contributing countries sending soldiers without the right equipment, badly trained, or totally baffled by what was going on around them. Only the British and the French battalions had a sense of purpose and confidence – though the locals of three factions could never overcome their disbelief that Britbat and Frogbat weren't going to fight their war for them.

The arrival of British troops quite simply confirmed our long-term presence: it's not cynicism which dictates that we're only interested in 'our own', it's convention, tradition and the national ties that bind. And in all the years we careered around the Balkans, there's also no doubt that we owed our lives to British soldiers on numerous occasions. Major Alistair Rule and his Cheshires once arrived in the nick of time as June Kelly, our radio correspondent, and our crew were about to be blown to nothing in the middle of a bridal shop. We'd misjudged the quiet of the town of Gornji Vakuf, and been summoned at gunpoint into the semi-derelict and ludicrously named Hotel Las Vegas, whereupon we found ourselves in the middle of a protracted firefight, and in the Bosnian HQ. As we lay on the floor, a polite Bosnian soldier set up his machine gun, using my back as an elbow-resting place. His efforts brought in a heavy reply from the Croats over the crossroads, all the windows of the shopping arcade attached to the hotel disappearing in a trice. The manager of the Las Vegas offered us coffee, which was a staggeringly ambitious gesture, considering that there was a battle in progress overhead and no electricity, but he crawled off to light a little stove and crawled back dragging a neat little tray with Turkish cups and a pile of sugar lumps. Five hours of firing ensued, and we crawled into the bridal shop which had glass fragments glinting on its scarlet carpet, and white satin-draped models festooned with bits of plaster and plywood. The ever-solicitous hotel manger crawled after us, waving his cordless phone. At the best of times, the phone system was fitful, so I ignored him. He persisted, leafing through the Yellow Pages and muttering about the local cement factory – where the British army had its base. He poked at the phone and then handed it to me. To my astonishment a voice chirped: 'Britbat Gornji Vakuf Corporal Jones here.'

Never. Gerroff. I didn't quite know what to say but pulled myself together and replied loudly above the din: 'Oh, it's just the BBC, calling in to say we're all still alive.'

'Oh, that's good, ma'am,' said the voice. 'We've been watching the fun and wondered how you were doing.'

I was a bit stuck for what to say next, and the phone battery was bleeping.

'Fine then,' I concluded – 'Oh, by the way, we're in the Las Vegas Hotel.'

'*Are* you?' said the voice, sounding as if it suspected that we were having a louche evening round the roulette table. 'Over and out then.'

Twenty minutes later a tank joined the action, and next door went up in flames. We lay on the scarlet carpet wondering if we should make a run for it – but hadn't a clue where to run to – when there was a gentle rumbling towards the crossroads. A minute later, Major Rule and his sergeant major charged into the building and rescued us. In darkness lit only by flashes of rifle shots and mortar explosions we all went headfirst into the back of the waiting Warriors and were carried to safety upside down among grunting soldiers back to the cement factory.

When you've felt very frightened many times, you appreciate even more those who carry courage naturally with them.

In the madness of Sarajevo in September 1992, Rory Peck was the *soigné* freelance who strode through town finding some of the odder aspects of war for his camera. To reach the hidey-holes of the Bosnian war effort, he propelled a bizarre BMW across the potholes of the city, driving uncompromisingly through the shelling. The BMW was a true Balkan war-horse. It looked impressive as it roared off into clouds of dust raised by mortars. It would have flashed its tail-lights in defiance, had it had any electrical system. Its approach was even more striking. It had no front and resembled a mangled, flattened wash-board. Sometime during the month it went on sale. Word had it that the price was £250. Whether that was what he got for it, or what he paid for the Bosnian black-market mafia to take it away, was never clear.

On the third of September he saved my life.

We had been waiting for Larry Hollingworth, the ex-British army king of UNHCR convoys, to make another attempt to get through to the besieged Muslim town of Gorazde. Several days running we'd got ready in the middle of the night, waiting for a call to say that the venture was on. The town had only had one supply of emergency aid, several months previously, and was being shelled continuously. We intended to join Larry as he set off from the airport, about a mile and a half away from our base at the PTT. At 4 a.m., for the fourth day, half a dozen of us gathered in the freezing cold to pile equipment and provisions into the faithful Miss Piggy. Colin Smith of the *Observer* and Didier François of the French newspaper *Libération* had hitched a ride with us, and I was checking we had bits of first aid kit, food and extra fuel. I always drove. Martin Bell and I shared a sense of determination to make decisions about how much risk we should take, and when to turn back. And with the cameraman in the passenger seat, we could both travel and shoot. Indeed, an inordinate amount of footage was recorded through the windscreen and windows of armoured cars, because of the lunatic amount of metal flinging about outside.

Rory arrived just as we'd got the call from Larry to say the convoy was on. We had about twenty minutes to get to the airport, along what was at that time probably the most dangerous stretch of road in the world. After 500 yards of a small back lane towards the main Sarajevo city highway, the route presented a right-angle turn up a slip-road the wrong way and on to a damaged motorway flyover. At the top of the slip-road, there was nothing for it but to do a three-point turn to get across the flyover. Travelling across that flyover was everyone's idea of Sarajevan hell. Sitting Duck Flyover. The Bridge of Spilled Guts. Shit Alley. It was as if you wanted to parade in front of all the warring factions and shout Here I Am, Shoot Now. There was no street lighting, of course; good thing too, with every so-called front line abutting and criss-crossing the half-mile stretch of the road ahead of us. No headlights either – You want to announce your arrival? However, the various fighting units had managed to contrive an ever-growing obstacle course in the horrible half-mile, in which the grandest obstacle was the remains of a tank, which stuck out at varying angles, depending on how it had been nudged by the most recent hit. Bits of cars which had failed to dodge the cross-fire, the wreckage of UN convoys and the odd mine all lay in wait.

I'd driven the road a handful of times, but always in daylight. I walked to the back of the vehicle, and – though not a superstitious or fey creature – got a hefty sense of premonition.

Standing next to the rear door, Rory said without prompting: 'You want me to drive?' For the first and only time when about to head into possible trouble in Bosnia I said Yes. I knew there was something ahead.

'Fine,' he said, took the keys, and off we went, me in the right-hand passenger seat.

The moment we lumbered up the slip-road there was a nasty chattering of automatic fire. Miss Piggy's engine laboured and there was absolute silence from the five people in the back. Rory executed a three-point turn which tested unknown bits of Miss Piggy. At what seemed like a hippo getting out of glue, we started to accelerate across the flyover.

Within a few hundred yards there were Croats – lying in the industrial suburb of Stup. To the left were the Muslims of Dobrinja. To the right, the Ilidja Serbs. And clearly every bastard wanted a piece of the action. There was tracer fire, single-flash mortars, and so much stuff heading for us that even through the armour-plating we could hear whooshes and whistles of the stuff that didn't quite hit us. Then we took five rounds. It was as if men with pick-axes were raining blows on the land rover. The nearly four tons of Miss Piggy heaved and rocked as Rory kept going, his foot flat on the floor. We took the final round and I was lifted from the seat and literally hit the roof. In the dark I'd seen a tiny scarlet spark down in the foot-well. Bouncing back on the seat, I realised I couldn't feel my right leg below mid-thigh. I yelled. Rory kept going. 'Airport soon,' he said casually.

'I – um – think I've been hit,' I ventured, too cowardly to put my hand down towards my leg. I wasn't sure if it was still there. In the back Colin Smith was wondering if he still had all of his brain. One bullet had struck the side of the vehicle immediately next to his head. I tentatively put a finger on my knee. Still there. Crept a hand down a bit further. Still there. But the entire limb was numb. No one was thinking straight, and the gunfire had not stopped. Rory never twitched, and thrashed Miss Piggy at full speed through total darkness over lumps of metal and shell-craters.

The airport – or the remains of it, covered with UN barbed wire – loomed up. We careered through the gate, surprising some dozy soldier who presumably shouted Stop in his own language. Finding Larry in one of the hangars making final preparations for the convoy, we piled out of Miss Piggy. The white paint with the letter BBC on both sides sported four large holes. The fifth could not be found. By now I had a tingling leg – and, in the orange glow in the hangar, it appeared to be a complete leg as well, much to my surprise. I sat down and removed a Doc Marten boot and a rather grubby sock. Eeny meeny miny mo, everything there. Then a tiny spot, a pinprick of blood oozed from just below the second toe.

'Congratulations,' said Rory, 'world's smallest war wound.' He seemed totally unfazed by the entire episode. The rest of us were in various states of frazzle. Mildly puzzled, I replaced sock and boot, then spent the next thirty-six hours travelling over logging trails, running around in Gorazde under mortar and sniper fire, lugging a wounded woman into a makeshift medical base, and interviewing people who were demented under siege.

Two days later my foot went mad, and a nice French naval surgeon who said British people don't want anaesthetics do they? sawed out a chunk of metal from my foot. It turned out to be a bit of the wheel rim of Miss Piggy, punched through by part of a bullet which slipped through a weld. The bullet bit remains. ('You want your toes, yes?' said the surgeon. 'So you keep ze bullet in zere.')

I know that had I been driving, I would have failed to keep going, so terrifying was the incident.

One year and one month later, Rory died while filming the attack on the White House in Moscow.

Keeping life and limb together preoccupied us; neither Martin Bell nor myself nor Nigel thought the odds of our surviving the Balkans were particularly good. But in a routine stint up in the northern town of Tuzla, something shifted in my mind.

Tuzla was a town of strenuous ugliness – every building delivered from some determined communist's drawing-board, calculated to sour and depress. Somewhere in its history, there had been salt-mines. There had also once been something of an orderly little Austro-Hungarian town, all pink and cream façades and curly balconies. But the keen modernisers of Tito's regime had managed to bulldoze away most of it. From the eleventh floor of the Hotel Tuzla, there was a relatively good view of the power station. The streets below were a symphony of concrete block and broken pavements. There was the odd splat-mark from the occasional shell. Tuzla had a very miserable and unexciting war.

Bianca Jagger arrived once, with much publicity and no transport. Celebrity visits were a feature of wartime Bosnia. Some undoubtedly did some good, highlighted particular causes, and no doubt raised consciousness and money. Other famous people came on the indignant bandwagon, pulled by a high horse. And it was remarkable how many were badly organised, with no idea about the place they were trying to save.

Mr Akashi, the UN's Special Representative, once turned up, declared the civil airport open, and flew away, whereupon it closed.

A UN diplomat arrived, and grew tetchy on being told that his request for reservations in a decent hotel in Srebrenica had not been fulfilled. He stumped up and down the airfield, a very short person with a big image problem. We debated whether to put a few questions to him on the lines of 'And how many stars would you like your hotel in Srebrenica to have? Would you like a view of the desperate people fighting to get out on aid lorries, or prefer the window on the hospital where the operations don't have a lot of anaesthetics available?'

As for Bianca Jagger, who was in the process of a high-profile rescue of some chosen child, none of the young British soldiers she pestered for lifts could work out what sort of Jagger she was. On learning the relationship, there was general agreement that the handsome British major whose land rover she was always trying to hijack 'was in with a good chance, sir, but mind you, those Jaggers are gettin' on a bit'. The major had the sense to realise that the world of glamour did little for a town like Tuzla:

exotic Nicaraguans didn't raise eyebrows in the seedy restaurant of Hotel Tuzla; only hardened warlords with mountainous bodyguards got decent service to accompany the awful food.

Tuzla's military airport also saw quite a lot of business which was denied by everyone. Flights of military transport? Shipments of arms? Heavens, what imaginations you journalists have. A lonely UN major, far from his African land, used to confide in me about the 'much flying and landing of big planes'. He was a charming man, utterly isolated. None of the locals would deal with him – not surprising when one thinks of the Bosnian ability to discriminate between identical-looking families; attitudes to other races were based on a practised system of prejudice. He mooched about the airfield, clutching his fawn gaberdine raincoat to him, shivering, but always producing a magical sweet smile. No one in Sarajevo would listen to his observations about the unscheduled air traffic, he said. 'Maybe it's because I'm so foreign.' Maybe. More likely, many of the people along the chain of command had a good idea about Tuzla's involvement in arms delivery from countries unwilling to declare their partisan behaviour, while participating in a multinational and supposedly neutral force.

Tuzla civilian airport (to be candid – the other end of the military runway) is still sleeping in its north Bosnian backwater, dreaming of metropolitan greatness. However, it used to be part of a ritual canter round the town during hostilities, for it was home to the Bosnian air force, all one helicopter of it. Plus its pilot, a man designated either the bravest Bosnian in uniform or the most unhinged, depending on your view of solo flights into enemy territory with very little ammunition and a wonky set of instruments.

Also on the Tuzla Places to Visit list was the military head-quarters – another place of dreams for most of its existence. Hard information rarely emanated from its mostly unlit interior. Grand campaigns were talked about, victories announced, and cunning strategies implied. More realistic were telephones that were banged down on the grey metal desks and didn't work. And the occasional eruption into the street of a gang of dishevelled and hollow-eyed soldiers, roaring drunk from some temporary success, in which they'd have overcome a field or two, and seized a farmhouse. That they were back in Tuzla celebrating indicated that the fields and farmhouse were even now being repossessed.

The next stop was the Hospital. A huge hymn to filthy concrete, a labyrinth of walkways and courtyards of hardened mud where grass did not dare to lurk.

Here, one evening, when nothing particularly significant happened in front of me, I shifted violently in my view of the encircling war.

We were standing in the doorway of the intensive care unit, a helpful woman anaesthetist rattling through the usual list of problems: lack of drugs, lack of dressings, lack of everything. In the ICU, inert shapes lay attached by bits of string to leaky drips. I wandered down the corridor. Next door, a glass window gave on to a ward full of more animated figures. Young men squatted on beds, all of them smoking. A couple of bottles were doing the rounds. And a couple of girlie magazines. Through the glass, I could see laughing faces, skinny and strained. I looked again, carefully. Of the eight men, five were missing a leg. Two more were squatted, stumps protruding across the sheets. One had an arm gone.

In a moment of horrible imagination, I saw them in a bar, healthy, drunk and randy, eyeing up the local talent and boasting what they might accomplish that evening. But they were here.

A nurse went past, young, sporting daffodil-dyed hair with the roots asserting rusty brunette. She glanced through the glass, scanned the young men, then grimaced and strode on.

I felt the pointlessness, the inanity of this particular war. I felt that most of the young men hadn't a clue what they'd done to their own lives. They were still in the grip of the macho, intoxicating spirit of fighting men. Even in this ward, they were reliving good times, and enjoying the brotherhood of the warrior.

They were going to be hailed as heroes, saviours of their country, honoured in eternity. Like hell.

These thoughts didn't occur at the time; simply, a chord was struck, or a single note which didn't have a tune with it. About two months later, sitting in Sarajevo in a café full of young men boasting, the tune suddenly played. I looked round the tables: young men bragging about their roles in Bosnian Special Forces. If all the young men who claimed such skills really belonged to an elite unit, then the Bosnian army would never have had an ordinary soldier in its ranks. Through the thick atmosphere, one of the young men at our table, chewing a pizza consisting of dough and tomato paste, banged on about the easiness of killing Serbs. About the rightness of the Bosnian government's cause, the only good Serb being a dead one. About the reason that victory was eluding them being entirely the fault of NATO, the British, the French, the UN and so on. And so on. Heard everywhere. Normally, I'd just have listened with half an ear, noting if any part of the familiar litany contained a new catchphrase, an indication of the latest piece of propaganda. But the tune suddenly played in my head. And I found I had less tolerance of the boasting, the wishful thinking, even the ideals.

A dangerous feeling. A view of events which curtails sympathy. Stimulates intolerance. A plague on all your houses.

You have to look closely at it. Make sure that your understanding isn't blunted by irritation. That a wider concern for humanity isn't blocked out by a personal impatience with the players in the scene in front of you.

Above all, you must not become indifferent, for then you cease to be able to report humanely. But you think all the time of injury – and survival.

THIRTEEN

At large in Libya

One of the editors of radio news in Broadcasting House used to say that he had a recurring nightmare in which one of his sub-editors – a man of vast experience, but mainly on Sunday tabloids – would be in charge the night royalty passed away, and would wake to the BBC announcing: 'Sixty-two-year-old brunette millionairess mother-of-four in palace tragedy . . .'

It's all a matter of training and experience, style and tone. Getting the words right. Whether you deal only in facts depends on who you're working for in journalism. The BBC is big on facts. But as for *training* for BBC journalists – there was none, thirty years ago. Technicians, engineers, producers and secretaries all went on courses full of BBC arcana: 'Remember, dear, the director-general is addressed by his Christian name but commissionaires at the door are always "Mr"; David Attenborough's wife is addressed as Mrs CBBC2; your personnel officer must always be told of personal debts; you may not have an affair with someone in the same department – it upsets the annual interview system; do not wear a hat to annual interviews.' Everyone got put through the BBC hoops – except journalists.

Hacks were in the main recruited from Fleet Street, and the only introduction they received was being made to sign the Official Secrets Act, after the MI5 official on the third floor of

BH had sniffed around their political activities and noted down interesting titbits about their private life. Having an eccentric lifestyle was no bar to joining the staff, and I've worked with a number of people who were certifiably mad, though highly entertaining. Odd behaviour merely made for a fatter 'starred file', a list of personal foibles which proved you were an interesting employee, the existence of which the BBC always denied. These files had a cousin – also denied – known as the Christmas Tree file, relating to a Tree doodle on the front page denoting its top-secret status and devoted to the exciting notion of subversion. Its existence was confirmed to me by my university professor, when he told me my Swedish defence ministry details had somehow found their way to the BBC. 'It's all rubbish, my dear,' he confided, 'but it keeps many a civil servant in employment. If the balloon ever really goes up again, they'll just round you all up and shoot you.'

Local radio's trainees were somehow omitted from the government's trawl of likely subversives – perhaps we were too lowly to be considered dangerous – and it was twenty years before a horrified squit from management squealed, 'You haven't signed the Act? Oh my God, that's terrible, we must get you to do it immediately.' I announced that I would publicly set fire to any copy placed in front of me and added, 'You can put that in the Christmas Tree file.'

Nevertheless, I often had twinges of guilt that I was without the automatic habits of many a reporter put through the rituals of training on a weekly newspaper, or these days armed with a three-year degree course in media studies. The greatest feeling of uncertainty used to occur on the way to a story: How do you start? Where do you start? I've never really found the answer. I suppose any reporter worth their salt reads voraciously so that likely events in the future don't come as a total surprise. And if you only read newspapers, then beware. Books, books, books. Reporters can become carried away with conviction that their fellow journalists are the source of all information, but most of us write for the moment, at the moment, and it's not enough for comprehension and context. And the more education goes in at the beginning, the more understanding later supports the bald text of the report on air. And the education never stops. Why and How are the two irritating questions never to be abandoned in favour of polite acceptance of press conference drivel and official spokesperson twaddle.

Having been asked frequently – usually in kind but puzzled terms by my family – 'Your report was only two minutes long – what did you do for the rest of the day?' I can sympathise with the view that we just indulge in a burst of frenetic activity, then retire to the bar or the beach, or behind the sandbags, anyway. Most reporting consists of long periods of hanging around outside meetings gossiping usefully, hours of walking round ruined villages trying to discover what happened, days in pursuit of a particularly important interviewee, and full-time observation, nosiness, watchfulness, enquiry, following up leads, ringing all useful numbers, acting on instinct and poking your nose in where it's not wanted. 'Nothing is ever wasted' is one of my little phrases. Time spent listening in bars to boastful fighters, half an hour with ersatz coffee while a housewife describes what has happened to her family as she goes slowly through the photograph album; a spare couple of hours at the tourist site – noticing the nervousness of policemen, the bus-drivers shooing their charges back to the hotel early; ten minutes in the morgue at the hospital – wondering where the bodies have gone to which would back up the official death-toll claims. Nothing ever goes to waste. Gossip has a kernel of truth, ranting speeches give a measure of the unreasonableness in the air, shopkeepers are the real barometer of the economy, and a peasant grazing his cows in a field can mean the local militia are nowhere in the vicinity: he'd never risk his most precious possessions. Look and learn.

Even so, writing scripts night after night about the events of the past few hours, it is impossible to imagine that you have any grasp of 'the whole story'. Television news, especially, is a truncated art form: the complementing of pictures and words, squashed into a couple of minutes. A postcard home, with a few succinct lines.

The frustration of being unable to convey any more than this is permanent. However, the quid pro quo is the opportunity to deliver a little solid pack of information to millions of people – particularly in the seventies and eighties, when the TV audiences went on growing until there were TV sets in almost every household, and in more than one room. It was a wondrous time to be working in TV news. Local radio had been fun, and regional news had been a strange introduction to the camera, but network television was an extraordinary opportunity. People switched on, night after night, a national and shared habit.

'Surely,' said one of my contemporaries, when we were discussing the question of ambition, 'you always wanted to do this – and you used to stand in your mum's bedroom, in front of the wardrobe door mirror, with a stick of rhubarb or a hairbrush in your hand?' I couldn't think what this was leading to. 'You stood there,' she went on, 'saying "This is Kate Adie, reporting for the *Nine O'Clock News*."'

I certainly did not. I'd never given the idea of journalism a single thought. And so I tended not to think very much about the nature of reporting. And I had never once assessed the job in terms of audience size. Seven years in local radio had taught me never to enquire – there was always the possibility that the entire audience had gone out for a curry when your programme was on.

I draw quite a lot of satisfaction from getting the words right in a report. Hitting the nail on the head. I'm prissy about individual words, and I'll hunt through a mental list until I light on the right one, even though a deadline approaches. Often I can see a gap in the mental list, but can't locate the word, so I end up interrogating the nearest editor or producer, in a manic game:

'What's it called when you feel tired and sloth-like and can't be bothered?'

'How about "knackered" – what are you trying to describe?'

'Princess Margaret going round a fish-farm.'
'Indifferent? Bored bloody rigid? Trout-faced?'
'No, got it: "looked mildly intrigued".'
Tone matters, as well as words.

Not everyone understands how hard we try to get the words right. Especially if those words do not please them, or do not fit their view of the world, or perhaps indicate that they are in the wrong.

It is not easy to sum up an entire country with one or two words. Perhaps it's not right to.

Libya had not been in my thoughts as I spent an evening of embarrassment sitting behind the skaters Torvill and Dean on an open-top bus during a triumphal tour of Nottingham one evening in 1984. I was wondering what words I could find which didn't cause offence to either Nottingham or the pair who'd just returned from the Sarajevo Winter Olympics, but which would convey the air of municipally inspired festiveness allied with the weird art of ice-dancing. In fact, I'd never given Libya any thoughts, for it was one of those countries which didn't welcome journalists and was, to say the least, odd.

The next day, during a small demonstration outside the Libyan Embassy in St James's Square, shots were fired, and PC Yvonne Fletcher was killed.

A full-scale siege developed almost immediately, with the Libyan People's Bureau – as their embassy was styled – containing both diplomats and firebrand revolutionary Libyan students, while outside the entire square was emptied of all except police.

Straight from Nottingham, I found myself trying to get a good view of the bureau and in consequence spending some time in Simpson's, the upmarket store which used to back on to the embassy building. The best shot was from the windows of the lingerie department, so we camped there for several hours among the bras. By evening, after a quiet word with a senior police officer, I was fairly sure that no Iranian-Embassy-style storming of the building was being contemplated, so we were probably in for a long haul. The office decided that we should find out how things were being seen from Tripoli, and I reached the Libyan capital twenty-four hours later after much haggling about visas.

We were met by a friendly but rag-tag bunch of officials in an airport which was the epitome of modern neglect: contemporary furniture (broken), conveyor belt (unmoving), glass display cases for duty-free goodies (none visible), immigration/visa office (man asleep amid filthy coffee cups). And this was one of the oil-rich countries with a population of only a few million. But there were slogans galore. The walls bore garish green signs proclaiming: No Democracy without Popular Congresses. In Need Freedom is Latent. Partners not Wage-workers. In Need Freedom Indeed.

What?

The information ministry chaps went for a long argument with customs about our equipment, and then took us into town in a battered minibus. The vista was a symphony of the twentieth century on the slide. Modern scruffy apartment buildings set amongst broken pavements and dusty, rubbish-strewn yards. Untended patches of grass with half the railings missing. Roads that started – and went nowhere. Vaguely Soviet, but baked in hot sun, so saved from dark ugliness and looking merely tatty. On the good road in from the airport (always a symbol of dictatorship – every boss likes to come and go in style, even if the rest of the country is a potholed mess), a ministry official pointed out Notable Sights. These included a ground-to-air missile battery – and a planetarium.

The Hotel Al-Kabir was large, modern and bugged. Not very efficiently, it has to be said, as the men who listened in to your phone calls were to be seen gossiping in the back office most of the day. But if you ever needed room service (which took an hour or two to serve a coffee) there was always the ruse of calling London, and complaining bitterly that you could never get a sandwich when you wanted one. This produced a knock at the door within minutes, for the ministry officials were adept at bullying room service waiters in the name of their country's image. The food was terrible, indeed the Al-Kabir Salad was a kind of museum piece, gracing the table day after day. The country being nominally dry, pear juice and a cherry-coloured liquid tasting of mouthwash and claiming to be alcohol-free Campari were the only drinks on offer.

Working normally was impossible. Libya wasn't like a country; it was a kind of mad boarding-school where the rules were unknown, but the punishments fearful. Try to take a cab from in front of the hotel, and the driver gunned his dented little Peugeot round the corner willingly enough – and then stopped in front of one of the few remaining Italianate colonial buildings behind the seafront boulevard. This was the central police station, to which taxi-drivers knew that all foreigners had better be brought – 'Well, you never know . . .' The officer on the front desk in the police station used to be quite charming, always apologising, blaming the taxi-drivers, and adding that it was only three minutes from the hotel, so have a nice walk back. He'd come out after you to ensure that the driver didn't demand a fare, and so the whole farce would replay, day after day – with the threat 'You never know . . .' unexplained.

Except that it was common knowledge that one Western embassy regularly heard shrieks from a nearby police station and had occasionally found severed limbs in its rubbish skips. Going out at night was discouraged, for the streets were eerie, and people disappeared – a phenomenon about which no mention was ever made in the public media, a straightforward propaganda machine.

As you walked out of the hotel, the information minders would lope after you, as if you were a wayward mongrel out for walkies on your own. Their main complaint was that *they* would provide transport if you wanted to go anywhere – 'Just ask please.' We asked; and much of the time they took no notice, partly because the information ministry had An Official Programme for the Visit of the Journalists, partly because of ineptitude, and partly because the minders were bone-idle and smoked pot in their hotel rooms for most of the day.

Most of the minders were well educated – many had studied in Britain, Italy or the United States – and well aware of how a free press operates, so they were (privately) genuinely embarrassed when having to explain, excuse or apologise for their country's wilder excesses. However, on occasions over the next decade, I regularly saw the minders terrified as some major event failed to go according to plan. If something were to happen to the foreign journalists, they confided, they would be powerless to extract the journalists from the revolutionary committees or the security services, and then their own heads would be on the block – or strung up, more likely. And for once, they seemed very sincere.

The Official Programme turned out to be an odd mixture of useful contacts with senior officials and a load of utter time-wasting crap. If ever I felt I'd need patience and tolerance, it was here. There were no news agencies, except for the absurd Jana, the nonsense organ of the regime. There was no resident foreign press corps – indeed, it was illegal for a foreigner to 'act in a journalistic manner' or 'communicate information to journalists outside the country', such activity being regarded as espionage.

We wanted to get proper reaction to the siege in London and we were promised an interview with The Leader, but no one said when we would see Colonel Gaddafi. No one else was made available and attempting vox pops in the street was to invite another chapter of farce: young men rushed up to start chanting slogans, ordinary people fled. We tried to film street scenes, and the minders screeched up with a minibus and took us somewhere 'more beautiful'. We headed for the souk – a last remnant of old Arabic Tripoli – and realised that the shops were not open, for at that time one of the Colonel's little homilies had included an attack on shopkeeping – so everywhere had shut down. After two days of no bread or anything else, there had been mutterings, and he grudgingly agreed to allow family-run businesses to 'half-operate'. No one knew what this meant, but interpreted it by half-raising their shutters so that customers had to crawl in. The Leader would have preferred everyone to use one of the seven supermarkets he'd had built, dusty dreary emporia meant to sweep aside 'nasty private leech-like enterprise', but he appeared to know little about managing them. He had staged a spectacular opening ceremony for the first of the seven, with Yasser Arafat wielding the ribbon scissors, probably without having looked inside at the mounds of cheap plastic toys and extra-size Bulgarian underwear. Now there were only six supermarkets, one having been blown up. By whom? 'You never know . . .'

If you filmed by the roadside, cars and trucks and minibuses stopped next to you. This turned out to be the Colonel's version of People's Transport – all bus services had been abolished, having being seen as another example of blood-sucking capitalism. So if you stood by the road, you had to be offered a lift. One of us had to be on permanent lift-refusal duty while filming.

And behind all the ludicrous outings and delayed interviews, there was the smell of fear. 'You never know . . .'

We managed to get to the British Embassy and found it closed up, with demonstrators threatening to set it on fire. At the British Residence the ambassador, Oliver Myles, and his wife could not have been more welcoming. He was an old hand at Libyan tactics, and was well aware that orchestrated street theatre was no indication of what the regime was really up to. But ambassadors had little contact with the Colonel – he regarded them as being of minor importance, and he rarely agreed to meet any diplomats. The embassy – when not being besieged – tried to look after the interests of around 5,000 British workers in the oil industry, most of whom were in distant desert locations and hearing only gossip and rumour from the cities.

The country ran on wonky lines. Nominally, there was a system of 'ongoing revolution', achieved through People's

Congresses to which three million Libyans supposedly belonged, and serving as a supposed democratic forum where some of them gathered for rambling rants and discussions and speeches. In reality, these theatrical talking-shops were window-dressing and educated Libyans needed a three-line whip from the Colonel's barracks to get them along. There was no real functioning civil service, and ministries were straight out of Kafka, their effectiveness wholly dependent on individual abilities and skill at circumnavigating some of the great Leader's odder notions – such as ordering three dozen flyovers to be built to improve the traffic flow without authorising any roads to join them up. Even so, no criticism was heard from the officials – 'You never know . . .'

Ordinary Libyans had come to expect their lives to be buffeted and irritated by the Colonel's schemes for improving their revolutionary awareness. In his time, he'd abolished savings accounts, ownership of more than one house, tourism, luxury cars and barber's shops. However, when he announced the end of primary schools, in the belief that parents didn't do enough to educate their own children, tempers got a little frayed. Then he announced that he was going to abolish money. Absolutely nothing happened – it seemed he wasn't keen to think up alternatives. But he was soon back on form, seized with the idea that he could generate more productivity by cutting a swathe through the Arab habit of gossiping for hours over a cup of coffee while seated on expensive leather chairs and shuffling paper on elaborate desks: he tried to abolish office furniture. Generations of indolence sabotaged that one.

Once, in a move of genuine radicalism, he did away with the police – an experiment which lasted just a few hours. However, he sneaked in a curious experiment in which he dressed children in police uniforms to control traffic. They proved to be remarkably effective.

Presiding over all of this was Colonel Gaddafi, who wielded absolute power in some areas, using the army to reinforce his authority, but was occasionally thwarted by the more extreme revolutionary organisations he himself had set up. 'Revolutionary renewal' accounted for a good deal of the unpleasant atmosphere, for though the membership of the revolutionary committees was technically secret, the qualifications appeared to be thuggery, ignorance and zeal.

There was a weird logic lurking behind the whims of the man in charge of this mess. He once boasted to me that driving standards had improved in the country after he'd passed just one law.

'You never see anyone go through a red light – ever, do you?' he asked me.

I couldn't recall seeing anyone do so, and asked how one law had achieved this.

'The penalty is to be shot,' he said. 'It works.'

On the other hand, I might argue that driving into a desert town far in the south of the country and having my driver pull an automatic rifle from under my seat and fire – while driving – at 'stupid traffic cops' somewhat challenges this system. I might have argued with the Colonel, but 'you never know . . .' – for as usual, this conversation took place in the small hours. Gaddafi is an owl, and really only gets into the mood for interviews late at night. The resultant hanging around is legendary, with visiting journalists stood by night after night, and falling asleep in the press conference room. One of the few methods of staying awake is to hold a sweepstake on what he'll wear: Army fatigues? Italian sharp suit? Naval commander with huge row of medals? Desert Bedouin blanket? Arabic lounge-lizard jacket? His entrance after the long wait always used to produce a lively reaction from the snoozy hacks – based on who'd won the pot of money under the table.

Over the years I grew inured to some of the crazy habits of a country that is small, rich and badly run. It's a dictatorship in which the Leader tells you he's 'not completely in charge' – and there are signs that this is true. Again late at night, he moaned to me about the indolence of his fellow Libyans.

'I run the place,' he reflected, 'because I'm the only one that does any work.'

Security is curiously discreet – weapons are rarely seen in public – but the atmosphere tells its own tale.

When you finally get to know people in the privacy of their homes, they turn out to be slightly frustrated by the system, but materially comfortable, with an easy-going Mediterranean attitude, much enamoured of Western fashions and pursuits. There's a high standard of education – and relatively easy access to ideas and attitudes from abroad. It was pure inefficiency that made foreign newspapers appear irregularly, there was no Gulf-type censorship. The Colonel himself goes infrequently to the mosque, though makes a show of piety when necessary, and there's a law which prevents imams from preaching politics. Fundamentalism is not to his taste. Middle-class Libyans are Westernised and long for their children to be educated in the States, or Paris, or London. The women are well on their way to a liberated status, and sigh with irritation as the British tabloid newspapers focus yet again on Gaddafi's habit of producing his nubile troupe of female bodyguards for the benefit of foreign cameras. His real protection is supplied by a handful of compact, unflappable military men, whose very affability is frightening.

While the siege continued at the embassy in London, those of us in Tripoli could only pick up hints of what might happen. Diplomacy was difficult – the normal channels of communication just don't function in the country, and the TV and the press parrot rubbish which would be laughable if it weren't so damaging. Television news has always been prone to influence from the Colonel's barracks, the conventional map behind the newsreader reflecting current political attitudes: Egypt for a long time was just a mass of felt-tipped splodges, illustrating Gaddafi's displeasure, while the British Isles just disappeared completely, having been wrenched off the wall; some time later, a peculiar scone-shaped bit reappeared off the coast of Norway – Ireland had been rehabilitated.

Eventually, our diplomats left, but not before we journalists shifted the grand piano and the royal portraits from the emptying Residence to a friendly embassy – 'You never know . . .' The embassy pet rabbit proved harder to shift, bouncing off round the tennis court during removals. As ever on these occasions, Honeybun's fate grew to be a major part of the story, with Mrs Myles eventually suggesting that it would have been better off being popped in a cooking-pot. A trivial moment – but a frequent problem in all stories where the politics is complicated and obscure, the tension is considerable and clear lines are not discernible. Rabbits, rescued dogs, neglected cats, injured horses, war-threatened zoos – there is a terrifying tradition that the fate of four legs produces more response in the British public than anything else. The first letter to me from a member of the British public after the Gulf War began: 'We've haven't heard enough about the abandoned cats and dogs in Kuwait . . .'

When eventually, after negotiation and questioning, the men who'd taken over the embassy in London arrived back in Tripoli, we were taken to the airport. A small group of young men chanted their way round the Arrivals hall, and we filmed the welcoming. 'Spontaneous demonstration' is actually a phrase in official use in Libya, and it denotes an organised ritual of shouting and banner-waving, usually under quite firm control. And even by Libyan standards the airport scene was low-key, though that was not how it was viewed in London, where newspapers talked of a triumphant homecoming.

Many months later I asked a senior associate of the Colonel about the negative impact of this scene in Britain, where considerable disgust and anger were felt by those who reckoned they were seeing Yvonne Fletcher's murderers feted.

'Well, it was their last celebration,' said my contact. He then showed me an indistinct photograph, purporting to support his claim that several of those who returned had been hanged. Another part of the Libyan puzzle – for I know for a fact that some are still around. 'You never know . . .'

What actually happened in the Libyan Bureau in London, and where guilt lies, are matters much disputed. The people involved are unlikely to tell the truth, and so the conspiracy theorists can have a field day. The Libyans' ignorance of how the rest of the world behaves leads them into trouble, and there were times when I thought the entire country behaved like a dreadful teenager who is capable of vicious violence, but can't work out why he's such a bastard.

I had occasion to return again and again to Libya – a rich state with a kink of craziness, ruled by a man with grandiose and fatuous philosophies and no grasp of the realities of world politics who can't stay out of trouble for long. Espousing the thoughts of Chairman Mao, he produced a whole raft of revolutionary innovations, wrote his thoughts in a little Green Book and decided to encourage every other revolutionary on God's earth to make trouble. Gaddafi is a man with limited knowledge of the world, who makes the mistake of putting his own country at the centre of the universe, unaware of the clownish figure he cuts.

As the result of more 'revolutionary renewal', during which he allowed young idiots to challenge both law and individual rights while demonising 'foreign powers', a number of people were either arrested on trumped-up charges or held illegally. After his initial enthusiasm, the whole episode became an embarrassment for the Colonel, especially when foreign residents fell foul of the thugs. But by then, the damage was done: the country was in a bruised and resentful mood, and the young bloods truculent.

A number of Britons were caught in the net, and so began a series of to-ings and fro-ings by British MPs, intermediaries and journalists. It was like investigating a sponge. Nothing substantial ever came out, and the further in you delved, the more empty spaces you discovered. Even the Colonel seemed diffident; having stirred up a storm in his own country, he was evasive about solutions, and on one occasion told me that he was unsure about moving against the movement he had begun. It was true that he had authority over the ultimate power – the army – but he was unwilling initially to confront the 'revolutionaries' over 'some foreigners'.

In one incident, two British men who'd been held for several months on illusory charges seemed destined for a longer stay after a delegation of British MPs had flown off empty-handed, completely baffled by Libyan obfuscation. The next evening a minder turned up at our hotel behaving like Humphrey Bogart in a bad film, anorak collar turned up, darting behind potted plants in the foyer, hissing to us to follow him. We piled into the usual decrepit minibus and found ourselves dumped in a derelict parking lot at the back of a justice ministry building. Feeling foolish, we stood around while the minder sloped off nervously; then suddenly, with a screech of wheels, a nondescript saloon stopped next to us. Peering out of the window were Mr Ledingham and Mr Bush, the two men who that morning had seemed destined for indeterminate imprisonment. The driver indicated that they should get out, and gestured at me as if I were deeply implicated in the whole matter. Then he roared off. Aha, so this is what a hostage release is like?

It took some time to convince both men that *we* were the safe hands into which they were being delivered.

Other British citizens were still being held on cooked-up charges of financial irregularities or espionage, but the four who seemed to be in particular trouble had nothing in common. Michael Berdinner was a lecturer who led a quiet life and appeared to have been bundled off to prison under some odd misunderstanding with students. Malcolm Anderson was an oil-industry worker, who'd been taking letters home out of the country for colleagues and had had them opened, at which point it was found that they – not unreasonably – contained criticism of the regime. Robin Plummer, a BT engineer, had had his car searched and a bog-standard map unearthed. And Alan Russell –

ah, not the Alan Russell whom we journalists already knew? Not a lot of British people are to be found playing the piano in the Hotel Al-Kabir. Mr Russell, part-time pianist and language teacher, was under suspicion of espionage.

We attended court hearings that made little sense, and watched as the Archbishop of Canterbury's envoy, Terry Waite, went off for long discussions with Libyan officials, who then told us privately that they had no authority whatsoever to make any deals, only to play host to Mr Waite.

We sat around for days, knowing that only a move from Gaddafi meant progress. The minders thought we needed cheering up, said so, and, without warning, pushed us on a minibus and took us to the airport.

This was one of the more alarming aspects of Libyan amusement: mystery trips in dodgy aircraft accompanied by excited minders unsure of the travel details. The last little outing had been into the desert at Sarir – a flight into nowhere, to discover several hundred other people also deposited in the middle of nowhere, including several foreign ambassadors and some important-looking Americans who were grousing loudly that This time he'd gone too far. Everyone was then invited to undertake a short desert trek. Looming in the distance was the sprawl of a vast construction camp, peopled entirely by South Koreans. The Libyan officials nominally in charge of our party ignored both the Koreans and our questions about why several thousand Asians were in this desert, pressing on towards a couple of grandstands erected in the sand.

With the dignitaries seated and night falling, nothing much else happened for quite a long time. Then Himself arrived, straight out of *The Desert Song* on a white horse at the head of a throng of local tribesmen, galloping past into the distance.

There didn't seem to be any running order for this occasion, and at the point where we thought nothing else would happen, the officials suddenly insisted that everyone should get up and move once again – we were all in the wrong place. We straggled out across the sand until we came upon a small cluster of pipes. Moments later the sand erupted round the pipe-cluster and a giant spout of water streaked into the air. We all stared up at it, and it then rained down on us. The horse-opera went bananas wheeling around under the gusher, Gaddafi waving and shouting and pirouetting his mount in what was now a sea of mud. We had apparently witnessed the inauguration of The Great Man-Made River Project, the world's second largest civil engineering project, overseen by American technicians and built by the Koreans. We plodged around in the mud, mightily unimpressed by the occasion, and gently sceptical that the desert waters would irrigate the whole of the Libyan coast and render it 'the agricultural wonder of the Mediterranean', as promised by the brochure, which arrived a year later.

So the prospect of another mystery tour into the desert hadn't exactly overwhelmed us. We sat in the VIP section of the airport as the minders went in search of the plane, returning to lead us to a small aircraft dripping new paint, with which Republic du Nord de Chad had recently been daubed on it. Protests notwithstanding, we were shovelled on board, and taken to another war zone in another country 'for the weekend – nice?'

We flew south for hours in a puttering aircraft bearing the name of an illegal regime, and laden with arms and boxes of ammunition. Over the disputed Aouzo strip on over the peaks of the Tibesti – curiously sharp and moonscape-like – until we made a couple of low passes over golden desert. Below us, sticking nose-in-sand absolutely upright, was another plane – apparently shot down by Chadian government troops in their last little engagement with the rebel northerners. We bumped to a halt and emerged to see the set from any romantic sheikh-filled film you care to recall: a crenellated fort, a camel caravan wending its way to a palm-fringed oasis, and the town of Faya Largeau, a former French Foreign Legion outpost and one of the great crossroads of the Sahara.

Business was bad, said the merchants sitting in the shade of the palms with everything from tins of sardines to rocket launchers spread out for sale. The Libyans, meanwhile, had disappeared intent on a mission, and soon re-emerged looking happier than I'd ever seen them, bearing crates of beer. This was why they liked coming to war: you could get a drink easily. Our hosts, the rebel army of northern Chad, which had been locked in years of struggle with the government, paraded a goat for my inspection ('pour Madame . . .') and then dispatched it in front of us. We drank bottle after bottle, staring at the hard rippled dunes which turned liquid orange at sunset. Sticking out of the sand were the reminders of the war – a helmet, empty ammunition boxes, and other shapes not bearing inspection. The night passed with the Libyans and the Chadian soldiers getting completely drunk and having a few firearms accidents. The next day we interviewed 'President' Goukouni-Weddi, who seemed rather nervous of his backers, the Libyans. I next heard of him when his death was announced from Tripoli – not on the Saharan battlefield, but in a corridor in the Hotel Al-Kabir in Tripoli. 'You never know . . .'

The habit of trying to 'amuse' journalists and thereby prevent them from doing a proper job was ingrained in the Libyan ministry of information. We were made to go on 'picnics' – lengthy drives along the coast to the admittedly wonderful Roman ruins at Leptis Magna and Sabratha. It wasn't worth refusing to go on these jaunts, as the ministry would ensure that absolutely nothing happened in your absence, and on one occasion a protesting journalist suffering from the hotel's attempts at cooking was carried bodily from her room and on to the coach. Picnics were part of The Official Programme.

Unofficially, there was an undercurrent of night-life, hidden from view. Behind high walls drink sloshed around, and as the main night-club – a relatively respectable establishment – was run by the Colonel's right-hand man, there was no reason to worry about the forces of law arriving to interrupt the evening's merriment. In a peculiar conversation about tourism, the Colonel had once painted a vision for me of the development of his Mediterranean coastline 'with many tourist villages'. I ventured that few people would cross the Med to drink pear juice. 'There will be alcohol, of course,' he countered – 'only I will have to find a way of stopping Libyans getting *into* the villages, otherwise no one will ever do any work here at all.'

Meanwhile, those who were still the unhappy guests of the Libyan revolutionaries spent a worried time – not physically ill-treated, but well aware of the reasons for being fearful in that land. We found ourselves in a highly awkward position when access to the men was finally agreed. We felt the need to confirm their situation and condition; however, at the same time – we had to see them and then leave them. Terry Waite held a short religious service with them, which added to the sense of awkward unreality, and as we were leaving one of the men clung to me, in a dreadful state. I felt a rat, walking out of the villa to which they'd been brought, unable to give them their freedom; but at least I'd extracted as much information as possible about where they were held and what the security was like, which I passed on later in London, suggesting that a rescue attempt would see them all killed.

There were weeks more of shilly-shallying, in which we trooped off to the People's Court for meaningless charades. The best occurred one Saturday morning, when, alerted by a contact to the court hearing of Malcolm Anderson, the Geordie oilfield worker, we turned up at the court with the minders to find it was all over. I was fed up with the ministry minions, especially the one who spoke English with a pronounced Welsh accent gained at Newport Polytechnic, and gave them an earbashing in the empty court-room, after which they disappeared. Fifteen minutes later, Malcolm reappeared in court and sat meekly in the front bench.

'You missed it,' he said. 'I was found guilty.'

Two minutes later, black-robed judges, with lawyers and interpreters, filed in, herded by our minders.

A man got up and began a long speech in Arabic.

'What the hell is going on?' I demanded.

The minder with the Welsh accent looked pleased.

'We got here late – I am admitting,' he said. 'So now we put it right – and we do all the trial again – just for you.'

All I can say in their favour is that they came to the same verdict, second time round.

The final release was a full-scale farce. ITN and ourselves had chartered a jet to return to Tripoli, having received an urgent message from the ministry of information that the event was imminent . . . just a few details to finalise. These included anxious enquiries as to whether the handover would be transmitted live on British television. It was due to happen at breakfast time, so, as we had a programme on air, we made a number of arrangements – and Libyan TV played ball (they would – the Colonel was involved).

On the Monday morning we turned up at the People's Palace (a remnant of old King Idris's regime) to find a crowd of officials, a table laden with food and juice, and Waite pacing the floor. I smelled a rat when I saw an official I trusted beckoning me into the next room.

'It's gone wrong,' he said, 'there's a problem with the revolutionary group, and His Nibs has got a crisis. Give it twenty-four hours and he'll have it fixed. Oh, and if you could just say there's been an administrative hitch, because you never know . . .'

Oh, really?

Explaining the situation on live television, pacifying Waite – who'd pinned a lot on this moment – and delivering guarded explanations to our newsrooms did not amount to a fun morning. I was worried, for Waite was announcing that he wasn't going to be humiliated and intended to leave; meanwhile I was getting odd little messages that the whole scenario was on for the next morning.

Late that evening, ITN having calmed down Mr Waite, I was asked to go to a meeting near the barracks. It was explained that the army was moving into a couple of locations and would be sitting very firmly on the revolutionary hotheads while the release was enacted. The atmosphere was very tense, said the nervous officials, and the Colonel was taking a gamble. Could I make sure that it was on television – live, as a kind of insurance for nothing going wrong again?

I felt highly uneasy, but had to balance this against the possibility that any wrong move on my part would jeopardise the hostages' situation. I got through to London and managed to get hold of Michael Grade, then Controller BBC1, asking him to authorise another expensive link-up live with Libya. I told him that I couldn't explain the reasons, except that it would help the hostage release. He was brilliant, and agreed without demur.

The next morning the pantomime began again, but this time when the official called me into the next room, there were the four men. They were all in a state of high anxiety, wondering if they were pawns in a nasty game. I promised them that I wouldn't leave the room and merely pushed open the door to signal thumbs-up to my crew. The next few minutes were highly charged, but finally officials opened the doors and led them in front of the cameras.

An hour or so later, while the four Britons were closeted with Terry Waite, I had a surreal conversation in which two of the Colonel's aides suggested that there might be a little deal necessary to ensure a quiet exit for the hostages, for there were serious rumblings in the city.

The Colonel was losing his bottle and needed to orchestrate things in his favour. He was over a hundred miles from Tripoli, and wanted to hold a big press conference – including the foreign journalists. I replied that everyone was going to accompany the hostages home when the British Caledonian plane arrived. 'It won't be leaving with anyone, if you don't go and see him,' I was told.

They added, 'He's with his father – who's in his hundredth year and not well, and he thinks there'll be trouble in the capital if he isn't seen to be in charge of the whole business.'

And also, 'Would it be possible for him to have someone in Britain thank him for his role in the release – such as the Archbishop of Canterbury?'

'What about his envoy, Terry Waite?' I suggested.

'No, a personal letter from the Archbishop – and could the Archbishop perhaps include a line of concern for the Colonel's father?'

While the rest of the press pack hurtled round trying to get through the cordon sanitaire Waite had erected around the released men, I sat in a blue funk wondering when reality was going to begin. I called my closest contact in the barracks, who arrived only to confirm all these bizarre arrangements.

I called Lambeth Palace, and arranged to see Robert Runcie.

Two days later, a British Caledonian plane arrived and most people headed for the airport. By then I'd managed to cook up reasons to London for not accompanying the plane, and found a small number of hacks willing to come to the interview. So we flew to Sirte, drove into the desert, waited for hours while being fed egg and chips – Libyans are partial to this kind of thing – and then saw Gaddafi. He made a point of showing his own press that the foreign journalists were present and ITN did a number of happy snaps with him. The Colonel looked content.

An army officer I did not know beckoned me silently into an office, and rang a number. He said: 'Ask in English who is this,' handing me the phone.

'Who is this?' I said.

'This is Air Traffic Control Tripoli.'

I handed the phone back.

Then, in Arabic and English, the officer gave the order: 'The British Caledonian can leave now, with everyone.'

Four days later, I met the Archbishop, who, I later heard from Tripoli, wrote a gracious and dignified letter.

*

As well as the undercurrent of fear in Libya, there were all the other allegations of nefarious behaviour attached to such a capricious regime. There was no doubt that there was naked endorsement of 'revolution' in all its forms. Gaddafi wasn't fussy about specific policies – you could find yourself in Tripoli sitting next to Nicaraguan leftists, Vanuatu rebels, sundry Palestinian groups and any number of oddball outfits, all of whom were hanging about in the hope of getting a bag of money, lots of public endorsement and perhaps some weapons.

The IRA did not appear publicly in the capital. The only time I heard a senior Libyan official refer to them was when he was with several army officers who concurred that the IRA were 'a problem', mainly because of their continued complaints about the isolation of the training camp in the desert, and its lack of booze.

Because of the Colonel's bombastic approach to foreign affairs, his penchant for interfering in matters of which he was ignorant, and talking loosely and luridly without any regard to consequences, he presented a sure target for the anger of countries strong on anti-terrorism. President Reagan led the pack – a man whose grip on foreign affairs, while markedly better than Gaddafi's, was not impressively so.

The mid-eighties were a time when hijacking and bomb explosions were horribly common across Europe. The Provos and the Red Brigades; ETA and Baader-Meinhof; the Red Army Faction and the PLO – all kinds of groups were delivering hypocritical justification for their contempt for human life as they indulged in car bombs, hostage-taking and random murder. But there is always a desire, particularly among politicians, to detect a simplistic conspiracy, ignoring both the deep roots of fanatical conviction and the eccentric thinking which drive individual acts of terror. Another unpopular line of enquiry is the murky area of finance and bomb-making and arms-dealing, which may have little to do with political views – and operates easily across ideologies. Libya was enmeshed in both areas – in stated encouragement and support of radical theories; and in terrorism itself, and in the supply of the means. Curiously, its own people tended to be middle-men rather than actively involved at the sharp end. There are a handful of incidents where Libyans appear to have taken part in terrorist acts – in central America, and in acts against the perceived enemies of its own regime – but I heard on several occasions that fear of the Colonel deterred most Libyans from undertaking any freelance work. So the assumption was, even among his own people, that he himself would be behind any major act of terrorism, should the finger be pointed at Libya – an assumption which came to haunt him when senior members of his intelligence outfit got greedily embroiled in the Iranians' revenge plans against the Americans for the shooting down of their airliner by the USS *Vincennes*. Initially unaware of their involvement in the explosion of the PanAm jet above the town of Lockerbie in 1988, he found no one believed him when he disputed any Libyan connection – and that he could mollify his accusers only by turning over for trial a couple of small fry who couldn't cause him any embarrassment.

Undoubtedly, the Libyan machine was always busy stirring up trouble, and time and again its citizens were found to be up to no good – in Syria, in Egypt, in Germany: active middle-men whose dirty work armed and fuelled the murderous idealists. Nevertheless, Libya was a fair way down the league of Middle East states involved in the efficient supervision of terrorism, despite its reckless, noisy and nasty cheerleading. Again, it was the behaviour of a teenager with a hatred of all that authority represents, but not a clue where his truculence and bad-mouthing and secret sniggering plotting will lead. A truly juvenile delinquent country – at least in its leadership.

For most of the nation wanted a quiet life; to get a crowd to demonstrate in Tripoli or Benghazi involved a ritual rounding-up of the usual suspects for a 'spontaneous demonstration', during which articulate students would shake your hand – in between shouting slogans – and ask politely where you were from. The only actual mob I saw in action consisted of peasants and workmen who admitted to being paid, and when they got over-enthusiastic were given a severe beating by the police. Mention revolutionary fervour to the middle class in Tripoli and they would quietly shrug and tell you that politics did not interest them, the Leader did that sort of thinking for everyone, and what did I think the chances were of sending their son to Birmingham University – and did I know John Cleese?

The obsession with John Cleese was national: *Monty Python's Flying Circus* was hugely popular and frequently shown on Libyan television. The Pythons must have been here, Libyans said thoughtfully, that's our country they're showing.

Most were aware of the dark side of their land, but felt they weren't the worst-off in the world, and that if the Colonel would shut up they wouldn't attract so much opprobrium. These remarks began to be heard much more freely in the mid-eighties, and the whisperings which constituted a guide to what was going on began to include mention of mysterious explosions and behind-the-scenes factionalism. There had been several attempts at assassination – nothing was completely secret in a country where the national prison was on the list of Notable Places and lit at night with fairy lights 'to cheer up the inmates'. Furthermore, the whole crowd in the Azzizya barracks were becoming a good deal more insecure, and the military were wondering discreetly if another little coup might be necessary; until, that is, Ronald Reagan confirmed the Colonel's rule for many years to come.

By late March 1986 there had been repeated threats from the Americans regarding Libya's role in international terrorism, the most recent based on the bombing of a discotheque in Berlin – an obscure and disputed incident, but enough of a pretext for President Reagan to claim justification for his stance. In that rather evangelical mode with which the United States feels quite comfortable, Gaddafi had been elevated to an international bogeyman and a symbol of devilry who, if removed, would take all the problems of terrorism with him. European voices were more sceptical, but the Americans were in an active phase and Gaddafi was an irresistible target for the president from Hollywood.

Try swatting a gnat, and you realise you need a lot of energy.

The US Sixth Fleet was just north of the Gulf of Sirte and there was no doubting that a confrontation was in the air. A considerable number of journalists made for Tripoli, and we found the atmosphere quite defiant – though ordinary Libyans were pretty ignorant about what they might be headed for. Gaddafi held a number of rabble-rousing meetings which he addressed with speeches full of ridiculous claims and insults – and was rewarded with a sharp attack on his military installations on the Gulf of Sirte by the American navy.

This merely roused him to greater anger, claiming victory against the Americans and calling Reagan a 'butcher'.

There was then a lull. Most of us were uncertain as to what might follow, for the attack had hardly given satisfaction to anyone; so the journalists left.

A week later there were more rumblings, and we arrived back to find that the Libyan military were on alert and the hospitals had raised their stocks of plasma and blood. But although the Jana news agency was churning out propaganda, the American threats of further action did not seem to be being taken too seriously by most Libyans. There was the usual failure to recognise the degree to which they were being seen as arch-terrorists abroad. We realised that the revolutionary committees were throwing their weight around: all the foreign TV crews had their stories about the disappearance of a Roman Catholic archbishop blocked by a mysterious new committee installed at the TV station. It later turned out that the committee stopped the story purely because *they* hadn't heard about it. Overt censorship was rare; most obstruction was due to poor communication, stupidity and the Libyan desire to work a one-day week.

We received no warning of the American air-raid; somehow the BBC, who had reported bombers taking off from Lakenheath in Suffolk, did not think to call us. Who am I to criticise Libyans for poor communication?

We'd had a quiet day in Tripoli, walking aimlessly along the crumbled promenade and contemplating another evening of wilted salad and pear juice. At two in the morning, the growl of aircraft, the first explosions and an eruption of chaos in the hotel sent me straight on to the balcony looking south over the city. I could see the planes, they were so low, and a second explosion, a pink-orange glow growing like ghastly sunrise behind a dark building, produced shock waves that made me hang on to the balcony rail. Immediately the corridor was full of cursing, for the electricity had gone off. I shrieked for the crew, and within seconds they were in the room and filming. In another room my colleague David Willey had had the foresight of a very experienced journo to tape his tape-recorder to the balcony rail earlier – just in case – and recorded everything.

The Hotel Al-Kabir is a large, ten-storey building. It shuddered as the bombs detonated, and although I have been under both Russian and Israeli bombing, this was the most severe I'd experienced.

We could not phone London. Eighteen months earlier direct lines between Libya and the UK had been suspended after one of the mysterious attacks by 'dissidents' on the main barracks, and the hotel subsequently used to take hours to get an international line out. So when David's phone rang as I got to his room, that line from London stayed open – with two lengthy breaks – for nearly a week (the receiver lay on the floor surrounded by notices threatening terrible things to anyone who put it back on the cradle).

In the dark there were explosions, shouting, confusion and, by now, loud anti-aircraft fire. Back on the balcony I already could see that the city was being hit in civilian areas. I knew the area well, and I also knew where the military installations were – the

Libyans were never shy of pointing them out. At one point, one of the American TV crews put on a camera light, highlighting the fact that I and my BBC colleagues were filming perfectly normally except for the small matter that none of us had a stitch of clothing on.

The next two hours were a scramble of shouting down the phone and attempting to get out of the hotel; but there were armed – and determined – soldiers at the door.

The anti-aircraft barrage continued for some time after the second wave of bombers had droned over. From the tenth floor of the hotel we could see flames and smoke rising from several locations, but the streets were completely empty. Then naval ships in the harbour joined in the barrage, and so it went on.

Just before first light, while another anti-aircraft barrage was in progress, three minibuses arrived at the hotel, bearing our frightened and ignorant minders. They told us candidly they'd been told by Gaddafi's office to take us to wherever there was damage. They would have been quicker, but, as usual, they couldn't get any transport. At least that seemed plausible.

The press piled in. We had a good idea where some of the explosions had been concentrated, so we directed the buses and headed for the residential district of Bin Ashur – where we drove into a scene of destruction. Casualties were still being pulled out of the rubble, small fires were burning, water mains overflowing, bits of building poised precariously. Families stood around in complete shock, some screaming, some frantically looking for relatives.

We roamed around, we filmed what we wanted, with no minders present. We interviewed people – a large number of younger Libyans speak good English – and checked on the damage. Further on, we recognised immediately that one of the buildings that had been hit was the French Embassy – we'd had a drink there only a few weeks previously. There's also what is known as Libyan security headquarters in the area, but it was unscathed, though three further embassies had been damaged.

It was eminently clear that a number of bombs had hit the suburb, not just a stray one.

We demanded to go to the hospital next, where we found the injured still arriving from several parts of the city. Many of the medical staff were non-Libyans – English-speaking Filipinos, Egyptian doctors, Bulgarian and Chinese nurses. All were deluged with work and merely looked up to give us precise information, defining injuries as 'shrapnel wounds', along with cuts from glass and severe shock. There were scores of people – including children, elderly men and young girls; we checked through to see if there were any military casualties in uniform, and saw none. I remember a Bulgarian nurse, a large dyed blonde with surgical forceps in hand, tweezing metal out of a teenage girl and asking me why war had started. She'd been brought up on communist propaganda, and asked me repeatedly if the Americans were also bombing her country now.

Later, at the children's hospital, the chief paediatrician, trained at a London teaching hospital, showed us two young boys in the emergency unit; his assistant, also London-trained, introduced himself as the Gaddafi family physician and said these were two of his sons, explaining their injuries precisely. Both doctors then described the death of the Colonel's daughter, Hannah – they had both gone to the barracks less than half an hour after the raid and found Mrs Gaddafi and some of the family in their wrecked apartment. (There was some confusion over the status of Hannah – 'adopted' was suggested, but as Libyans do not have adoption as such, it was evident that she was the daughter known to have been born as a result of his liaison with a Libyan army officer, and brought up with his other children.)

We went to see bodies in the morgue; we even turned them over to check that their injuries were consistent with a bomb blast, and not accident victims sneaked in to inflate injury figures. Having been fed red herrings, lied to, and shown stage-managed propaganda for more years than I can remember, I bring a cold eye to even the most graphic of scenes. In Libya, none of those of us present had a shred of doubt about what we were seeing.

I sat for longer than usual looking at our pictures, knowing that we hadn't managed to get to more than a handful of locations, that we had only 'official' reports of what had happened during the raid on the other large city, Benghazi, and that we did not yet know officially about Gaddafi himself – though I was told very soon after the raid that he had survived, otherwise, said my source, we would have been witnessing armed chaos. So I stuck to reporting what I had seen – which amounted to extensive damage to residential areas and a large number of civilian casualties – plus a direct hit on Gaddafi's headquarters, two miles from the district we had visited.

When I wrote my story – the first of fifty-six reports from Tripoli – I did so entirely from the point of view of an eye-witness, cataloguing events, but mindful of the unusual nature of the country and the need to explain to people at home the precise result of the British involvement in a botched American raid.

Two repercussions.

I nearly lost my job due to political pressure from politicians responsible for authorising the use of British military facilities for the raid. I said at the time that I stood by every word of my broadcast reports. Every single allegation made against those reports proved groundless.

Colonel Gaddafi is still in power – and both he and his people saw the American bombing as an act which confirmed and strengthened his authority.

FOURTEEN

A Chinese square

'In 1989 when spring was passing into summer . . .'

What a pretty phrase. The opening words to a cruel rewriting of history, in which the old and evil men who have run China turned truth on its head and proved they have no shame.

Entitled *The Truth About the Beijing Turmoil*, it is a glossy publication: ninety-four pages of colour photographs and very detailed text. Just so there's no doubt about the editorial provenance, the book is produced by The Editorial Board of *The Truth About the Beijing Turmoil*.

When I first looked at it, I knew yet again that what we – the visitors, the journalists – saw in June 1989 in Beijing was but a fraction of what happened when the Chinese authorities decided to end the three-month-long student protest. There are pictures of burning military vehicles, charred corpses, a body swinging from a flyover, injury and destruction. They were taken in both daytime and at night, and in several different locations in the capital. The text states that 'over 1280 vehicles were burned or damaged, including over 1000 military trucks, more than 60 armoured cars, and over 30 police cars . . . and more than 6000 martial law officers and soldiers were injured and scores of them killed.'

Read on.

'Such heavy losses are eloquent testimony to the restraint and tolerance shown by the martial law enforcement troops. For fear of injuring civilians by accident, they would rather endure humiliation and meet their death unflinchingly, although they had weapons in their hands. It can be said that there is no other army in the world that can exercise restraint to such an extent.'

It can be said that no other government in the world showed such effrontery in the last years of the twentieth century when describing the butchery of its own people.

I make no claim at all to being a 'China watcher'. As on so many other stories, I brought only curiosity and a layman's knowledge to this vast country. I know nothing of the language, except its tonal complexity and the tradition that a phrase directly spoken is impolite – a tradition eroded by the communists, led by a peasant brute called Mao, a man of phenomenal determination, who had no feelings for the millions who starved as his revolutionary ideas flew in the face of nature and common sense. His body, with his blackened rotted teeth, may – or may not – lie in the mausoleum which overlooks Tiananmen Square at the heart of Beijing. In the days following his death, the atmosphere in the Forbidden City, the enclave of power which abuts the square, was so poisonous and fearful that no one wanted to take any decisions, including what to do with his bloated body. When they finally decided to have him stuffed and mounted, after scouring the world – and Madame Tussaud's – in search of the finest preservation techniques, it was rumoured that there wasn't much left to deal with, and one of the wax models was substituted.

Tiananmen, therefore, is loomed over by all that is opaque and powerful; and yet it is a only a stretch of concrete of hideous proportions, somewhere the modern emperors can stare at, while their minions in their millions perform for them. When small families stroll across it, the precious 'one child' permitted by the state held between the parents, they are like insects venturing on to a vast plate. And, as with insects, the state has no concern about swatting them.

It takes the briefest of encounters to realise that the way life is lived rests on foundations constructed very differently from those of Western culture. The sense of the community above the individual is ancient. Nearly 400 years ago, the Chinese were already operating the *baojia*, a system of mutual responsibility which underwrote law and order: households registered in groups of a thousand, and then were subdivided and made responsible for keeping an eye on each other, with the idea of everyone being held equally liable for a crime or social misdemeanour. The communists merely reinforced and refined the system. No wonder we were occasionally met by officials with the greeting: 'Who is your group leader?' The concept of the group, the mass, has an emotional tug which a Western crowd does not parallel.

The demonstrations which began in 1989 had been world-wide news for months, prompting speculation abroad that China was heading for some momentous change. Week after week pictures appeared across the world of the students camping in Tiananmen, arguing, debating, writing posters and parading banners. That part of the story was there for all to see. But what the elderly men shuffling round the levers of power were up to was anyone's guess. Reading the runes in China is a full-time occupation, a matter of nuances and symbols, with the stage-managed political events containing only hints of internal plotting and manoeuvres. What was certain was that the colour-ful mayhem in the square (highly conservative by comparison with student behaviour in Europe), with the accompanying litter and air of spontaneous excitement, was anathema to the gerontocracy. Tiananmen was where they liked to see the grandeur and unity of China displayed: serried ranks and orderly extravaganzas at which they could flap an arthritic flipper and beam in pretence of geniality. The sight of the students – and the knowledge that the world was sharing in this sight – laid down layers of resentment over the months.

I'd not seen the early demonstrations – except on television – for I was only called to go to China as the weeks of protest turned into months. The Soviet President Mikhail Gorbachev had come and gone, and still the students hadn't moved. Indeed, many news organisations were beginning to scale down their presence, and it wasn't clear if there would be any significant developments. However, the summer days were warm, the square was a social magnet, and the students were as enthusiastic as ever. And there were no overt indications of government action.

I started from Hong Kong, with a dodgy visa acquired by normal Hong Kong methods (fifty dollars to a man in a back street), and headed for Shanghai. There, at Fudan University, the students were also agitating; but here there was none of the open and freewheeling atmosphere that one associates with student protest, just tension and intensely spoken wishes, and whisperings in the tiny and spartan accommodation blocks. They were desperate for information, but could only rely on word of mouth, for the national media were a mere government mouthpiece, an instrument of instruction and admonition.

Because one of our correspondents had lost his voice, and another had to return home, I flew to Beijing, and headed straight for the square early one afternoon. It was a huge, messy, sprawling sort of carnival; but instead of funfair and jollity, there was passion and debate, knots of young people engaged in discussion and endless poster-writing. Food was a preoccupation: pennants fluttered from small tents plastered with bits of paper – testimonials from the hunger strikers inside. Next to them, bespectacled lads picked their way through bed-rolls and crumpled newspapers and wooden stools and bags of rubbish, delivering bamboo boxes of noodles and sacks of buns. It was organised chaos, rather serious, and fuelled by argument and critical question-sessions.

Television crews from many countries roamed around, finding the students who spoke English. That in itself was a sign of the square's unique atmosphere: trying to report in China has always been difficult, and to find oneself free to ask questions, with young people eager – and unafraid – to talk, was extraordinary. The American crews always homed in on the white plaster Goddess of Democracy which poked up among the tents – an echo of the Statue of Liberty, but not quite the precise symbol of a unified desire for freedom and democracy between East and West that many foreigners wanted to believe. 'Democracy' was a word used loosely by everyone; but the words 'reform' and 'anti-corruption' were used much more frequently by the Chinese, and it was clear that the Chinese road to democracy was viewed by the students as very different in concept from that of the West.

I have no grand ideas about reporting. You make your way to the centre of the action, look and listen, ask questions and verify, and shift the story as fast as possible. You can never report everything, and what you see may be unrepresentative of the whole. On the other hand, you may underestimate the scale of what you see. And trying to gauge the significance of any event while it is in progress is a dangerous game.

Even at the time, on the night of 3 June, I knew that we could not adequately convey what was happening in Beijing. At one point, standing in a darkened side road, out of range of the machine guns, I took a minute or so just to listen. Normally, Beijing, still then a city of bicycles, was as silent as a country village at night. On 3 June, I could hear the rumble of military vehicles five hundred yards to the south of me – also, unmistakably, the sound of gunfire echoing from all sides – and from a very great distance as well. The guns spoke of citywide trouble, continuous and violent. An hour later I listened again, and the volleys were non-stop, chattering across the city – some very far away. To be unable to show the full extent of what happened is not only frustrating, but a measure of the arbitrary and piecemeal nature of any reporting. That night, I felt it more strongly than ever before – or since.

There had been warning signs. In the early hours of 3 June, columns of soldiers had made their way towards the city centre, but were stopped by local people. The troops were unarmed, and appeared rather unsure of themselves. What was significant was the number of non-students – ordinary Beijing residents – who demanded of the soldiers that they leave the students in peace: a gesture of support not lost on the authorities. Students were one thing – but the workers? The old men grew alarmed.

The day passed and nothing untoward happened. It was warm and muggy, and as usual we could gain no information whatsoever about official reactions from the leadership, which lives next to the imperial Forbidden City in a compound known as Zhong Nan Hai – a modern version of imperial hauteur, all high walls and secrecy. But towards evening that Saturday, another column of soldiers had a much noisier confrontation with civilians at a flyover a mile from the square – and again, there were passers-by and bus drivers and old men on bicycles arguing with the military. All over Beijing – but unknown to most of us at the centre – similar scenes were played out for several hours, and any move the soldiers tried to make was blocked by swarms of angry citizens. We were out getting pictures all evening, conscious that the appearance of uniforms marked another step up the ladder of tension. However, the students in the square merely went deeper into discussion, and there were still sightseers and Chinese families wandering over the concrete expanse, revelling in the strangeness of it all. By this time, most of the foreign TV crews had headed for Tiananmen, including our American colleagues from NBC, who had two-way radios.

Just before midnight, I sat on railings at the edge of the square, nattering to a couple of students who spoke excellent English. They were both children of academics, and relatively sophistic-ated, gigglingly admitting to being boy- and girlfriend, asking shyly if it was rude to hold hands in public in Britain. They weren't sure where the demonstrations were leading – but they were sure that the country's new-found economic wealth had been grabbed by the inner circle of privileged party members, who had no compunction about snaffling the best jobs on offer. They spoke with the irritation of relatively well-connected young people, sensing that unseen corruption might just impede their own ambitions. They both dreaded the end of their studies, for the system was still operating that deployed graduates at the state's behest to work anywhere in the country, so they couldn't guarantee to stay in Beijing, or together. 'Are students in Britain ordered to different cities to work?' they asked. I wondered where to begin.

They perched on the railings, holding hands and dreaming, both smartly dressed and bathed in the strange tangerine-orange lights of the square. At that moment I got an odd feeling. I'm not overtly superstitious, but occasionally there is the unmistakable frisson of *something* – something which passes broodingly overhead, unseen but emanating darkness.

At a quarter to midnight, I headed with the crew back to the Palace Hotel. A swish bit of chandeliered modernity, it lay a quarter of a mile back from Chang An, one of the main roads leading to Tiananmen, and we had our editing machines and extra phone lines there; we'd also bagged a few rooms in the gloomy old Beijing Hotel which fronted Chang An, and had a view of the square from its balconies.

At seven minutes past midnight, I overheard an NBC radio crackle with the words, 'There's shooting, there's shooting at Fuxingmen.' I knew in my bones that this was no false alarm; it was as if a siren had sounded. Grabbing Bob Poole, our camera-man, and his sound recordist Alan Smith, we hurtled out, finding one of the drivers we'd used before who spoke a little English. We decided to avoid the main roads, and head for the location round the back of the Forbidden City. There was clearly some-thing very odd going on – hundreds of people were creeping out of their houses, pointing and shouting. Beijing at that time was usually silent at night; there was no 'night-life' and policemen discouraged any loitering.

We got our first sight of army trucks heading across the end of a small street, and we abandoned the car to walk down and join the little crowd watching a fire a hundred yards in the distance. Puzzled, we saw two of the crowd fall to the ground. There was consternation, with people bending over trying to lift them up. I couldn't figure out what was going on, for I was standing in the middle of the lane transfixed; an armoured personnel carrier had roared by, and a truck on the main road was on fire. There was thunderous noise, and petrol fumes and smoke. The fuel tank blew as I watched; when I looked back, I saw two inert bodies being carried away helter-skelter. Only then did I realise the gunfire was continuous, and as we scuttled to the edge of the main road a truck went by with soldiers standing apparently ramrod-stiff. It took several seconds to realise that they were holding their automatic weapons absolutely straight and hammering bullets relentlessly along the pavements and down all the side streets. We took a couple of shots, and wondered how long we could stay in any one position. I looked into the distance up Chang An and saw scores of trucks and APCs heading towards us. A second truck went by – and swerved as something was hurled at it near the blazing vehicles. The soldiers went on firing. This is what an invading army looks like, I thought, shaking with helplessness. We raced away down the lane, past the small cottages which make up the traditional maze of housing, looking for our car. We spotted the driver, who was surrounded by a shouting crowd; seeing our camera, a man detached himself and pulled us into his cottage doorway. A tiny room, with every household article stacked neatly, a bare floor well swept, and a blue-screened TV on a lace mat with an old-fashioned rabbit-ears aerial. On a low chair was a woman, a huge blossoming peony of blood in her stomach, the bullet exit wound. The man was quiet, blinking, with a questioning look on his face. He crouched in the other chair, evidently trying to explain that they'd been watching together when . . .

There was another commotion at the door: the driver asking if we could help. Outside a woman was being carried by her family – they wanted to know if we could take her to hospital. There was an air of panic as we tried to cram ourselves into the car and take her on the back seat with several relatives refusing to be left behind. Her skull was a mangle of brains and hair, though she was still alive. We careered down dark streets to the children's hospital; we found ourselves heading into hell.

Scores of people were jamming the entrance, all distraught, screaming, demented – and in a state of disbelief. In the twenty minutes we were there, forty casualties were brought in: by bicycle, by rickshaw, carried in on a park bench. All the injuries were bullet wounds – in some cases, multiple. There were elderly women, teenagers, children – not one seemed to be a student. We pushed our way into the operating theatre. It was a scene of mayhem, the living and the dead alike fetching up on the tables, with the staff slinging corpses on to the floor. The whole floor was red with running blood. As well as panic, there was fear. Staff clutched at us, pointing to the camera and begging us to take pictures – but quickly. After a few minutes, two men erupted from another door and shrieked at us. The staff made it obvious that these were officials, and we were in trouble. I wanted to stay to get more evidence, but we legged it, for the atmosphere was wild, and the camera was precious.

We tried time and again to get near the square, eventually abandoning the car, and although I desperately wanted to see what was happening there, it began to dawn that the killing was taking place well away from Tiananmen. Ordinary citizens were being killed in their homes, the bullets ripping through the soft bricks. Onlookers, the curious, the disbelieving, and the frightened venturing out into the narrow lanes were being mown down. At one point I found myself between two men about three hundred yards from the endless passage of army vehicles. The man on my right was crying and gripping my arm; on my left, the other man had a few words of English. As I turned to him, I felt the grip on my right arm slip – and at my feet was a silent heap, absolutely still.

At that point I wondered if we were going to survive. The odds seemed terrible, and still I felt that we had not got enough evidence of what was happening. I had a brief and halting conversation with Bob Poole:

'Should we stay out?'

'Course we should.'

'I agree.'

We both knew we had gone beyond the boundary of risk where we would normally call it a day. The Chinese army was killing indiscriminately with powerful weapons, and added to that, the secret police and other officials were hunting for foreign journalists: in the hospital, and also when approaching groups of onlookers, we had seen people scatter as anonymous men barked at them and then turned to head for us. However, one of my worries at that point was that after over two and a half hours on the streets, we had seen just one other member of the media – a Canadian TV cameraman. For the majority of the press, I later learned, were still gathered in the square – or, like my own colleagues, had stayed in the Beijing Hotel to watch events from the balcony.

From the hospital, I managed to call the office and alert them to the scale of events, and made clear our intention of staying with the story for as long as possible.

'It's appalling, it's dreadful,' I said, for the first time having to find words, however inadequate, to describe what we were seeing.

And still the troops came in – and now tanks: the 38th Army and the 27th, tough professionals, who nevertheless managed to shoot each other in a major cock-up in the suburbs, and whose orders, it's now believed, were unclear and wrongly executed. Be that as it may, the force now let loose on the streets was a body of men completely ignorant of the situation in Tiananmen, fed the line that they were on their way to 'put down a rebellion' which was led by 'counter-revolutionary thugs' – and with every intention of shooting their way to victory.

Along Chang An, we could see signs of resistance – stones littered the road, and the number of vehicles on fire was growing. As we finally made our way to the edge of the square, having taken a roundabout route on foot, we were having problems with students calling attention to our camera. They were so desperate, they clung to us and shouted to their mates and tried to drag us this way and that, to show us another body, or a wrecked vehicle. This only made us more vulnerable, drawing attention to the camera and alerting the creepy secret police; but we were eventually lucky.

A pony-tailed man who said he was called Li attached himself to us and proved a marvellous friend. He was too old to be a student, and had a dark, characterful face; he spoke a little English and instantly understood the problem, shushing the students, and guiding us nimbly through back alleys and courtyards. I put my faith in him – and prayed that he wasn't a secret policeman. Instead, he got us to the edge of the square, which by 3 a.m. was partially under the control of the army, though we could only see lines of troops blocking our access. There were still thousands of students standing defiantly, confronting the soldiers, and as we walked nearer I realised they were singing the Internationale.

As they sang, there was a tremendous roar of gunfire, which lasted for minutes, starting a stampede, with bicycles and rickshaws intermingled. Li pointed to the far side of the boulevard – and we dashed across a couple of hundred yards while people fell around us. In the shadow of a government building, we lay on the ground and considered our options. We were breathless and bewildered and outraged. I knew that I had to get on a phone to London for the main news bulletin, and that there was only an hour or so before the deadline; I felt it imperative to deliver an eye-witness report, for clearly the killing was going to continue, and such action should be exposed as soon as possible.

The crowd soon reformed in front of the soldiers and we risked a 'stand-up', just a few seconds of me talking to camera – but we were interrupted four times by immense volleys and rushing students. Over an hour later, we got a take, having witnessed ambulance drivers being injured and white-coated medical staff being shot. I decided to head back to the hotel with the one precious cassette, for I was getting worried that if we lost it to some soldier, the whole night's work would have been in vain. Bob and Alan opted to stay in the lee of the building, because it was obvious that the only way back to the hotel was across a long expanse of open ground, running parallel to the soldiers' line.

I set off at a hard run and had gone only fifty yards when the firing began again. There was chaos, hundreds of people blundering in all directions. My arm flipped upwards and I lost the cassette, and simultaneously a young man cannoned into me. I went full length over him and lay with my face on the tarmac, watching little scarlet ticks flashing on the ground just a yard away. I had no notion that they were bullets. I crawled after the cassette, and turned to apologise to the young man. He had a huge seeping hole in his back – and I had blood running down my arm. The bullet which took a nick out of my elbow had killed him.

I set off again, possessed with fear and rage. I ran towards the Beijing Hotel just beyond the edge of the square, hoping the BBC was somewhere in the rooms we'd rented. A safe haven, I was squeaking to myself, and then I found the gates fastened shut with wire.

Bugger that, I thought, and, like an animal, went for the wall.

I got up it in one go, clawing at the stone, and only when I got to the top did I realise it was at least eight feet high. I half slid down the other side, too chicken to jump, and trotted across the compound, which was eerily silent, clutching the tape. The lobby looked dimly lit – too late, I saw three policemen inside. Also coming across the lobby were two non-Chinese, shouting as the glass door was pushed open: 'Run for it – they'll arrest you!' By then I was halfway through, and mad.

A policeman went for the tape in my hand. I kicked him in the groin, punched the second with my left hand, and body-charged the third. I'm no fighter, but surprise and a sense of outrage are enough. I then hurtled to the stairs, with the two strangers shouting 'Go for it!' as they deliberately got in the way of the cops. I streaked up the stairs – realising I had no idea on which floor we had our office. I tried two floors, hammering on doors, until I struck lucky, cannoning in on *Newsnight*'s Julian O'Halloran. I looked a complete fright, blood and grit everywhere, and with my fingers locked so rigidly round the cassette it had to be prised free, but I was staggered to find the entire BBC operation hotel-bound, viewing the carnage from the balcony.

I mustered everything I could to find the right words, the words which would both paint a picture accurately and convey a sense of the scale and the atmosphere – for we could not send TV pictures directly: all we had was a telephone line.

After such a night, there should have been some respite; but neither the Chinese army nor the protesters had given up. Even though the streets had quietened down, and the students had been marshalled from the square under army guard a short time after I had left, with Bob and Alan making it safely back, the next few days saw a city in defiant mood. There were frequent bursts of gunfire – so much so that it became the norm, like Beirut in wartime.

Though the population was threatened and exhorted and lied to by the authorities, there were enough people who had seen or heard what had happened to spread information by word of mouth. Tanks growled down the streets, but still there were determined sallies against the army. Vehicles burned on street corners and soldiers taking action against a crowd found themselves repeatedly defied by a lynch-mob mentality – and indeed, several uniformed bodies swung from bridge and lamp-post and tree. Rocks were hurled at passing APCs – and all the while, the army's guns were in action.

Our stories were 'pigeoned' out the next morning – taken to the airport by a roundabout route and smuggled abroad, for the TV station had closed down its satellite operation in late May, the state-appointed management conscious that direct transmissions might not work in their favour. Ordinary drivers risked their lives to help us, and friends of people who worked in our local bureau bamboozled officials and fought off plainclothes secret police to protect our tapes.

Foreign journalists were threatened and hassled; every move we made was technically illegal. Martial law was in force – draconian measures which included the potential for shooting foreign camera crews on sight.

The city was prey to rumour and fear: patients were being hauled out of hospitals, the crematoria were working overtime – was it true they threw the injured in, still alive, along with the dead? Blood and medicine supplies were low, hospitals were short of medical staff – no one dared count the number who'd been killed on the streets.

Hospitals were out of bounds to foreigners. Even so, I thought it necessary at least to have a go, and sneaked into the Beijing Medical Union Hospital, having been refused authorised entry after lengthy negotiations with officials.

Inside the front door nervous young doctors immediately guessed what we were up to, and shepherded us to a small room in which were several patients with gunshot wounds, then down a corridor to another ward, passing another, curtained corridor in which a score or more people lay on the floor. The doctors were frantic that we should see what they were having to deal with, but also terrified – officials were roaming the building, they said, and patients and bodies had been removed without the permission of families – who knows where.

We scampered around in an atmosphere of threat, when suddenly we heard shouting and saw uniformed men heading for us. A nurse screamed, 'They kill you!' and a young woman doctor shouted, 'With me, with me!' and set off at breakneck speed. We galloped after her, hearing men shouting orders – presumably at us. The doctor dived down a narrow set of steps and pelted through a basement full of God knows what. We knocked into stores and old equipment as we ran for our lives, ending up in the coke cellar, where this young woman, tears streaming down her face and shouting 'Run, run!', pointed to a window of light at the top of a heap of coke. We scrabbled out, finding ourselves in a side street we knew, and ran for dear life.

And so it went on: days of gunfire, the crushing of resistance, the refusal to countenance defiance, and the inexorable advance of the state machine, churning out the propaganda, rewriting history. The old men had held on to their antimacassared armchairs of power through simple brutality; now they had scores to settle.

On the afternoon of 4 June, having spent the morning broadcasting over the phone to London and cutting the story to send to the airport, I went to my hotel room. I cried uncontrollably for a long time. I kept thinking not only of those who had wanted to change their country and been blown away, but of those who had risked everything for us – the strangers, the mere journalists.

No one has ever been able to put a number on those killed in Beijing in June 1989. In a country where millions have been sacrificed to the whims of the leaders – in living memory – what are a few thousand more? Perhaps two to three thousand died, with many more injured. A regime which lies to its own people as a matter of course – and has most likely destroyed any detailed evidence – cannot even bring itself to admit that it might have made a mistake.

Instead, it produces glossy publications such as *The Truth About the Beijing Turmoil*, and writes: 'The measures adopted by the Chinese government to stop the turmoil and put down the rebellion have not only won the acclaim and support of the Chinese people, but they have also won the understanding and support of the governments and people of many other countries.'

Liars.

That's why it's worth being a reporter.

FIFTEEN

How to be a Ponti

When I was a Brownie, like millions of other little girls, I cantered about a church hall singing: 'Here we are, the laughing Pixies, helping people when in fixies.' I quite liked the games, and because Big Fatty Robson and Small Fatty Robson were in our pack (oh, the cruelty of children, and I can't even recall their Christian names), I rose to the exalted rank of Pixie Seconder, due to the inability of the Two Fatties to run, jump or skip, never mind amble helpfully towards people in fixies.

I took a hearty dislike to the uniform. Why were we dressed as brown paper parcels, tied in the middle? School uniform was just about bearable, as long as you didn't mind being addressed as a bunch of hairy greyhounds by other schools, but a tan sack surmounted by a brown knitted Thing? I ask you. So when approached to 'fly up' to the Girl Guides, I first enquired about the dress code, only to discover a larger blue sack, tastefully decorated with badges denoting thrilling activities such as Proficiency in Darning. I said No thank you, and set my mind against uniforms, and the batty things you appeared to have to do when wearing them.

I held out for thirty-five years until 1990 and an evening in Saudi Arabia, when I realised the old nightmare was upon me. The only woman in the two-dozen-strong press team with the

British army in the Gulf, I was facing a table heaped with Uniforms, Size Various. Female antennae waving, I shoved past the bespectacled RAF clerk who thought himself capable of holding up bits of clothing and 'guessing' my size and burrowed through the mound of clothes on his table, years of experience at the sales putting me well ahead of my colleagues. Armed with a monstrous heap of 'desert combats' – curious camouflage resembling a herd of pale Ayrshire cows – I tried on a dozen bits and pieces. The RAF looked on bemused, completely unable to grasp that if a woman is going to have to go into the desert and live with a front-line unit of two thousand men, several hundred miles from a bathroom and a hairdresser, never mind the shops, she is at least going to get a uniform that fits.

In between acquiring 'bits of kit' – most of which seemed to suggest that a pack animal might come in useful – we were all being told to fill in lots of forms. Military paperwork has much in common with BBC paperwork, being copious, detailed, legally meticulous and destined to be stuffed down the back of the sofa or used as kindling for camp fires when the real action starts.

One form gave me pause for thought.

Next of Kin, it stated – leaving not one, but several lines to fill in, clearly suggesting that in the event of your demise your many relatives would all get a bone each.

I wondered what to do.

Having had one or two narrow squeaks in the course of my work, I've had cause to think about survival, and luck, and providence. I'm not overly superstitious, but I touch wood and don't walk under ladders and throw salt over my shoulder. Long live medieval talismans, say I. The strength of childhood religious ritual has never quite dissipated, even though it wasn't a particularly fervent religious childhood and no one actually mentioned belief or theology; it was all a matter of form and seating-plans. The Church of England seemed a reasonable middle-of-the road outfit to me, as I toured the various chapels and missions and churches; the Methodists, of course, had the music, but the C of E had the glory of Durham Cathedral.

As a radio producer I began to see that the BBC played a not insignificant part in upholding religious tradition, and that for all the falling attendance figures on Sundays, the audience cleaved to the idea of the BBC going through the motions for them – a kind of national religious insurance policy, reinforcing comfort at times of distress and disaster. What I hadn't expected was the number of funerals that I would have to attend. From bulldozers shovelling scores into a mass grave in Italy, to a funeral pyre of hundreds of rotting corpses in Rwanda, to a jolly lunch held by Armenians atop the freshly filled funeral-plot, I'd been made to think about mortality.

A week before I flew to Saudi Arabia I'd been in Sunderland at Maud's burial. An adopted child, I'd been her daughter for over forty years, happy and secure. I'd always known about the adoption; I was a child of war. I'd been curious, but not disturbed about my origins, though at school I'd been privately intrigued by the drama and shame and social horror which seemed to surround unwanted pregnancy. It appeared to take two forms: the 'never darken my door' Victorian novel variety, coupled with incomprehensible whispers which implied that someone's elder sister 'was having to go away to Scotland for a while', balanced by a reading of history which seemed to suggest that bastards did pretty well – they kept turning up in royal family trees and even in the cast list of Shakespeare's plays. All this possibly planted a few thoughts about tough social conventions and the importance of roots, but I never dwelled or brooded on it, nor did I cling to any fantasies or expect anything else than to make my own way in the world. After Maud's funeral, Wilfrid, her husband, was lost without her, and had retreated into his own world.

Now I stared at the military form in front of me and realised – for the first time – that I had no close relatives. It had never struck me before. Some people have large families, some don't – I'd never really pondered the matter. I felt awkward.

It's not something you make a joke about: who will bring your body home?

I think I left the form blank, and felt a little curl of angst in the bottom of my stomach.

It had all seemed such a switchback of events in the past few months, and I hadn't stopped to consider what might lie ahead.

Nigel Bateson and I had been in Trinidad in July, trying to make sense of a puzzling hostage-taking-cum-coup carried out by a Muslim fundamentalist who'd burned down the central police station in Port of Spain and taken over the parliament building. Initially, I couldn't believe my luck: a Caribbean island? Decent weather? My oh my – this was a change from crawling around a Romanian television station while Mr and Mrs Ceauşescu were being shot, or spending a day on the floor of a Jaffna hospital as the Tamils decided to take on the Sri Lankan army ward by ward.

Sadly, most of Trinidad seemed to be under curfew, and the hotel with the best view of parliament was located in the docks. And it rained a lot. Also, disconcertingly, various Trinidadian hostages were willing to give us phone interviews while casually mentioning that Mr Abu Bakr, the Muslim leader, was holding a gun to their heads. We filmed the rebels' surrender in a magisterial tropical downpour, and transmitted the story from one of our colleagues' satellite dishes on the hotel roof. It then became abundantly clear that we were trapped – all flights having been suspended. The hacks' eyes glazed – 'marooned on an island in the West Indies . . .' – and we headed for the bar for a monumental session.

At some undefinable point in the evening, our celebrations were interrupted by a demented reporter staggering round the room clutching a radio and shouting incoherently. Everyone ignored him. So he took to rugby-charging groups of hacks and shrieking. Eventually we gathered round to prevent further damage, at which point we made out the word:

'SaddamHusseinsinvadedkuwaitandwerehalfwayroundthewor ldinthewrongplace.'

Indeed he had. And indeed we were.

Overnight, the hotel rang to the screams of desperate journalists, convinced that war was going to begin in the Gulf the next morning, and we were on a tropical island, the wrong side of the globe, with no plane. By 4 a.m. the Americans had chartered an immense aircraft from some doubtful outfit in Florida, and we'd all paid for a seat, and possibly for its owner eventually to have it gold-plated.

No one suggested on the first of August that the war wouldn't happen until the next year.

I went to Saudi Arabia, having reported in the previous weeks on the exodus of refugees from Iraq to Jordan, and then having spent a very short time in Baghdad before being called home with the news that Maud had had a heart attack.

Flying into Dharan, the scruffy east coast town which the Saudis regard as a convenient place to keep contaminating foreigners away from the rest of their country, I felt very apprehensive. This was a much more formal 'going to war' than I had ever encountered, with a great deal of time to contemplate what might happen. Under normal circumstances, we reporters usually found ourselves shoehorned into some plane with a hazy idea of the front-line positions and with hostilities already going at full tilt – or visiting a conflict which had been in progress for so long that war was a way of life.

Sri Lanka's long-running problems with the Tamil insurgency in the north of the island, for example, had left the country's army relatively indifferent to journalists. A casual enquiry got you a seat on a military plane – a Chinese flying horror with metal park-benches riveted to the floor, but provided with gold-tasselled scarlet plush velvet cushions – and you took off with some major yelling in your ear, 'They are shooting on the runway up north – we are thinking you should be getting out first while we observe the situation.' In such circumstances, risk assessment is a sharp operation involving quick decisions and very little imagination. You and your crew agree and then run like hell.

In Saudi Arabia we had a lot of time to think – and to become only too aware that before anything actually began, there was likely to be a small war with our allies the Saudis. We found ourselves trying to operate in a country which is hostile to journalism, and which initially refused to grant visas to the foreign press; indeed, the attitude of many ordinary Saudis was an arrogant irritation that foreigners had to be admitted to their a country. This included not just the press but the allied military force as well, and American and British soldiers were frequently told by sneering passers-by, 'Why are you on our streets? We pay you to go and fight,' as if their oil-money had hired half a million mercenaries to do their bidding and defend their autocratic and primitive regime.

There were bad-tempered incidents, with the presence of women in uniform – both women reporters and energetic young soldiers – constantly showing up the narrow and unpleasant atmosphere. The diplomats were having kittens – and there was a major downplaying of the assaults and insults that came the way of the foreigners. One morning our makeshift BBC office in a Dharan hotel was informed that a local princeling was intending to pay us a visit. A few minutes later his entourage swept in, fat men in white dish-dashes showing their vests and pants underneath. The plump head honcho, followed by a local TV crew catching his every gracious move, beamed grandly at us, asking who was in charge. I stepped forward and held out my hand, watching as this minor member of the Saudi royal family made a split-second decision whether to advertise his ease with Western ways, or treat me as an untouchable second-class citizen. His teeth fixed in a cold grin, and he brushed my hand rather than shook it – but even this was too much for the camera crew: the camera light was switched off, the camera heaved off the shoulder, and – as the prince turned abruptly away – all three members of the crew shoved me physically aside and hissed abuse, fortunately in Arabic.

On the streets the religious zealots, the *mutawa*, charged with upholding what passes for morality, took out their frustrations on individual women, sneaking up behind them and hitting and slapping and screaming. Then from the administrative capital, Jeddah, came the story of a middle-aged, middle-class university lecturer and her friends and colleagues who decided to take advantage of the international spotlight shone on the limitations imposed on women by staging a demonstration. About forty women drove their cars decorously through the capital – an illegal act. (They're always expected to have a male driver, supposedly a 'more comfortable and dignified' way to travel; in reality, they are spied on, and a woman is almost without the means to conduct her life without male permission, or being informed on.) The story got into the press, to the horror of everyone (especially the governments) trying to pretend that these little cultural problems were irrelevant. What did not get into print was that the lecturer was summoned in front of her entire family that evening, whereupon her father shot her dead.

I drove our four-wheel-drive vehicle around Dharan with added determination. There was little proper reporting to undertake, except for the military build-up. Local people would not be interviewed, and the large expatriate community was hospitable but kept its head down, living in foreigners-only compounds. The only advantage of these ghettoes was the absence of roaming religious busybodies – and the potential to get much alcohol down the collective foreign throat, to the shrieking envy of young Saudi men, who were forced to drive across the seven-mile causeway to neighbouring Bahrain on Thursday nights, for a Muslim weekend of scotch and as many vulnerable Filipina housemaids and hotel-workers as they could coerce. Dharan was a dump; the interface with the West that the Saudis had to maintain in order to keep their oil industry going and to administer the hundreds of thousands of poverty-driven third world workers who service the country – all of whom are denied basic rights. The grandiose and cool marble palaces and mosques which oil has built were elsewhere across the desert, and the Saudis, terrified that they were the next snack for Saddam

Hussein's appetite, must have been grateful that most of them could stay well away from Dharan, and did not have to be bothered with too much contact with those dreadful military people who were about to save their skins.

All this was an undercurrent to the military preparations which were, by any standards, immense. Every few minutes giant American Starlifter transport planes blotted out the sun like monstrous albatrosses as they flopped on to the Dharan runway. At the port of Al-Jubail a few miles north, ships disgorged every kind of vehicle and weapon, along with enough provisions and support equipment to keep several small countries going for a decade. The scale was indescribable – literally, for in a flat landscape it was almost impossible to convey the picture of acre after acre of sand being covered with hardware. Up the main supply route (MSR to the army chaps – and the acronyms kept coming) went an endless line of military vehicles, twenty-four hours a day, seven days a week. The Americans seemed to have brought *everything* with them – including trucks which appeared to be carrying plywood telephone boxes in groups of four. All was explained later in the desert. No American soldier leaves home without the portable loo (communal four-seat variety).

As we counted guns and tanks and APCs and wondered where Americans kept all this stuff back home, the ever-growing press corps circled the military press officers inquisitively, wondering how we were going to report this war – if it ever happened. The military was clearly not going to take everyone with them, and the Saudis were making it plain that they'd deal nastily with anyone they found trying to do a decent job of reporting on their own.

Meanwhile, a number of jaunts into the desert were on the cards.

The British – both the soldiers and the press – liked things that went bang. UK 'facilities', as these PR outings were called, tended to be held in a rugby-club atmosphere, with a lot of cheering and bouncy behaviour, accompanied by a certain amount of 'sorting out the men from the boys'. This involved inviting gung-ho journalists to reveal their true wimpy colours: 'Just pop on to that Warrior and we'll go for a look-see.' A Warrior is a mammoth armoured personnel carrier, thirty-five tons of tracked vehicle covered with dangerous sticky-out bits which may possibly fire something. Proper soldiers ride inside them; extras, such as journalists, find themselves treated as roof-rack material. There are no stepladders incorporated (a major design fault in the view of the press), and 'popping on' to a Warrior was akin to mounting a rhino at full charge. Once aboard, you hung on for dear life while some officer, hand on hip, gestured languidly at various desert Points of Interest and the Warrior's driver (the corporal from the To Hell And Back At Speed school of military driving) tried his best to dislodge the clinging journalists, by looking for sandy ridges and holes and anything that would deliver a roller-coaster experience. I gave up nail-polish.

We'd reach the middle of nowhere and the army would then explode something, languid officer chaps managing a small smirk as unprepared journalists yelped in fright and fell off the Warriors. In time, we learned to grow fond of these games – more so when our bored American colleagues were invited along. They, now that hundreds of thousands of US troops were in theatre, were being treated as The Enemy by their press officers. The relationship between the American media and their military started at rock-bottom and then deteriorated. The US army's 'public affairs officers', as their press liaison staff were termed, seemed to consist of very weird reservists straight out of a bad movie: guys who wore sunglasses at night, and talked a lot of 'shootin' sumpin' *soon*', but whose idea of a press facility was to haul their huge press pack into the middle of nowhere and show them A Military Post Office. None of them was ever allowed near anything that went bang; for a start, the list of 'accidents' occurring within the US lines was already climbing to the hundred mark, and included a number of deaths that weren't road accidents or suicides: fights and brawls involving weapons occurred, and rape was not unknown. Getting hard evidence of what went on was impossible – this wasn't the sort of 'news' that public affairs officers intended to handle: they liked 'positive material', and were certainly not going to discuss social and sexual tensions among the ranks. So we found several score American reporters nosing around the British, wondering what we were up to, an innocent curiosity which led to their being welcomed with coffee and scones one morning by the Royal Engineers; just when they'd all relaxed, the ground around them blew up.

The desert was uninviting; not the golden sands and shifting dunes and wondrous purity so lauded by Lawrence in *The Seven Pillars of Wisdom*, but a flat stretch of grit, interspersed with mucky sand and the odd dune-ish bit, and absolutely bestrewn with the rubbish left by the Bedouin. Noble nomads of ascetic culture? Nope; drivers of beat-up pick-up trucks, whose encampments produce more plastic garbage than an American housing development. Blue plastic flapped across every vista, streamed from thorn bushes and hung on telegraph poles. The sun glinted on a million plastic water bottles, discarded to last for ever, bouncing across the grit. And then there were the camels. Or Four-Stomached Financial Opportunities. With gunners scouring the supposed wilderness for suitable practice ranges, you'd have thought there was enough room for everyone. Certainly not, according to the camel-owners. Every time a gun barrel was trained on the far horizon, a tatty humpy beast wandered into view, followed by a monetarily astute local, well versed in arguments about compensation. War has always been a time of opportunism, and the desert was no different. Any wildlife appeared to have been done to death by rich young Saudis unwilling to give anything a sporting chance: desert jackal *v.* Chevrolet and four young bloods with semi-automatics equals relegation of wildlife to history. In five and a half months I saw one desert eagle, and 7th Armoured Brigade managed to corner and cherish a family of tiny jerboas – the original Desert Rat, and the Brigade's symbol.

Our machinations continued as to how we were to deploy, leading one British colonel to remark that he saw more aggression and violence among the press than in any other part of the war. Eventually a number of small units were formed, courtesy of civil servants in London: a hopelessly uneven mixture of pared-down TV crews, no radio, a clutch of provincial newspapers and an eclectic selection from Fleet Street. Dharan echoed to cries of Rubbish and Unfair. And a bizarre knock-out contest ensued, with everyone trying to think up reasons why someone else's reporter would be a major disaster on a front line. Vicious allegations were made, the army looking on bemused as a tabloid newspaper savaged Sky News ('Our readers might move their lips, but at least they're counted in millions, and Sky would save money by bringing its viewers out here in a minibus'), and it took days to hammer out a compromise, complicated by bleatings from Whitehall – 'Do the TV people really need a cameraman?'

And all the time, the story ebbed and flowed, with diplomatic missions shuttling around the Middle East, threats and teasing from Baghdad, UN envoys and summits, compromise formulae, and a mendacious PR campaign by the Kuwaitis – a diplomat's daughter getting her cooked-up tale of Iraqis dragging babies from incubators told round the world, while actual information from Kuwait City was almost impossible to obtain. It was interesting – and in the end quite alarming – to observe the inexorability of a military build-up, the detailed plans, the determination to cater for every eventuality: mobile hospitals, chemical warfare precautions, and American body-bag units (rumoured to be staffed entirely by Spanish-speaking Puerto Ricans, who were less likely to communicate information as to numbers of dead).

It was a peculiar time. Saudi Arabia is remote from the normal world, an artificial state – much like Kuwait, built on oil money, with the hard work done almost entirely by foreigners. In this atmosphere it was difficult to formulate thoughts about waging war on the grounds of 'defending a people' or any noble ideals of sovereignty. Large numbers of Kuwaitis spent little time in their featureless and rather joyless city, preferring Western capitals, and although much was made of having 'our Arab allies' on board, it was an exercise of political tiptoeing through the Middle East minefield. At one point, Colonel Gaddafi's chief adviser contacted me from Libya, saying the Colonel was uncertain which side of the fence to choose, having an equal dislike of 'American imperialists' and what he termed 'fundamentalist Gulf layabouts'. I suggested that if the Colonel wanted a few bombers diverted west over Tripoli from the massive allied-force gathering in Saudi, he could do no better than to back Saddam Hussein. A call came back a day later saying the Colonel was going to sit firmly on his fence – and for once, he shut up.

Grand speeches about territorial integrity seemed out of place in the Gulf, where for the last hundred years families and tribes have shifted around according to conflict and opportunity. But the office in London was obsessed with the notion that the gathering allied armies spent their time musing on the reasons for an impending war – 'The Big Questions' – and insisted we search out 'the ordinary soldier's view'. We spent an entire morning with several thousand American GIs – 10 per cent women, over 30 per cent black, and 100 per cent dim. The idea that they'd be sassy, articulate, characterful individuals from the Land of the Free is straight from Hollywood. The US army takes unpromising material, and moulds it ruthlessly into a dull unit that responds to orders, or, to use the only phrase we heard forty-four times that morning, 'does its dooty'. Dozens of these large, overfed and slightly lackadaisical troops stared blankly as we asked them: 'Why are you here? Why are you going to fight?'

One of the main stumbling blocks was not a political or philosophical conundrum, but the word 'here'. They knew they were not in America, yessir. Some were faintly aware they might not be in that place where they were based – er – um – yes, Germany. Some thought they might be in Israel, a country they thought constituted most of the Middle East. One unit eagerly produced their candidate with the light-up brain-cell, an overweight corn-fed specimen whose glasses steamed up in excitement when he told us that they were all ready 'to whup those guys who took our guys hostage'.

Puzzled, we asked, *Which* guys?

'Those Eye-rannians,' said our lad, to much applause and whooping from his mates.

Later that week I spotted the American boss General Norman Schwarzkopf at a briefing, and wondered whether a question on the lines of 'Who are *you* planning to fight?' would be apposite. Perhaps not.

We spent the afternoon with a bunch of British Staffords, who were busy under their Warriors producing home-from-home in the desert – brewing tea, their socks and T-shirts drying crisply over the 30 mm cannon – and who were deeply unimpressed with our questions, and not a little bit put out that the BBC needed to find out why all of them were 'here'.

'Oil,' they said. 'Fancy you not knowing that.'

At least we'd got one answer from the Americans, which was more than we subsequently managed as they continued to pour off the planes and ships. One particular unit arrived at the port of Al Jubail to stare at our cameras and grunt in aggressive fashion; the mob of regional TV American crews, 'the affiliates', were desperate for new material to satisfy the home-town appetite. They corralled some square-jawed men and began:

'Soldier, could you tell us your name?'

'Can't say, sir.'

'Why not?'

'Sir?'

Another reporter stepped forward, cute and curvaceous, and tried her skills: 'Like to say Hi to the kids?'

'No, ma'am.'

'OK – your wife – your girlfriend?'

'Ma'am?'

A grizzled hack interrupted: 'OK, just tell us where you're from.'

'Can't say, sir. If I tell you, some sneaky Iraqi spy might come and git ma family.'

The prospect of the Iraqi secret police crawling all over Kansas or Idaho in response to a vox pop in Saudi Arabia was interesting.

When the time came to get into uniform, there was a sense that this on-off war was beginning to look more likely, especially when the subject of anthrax injections arose. Years later, the threat which then dominated our thoughts has almost been forgotten. I've seen the only footage which exists of the chemical attack on the village of Halabja in northern Iraq, when Saddam Hussein reduced a village to a silent scene of bodies curled up or flattened to the ground, all clearly trying to escape some ghastly invisible invading death. And we knew there were extensive preparations to deal with nuclear/biological/chemical (NBC) victims, who would probably be taken to Cyprus by special airlift, rather than back to Britain. No one discussed the details much, but there was no doubt we'd have all preferred to be shot rather than end up a heap of dissolving tissue. So we swallowed the pills, had the injections and went through endless 'NBC drill', with cunning officers yelling the alert of Gas Gas Gas at every possible awkward moment, watching us heaving on an entire array of protective gear in a terrible scramble, while stopwatches clicked and we were pronounced 'too slow, and dead by now'.

(At least this took place in the desert, and we were spared the spurious alerts which occurred in downtown Dharan, leading to an unfortunate member of the press corps racing into his hotel lift fully kitted up, gas-mask and all, to find himself surrounded by puzzled hotel-guests and fellow hacks, all of whom took photographs.)

The intensity of the preparations, the sheer numbers – building up to nearly three-quarters of a million people in uniform – the constant whine and roar and rumble of military aircraft and tanks made the days speed by. At night – freezing cold; something else we hadn't bargained for was frost on the sleeping bag – we'd stare at the stars, not romantically, but searching for our very own satellite which had actually been shifted in space to accommodate our needs. An expensive operation, but when the BBC War Chest opens, bits of equipment which have hitherto been just a dream in an engineer's eye arrive like Christmas parcels; and the smart engineer remembers to ask for lots more, while the going's good.

By now we were in uniform, an unlikely band of Official War Correspondents. Some took automatically to the role – Martin Bell instantly appeared officer-like and soigné, adjusting his desert scarf as a cravat and looking as if he'd been in and out of sandy trenches for years. His cameraman Nigel Bateson, who soon discovered that most of the desert spent much of its time trying to get into the working parts of his expensive camera, is a man for whom flak-jackets were not invented – his army-issue number covered his manly chest rather like a bra. Duncan Stone, our tape editor, looked suitably dashing, but insisted on maintaining individuality by going to war in a pair of purple trainers. My cameraman, Ian Pritchard, had acquired a superb set of desert boots, which I coveted; I remarked on this to one of our officers, who immediately said: 'Tell him you want them. If he gets shot, it saves a lot of argument.'

It was fascinating to see how the rest of the hack-pack seemed to be surreptitiously realising boyhood dreams, festooning themselves with colourful keffiyeh and sporting an array of water-bottles and large watches with many dials for telling you where you were and what the time was in Baghdad.

As for myself, I was permanently preoccupied with having lost bits of kit – water-bottle, penknife, compass, torch, spare dressing pack, helmet, floppy hat, NBC kit, tiny make-up bag, hair-brush, nail-file, and another dozen things without which the army doesn't think you should get out of bed. Eventually, I was introduced to the most essential element of the British army:

string. Major Rayson Pritchard of the Royal Marines (no relation to Ian, but another Welshman with enviable boots – was there a Celtic store somewhere?) tried to sort out my incompetence, and I gave in and attached everything to me with String, Essential.

I was also bothered by the attentions of the tabloid press. It comes with the turf if you're in the television business – not that it in any way affects your reporting if you spend your life well away from Fleet Street's Finest (or at least its Best-Paid); no one recognises you on the streets of Beirut or in the wilds of Afghanistan. However, obsessed with the idea that a Woman Was Going to War, at least one paper had sent a reporter to track my moves and get 'a few embarrassing snaps'. And at home, a woman MP wrote a snide piece containing the ridiculous fiction that I'd lost my pearl earrings and 'soldiers had been hunting for them in the sand'. Still, no hard feelings – I've still got the earrings, and she's no longer got her seat.

The feeling of being sneaked up on by a fellow hack intent on making life difficult was unsettling. I was finding things quite hard, despite the fact that the army had not once showed me any prejudice or seemed in the least irritated by having to accommodate a female in a unit of two thousand men. I was in my midforties, relatively fit and keen to do my best, but I was worried that I'd have a stupid accident, or fail to make the grade in some way. And if I did, I felt that I'd have let down a lot of women back in Britain who thought that I ought to be able to hack it. I didn't want to stand out and 'be the exception', I just wanted to get on with the job – and I didn't want to complain: a whingeing woman was just what the tabloids would have loved.

As we went through a particularly lengthy NBC exercise, I was wondering if I was really going to be a bit of nuisance when an officer came up to me.

'You look a bit worried,' he said.

'I don't really know if I'll get through this.'

'You're going to,' he replied, 'because all of us are going to make sure you do – and you shouldn't worry.'

He then disappeared in a cloud of gas as we threw ourselves into the usual contortions of getting our NBC kit on; however, he'd said his words with enormous kindness and sincerity, and a weight lifted off me. I've no idea who he was, but he gave me the confidence to forget the comments and the backbiting at home.

Unknown to me, the rest of the lads in the unit were also on the lookout, a lot of them irritated by the constant portrayal of them as mindless thickos desperate for parcels of red-top papers bustin' with Page Three lovelies; they were far more organised than any London editor had imagined, attested to by the yelps of delight which regularly issued from the tent which housed the enormous and interesting video collection that travelled with them. They were also fed up with being asked to pose for little stunts dreamed up by those editors who treated soldiers as useful objects to grace their front-page notions of 'Our Lads'. And when a creepy hack was found going through my kit one day, an unceremonious removal took place.

Having filled in the forms and signed up to join the British army, there didn't seem to be any perks coming our way. No pay, and a rather woolly status somewhere between a completely useless recruit and a very dim officer. Early on we heard that we were referred to as PONTIs – an official army acronym, no less. This was it, recognition! A long time later we learned that it represented what the army really thought of us: Persons Of No Tactical Importance.

However, the man in charge of British troops, General Rupert Smith, took us seriously, so much so that weeks before most of the military were told about the exact nature of the Battle Plan, we were briefed with the details. The little group of Pontis left our meeting with General Rupert filled with information and not a little apprehension. Astutely, the general had decided that journalists entrusted with enormous amounts of confidential information are far less likely to squeal than journalists denied any information at all, who pounce on snippets and rush to divulge them.

Censorship and journalism, especially with regard to military matters, are uncomfortable bedfellows. But, by deciding to be alongside the army in uniform, we had at least signalled to viewers that we had in some way 'done a deal', and changed position from that of completely independent reporters to that of Official War Correspondents. We got the inside information and were privy to sensitive discussions; in exchange, we recognised that telling the world of such matters would endanger the lives of those we were alongside – and ourselves, by the by. National sentiment, loyalty, patriotism, being 'on side': all are issues involved in the decision to be with, rather than report on, an army. In this instance, it was judged that we should make it very clear that we had shifted position – but also state baldly when we were unable to give out certain information.

Early on, I had a brief discussion about censorship with the officers who were in charge of the press unit – and, literally on the back of an envelope, wrote four words: Strategy and Tactics, Taste and Tone. The first two would determine decisions made by the army as to what should be withheld; the latter two would be the preserve of the media. It was an absolutely off-the-cuff plan; and it worked, partly because the officers on the ground had ten times the nous and common sense of the politically influenced Whitehall-based officials, who continually attempted to interfere with the media, and had none of the precise judgement, confidence and responsibility of those in theatre.

We encountered precisely two instances of censorship in the entire campaign. A new American ground-to-air missile fired one night was omitted from our report, due to American insistence that its capabilities should not be identified by the Iraqis. And then there was Christmas.

The Foreign Office barged in, fluttering diplomatically that 'our Saudi hosts' had 'sensibilities'. Could have fooled us – though at least they had taken to holding their regular weekly public executions away from the allied troop concentrations. But Christmas, in a land where the wearing of a cross constituted a crime and where army padres had been turned into 'welfare officers', was obviously too much for them. Edicts went out from London – no trees, no carols; no celebrations.

The kow-towing to an intolerant regime was stomach-churning – especially as young men and women might have to lay down their lives in this war. So all around the desert, tiny trees twinkled in defiance, and the strains of 'Silent Night, Holy Night' were heard with more than usual emotion.

Other than this, it was the Americans who experienced real trouble with censorship, so giving the impression that the whole war was directed by a Pentagon PR team. In the field, the relationship between the US press and their military minders was a form of war. They despised each other and were ready to trade insults about Vietnam at any given moment. Those of us deployed in the desert had no idea of the appalling management of information achieved back in the isolated Saudi royal capital of Riyadh, where press briefings, accompanied by cutely edited videos, were fed to a massive and frustrated press corps. Part of the problem lay in the appeasement of a primitive and repressive regime that would not countenance the idea of reporters roaming freely. The result has been the impression that the Gulf was a 'TV war', consisting of tightly censored images, filtered through the Pentagon. For us, though, it was a standard operation under clearly stated restrictions, which sought neither to deliver PR nor to gloss over reality, and had the added bonus of a live satellite dish, through which we talked directly to our audience – without any interference from army personnel. Perhaps the very brevity of the ground action led to a number of the press corps, penned in Riyadh, feeling that the war had been 'hidden' from them. We in the field did not think so, when we saw the crisped corpses and napalm-blackened trenches in the final days.

Two small media groups accompanied the 4th and 7th Armoured Brigades; the third one was to act as the Media HQ, centred on a mobile satellite dish and TV editing equipment. This was the FTU – the Forward Transmission Unit (at least,

I think that's what we were; I heard the phrase Fuck iT Up unit more than once). Attached to us were a very game lot of people, willing to share their war with the headless-chicken journos; a group of officers – unfailingly charming and not a little eccentric – who were so determined not to miss the war that they were prepared to 'look after' the press (as in 'herding un-housetrained cats'). In charge of all of us was Corporal Walls, to whom officers and hacks alike deferred. Wallsy was a sensible Yorkshire lad, saucer-eyed at our attempts at trench-digging and despairing of my lack of familiarity with Woollite (I was led off for a lesson in cold-water laundry, hitherto a mystery to me).

We had been given our own tent – probably because no one else was willing to share with a dozen people thoroughly incompetent in matters of self-preservation and hygiene. Erecting the tent took all our efforts, and even then, there always seemed to be something missing, like an entrance, or stability. We were lectured on the dangers of crutch-rot and gangrene, and given continuous training in first aid (not helped by a distinguished colleague fainting at the sight of an orange stabbed with a syringe). Days were crammed with instruction and training, mainly aimed at keeping us alive and stopping us from being run over by tanks. It was another world for me: OK for the boys who'd always wanted to play with the Big Toys, but for a woman whose education included embroidery and ballet and never extended even to an Airfix kit, there was a lot to learn. The very idea of following an order was a problem to someone fresh from a couple of decades in an organisation in which it would have been suicide to follow management's instructions to the letter (idiot-recognition is a central part of BBC training). I had a habit of 'considering' instructions rather than acting on them, and of asking a lot of questions. Finally, Colonel Chris Sexton decided to make things clear:

'Kate,' he said, 'Why? is not an Army Question.'

Nor, I discovered, was Where? The army took us on convoys overnight, our tent dismantled, our equipment packed up, complicated routes and signs involved, me and Duncan our video editor driving our pick-up truck miles in a huge column, only to see dawn break and our final objective – the place we had started out from. I found the army odd.

They found us peculiar. 'A bit lemming-like,' said a captain; 'you have no idea about survival.' We thought this unfair and flounced off, tripping over tent guy-ropes, to continue falling into trenches and standing behind reversing Warriors.

We were a curious mobile broadcasting unit, something of an experiment, for the new small satellite dishes had not been in use very long, and had certainly not been lugged into a war zone – at about a quarter of a million pounds each, it represented a considerable act of BBC faith to allow one to perch in the sands, and bounce around in the back of the pick-up truck. I drove the pick-up piled high with editing equipment. For several years we'd edited 'in the field' on small portable machines, sending back 'news packages' to the UK contrary to the general belief that scripts are mulled over – and pictures selected – by senior staff in London. In reality, the 'package' skips into TV Centre by satellite mere minutes before the start of a bulletin. The engineers had a four-wheel-drive with the rest of the equipment crammed in it. They were a TV transmission station on the move, with a smart red rat shouldering a camera painted on the door panels – the ultimate accolade from the men of 7th Armoured Brigade, signifying that we had joined the family.

We were one up on the American media pool, who had had their dish banned from the desert by General Schwarzkopf. Knowing this, we felt some anxiety as the British generals headed for our set-up. However, General Sir Peter de la Billière seemed to be made of tougher stuff than the Americans, unfazed by the idea that we had the capability to broadcast live from just behind the front line. Ian, our cameraman, and Pete and Rob, our engineers, were primed to answer any question that might arise; still, we were not prepared for the query: 'What happens if you're captured by the Iraqis?' (Up to then, I'd assumed we were confident of winning . . .) The general eyed the yard-diameter dish, painted a fetching sand colour, peeking out from under an equally fetching camouflage net, as I groped for inspiration: 'I'll tell the Iraqis we're mere journos and we're self-catering and that's our wok.' He gave me one of those looks acquired over years in the SAS, and then said Carry on.

There was no mistaking that we were in a world that was not only alien to the media, but presaged the possible onset of war; a unique mixture of the hilarious and the serious, of humour and ruthless intent.

Daily life was a relentless round of mystifying army routine, blended with moments of panic as I realised I'd yet again forgotten essential (according to the military) bits of kit. Having to turn up at the field kitchen for breakfast carrying everything needed to survive a chemical attack, not forgetting penknife, helmet, flak-jacket, notebook, assorted bits of string and compass (to reach the field kitchen? Remember: Why? is not an Army Question) was one thing. Having to devise methods of how to get bra and knickers on while having a conversation with a dozen male hacks also wrestling with underwear in a small tent was another.

Added to this was the interesting situation of finding oneself in a flat desert with two thousand men and no trees. At a critical point – about six hours into our deployment – there were hard decisions looming. For the chaps, there were little 'desert roses' – funnels on stalks – placed at convenient intervals about the camp, and there were also some of the odd US 'phone-box' comfort stations, all of which were literally public conveniences, men staring thoughtfully at the horizon while seated.

For the first three days I hung on until nightfall, limiting my water intake – then set off like a desert fox into the darkness, terrified of becoming detached from the near-invisible humps of camouflage nets which designated our unit, and trying to follow Army Rules: don't go further than two hundred yards (possible Iraqis lurking?), always follow tracks in the sand (you want to stand on a mine?), take a shovel (don't leave evidence for the enemy) – also compass and NBC kit (be prepared for war at any time), and loo roll (obvious). A veritable expedition *à la* Captain Oates. Then came the peculiar decision of which direction to face, even though in darkness, for it's very unsettling to squat in a vast wilderness.

Three nights of expeditions and I thought I was getting the hang of it; but on the fourth morning, one of the colonels said he wanted a word. He launched into a description of the properties of the standard-issue army rifle, the SA80. Deeply puzzled, I interrupted, pointing out that the army seemed wisely to have decided that the press pool didn't need guns, being capable of arguing any enemy to death.

'Indeed,' said Colonel Sexton, 'but let me merely add that you seem to be unaware that the SA80 incorporates a first-rate night-sight, and Kate, they're all using it so don't bother to wait until dark.'

Two days of embarrassing sorties ensued, not helped by encountering the same Kiwi lieutenant-commander (no, I've no idea why the New Zealand navy was in the desert) three times in the same Army Male Public Loo; nor by being enthroned, with three chaps waiting outside, when an NBC alert took place, which led to a bizarre shouting-match in which four desperate people disputed priorities – to crap or to die, that is the question; whether 'tis nobler . . . etc. while a Scud missile hurtled overhead.

Then Bruce arrived. A brilliantly organised, laid-back Argyll and Sutherland Highlander ('No, ma'am,' said Wallsy knowingly, 'Argyll and Bolton Wanderer') who introduced himself with the words: 'I have a land rover *and* a solution to Your Problem.' Meaning that when nature called, we would leap into the land rover, drive for a mile, and then Bruce would gallantly stare at the horizon while I disappeared round the back. Which was perfect, except for our driver, a bespectacled Belfast Protestant, an ever-helpful boy scout Signaller, who would insist on hovering with offers of 'Youse needin' more bog roll then, ma'am?'

I harp on about loos because they're necessary, and cause more grief to women journalists than almost any other single item. You find yourself on twelve-hour journeys in Bosnia? The lads hop out of the vehicle and head for the traditional rear wheel position. You fling yourself in a ditch, discover it's a bog, and then say good morning to three passing shepherds, who stop to stare. You retreat from a lengthy meeting in a government building, a barracks or a factory – the Gents is the door opposite, the Ladies is a half-mile trek, and, if you're in the Far East, a family of four will be living in it. Nemesis used to take the shape of an aircraft carrier: several thousand men and Absolutely No Place For A Woman, literally. Thank heavens for women in the navy now.

Saudi Arabia managed another variation on the Loo Theme. Stop at a roadside filling station – Western-style, except for the mini-mosque between the loos – and discover that the Ladies is always used by the local blokes as the pre-prayer ablutions room; discover this while inside one day, and find oneself descended on by aggressively screaming, half-dressed, sopping-wet Saudi soldiers until rescued by a gallant British officer, hugely satisfied by having a reason to point his gun at Arabs at last – *any* Arabs.

But the world is changing – and one of the great advances brought by women's progress to true equality is the recognition that Women have a right to Ladies – conveniently situated.

When the air war began, we were all asleep in our tent, woken by Wallsy saying in precise but unemotional tones: 'Lady and Gentlemen, yellow alert, we are at war, this is no joke.' Wallsy had a sense of occasion.

For the next few seconds we lay in the dark, wondering what on earth we were meant to do. Surely one should do *something*? A radio went on – and for half an hour we listened to reports tumbling in from all over the Middle East. We were in the dark, because a lengthy bout of convoying and tent re-erection the previous evening had left us too knackered to rig up a light-bulb –

'Oh, we'll do that tomorrow.' One learns many lessons in life, but starting a war without a light-bulb, when someone shouts Gas Gas Gas at four in the morning and you have to find your uniform and your entire NBC kit in the dark, and you think Saddam Hussein has a Scud missile bearing down on you personally carrying mustard gas or plague, is not advisable. A dozen journalists squeaked and swore and fell over camp beds and each other, pulling on boots and overboots, unable to find flak-jackets and protective gloves and totally, utterly in a panic. Only half-dressed, we were ordered out of the tent, where someone promptly threw me in a trench. 'Welcome to war,' said the man I landed on.

For weeks we watched the horizon at night become a streak of crimson ballooning into orange globes. The bombers went in, tiny red fireflies snapping off their lights as they crossed the border into Iraq. Between sending reports through the evening, we'd usually stand silently, watching the remote vaporising of life. At such distance it was impossible to imagine, never mind describe, what might be going on. For thousands of Iraqis there was never any reference to what they endured, for their president was indifferent to them, their media carrying almost no mention of the effects of the dreadful pounding by allied aircraft.

For us, there was continuous work – the appetite for news, any kind of news whatsoever, becomes manic in war. The pace of daily life hotted up. We were on the move frequently, and found ourselves digging trenches in the rain, sleeping outside with ice on our sleeping-bags, getting grit and sand in equipment and ourselves, while overhead the bombers never stopped. Huge columns of tanks and APCs went past us continually. One night, while were sleeping in a hollow, we heard an American tank whining and roaring ever closer, until it filled the very air around us – and we then heard it suddenly squeak to a standstill. The next morning we found its tracks on the lip of the hollow, where it had stopped, part of its sixty-odd tons overhanging our sleeping bags.

One night there was a set-piece dinner, an evening of formality and reflection, with little candles on the trestle tables in the tents and a lone piper playing – and quite a lot of frozen shrimp which had mysteriously found its way from the American lines (so mysteriously as to suggest the noble army tradition of 'proffing', conducted on the principle that anything not nailed down or attached with string may well find itself a new owner. I was the getaway driver on our regular proffing raids, based on the premise that No-one Will Notice a Woman or Suspect Anything . . .). Anyway, we judged that the American military didn't need to eat real food; they had MREs – 'Meals Ready-to-Eat' – instead, brown plastic sachets which had spent ten years maturing in a warehouse in Kansas, and were rightly termed Meals Rejected by Ethiopians. Shrimp was wasted on MRE-eaters.

We watched multiple-launch rocket systems, saw men fired with battle-fury on the artillery raids, took part in night manoeuvres lit intermittently with flares like a painting of hell, the infantry dashing around, the tanks grinding past us. We all became more nimble, we concentrated on essentials, and we rattled off reports every hour, editing pictures in conditions of sweat and pressure. The huge move forward was under way, and we found ourselves a minuscule unit – just a number in a huge flowing river of armoured might. One night, we were part of a convoy of 1,200 vehicles. After the fifth stop, in the dark, having followed the dim red tail-light of the vehicle in front for five hours, I fell asleep – and so did Duncan. I woke to the ultimate nightmare: a grey dawn desert filling the windscreen – and not a vehicle in sight. Except in the wing-mirror, which showed that everyone was patiently queued up behind us. I screamed, Duncan jumped, and, incoherent with fear, I headed off in a grand prix start towards the horizon. After about five minutes of absolute terror ('Woman delays invasion? Reporter gets several thousand vehicles lost? BBC shot at dawn?'), we spotted a tiny spiral of dust, and, with a galloping convoy lurching in our wake, we caught up.

More than anything, I had no wish to lose touch with the field kitchen. I – like many before me – realised that I marched on my stomach, and the field kitchen was not only a miracle on wheels producing mounds of tasty cholesterol, but also the best intelligence source in the Middle East. In the morning we set off to head further north – perhaps over the border, who knew? – and breakfast was unbelievably generous, with mounds of fried bread. We thrust our paper plates forward, observed by a resigned-looking chief cook.

'Better eat it all up,' he said.

'Mm?'

'You're all off over the border and you're all gonna die,' he replied.

The plan to breach the huge sand wall – the berm – and the defences on the Saudi–Iraq border was meticulous, with each vehicle assigned a numbered column (ours was 14), a lettered breach (L) and a parallel column (we were meant to have non-tracked unarmoured vehicles such as supply trucks rolling next to us). In the event, we went through P in an unknown column, and I found myself driving hell for leather with one foot between me and a line of American M1A1 tanks. Stuff the plans, we all went for it – a huge surge of armour and noise and flashing lights and thunderous firing just ahead of us. Figures in helmets and goggles and scarves loomed in the dust waving neon batons as guidance, but the thrust was inexorable, the vehicles speeding up as we hurtled into Iraq. The sheer scale was indescribable. Roughly half a million people massing northwards at a far greater speed than had ever been envisaged. You kept your wits about you in the dark, in the din, in the haste. The adrenaline was surging, the dust choking, the noise a continuous roaring, punctuated with explosions. And that odd feeling, after so many months of waiting: we were in the enemy's territory – we were invaders.

Our first obstacle was unexpected: a group of tattered, frightened men in unrecognisable uniforms moving towards us, arms held high, pleading. The media had thought of many potential scenarios, but having to take people prisoner wasn't one of them. One of the Iraqis staring at me suddenly realised I was a woman – his jaw dropped – and I expected him to be angry or ashamed – instead he gave me the sweetest fleeting smile. We offloaded our 160 miserable Iraqis on to an obliging and rather dim American unit with empty trucks, and set off again – only to get entangled with another American unit, a set of South Carolina National Guard who were gung-ho and up for it, but were going to war in the wrong direction, heading south for Saudi Arabia.

The confusion of war was all around – flashes and booms ahead, and to left and right the ugly piles of abandoned guns and burning tanks, belching red-black clouds of fuel on fire. Mile after mile the detritus of war lay scattered, as if a monster had swept aside these mighty defences like so many bits of Meccano, tossing and chewing them, then breathing fire to char and kill.

The whole swift advance was taking hours, where days, maybe weeks, had been envisaged. Two of us managed to grab a ride on a helicopter taking General Smith into Kuwait; we skimmed under electric pylon cables and hopped over hundreds of smashed artillery pieces and sandbagged trenches, everything blackened and desolate and with indistinguishable sooty shapes like charred barnacles dotted everywhere. It was a battlefield of defeat, strewn with human leftovers. And then the sky ahead began to grow dark, with the navy pilot unable to make out a single feature – for we were flying straight into the smoke of the burning oil wells.

Scorched desert, blackened sky.

Most people recall the stream of vehicles abandoned on the Mutla Ridge north of Kuwait City as the symbol of the war's end. In the demented scramble to escape, ordinary Iraqi soldiers had been caught in a tank battle between the US Armoured Cavalry and a handful of Iraqi tanks next to a police station. The cars, trucks, vans, buses, ambulances, even a fire engine – all stolen from Kuwait City – piled into one another, the whole scene shrouded in smoke from petrol tanks on fire. Some drivers died in their vehicles – we counted a dozen or so, as we went through the wreckage before the rest of the press came up from Kuwait – but most had fled on foot; and it was much further north that they were spied by the US helicopter gunships and chased in an ugly turkey-shoot. Forty-odd bodies were laid out on the ridge – Kurds and Turkomen from the far north, press-ganged into the war only six weeks before by Saddam Hussein, but men who'd fought to the last.

But it was the blackened desert that I remember most vividly. There were scraps of black-edged school notebooks drifting out of the bunkers. Looted ornate tapestry chairs, dirtied and singed, lying in the sand. Ammunition and bits of clothing – gas-masks too – scattered about. And every so often, an unrecognisable melted bundle of humanity, a man who had died – maybe praising, possibly cursing Saddam Hussein.

To survive a war is a blessing. It made me understand better why my childhood had been full of people who were just glad that it was over.

What I did not know was that the training in survival and the discipline under fire would be life-saving in the coming decade – with two more bullets to prove it.

And that the question of Next of Kin had been the most important one of my life, to be answered also as a blessing.

SIXTEEN

Postscript

I sat reading by torchlight in Sarajevo, shells thumping, the ping of sniper fire every so often. To get a few quietish moments in the city for reading – or sleeping – it was wise to take yourself into the bathroom, sit in the bath and cover yourself with a duvet. That way you weren't too bothered if the bedroom window shattered again, and there was a belief that an iron bath gives you a little more protection against incoming mortars.

If reading was interrupted by part of the ceiling walloping into the washbasin and two inches of plaster dust settling on the book, I would still be able to tell my family that I at least tried to live a normal life, give or take the odd detonation and whizz-bang. For I was now part of a much bigger family, having met my own mother and a wonderful, welcoming tribe of kind and fascinating relatives. And they were only just getting used to someone who disappeared into war zones and whose phone calls home were punctuated with the sound of explosions.

I was rereading Martha Gellhorn, that most distinguished American war correspondent who covered most major conflicts for more than half of the twentieth century. She was writing about the civil war in Spain.

'There was smoke in the room and the hotel had been hit several times,' she wrote, 'so we took our wine glasses next door, on the agreeable and traditional theory that if a shell came in the front room it would not bother to come as far as the back room, passing through the bathroom on its way. We counted six hundred shells and got tired of it, and an hour later it was all over. We said to one another, "Well, that was a nice little shelling."'

Her subsequent description of the war around her made me shiver. She could have been next to me in my bathroom, over half a century on, writing about Sarajevo instead of Madrid. And it wasn't just the bizarre and horrible and complex nature of warfare which seemed familiar, it was the way she reported. Every conflict needs a Martha Gellhorn, with a clear eye and an unfailing grasp of what she was doing, why she was doing it, and the guts and style to do it well.

I met her just before she died. She was stunning – and still reporting: stylish and perceptive, wise and witty. It became immediately clear that the precepts and principles which she had held for decades were enduring and relevant. She didn't just write of the military manoeuvres and the tactics of war. She described what happened to everyone around her, and was commended by that other wonderful journalist, James Cameron, for having 'a cold eye and a warm heart'.

Martha Gellhorn, of course, wrote for newspapers, and her method of reporting was relatively untouched over the years by advances in technology, except for the spread of telephone lines into distant lands. I found myself at one with her on the nature of reporting – the supremacy of facts couched in humanity and the urgency of communication. But in nearly a quarter of a century of television reporting, I was buoyed up by an expanding medium which embraced ever more efficient communications and put TV news at centre stage in its output.

Nothing is set in stone, even though the meat and drink of the news messengers has changed little over the centuries: murders and acts of God; wars and miracles; gossip, power-broking; the royals and the weather. However, the way we 'choose the news' – for every bulletin is an act of selection and rejection – and the way we present it are vulnerable to both commerce and intellectual fancy, and to fashion and technology. As the twentieth century drew to a close, and we pursued murders and acts of God and so on, the ground began to shift under our feet, and we realised – in a rather fuzzy way – that change was taking our work in a new direction; and that reporters were not immune to the new order.

The moment when this change caught the public's eye was the death of the Princess of Wales. What we saw on television – the personal grief expressed so openly, the public criticism of the royal family, the status given to baseless speculation surrounding the car crash – all this reflected a change that had already taken place in television's attitude to royalty. A change which merely reflected a less decorous, a less fawning and a somewhat more sentimental attitude which had begun to infuse newsrooms. Diana's death highlighted how TV news had been becoming less touchy about tabloid-style stories.

Time was when a large bargepole appeared whenever a 'less-than-proper' Wales story begged to be included in a major news bulletin. As someone who resigned the post of Court Correspondent after a management refusal to accept that the Queen might have commented (mildly) on the miners' strike, I watched with interest the gradual shift to coverage with less cringing, but more speculation. As the Waleses' marriage got into greater difficulties, there were endless arguments in the newsroom about the less savoury details – the publication of intimate conversations, the acknowledgement of other partners, the gossip that was a daily mainstay of the red-top press. Each time there was a 'revelation', cautious decisions were made by nervous news editors, but gradually the frontiers were being pushed back. Admittedly we in the BBC were days, sometimes weeks behind in using the terminology current everywhere else: lover, mistress, divorce. This was partly because it was judged that our viewers were not pushing for change, and partly because the standards of the tabloids were understandably different from those of a public service broadcaster. But by the late nineties a shift had been made, even though the tone of reporting was still restrained. And the week following the fatal car crash in Paris saw a sombre cavalcade of the more personalised, emotional and populist reporting that was gaining favour in the industry.

Alongside the royal stories, there was a perceptible loosening-up in the rest of the 'news agenda'. Some bulletins, without any public discussion or announcement, began to acquire a more 'popular' feel: more consumer-orientated, more feature-driven, and with a determined suppression of pictures of violent reality. Not a corpse to be seen before nine o'clock. What was happening?

Technology was the first and obvious force for change: in the age of satellite, the internet and mobile phones, reporters can fill idle hours speculating on how events might be affected by technology (always ending up with an argument as to what might have happened if the evacuation of Dunkirk in 1940 had been broadcast live on television). However, the equipment *is* now available to deliver live pictures from war zones; so will the audience respond by demanding a halt to the barbarities – regardless of the cause of war? Or will the military keep pace and deliver their own version of events – on video – while conveniently excluding the press from 'operational areas'?

When the politicians emerge from hours of negotiation to announce an agreement into the microphones, do they now have to be prepared for instant rejection from an aggrieved faction hooked up to the outside broadcast? Before detail has been explained and reasons are given?

At the scene of a disaster, are the facts made public so quickly that blame is apportioned and public relations machines have generated defences before the victims have all emerged from the wreckage?

The humming of the satellite links, crunching information and flitting it round the world in nanoseconds, is now a staple of news-gathering. Poorer countries may not yet have the means to operate their own equipment – but a cheap dish can catch the richer foreigners' messages, and all can stare at the bewildering non-stop ribbon of pictures. For technology and commerce have combined to deliver news non-stop, round-the-clock: the 24/7 newsworld.

During the second half of the twentieth century, television news in western Europe gathered speed and confidence – and audiences. The Americans were ahead of us in Britain by about ten years; so far ahead that by the end of the eighties, they were the undisputed leaders in the TV news world. We Europeans used to dribble with envy when the Big Three Networks rolled into town – or rather, into battle zone and disaster scenario and superpower summit. For two decades, the US Big Three had had More of Everything. More money, more people, more equipment – operating out of several dozen bureaux flung worldwide. Cameras, telephones, editing equipment, lighting and a mind-boggling amount of Coca-Cola thundered into remote villages in El Salvador, spewed out of planes into African jungles, formed oases of Americana in Middle Eastern deserts, and always, always occupied the best suites in five-star hotels right next to the conference centre. The BBC and ITN could only dream, while we drove ourselves out of foreign airports in dodgy hire cars, only to be overtaken by the NBC/ABC/CBS stretch limo, at the wheel a local madman whose family was henceforth assured of a lifetime of comfort, courtesy of naïve American largesse.

We liked to think that we didn't need the US network circus, but we cuddled up close every so often, to obtain extra titbits of footage. And we were gracious in declining offers of room-service hamburgers and oceans of fizzy drinks from our transatlantic cousins. After all, we Brits had constitutions of iron weaned on years of curried goat; and no self-respecting crew left London without filling a camera-tape box with real drink, labelled For Medicinal Use of Crew.

Back in the United States, audiences were treated to the fastest news operation ever. Presented with style. The 'anchors' – grizzled (but craggily handsome) veterans – delivered the nightly news with smoothness and confidence. Years before the British managed to shoehorn a newsreader into a reasonably cut suit and get him to stare at the autocue without too much hostility or fear, the Americans had teams of cutely smart people with years of on-the-road experience under their belt. We still had former actors and announcerettes in the studio, and paraded a range of either scruffy or raffish correspondents who did not take kindly to advice about personal appearance. Not that any advice was forthcoming.

The language of the US networks' bulletins across the pond was terse and clear; the phrases short and telling. The Americans knew their audience, and served up news in a form that paid sharp attention to cultural tastes and limitations. Years of competitive writing and a solid tradition of academically overseen training shone through on screen. The British valued the 'trusty old hack' tradition, which eschewed professional teaching and was firmly grounded in grimy provincial newsrooms, backed up with mysterious references to 'a nose for news'; and in the BBC there was always, hovering among the typewriters, a sprinkling of 'bookish chaps' who could argue the hind legs off the *Oxford English Dictionary* and who knew how verbs were conjugated.

In the field, it was not difficult to categorise the US on-camera personnel. Washington DC-based reporters shopped on a different planet from us. They wore a unique uniform of elegantly casual jackets and good cotton shirts, above bum-hugging, well-cut jeans. They had haircuts either sleek as mink or neatly floppy. The female of the species had great teeth, perfect make-up at three in the morning and no concept of diffidence.

They all responded to us with restrained disbelief: *You're* on camera, oh *really?*

When I joined TV News, clothes were never mentioned. I was completely at a loss to know what should be worn on screen. Any queries were met with an embarrassed shrug, as if I'd suggested nudity. My male colleagues dressed according to ingrained British habit and class. The confident old stagers wore baggy suits probably tailored for their father and the young bloods wore puffy anoraks. The one truly aspirational working-class reporter on the staff was easily identified by his brass-buttoned blazer and poncey tasselled shoes. Moulting sheepskin coats and tartan lumberjack jackets lurched on to screen without warning, and ancient mackintoshes were paraded because their wearers had 'had it for – let's see – twenty-two years now'.

How a female was supposed to dress posed problems. If someone commented on my clothes, it was deemed that I'd committed some kind of gaffe. So I decided to non-dress, to wear unremarkable clothes – something that looked 'right' but didn't deliver its own message on screen. I was just beginning to think I'd got it right when, in the midst of a howling riot in Northern Ireland, I bumped into my colleague Brian Hanrahan at three in the morning.

Pointing to a figure picking its way carefully down the middle of the Falls Road, he said, 'That's what we should have more of,' as we fell behind the remains of a fountain in a bottle-strewn park under a hail of petrol bombs and rubber bullets.

'More of what?' I peered at a truck ablaze and dark silhouettes striding around in the glow.

Crawling nearer, I recognised a Brazilian TV reporter who'd been at an Ian Paisley press conference earlier; she'd asked me why the BBC had been addressed as 'a harlot' and what did it mean, and I'd said it was a political phrase and of no great significance. And here she was, fluffing her hair and smoothing her glossy fur coat which glinted and rippled in the dancing orange firelight. Dozens of little creatures must have lived and died expensively to create her mantle, which swung luxuriously inches above the rivers of petrol, broken paving slabs, glass shards and the remains of a smashed lavatory. I sighed thoughtfully, knowing that a fur coat would see me nailed to the newsroom wall in it.

Confident, generous, well resourced: for a quarter of a century, American TV news was king of the road. And during the eighties, the networks were rewarded with huge audiences. The States were media-savvy. There was increasing use of television by the politicians to get their message across, to run campaigns, to conduct elections. Their officials actually knew about cameras and soundbites. During the Falklands War, I waited in a Luxembourg hotel for the outcome of talks between General Al Haig and the new British Foreign Secretary, Francis Pym. I'd secured my interview spot among the three US network women reporters: three lots of Farrah Fawcett hair and an alligator's worth of teeth.

In came the official party. On went the TV lights. A figure strode towards us. Al Haig exuded bounce and his tan glowed. His suit was palish blue, he looked as if someone had pressed him after he'd got out of the car. He leaned towards us: 'Hi, ladies,' he purred, 'I'm the general. Anybody got time for a game of tennis?' There were shivers of lust in the reporting line. Instead of meat-axing him with cold enquiry as to why the negotiations had apparently got nowhere, there was a communal soft bleating for him to 'tell us how he'd got on'. Yet another battle won by the general.

Several yards behind him lurked the British delegation. Bereft of the recently resigned Peter Carrington, they had produced a new Foreign Secretary. I peered through the pool of TV light and espied a hunched figure.

'Mr Pym!' I squawked. An adjacent dark figure slid forward. 'The Foreign Secretary does not intend to give interviews,' hissed the man from the FO.

General Haig put out a bronzed hand and patted my microphone, then turned and waved the hapless Mr Pym next to him. Into the light tiptoed Mr Pym, a serious politician in a crumpled, ill-fitting navy suit, with a little dandruff. He looked grey and tired. Most of all, he was clearly appalled at the line-up of cameras. After a few perfunctory words, he made his escape. Not surprisingly, his contribution to events during the talks had been the more significant – but the British government was some way behind in what have become known as Presentational Skills.

Back in London, American correspondents, fresh from reporting their President's words from the lawn in front of their well-appointed press room next to the White House in Washington, were engaged in a fruitless struggle with Number Ten Downing Street: 'No, there is no lawn to stand on. There is a pavement – this "sidewalk" opposite the Number Ten front door, ladies and gentlemen. No, there is no press room. Yes, it rains quite a bit here in London. No, there is no possibility of If Wet, Inside. Mrs Thatcher is not afraid of rain.'

Television news in Britain was deemed serious, but not worthy of special treatment, and significant stories were as likely to be broken to the print press as to the cameras. Nor were official announcements delivered with TV deadlines in mind.

Through the sixties, seventies and eighties, the global tension between the Soviet Union and the United States meant that American TV news followed American interests to the four corners of the world: from Nicaragua and El Salvador to Cambodia and Angola, with the Middle East and Moscow permanently in their sights. Not only did they have the latest video kit, they reflected social change back home, pushing at the conventional make-up of news crews. It became something of a joke that each team had to represent a particular minority, and that WASPy males were having to give way to black sound-recordists, Puerto Rican tape editors and – gasps from British union-stalwart technicians – camerawomen.

I used to wonder if we could ever catch up with the US networks. Particularly when Chicken Noodle News came along. Ted Turner's brainchild, brazenly adding itself on to an already dominant US media machine, was ridiculed at first; but CNN persevered and marketed itself like a world-bestriding washing-powder.

And then something happened to the US TV empire. Several things, in fact.

As the decade changed, and the Soviet Union began crumbling behind the Berlin Wall, there was a reassessment of international concern and responsibilities. Not an immediate decision, but debate and ideas about the End of History, the New World Order, a World's Policeman. And the audiences for television news in the US shrank. The only exception was the sudden flourish for the Gulf War, when the three networks flung everything they had at the story and CNN made a strong bid to claim a significance in the conduct of the conflict itself. The result was near-bankruptcy for the Big Three, and a set of headlines for CNN which were more a tribute to self-promotion than an endorsement of significant heavyweight journalism. Hundreds of US media personnel had found their way to Saudi Arabia; what none of us realised was that it was an off-key swan-song for big-time American news coverage. Throughout the nineties CNN continued to bid high, tending to throw all its eggs into one particular basket, majoring on one situation to the exclusion of all other news stories at any one time. But worldwide, the US TV presence waned.

There were mutterings of isolationism, and of a TV business in the States which was no longer controlled by media people. Takeovers and mergers had made the news organisations mere building blocks in industrial conglomerates more interested in the entertainment industry. Men who ran mega-industrial complexes involving washing-machines were not entranced by the drama of journalism. Technology might be enabling TV to bring the rest of the world into American living-rooms, but the ratings were taking a dive; the advertisers didn't think much of the pulling-power of news.

Shrewd commercial judgement replaced editorial power. The bureaux which had spanned the world closed; the plush offices in Frankfurt, Rome and Paris contracted to modest premises in London. Only a handful of international outposts remained. The equipment was no longer the ritziest on the block.

Meanwhile, somewhat ironically, the Europeans were ex-panding, and experimenting. We were finally catching up – and so was the rest of the world. We'd noticed, even during the Gulf War, that the British and French had had better mobile satellite ground stations – the nifty up-links which enabled us to accompany our fighting troops into the desert. The Balkan conflict hardened and sharpened a myriad TV organisations. Sarajevo saw the rise of the TV agencies, Reuters and AP, drawing their strength from local camera crews; soon they had hundreds of crews worldwide. Small news stations – Catalan TV, RTL Luxembourg, even hitherto moribund French telly – earned their spurs, and showed that they were up with the best on the front lines. The grammar of television was becoming universal, though it meant a flattening of individual styles, and a spread of conventional TV packaging.

Because of the technology, the way we reporters went about our business began to change. Those of us who'd spent years overcoming every kind of obstacle to claim we were first on the scene in foreign parts found that pictures were heading back to London before we'd even negotiated the M4 to Heathrow. The agencies had their local camera crews on the spot – in almost every significant city, and on every front line. The dominance of the Western cameras diminished as young people in the poorest countries acquired the skills and scraped up money for professional equipment, knowing that they were joining an international and expanding business.

All those years wheedling a place on an unreliable aircraft, facing down venal immigration officials, hiring – nay, buying – taxis, lorries and ox-carts began to recede into a past world.

At the end of the eighties, it had taken days for us to reach Armenia to cover a massive earthquake. The Western press scrambled to overcome Soviet barriers, non-existent transport links, ruined roads and the lack of electricity supply. It took over a week to sort things out, with chaos everywhere and hopeless communications. Soviet television reacted with about the same speed as a writer thinking about covering the Crimean War.

At the end of the nineties, as the Western press scrambled out of its bed to head towards the airport en route to another huge earthquake, this time in Turkey, two Turkish provincial TV channels were scrapping publicly about who had transmitted the first pictures to the world. Was it the one which went on air twenty-three minutes after the tremor, or had it been beaten by the station which claimed to have had pictures nine minutes earlier?

Over in the States, it had become a darkly muttered fact that the staff in the BBC Washington TV bureaux resembled furniture. They never moved from the office, taking in stories by satellite from Florida to Alaska. You no longer even needed legs to get to the White House or State Department, for press conferences were put out live, and you just hooked up to the electronic feed. As for raising your butt from the office chair and heading into the open air in order to stand in front of the elegant Capitol Building . . . why bother, when your video library carries a variety of background shots – sunny summer, cloudy fall day and so on – of all major Washington locations? You can just rearrange the hairstyle in the comfort of your own washroom, and stroll into the studio to stand in front of the back-projection. Why bother going to the location, when it can come to you? At least the ozone layer has been conserved by this development – less hair-spray is necessary when indoors.

By the mid-nineties in London, the regular mad midday dash on to planes to file from Rome and Paris and Bonn for that evening's bulletins became redundant, because the pictures were already being hoovered up by our European counterparts. Even French TV news had begun to function properly, after years of political shenanigans in which senior management posts went to politicians' mistresses' cousins. Italian cameramen had ceased to wave cameras in demented and unusable fashion (known as 'hose-pipe vision'), and were content to deliver footage without attempting to be Fellini. The Germans still shut up shop round about teatime, but enterprising freelance outfits were filling the gap. And they all had access to satellite links, so were only minutes away from delivering their work to any TV company in the world. The race to the airport became rare, as the screens lit up with events already being covered and transmitted by the locals. And the accountants could be heard kissing their calculators, as more and more news slipped cheaply on to screen via satellite, without all that money being spent on sending someone to see for themselves what was really going on.

And, as the technological developments changed the way we reported news in the last decade of the century, so the news itself changed as well.

For three decades, up to the end of the eighties, British television developed news coverage to serve increasing audiences, so that almost a quarter of the adult population sat down every night to view one of the two main TV news bulletins. In thirty years we changed from laborious film-processing and hand-drawn illustrations to satellite video transmissions and electronic graphics as the audience initially thrilled by 'live from New York' gradually grew to expect electronic miracles, taking a globally accessible world for granted. We may have lagged behind the Americans and envied their budgets – but we were running hard in second place.

We also reflected a world where nuclear war was a possibility, and much of the conflict all over the globe saw the superpowers either involved or interested. From Angola to south-east Asia, central America to the Indian subcontinent, there was always the fear that greater trouble could erupt which might affect us all; so we felt it proper to send British reporters to Vietnam, to El Salvador, to Beirut, to Zaïre, to Nicaragua, to Afghanistan.

It was also a period of change in a string of countries where hitherto the British had had colonial interests: Zimbabwe, Anguilla, Uganda, Nigeria, South Africa, Pakistan. We had a strong sense of connection, so we watched what happened there.

Revolution was in the air all over. Students marched, workers protested, terrorism flourished. These were decades of acronyms and colour-coded violence: ETA, IRA, Red Brigades, PLO, INLA, Baader-Meinhof, Black Panthers, SLA, PFLP, the Japanese Army Faction. Looking at rubble and wreckage was a near-daily habit. I used to remember airports by whether you could see a hijacked plane from the terminal building, or needed to crawl round three miles of barbed wire to get a decent shot.

We reporters all had vocabularies honed to discretion when reporting atrocity. And we all went to a lot of funerals.

There was social upheaval – revolting students, the women's movement on the march, demonstrations for racial equality. Reporters had to be able to walk miles to keep up with demonstrators, then be able to run fast when the demo met the police. We sat in bars nursing bruises, debating whether the Berlin police should get the Violent Suppressors of the Month Award, or whether the Belgian police had acquired it permanently. We acknowledged that the US National Guard made regular efforts to be in contention.

All in all, the world turned in front of our cameras, and the East–West tension bound it to our audience at home. The sixties, seventies and eighties – days of exciting pictures, great television, making for riveting nightly viewing.

Then, in 1989, in front of the cameras, the Berlin Wall came down. Great television; but, unexpectedly, it altered the way we saw the world – for those who bothered to see it – for it ushered in the beginning of an era of lesser TV news. Not less in volume – we were now running 24-hour channels – but less in impact, in great events, gripping issues.

In France, Claude Moisy, the veteran ex-head of the AFP agency, remarked that 'the less we fear that foreigners are going to kill us, the less we're interested in them'. It was a simple but profound remark when applied to news coverage.

In America, the shrinking of the networks had been under way for some time, with a non-American story a rarity on the nightly bulletins. News from foreign parts now made it across to the States only if it had the President or a bunch of GIs attached to it. And the Americans continued in their comfortable isolation for over a decade – until the outside world struck home savagely with the attack on the Twin Towers in New York in September 2001. True, the technology delivered incredible pictures – live – and a multiplicity of channels was able to devote hour upon hour of screen time to local reaction and comment transmitted in from around the world; but the events and their immediate aftermath also showed that for years American TV viewers might not have had the slightest inkling of what lay behind the terrorists' actions. They had not been interested in foreigners, for they had not feared them.

In Britain, the change in the 'new news agenda' crept up slowly during the nineties.

The BBC had snoozed for years in a protected stockade of cultural and political arguments which debated the supremacy of an independent institution which reflected the educated and liberal mind, tempered by fits of creativity and bursts of righteous pompousness. Experienced in repelling attacks from puritans, radicals or political jackals, it did not expect to find its very foundations being dug away by people who thought that 'institutions' were a Bad Thing. The zealots came in under the fence to dismantle from the inside. Armed with ridiculous management dogma and concealing an embarrassing itch for the world of money-making, they caught out a body of people who were dogged programme-makers ignorant of the profit motive, and who naïvely failed to recognise that 'public service broadcasting' caused amused sneers among the new lords of broadcasting. The News Department got a 'make-over': first, a bureaucratic upheaval which deposited layers of management on a puzzled newsroom, accompanied by gnomic statements about a 'mission to explain' – without explaining what this meant; and second, a cultural upheaval which demanded 'accessibility' and a populist agenda.

Not that any of this impinged immediately on grubby hacks lying in ditches in Bosnia. But while we ran for our lives in Mostar and Sarajevo, the audiences slid from the giddy peaks of the eighties, and 'boring Bosnia' began to be edged off the screen in favour of gentler, more consumer-friendly items.

Seen from the London newsdesk, in a world of distant wars and insoluble famine, priorities were different. Consumer affairs, money matters, crime, education, health and house prices – *your* life, *your* preoccupations – with a leavening of sport and a sprinkling of celebrity gossip. All presented in a more intimate manner – lots of Hello Mike and Thank You Debbie – Take Care Now! The reporter was to act the role of a 'facilitator' of information, eager and chatty and occasionally earnest and concerned. Or moved. Or sombre. No longer a straight conduit of facts, but a flexible conveyor of impressions.

And reporters were moving *into* the story: popping up on screen to chat to newsreaders, walking around, and frequently asked to explain how they themselves felt about the situation. After years in which objectivity had reigned, there was a move to the more personal, to involvement in the story: just how did the reporter react to events? Personal feelings were subtly interwoven into the replies in 'on the spot' interviews. Emotion was deftly encouraged – for there was a sense that the news should be more 'accessible' – and perhaps the reporter was needed to guide a viewer to the true reaction to the story.

Increasingly, hacks were tethered to the satellite dish, always on hand to deliver the 'live spot', in a curious belief that rabbiting on live is a more relevant and informed kind of reporting; in reality, someone stuck next to a dish for hours on end is the last creature on earth to have learned anything new, and probably unaware of a corpse twenty yards away.

Eventually it became clearer that the audience was now being catered to – given what it was *thought* it might like or consider important, rather than being dosed with what was judged significant. News bulletins ceased to exist; the string of significant items had metamorphosed into a programme of interesting 'packages'.

Audience figures took on new importance. Hitherto, the average reporter had consoled him- or herself with the idea that if someone, somewhere heard your story, it had all been worthwhile. Now reporters found themselves drawn into a programme format and much more involved in delivering a product which would complement the programme's 'style' and satisfy the 'target audience'. Instead of staring at the wide world and wondering what's going on, at least one eye had to be firmly on the audience.

Winning prizes also began to matter, with expensive announcements made in the press every time an awards ceremony saw your firm's name attached to various peculiar trophies. Hitherto, such competitions had been something of an in-house ritual, with the management rather embarrassed about competition – so much so, that when what was considered 'the Big One' took place – the Europe-wide Monte Carlo International TV Festival Awards – there was a half-hearted search in the BBC for someone to go and find out if we were among the winners.

I was dispatched some months after returning from China to see if our coverage of Tiananmen Square had caught the judges' eye. Monte Carlo – wonderful. I skipped off quickly before the management realised that it had sent me to a decent place.

'You have been here before?' asked the superior receptionist in the posh hotel.

Unthinkingly, I gave the usual reply: 'Yes. I buried Princess Grace' – a curious forerunner of Diana's death, with a horrendous traffic accident giving rise to gossip and accusation.

The receptionist clearly decided that people who visited for funerals were either royalty or ratpack – and made the correct deduction, giving me a very small room.

That afternoon, there was a rehearsal for the awards ceremony which found a dozen assorted potential prize-winners carted off to the Monte Carlo Sporting Club and harangued by a stressed Dutchman. We stood on stage, a gaggle of European producers, cameramen, writers and directors, completely baffled about our role. The Dutchman's instructions grew more hysterical as he spotted the evening's star presenter, a still-glamorous French film actress *d'un certain âge*, apparently talking to a large potted fern. While we were meekly enquiring exactly what we were supposed to do, The Entertainment turned up: Shirley Bassey's personal orchestra, a vast horde who immediately began rehearsal. While the musicians blared through 'I Who Have Nothing', the French actress was patting the fern and apparently asking it questions, ignoring the Dutchman's approaches. An officious stage manager then shooed us all away, and we returned to our hotel to prepare for a mystery evening.

There were two thousand people gathered at the Sporting Club, including Prince Rainier and an extraordinary array of stick-thin women of pensionable age submerged under blankets of mink and diamonds, all parading past live TV cameras from several channels. Our little group got ready to march into the grand entrance, and were immediately treated like errant steers and stampeded into a side entrance which gave on to the wings of the stage – a dark jumble of unwanted furniture and old props. In the gloom behind the black drapes the Dutchman reappeared, waving a list which he said was the Order of Play. With his droll and completely inaccurate cricketing analogy, he managed to enrage and confuse all of us, who were growing nervous – we felt like Christians about to be fed to giant mink in the full glare of our own profession.

The French actress reappeared. Announced that she couldn't read the script. And wandered off.

The orchestra was trumpeting loudly by now, Award Ceremony Style. A German grabbed the Order of Play and started to shove us into a vague queue; someone from eastern Europe whimpered with fear; and the British contingent made a final effort: the distinguished novelist and scriptwriter David Lodge and myself demanded to know what we were meant to do.

The Dutchman grabbed his list back, stared at David Lodge and accused him of being a writer. Mr Lodge politely agreed, only to be propelled to the back of the queue with the words: 'Writers are last man in.'

'Reporters?' I said.

'Third, you are third, only third.'

I assumed I hadn't won, and wondered whether I should leave.

'Do not make a speech,' said the Dutchman. 'Just go up to Michael and take it and walk off.'

By now, the French actress was extemporising out front, clearly in a world of her own and addressing her remarks mainly to the conductor and the faithful potted plant. The stage manager decided to take charge, shunting out the first two in the queue to tentative bursts of applause.

'Michael who?' I said.

This was the straw that broke the camel's back. Whisking the drapes aside, he gripped my neck and pointed to the other side of the stage. 'You are the only one not knowing him?' he squeaked.

I could see nothing in the bright stage lights as I was shunted into them, but I distinctly heard the words: 'You don't know Michael Douglas?'

Well, er, no. Not *personally*.

Two seconds later, I was three inches from him under the main spotlights. He looked serene, smiling and calm, and then said very quietly: 'Have you any idea what we're meant to do?'

'Not a clue,' I replied – 'but what's that?'

He was carrying an object which appeared to be a half-dressed woman on a slab of marble.

'Would you like it?'

'Why not?'

As the band played, we executed a pantomime of surprise and gratitude, and Mr Douglas said very politely: 'May I kiss you?'

I assented with disgraceful eagerness.

We found ourselves marooned in a sea of blinding light and noise and wondering what to do next.

'OK, when in doubt, exit downstage left, look confident and keep smiling.' Mr Douglas is a pro. We swerved to avoid the French actress and missed going over the edge of the stage by only about six inches.

Awards ceremonies never quite resonate with the reason for them. It's great when they're fun, but winning odd-shaped lumps of glass, metal and marble isn't what the job's about. Nor is it about influencing history. I have grave doubts that any world leader of any stature trembles at the arrival of The World

Famous Hack Who Bestrides The Globe. For all the claims that confidences are divulged exclusively, the souls are laid bare and the 'real person' is revealed to the visiting reporter, the reality is that you're one of a vast swarm of gnat-like visitors who are mutually indistinguishable.

I did once wonder if I'd invented the Latvian navy. I encountered a very charming man in a tiny attic office in Riga while trying to find out whether the country had yet got itself a functioning government after the demise of the Soviet Union. Speaking excellent English, he explained that his empire ran to a desk, a telephone (not connected), a map, a chair and a wastepaper basket.

'What do you do?' I asked.

'I am the minister of defence.'

'Are you a soldier?'

'I'm a lawyer.'

We chatted generally for a few minutes, and then he turned to the map.

'Do you think we should have a navy?' he enquired.

On the basis that Latvia has a coastline and the Russians have never been their best friends – not exactly an intellectual approach, but time was short for reflection – I suggested that something small and effective afloat might be a good idea.

'Thank you very much,' said the lawyer. 'Now I have a strategy.'

I've always thought that being a reporter is rather like being a gun dog. You don't know exactly what's going to happen; you're not in charge. You're a bit nervous, but keen. A shot rings out, and off you hare to sniff out something interesting and bring it back. And you bring back something which is part of a much wider scene – a small but *pertinent* trophy, with smell and colour and texture, and a history – which you lay in front of someone hoping that the way you carried it hasn't changed or damaged it. What I didn't ever fancy was being a poodle chasing after a ball and obediently fetching something already familiar in order to fulfil limited expectations.

Unless you focus all your wits on the unexpected and complex and baffling and frightening events which happen daily, the audience is not well served.

I've always been apprehensive when going on a story. I've never quite accepted that you can do justice to what you're about to witness. You get there, gather the facts, and always pick up little asides and curious incidents which are part of the tale, but sit oddly in the wider picture. In the middle of the night in Zeebrugge, listening to survivors gulping out their descriptions of mayhem in the bowels of a ferry turning turtle, not all the stories were the same. As dawn broke, the radio airwaves were full of voices praising a man who'd made himself 'a human bridge', allowing others to scramble to safety; there was the natural emphasis on heroism and sacrifice – it helps us cope with such a disaster, and we all cling to the wreckage of decency. We'd also, completely by chance, been filming at a hospital bedside when a doctor entered urgently to confirm a name with the patient, only for everyone to realise that this was the frightening moment when a mother learned of her child's survival.

I had also been listening to a number of people who described the darker side of panic, and its natural companion, the instinct for survival. As the huge ferry rolled in darkness, and every plate and chair and human being tumbled and crashed in an upside-down world, there was another force emerging. Superhuman determination to survive took hold in some – something which does not automatically recognise the plight of others, nor baulk at using every means available to cling to life. Anything – anyone – was grasped at, stood on, clambered over, used as a step upwards, shoved out of the way. It was one of the little images which sat in the wider picture – just as every portrait has shadows. Survival is a terrifying life force – and often not pretty to hear about.

In Sarajevo, I once felt the push of the survival imperative myself. I'd fallen badly while negotiating an unlit and ice-covered rat-run between derelict buildings at night in a sniper zone. Not a sensible set of circumstances; but needs must when your colleagues have taken the armoured land rover to a riotous party with the French Foreign Legion and you've been asked to dinner by the Archbishop of Canterbury (yes, everyone who's anyone paid a visit to the city at some point). Lying in the snow, having heard the appalling sound of leg and ankle bones snapping, I realised that at minus ten degrees my chances were not good. Later, having been through a surreal evening involving a traffic accident, a murder incident and some hands-on first aid from the SAS, all while prone and bleating, I realised that I'd crawled through the snow for over 300 yards on hands and one knee, in order to reach a building with lights on. The survival instinct is an interesting phenomenon.

I've wondered if reporting is like putting together one of those irritating jigsaw puzzles which builds a scene out of a thousand tiny scenes; from a distance, it's just a kaleidoscope of different colours and edges and shapes; close to, there are individual pictures, many of which jar with the overall effect. And all the time, you must not let one of those tiny images knock the bigger picture out of focus. If you're injured or intimidated in a nasty and jarring moment, you have to stop it from informing your entire view. When standing by a graveside, you have to take note of the individual comments, but attempt to appreciate the wider significance of the death; even the funeral of a saint is not without the remark that 'the crafty old trout must be having a good laugh'. (Not everyone adored Mother Teresa.)

Trying to bury Gracie Fields in 1979 was an exercise requiring considerable restraint. An interesting woman who was the highest-earning British entertainer in the 1930s, yet whose image was resolutely down-to-earth Lancashire lass, with a voice like a corncrake on speed, she had early in her career acquired a property on the Italian island of Capri. Having spent the war years mainly in America, she married as husband Number Three an Italian called Boris Alperovici. She never quite got Vera Lynn status as a national sweetheart, but nevertheless was a phenomenally successful singer who had a special place in many people's affections.

Her funeral was to take place on Capri and, as usual, we were dispatched to cover it at the last minute, driving overnight from Rome to the ferry via the back streets of Naples as dawn lit up sleek, giant rats promenading the port. I'd wondered what we might expect; as we hadn't told anyone we were coming, I envisaged a solemn little service viewed from afar, with perhaps a few ex-pat mourners.

We fetched up on the island and enquired of a taxi driver the whereabouts of Our Gracie's villa. He looked perplexed: 'Whicha one?' It turned out the 'umble lass from Rochdale had four.

'The one with alla the grande visitings?' suggested the taxi driver, who then regaled us in true taxi-driver tradition with his knowledge of Señora Alperovici – 'Strange lady – but lotsa money so go from one villa to next when it need cleaning. Dona lika see cleaning.'

I wondered if I'd stumbled upon a secret psychological key to Gracie Fields' character, or merely succumbed to taxi-driver lore.

We hurtled up a purply-green early-morning hillside dotted with delectable housing and were deposited outside very grand gates, beyond which milled scores of mourners like a bouquet of carnations – white silk and scarlet, with emerald hats and swirls of black lace – all of them carnation-thin and working their way down tables laden with bottles and goodies. Dishevelled and lugging our tripod and camera gear, the three of us looked like scruffy spectres at an exquisitely dressed feast.

La crème de la crème of Capri parted in a ripple of silk and linen to allow an elegant man to stride towards us.

'Erm,' I began, '*buon giorno, siamo BBC dalla Londra* and although we weren't invited . . .'

'Come in come in welcome welcome and you shall be the first to see her.' So Boris began – and with charm whisked us towards the French windows across the cliffside terrace.

A disquieting noise came from my sound-recordist.

'I don't do lyin's-in-state sort of fings.'

Too late; we were already at the French windows and there in front of us was a gigantic coffin in an ocean of flowers.

Boris propelled us forward.

There was another choking sound at my side.

'Close your eyes,' I hissed, 'I'll tell you when time's up.'

Gracie looked about thirty – a spin of blond hair around a perfectly made-up face under an exotic black lace veil and no hint of eighty-one years on this planet. I counted slowly to twenty, not having a clue how long was thought proper to gaze. Very odd, I thought. Millions have seen her in life – and I never did, but saw her in death.

'Been at the peroxide, then,' said the cameraman, a creature of observation, though not of discretion, as the remark was addressed to Boris.

I hauled the crew back on to the terrace, where we found ourselves accorded great courtesy in a situation where I thought we might have been asked to leave.

Several breakfast-glasses of chilled white wine later, there was a general and noisy move towards the gates, and a small, squat, be-goggled workman bearing an acetylene torch ambled out of the French windows, jabbing his thumb in the direction of the coffin and helping himself to wine.

A gentle comedy of errors ensued. There appeared to a slight mix-up about cemeteries. The 'English' cemetery hadn't been used for some time, and someone had suggested the Catholic one – but Boris was having none of this, so after a quarter of a mile the coffin did a U-turn and the priest and Boris had a very animated conversation. The 'English' cemetery did for the lady-guests' gorgeous shoes and tight skirts, being a riotously neglected patch of scrub, cactus and lurking head-stones. The procession began to resemble a Hollywood B-movie, in which the jungle is hacked through by a motley group of plane-crash survivors.

Eventually, a splendid little service took place, full of feeling and a sense of a life fully lived.

I kept wondering how I would convey the overall effect to viewers at home, who associated Gracie with cobbled streets and factory hooters, sentimental ditties and grey back-alleys. Especially when the coffin was borne to the graveside by six of her employees – Our Gracie had been an astute businesswoman, and owned a successful restaurant on Capri. Her coffin approached its final resting place with six orange-jacketed waiters bearing her at a high, odd angle, like an oversized tray of drinks.

You put together a story which gives the flavour of the occasion, bearing in mind that each little vignette, your own reactions, the delightful oddnesses all play a tiny part – but remembering that most viewers will be recalling fond memories, and feeling sadness that it is a funeral they're watching.

Getting close to a story – getting to know participants, visiting homes, hearing confidences – can both confirm your judgement and also unnerve. Just as you think you're approaching the heart of the matter, you're thrown off-course. I spent an afternoon with a Bosnian family in Sarajevo, three generations of the educated middle class – an architect, a doctor, a teacher among them – while mortars thumped and boomed round their Ottoman-decorated house, a confection of ornamental woodwork and painted tiles. While eating War Cake – a disgusting glob of rice, honey and possibly sawdust – we discussed, as you did in Sarajevo, the usual things: history, politics, the future, more history. Conversation lacked the ritual clichés of village life, the unthinking mantras mouthed by most of the combatants. They were a thoughtful family, cosmopolitan and well travelled, and the grandfather's most vehement feelings were vented against those whose military shenanigans prevented him from visiting his beloved bees in their hives on what was now a Serbian field. A refreshing afternoon of civilised conversation which restored a sense of hope, and let in a shaft of reason through the murky old prejudices.

As we were leaving, the middle-aged architect caught my arm and said in a low urgent voice: 'What we really need are more arms – then we can finish off the Serbs for good.'

When you get to the heart of the matter, you find it isn't a sweet pink shape, flat and simple, but a complex, pulsing thing, a billion unseen particles of nature, with a life of its own.

I never expected to be a reporter, nor, when I found myself embroiled in journalism, did I see it as a crusade. It's an honourable trade, whose practitioners exchange a privileged position at significant events for the obligation of telling others exactly what happens. How we see our world and tell others about it will always be changing. Fashion and commerce modify the menu and the style, and technology galvanises the speed of delivery and the spread of information. The printing press and the satellite alter the means; education regulates the understanding. Interest in the further corners of the earth ebbs and flows, while the sound of conflict resonates continually.

You witness other people's grief and anger and excitement and joy, and you also feel it; however, rather than becoming part of the scene, you take away with you a sense of wonder that survival and humanity are stronger than violence and suffering. You're a bystander, a witness, and although you alight very briefly on other people's lives, there is fascination and delight to be found.

Occasionally you get a little too close to stories and your fellow man tries to swat you out of existence. I've been very lucky – three bullets doing little damage and a fourth fired by a Libyan army commander who was in two minds (both of them drunk) whether to murder me or not for refusing to act as an intermediary between the Libyan and British governments. Eventually he shot at me from point-blank range, nicked my collar bone and demolished a sizeable slab of his drawing-room wall. I stalked off as best I could and – sounding like a British nanny delivering a ticking-off – announced: 'We don't behave like that in my country – and anyway, I'm only a reporter.'

I just stick to the facts.

Index

Index

Index

Index

Index

Index

Index